Street by Street

EAST KENT

ENLARGED AREAS ASHFORD, CANTERBURY, DOVER, FOLKESTONE, MARGATE, RAMSGATE

1st edition May 2001

© Automobile Association Developments Limited 2001

Published by AA Publishing (a trading name of Automobile Association Developments Limited, whose registered office is Norfolk House, Priestley Road, Basingstoke, Hampshire, RG24 9NY. Registered number 1878835).

Mapping produced by the Cartographic Department of The Automobile Association.

A CIP Catalogue record for this book is available from the British Library.

Printed by in Italy by Printer Trento srl

Ref: MD102

Key to map pages ii-iii

Key to map symbols iv-1

Enlarged scale pages 2-13

Street by Street 14-239

Index – towns & villages 240-242

Index – streets 243-270

Index – featured places 270-276

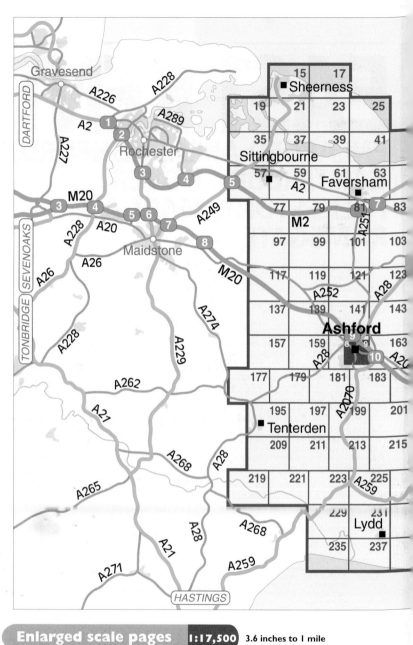

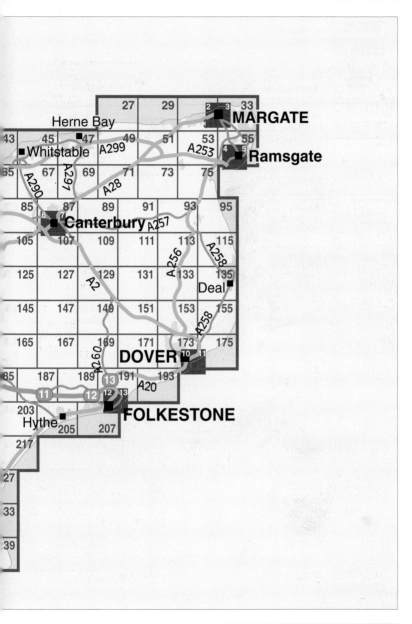

27   29   2 3 33   **MARGATE**

Herne Bay

43   45 47   49   51   53   55   **Ramsgate**
 Whitstable A299   A253 4 5

65   67   69   71   73   75
 A290 A291   A28

85   87   89   91   93   95
 6 **Canterbury** A257

105   107   109   111   113   115
  A256 A258

125   127   129   131   133   135
  A2   **Deal**

145   147   149   151   153   155
  A258

165   167   169   171   173   175
  A260   **DOVER** 10 11

85   187   189   191   193
 11   12   13   A20
  12 13   **FOLKESTONE**

203   205   207
Hythe

217

27

33

39

2.5 inches to 1 mile   **Scale of main map pages** **1:25,000**

0   1/2   miles   1   1 1/2

0   1/2   1   kilometres   1 1/2   2

iv

Junction 9	Motorway & junction
Services	Motorway service area
	Primary road single/dual carriageway
Services	Primary road service area
	A road single/dual carriageway
	B road single/dual carriageway
	Other road single/dual carriageway
	Restricted road
	Private road
← ←	One way street
	Pedestrian street
	Track/ footpath
	Road under construction
⊢ = = = ⊣	Road tunnel
P	Parking

P+	Park & Ride
	Bus/coach station
	Railway & main railway station
	Railway & minor railway station
⊖	Underground station
⊖	Light railway & station
++++++++	Preserved private railway
LC	Level crossing
•—•—•	Tramway
---------	Ferry route
....	Airport runway
— · — · — ·	Boundaries- borough/ district
⌄⌄⌄⌄⌄⌄⌄	Mounds
93	Page continuation 1:25,000
7	Page continuation to enlarged scale 1:17,500

	River/canal lake, pier	♿	Toilet with disabled facilities
	Aqueduct lock, weir	🅿	Petrol station
465 ▲ Winter Hill	Peak (with height in metres)	PH	Public house
	Beach	PO	Post Office
	Coniferous woodland	📖	Public library
	Broadleaved woodland	ℹ	Tourist Information Centre
	Mixed woodland	♜	Castle
	Park	🏛	Historic house/ building
	Cemetery	Wakehurst Place NT	National Trust property
	Built-up area	Ⓜ	Museum/ art gallery
	Featured building	✝	Church/chapel
⊓⊔⊓⊔⊓	City wall	♔	Country park
A&E	Accident & Emergency hospital	🎭	Theatre/ performing arts
🚻	Toilet	📽	Cinema

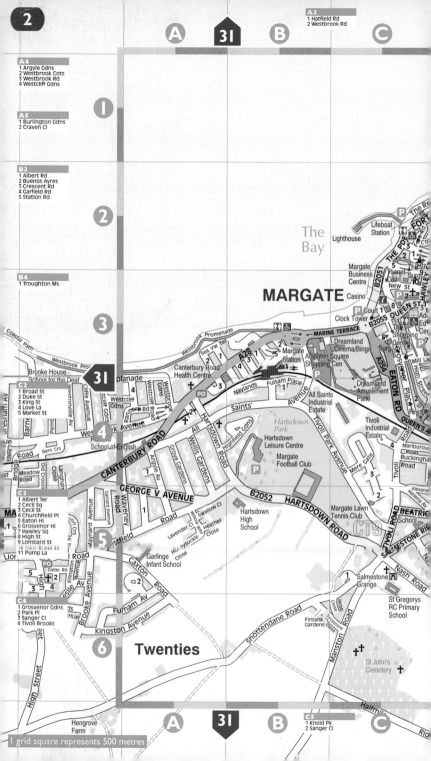

A 31 B C

MARGATE

The Bay

The Pde

Lighthouse

Lifeboat Station

Margate Business Centre

Casino

Clock Tower

Marine Terrace

Dreamland Cinema/Bingo

Arlington Square Shopping Cen

Margate Station

Dreamland Amusement Park

All Saints Industrial Estate

Tivoli Industrial Estate

Hartsdown Park

Hartsdown Leisure Centre

Margate Football Club

Margate Lawn Tennis Club

Canterbury Road Health Centre

Westbrook Promenade

Brooke House School for the Deaf

Royal School of English

GEORGE V AVENUE

CANTERBURY ROAD

HARTSDOWN ROAD

B2052

Hartsdown High School

Garlinge Infant School

Hengrove Farm

Salmestone Grange

St Gregorys RC Primary School

Firbank Gardens

Snottendane Road

Kingston Avenue

Fulham Av

St John's Cemetery

Twenties

B2051

B2055

QUEEN ST

EATON RD

QUEEN'S A

HAWLEY

New St

Tivoli Road

Buckingha Road

Marlborou Road

Alexand

Helena R

BEATRIC

SALMESTONE RI

Nash Road

Manston Road

Halfm

CT9

High Street

Lion

A28

A254

A 31 B C

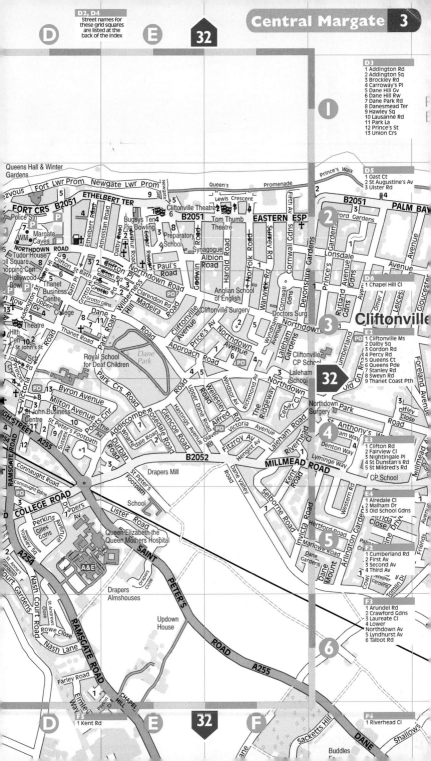

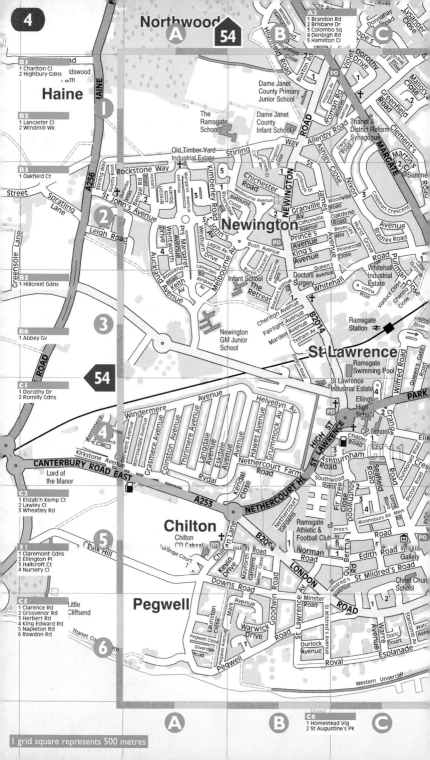

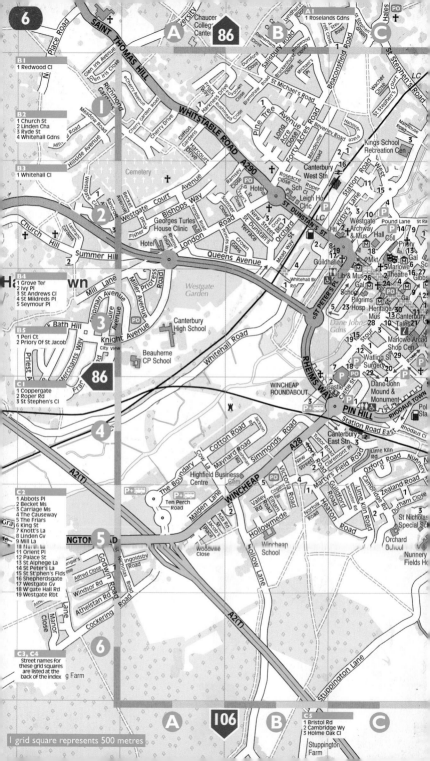

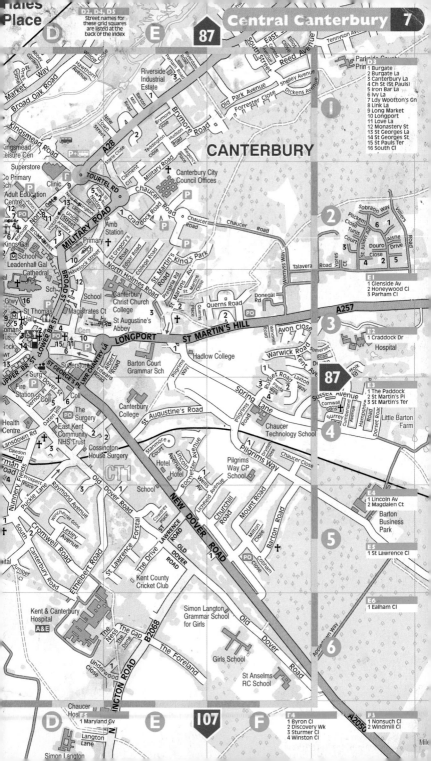

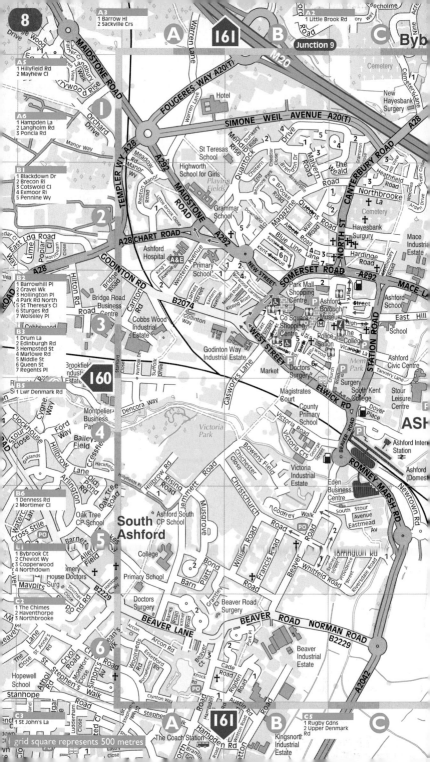

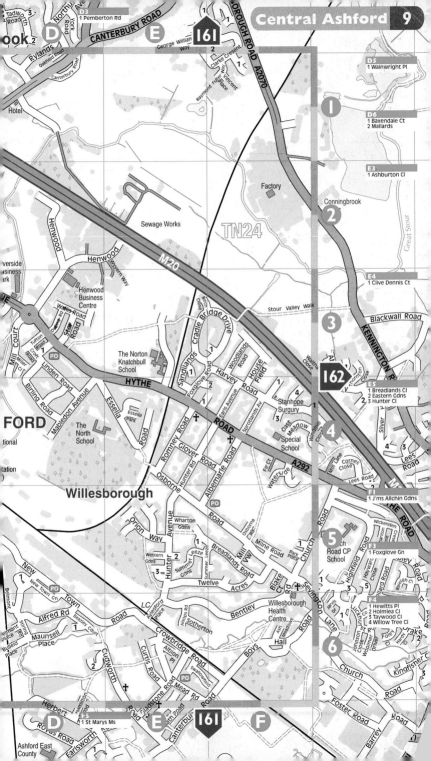

Tadworth
Road
York Ave
Northm
D
Rylands
Oakfield Road
Canterbury Road
E
CANTERBURY ROAD
D3 1 Pemberton Rd
George William Way
Clarke Crescent
St Vincent Place
Raymond Fuller Place
BOROUGH ROAD A2070
161

Hotel

D5 1 Wainwright Pl
I
D6 1 Baxendale Ct 2 Mallards
E3 1 Ashburton Cl
Factory
Conningbrook
2
Great Stour

Sewage Works
TN24
M20

riverside business park

Henwood
Henwood
Jarvent Way
Henwood Business Centre
Watts Road
Stour Valley Walk
E4 1 Clive Dennis Ct
3
Blackwall Road
162
KENNINGTON R

Mill Court
Turton Close
Miller Road
Linden Road
Birling Road
Mabledon Avenue
Essella Road
HYTHE
The Norton Knatchbull School
Sandilands
Cradle Bridge Drive
Birch Close
Foxglove Road
Harvey Road
Woodlands Road
House Field
Stanhope Surgury
Oak Meadow Close
Windmill Close
Thornton
E5 1 Breadlands Cl 2 Eastern Gdns 3 Hunter Cl
Silver
Lees Road
4

FORD
The North School
Essella Park
ROAD
Romney Road
Glover Road
Hunter Road
Earls Avenue
Spratlands Av
Albemarie Road
Special School
Fir Ct
waterside
First
Mill Lane
Corner Close
Lees Road
A292
F1 1 J'ms Allchin Gdns
ME ROAD

Willesborough
Osborne Avenue
Wharton Gdns
Orion Way
Western Gdns
Hunter
Leeze Feeze
Summer Gdns
Twelve Acres
Breadlands Road
Mill View
Milne Road
Osborne Road
Park Place
Church Road
Wickenden
Charlton
Hayward Road
5
Road CP School
E3 1 Foxglove Gn
Highfield Road
Silver
Brisley Road
Road

New Town
New Town Gn
Alfred Rd
Maunsell Place
Belmont Spring
Bullield Place
Road
Beazley Court
Aylesford Place
LC
Abbots Rd
Sotherton
Bentley Road
Blake Cl
Willesborough Health Centre
Hall
Ash Meadows
Sevington Lane
F4 1 Hewitts Pl 2 Holmlea Cl 3 Taywood Cl 4 Willow Tree Cl
Johnson Close
Woolmer Drive
Foley
Drake
6
Church Road
Kingfisher

Belmont
New Town Road
Crowbridge Road
Curtis Road
Cudworth
Gladstone Road
Albion Pl
Mead Rd
Swallowfield
PO
Canterbury Road
Boys
D Herbert
Royds Road
Earlsworth
E5 1 St Marys Ms
Hamilton Road
North Road
E
161
F
Foster Road
Barrey Road

Ashford East County

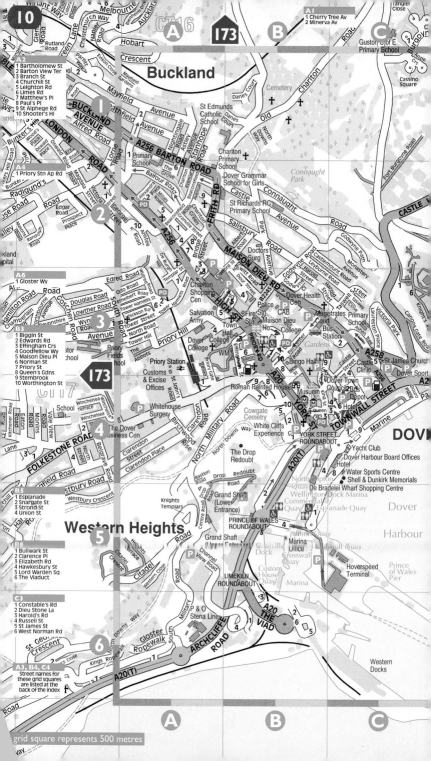

Dunkirk
Square

Lucknow
Close

Heights

D

D3
1 Athol Ter
2 East Roman Ditch

E

174

lamein
lose

Kohima
Place

A258

JUBILEE WAY

A2(T)

1

Cliff Road

Upper   Road

Upper Road

Saxon Shore Way

Langdon
Bay

2

Bleriot
Memorial

Upper

Back Road (East)

Saxon Shore Way

Camber Way

Cliff Road

The Fan

Keep
Dover Castle

Godwin

East Ramp

Road

3

rtimer
Road Pharos

P
2
P

Road

Exit

Road

174

Police
Station

Dock

Eastern Docks

Queen Elizabeth Road

uins)

East Cliff

Parade

Marina

Centre

de

R

4

CALAIS

5

6

CALAIS   OOSTENDE

D

CALAIS   **E**

F

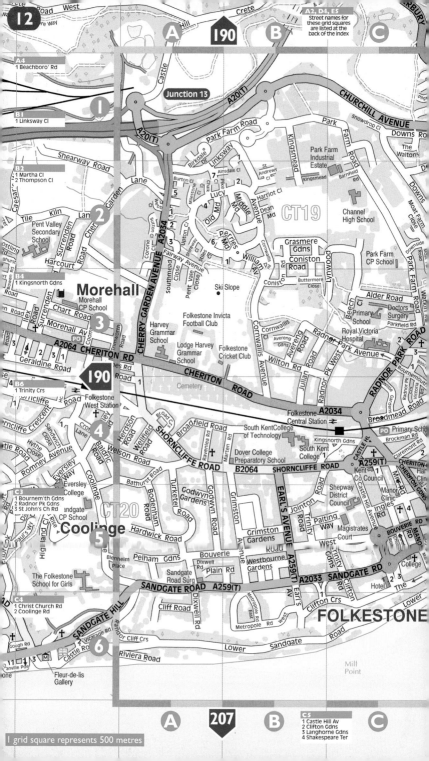

F8
1 The Crescent
2 Labworth Cl
3 Lowfield Rd
4 Pleasent Pl

H8
1 Magpie Ct
2 Mallard Ct
3 Stiles Cl

J8
1 The Maples

K8
1 Petfield Cl

Sheppey
Yacht Club

Barton's
Point

Marine Parade

The Commodore
Catamaran
Yacht Club

Marine Parade

Minster
Marshes

Scrapsgate

The Leas

Scarborough

Southsea
Drive

Augustine

The Broadway

Sexburga Drive

Minster Drive

Scarborough Road

Clovelly Drive

Wards

Seaside Avenue

The Glen

The Glen

Ripney Hill
Farm

Woodland Avenue

Hillside Road

Minster
Community
Hospital

Sheppey
Golf Club

Sheppey
Rugby
FC Club

Elliott
Park
School

Waverley Avenue

The Chase

Minster In
Sheppey
CP School

Brecon Chase

Union Road

Crescent Drive

Halfway Houses

Power Station Road

Drove Road

Marian Avenue

Johnson

Queenborough

Abbeyview

Shurland Avenue

Saxon Avenue

Collinwood Drive

Bellevue Road

MINSTER

Minster
Abbey

Queens
Road

Museum

HIGH ST

CHAPEL

Danley
Middle
School

B2008

Minster
College

Noreen

Avenue

Sunnyside
Avenue

Oriva Medical
Centre

Riverdale Avenue

Porters
Close

Minster Road

Highfield Road

Parsonage Chase

Darlington Drive

Sansparell Avenue

Summerville Avenue

Halfway Road

Dreadnought Avenue

Norwood Close

Blatcher
Close

MINSTER ROAD

B2008

New
Road

Hopsons
Place

Avenue

Nelson

Drake

Elm Lane

Thistle Hill
Way

21

A   B   C   D   E

1

2

3

4

◄ **15**

5

6

7

8

Royal Oak Point

Bugsby's Hole

East End

Punnetts Farm

Cripps Farm

Plough Road

Kingsborough Farm

St Georges C of E Middle School

CHEQUERS ROAD

Pigtail Corner

Tadwell Farm

Minster in Sheppey CP School

HIGH ST

CHAPEL ST

A   B   **22**   C   D   E

The Mount

EASTCHUR

1 grid square represents 500 metres

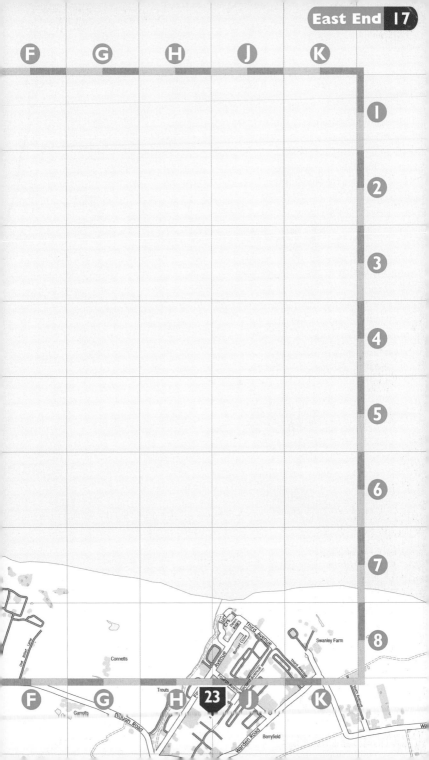

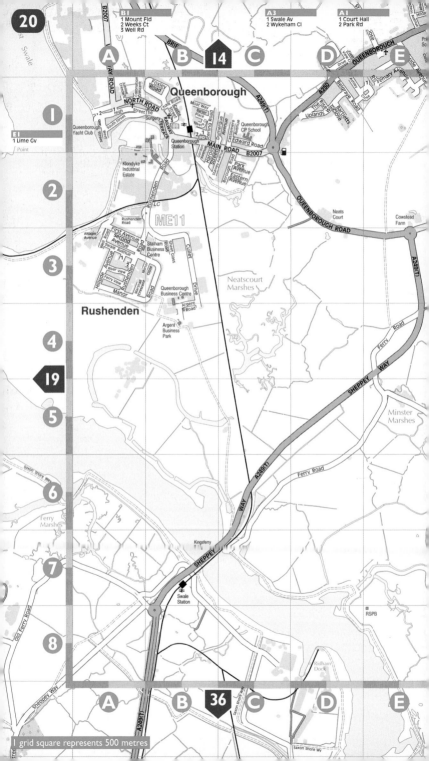

H1
1 Allen Ct
2 Brasier Ct
3 Menzies Ct
4 Miller Ct
5 Murthwaite Ct
6 Nautilus Cl
7 Turmine Ct

F   G   H   15   J   K

MINSTER ROAD

MINSTER ROAD

Sansparell Avenue

Summerville Avenue

Parish Road

Barton Hill Drive

Hilltop Road

Dover Road

Scocles Road

BellFlower Avenue

Blackthorne Road

Orchid Close

Scocles Farm

South Lees

Thistle Hill Way

Nelson Avenue

Elm Lane

Drake Avenue

I

2

3

Elmley Road

4

Poors

22

Windmill Quay Road

5

Wallend

Southlees Marshes

6

7

Isle of Sheppey

8

Stray Marshes

The Dray

F   G   H   37   J   K

Elmley Island

31   LOWER   ROAD

FORTY ACRES HILL

B2231

G3
1 Bramley Cl

G5
1 Roll's Av

Swanley Farm

17

I

H3
1 Squires Ct

Donnetts

Trouts

First Avenue

Fourth Avenue

Second Avenue

Third Avenue

Sixth Avenue

Berryfield

Garretts

Plough Road

Warden Road

Rayham

Eastchurch C of E
Primary School

High Street

Church Road

Rowetts
Farm

ROWETTS WAY

Doctors
Surgery

Leysdown Road

Cheyne Road

Anne Boleyn
Close

Eastchurch

B2231

LEYSDOWN ROAD

Harty Ferry Road

24

Parsonage
Farm

St Georges
Avenue

Church Road

Kent View Drive

Orchard Way

Range Road

Longbrant Drive

New Rides

Old Rides Farm

Capel Hill
Farm

Great
Bells

39

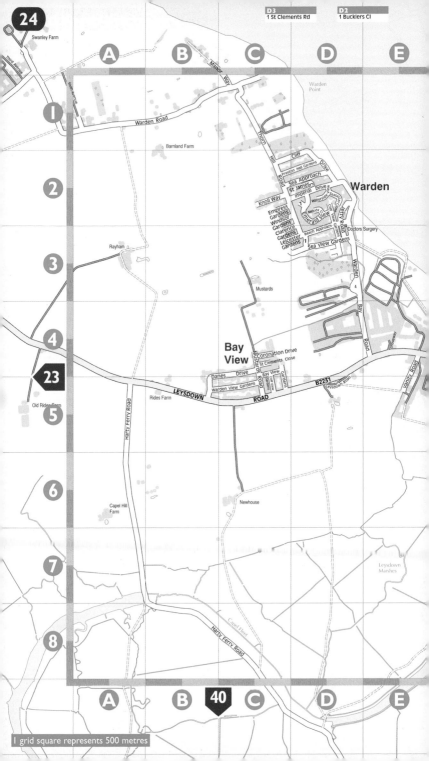

D3
1 St Clements Rd

D2
1 Bucklers Cl

Swanley Farm

A   B   C   D   E

Third Avenue

Sern Avenue

Manor Way

Warden Point

1 Warden Road

Barnland Farm

Thorn Hill Road

Cliff

Preston Hall Gardens
Drive

Sea Approach
St James
Imperial Drive

2 Warden

Knoll Way

Waterside Crescent
Melody
Emerald View

Ferry Road

Empress
Gardens
Windsor
Gardens
Clarence
Gardens
Leicester
Gardens

Beach Approach
7
Sea View Gardens

Doctors Surgery

Rayham

3

Mustards

4

Warden Bay Road

Mustards

4

Bay View

Coronation Drive
St Clements Close

23

Danes   Drive
Warden View Gardens
Drove
Bay View
Gardens

B2231

Vanity Road

Leysdown Road

Old Rides Farm

5

LEYSDOWN   ROAD

Rides Farm

Harty Ferry Road

6

Capel Hill
Farm

Newhouse

7

Leysdown
Marshes

8

Capel Fleet

Harty Ferry Road

A   B   40   C   D   E

The
Bay

**Leysdown-
on-Sea**

Grove
Avenue

Leysdown
Road

The Promenade

Manor Way

Doctors
Surgery

Park Avenue

Wing Road

Shellness Road

Shurland Avenue

Shellness Avenue

Priory
Hill

Muswell
Manor

Shellness Road

41

ty
shes

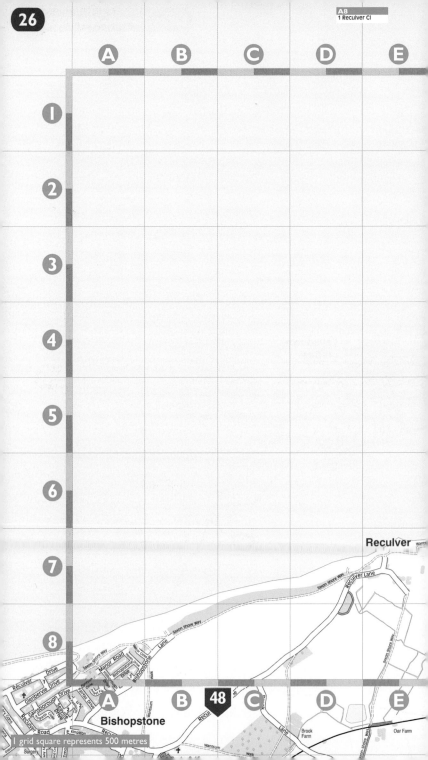

A B C D E

1

2

3

4

27

5

6

7 Wantsum Walk

Wantsum Walk

Wantsum Walk

Plumpudding
Island

8

Wade
Marsh

A B C D E

50

1 grid square represents 500 metres

Street names for
this grid square are
listed at the back of
the index

Grenham
Bay

Minnis
Bay

A8
1 Newbury Cl

A7
1 Cambridge Cl
2 Crispe Park Cl
3 Dovedale Ct
4 Edenfield
5 Melsetter Cl

A6
1 Beverly Cl
2 Hawkhurst Cl
3 The Retreat
4 Tudor Cl

South
Channel

A   B   C   D   E

1

C6
1 Carlton Rd East
2 Westleigh Rd

2

C7
1 Collingwood Cl
2 Hundreds Cl

3

D5
1 Ethelbert Ter
2 The School Cl
3 Wellington Cl

4

St Mildred's
Bay

29

Epple
Bay

5

D6
1 Osbourn Av

Westgate Pavilion
& Theatre

St Clement's
Rd

Royal School
for deaf
Children

Westgate
on Sea

Esplanade

Thanet Coastal Path

Sea Road

Carlton Road West

Ryder's Av

Cuthbert Road

Westgate Bay Av

Westgate-on-Sea
Station

Hockeredge
Gardens

Spencer Road

6

Thanet Coasta

Epple Bay
Avenue

Ocean Close

Queen Bertha's Avenue

St Davids Cl

Elm
Grove

School

Westgate &
Birchington
Golf Club

WESTGATE

ROAD

D7
1 Prospect Cl
2 Wellesley Cl
3 Wellesley Rd

Shakespeare Rd

cross Road

A28

CANTERBURY

Health Clinic

Ursuline Convent
School

St Augustines
College

Linden Road

Recculvers
Road

7

Alpha

CANTERBURY ROAD

York Terrace

Marilyn

Anne Close

The King
Ethelbert School

Limington

St Jean's
Road

St Benet's
Road

Birchington

E5
1 Beach Ri
2 Courtlands Wy
3 The Grove
4 Norman Rd
5 St Mildred's Gdns
6 Waterside Dr

Charlesworth Drive

Dovedale

Braxton Way

Barrington
Crescent

Ursuline
Drive

The Warren Drive

Southwold
Place

Allen
Avenue

Dunstan
Avenue

8

Birchington
Primary
School

Woodland
Avenue

PARK

Silver Avenue

King's Road

Park Road

Queen
Park

Park Road

LANE

A   B   **52**   C   D   E

E6
1 Chester Rd
2 The Grove
3 Queen's Rd

Two
Chimneys

Waterloo
Tower

I grid square represents 500 metres

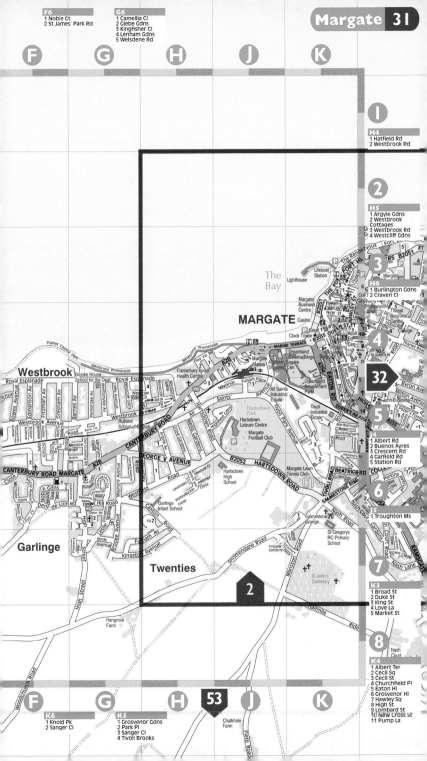

F6
1 Noble Ct
2 St James' Park Rd

G6
1 Camellia Cl
2 Glebe Gdns
3 Kingfisher Cl
4 Lenham Gdns
5 Welsdene Rd

H4
1 Hatfield Rd
2 Westbrook Rd

H5
1 Argyle Gdns
2 Westbrook Cottages
3 Westbrook Rd
4 Westcliff Gdns

H6
1 Burlington Gdns
2 Craven Cl

Westbrook

MARGATE

The Bay

Garlinge

Twenties

J4
1 Albert Rd
2 Buenos Ayres
3 Crescent Rd
4 Garfield Rd
5 Station Rd

J5
1 Troughton Ms

K3
1 Broad St
2 Duke St
3 King St
4 Love La
5 Market St

K4
1 Albert Ter
2 Cecil Sq
3 Cecil St
4 Churchfield Pl
5 Eaton Hl
6 Grosvenor Hl
7 Hawley Sq
8 High St
9 Lombard St
10 New Cross St
11 Pump La

K6
1 Knold Pk
2 Sanger Cl

K5
1 Grosvenor Gdns
2 Park Pl
3 Sanger Cl
4 Tivoli Brooks

A6
1 Oast Ct
2 St Augustine's Av
3 Ulster Rd

A4, A5, A7
Street names for these grid squares are listed at the back of the index

A3
1 Booth Pl
2 Clifton Gdns
3 Clifton Pl
4 Ethelbert Gdns
5 Fort Paragon
6 Trinity Hl
7 Trinity Sq
8 Walpole Rd
9 Wellington Gdns

B3, C4, D3
Street names for these grid squares are listed at the back of the index

B4
1 Clifton Rd
2 Fairview Cl
3 Nightingale Pl
4 St Dunstan's Rd
5 St Mildred's Rd

B5
1 Airedale Cl
2 Malham Dr
3 Old School Gdns

C3
1 Cumberland Rd
2 First Av
3 Second Av
4 Third Av

C5
1 Riverhead Cl

C6
1 Kent Rd

D4
1 Rutland Av

D5
1 Amherst Cl
2 Northdown Wy
3 The Paddocks
4 Tenterden Wy

D6
1 Balcomb Crs

E4
1 Lyngate Ct

E6
1 Hinchliffe Wy
2 St Christopher Cl
3 St Francis Cl

Palm Bay

Cliftonville

Woodwood

I grid square represents 500 metres

F G H J K

I 2 3 4 5 6 7 8

Botany Bay

Kingsgate Bay

The Ridings
Knockholt
Springfield Road
Staplehurst Gdns
AV B2052
Headcorn
Meadcorn
Summerfield Rd
Way
Marina Drive
Second Av
Percy Avenue
Kingsgate Avenue
Cabel Avenue
Fitzroy Avenue
Oakridge
Joss Bay Rd
Whitby Green
Whiteness Road
B2052
George Hill Road
GREEN LANE
Sedano
George Hill Road
Rosetower Court
Lerryn Gdns
North Foreland Golf Club

Kingsgate

Reading Street

Convent

Joss Gap Road
Kingsgate Bay Road
Joss Bay

Avenue
Elmwood Avenue
Crescent Rd
North Foreland Road
North Foreland Avenue
Cliff Road
Crafton Road
Victoria Ave
Albert Road
Whitfield Avenue
Camden Road
Reading St
Old Green Road
Foster's Av
Hugin Avenue
Coronation
Linley Road
Cedar Close
The Paddock
The Vale
Fig Tree Road
Beacon Rd
Westcliffe
Bracken
WESTOVER ROAD
Northdown Ind Estate
Orange Road
Junior School
Lanthorne Road
Guy Close
Laking Avenue
Francis Road
Stone House
CT10
Thanet Wanderers RUFC
Rhodes Gardens
Cornwallis Gardens
Fig Tree Dardens
The Foreland School
ALBION ROAD
Norman Road
Albion Road Surgery
Sea View Road
Bradstow Sch
Bishop's Av
Castle Avenue
Park Road
Stone Bay Special School
Lindenthorpe
Queen's Avenue
Knight's Av
Oakwood Road
ST PETERS
St Pete Court
Selwyn Drive
Warre
Rise
Bradstow
Cumb
Rectory Road
Dickens Road

BROADSTAIRS
Broadstairs Station

55

F6
1 Thrupp Paddock
2 Woodland Wy

BROADSTAIRS ROAD

B3
1 Crouch Hill Ct

A8
1 Frankapps Cl

A3
1 The Green

A B **18** C D E

1

2

Saxon Shore Way

Barksore
Marshes

Funton Creek

3

Lapwing Drive

Saxon Shore Way

Barksore

**Lower
Halstow**

*Callum
Park*

Breach Lane

Landrail Road

The Street

Blunden

Vicarage Lane

Cumberland Drive

School Lane

4

Lower Halston
CP School

Wardwell Lane

Elm Farm

5

Boxted Lane

Bro

*Hawes
Wood*

Belnor Avenue

Great Norwood

Little Norwood

6

Wardwell Lane

Bog Farm

High Oak Hill

Oak Hill

Cemetery

7

School Lane

Newington
C of E Primary
School

St Mary's View

Denham Road

Newington
Station

Cold
Harbour

Cold Harbour Lane

8

London Rd

Bull Lane

Orchard

Burntoak Road

Playstool

Wises Lane

Church Lane

HIGH STREET

James Place

Gallways

Lane Traces

BOYCES HILL

Keycol

A2

Cold Ha

Rook Lane

Leafields Close

KEYCOL HILL

Newington

**Cold
Harbour**

Newington
Manor

A B **56** C D E

A   B   22   C   D   E

1

2

3   Wellmarsh
     Creek

Windmill Creek

Spitend
Marshes

4

37   Peg Fleet

5

6   Saxon Shore Way

Fowley Island

South Deep

7   Swale Heritage Trail

Conyer Creek

8   Conyer

Teynham Level

A   B   60   C   D   E

Eastchurch
Marshes

Conyer Road

Brunswick
Field

Saxon Shore Way

1 grid square represents 500 metres

F G H 23 J K

I

2

3

4

40

5

6

7

8

Great
Bells

Bells Creek

Dutchman's
Island

Spitend Point

Uplees

Uplees Road

Nature
Reserve

F G H 61 J K

A   B   **24**   C   D   E

Capel Fleet

Harty Ferry Road

① ② ③

39

④ ⑤ ⑥ ⑦ ⑧

Isle of Harty

Elliots Farm

Harty Ferry Road

Mocketts

Sayes Court

The Ferry Inn

Harty Ferry Road

Nature Reserve

A   B   **62**   C   D   E

Nagden Marshes

F G H **25** J K

I

2

Nature
Reserve

3

4

42

5

6

7

The Swale

Saxon Shore Way

8

Cleve
Marshes

F G H **63** J K

Shellness Road

Harty
Marshes

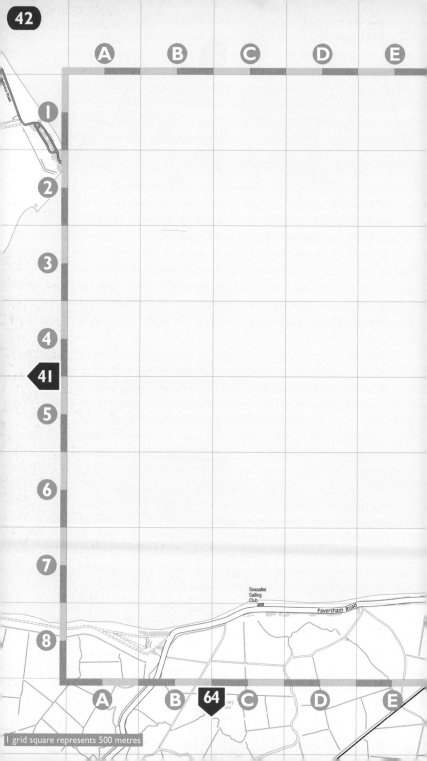

Seasalter
Sailing
Club

Faversham Road

41

64

1 grid square represents 500 metres

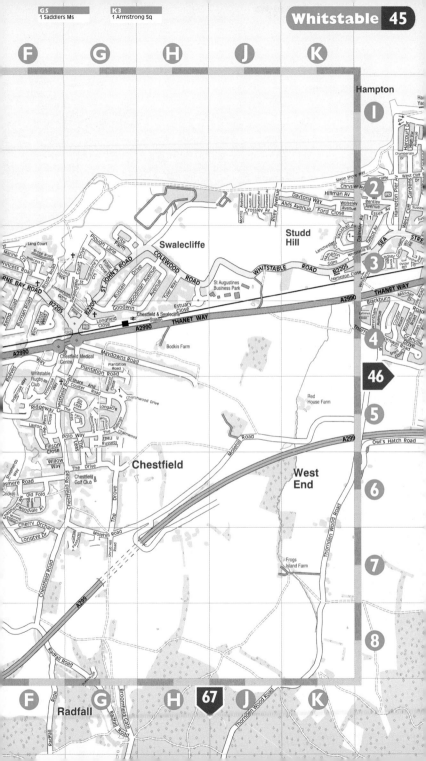

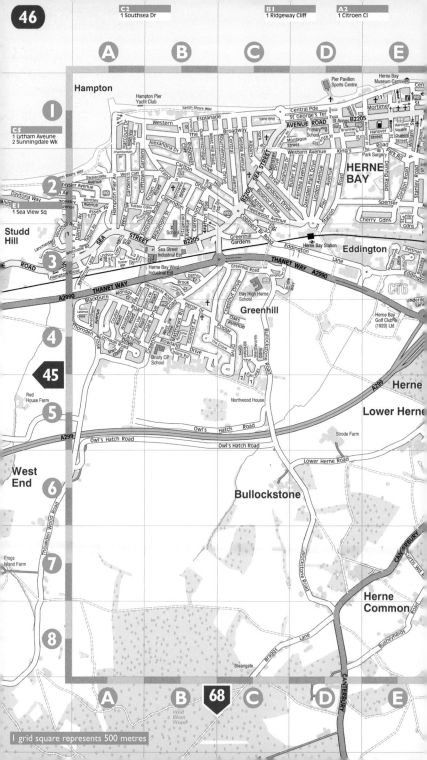

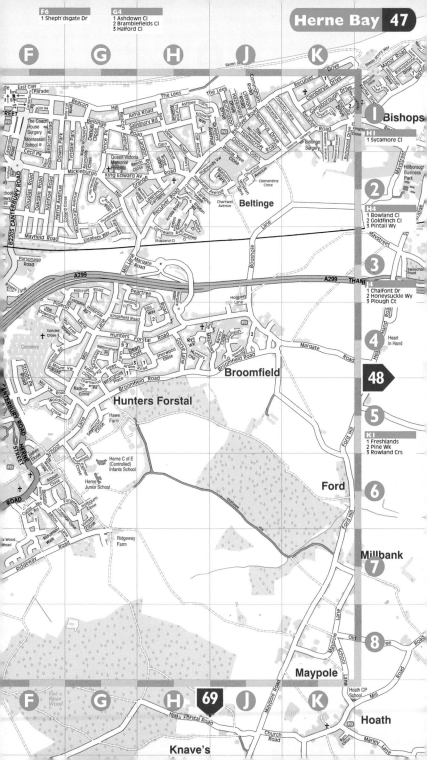

F   G   H   **27**   J   K

I

Wade Farm

2

C...
Wall

Bar...

THANET WAY A299

THANET WAY

A299 THAN... ...Y   3

Warehorn

Wagtail

River Wantsum

Wantsum Walk

Belle Isle

St Nicholas a...ade   4

50

5   ...Down

Chislet Marshes

6

Wantsum Walk

7   **Sarre**

Walk

Wantsum Walk

Old Road

8

ISLAND ROAD   A28

Surre ...

F   G   H   **71**   J   K

Wall

F G H 29 J K

Great Brooksend Farm

CANTERBURY ROAD BIRCHINGTON

PO

I

Brooks End

College Farm

A28

B2049 HILL

2

Coney Close

CT7

Crispe Road

THE STREET

Nursery

3

Acol

Seamark Road

Dilton Lane

Monkton Road Farm

Road

Plumstone

4

52

Plumstone Farm

Mill

5

Seamark Road

A299

A25 6

A253

Minster-Thanet Cemetery

Millers Lane

Willetts Hill

Parsonage Fields

Fair Road

7

Edgar Gardens

Collards Close

Monkton

Prospect Gardens

Greenhill Gardens

Brockmans C

Prospect Road

Monkton Street

PO

Monkton Street

Hoo

Sheriffs Ct Lane

Monkton

Rose Garden

Kenton Gardens

Edgar Road

Augustine Road

Emhurst Road

Epbert Road

8

Thorne Road

Molineux Road

Minster Primary School

F G H 73 J K

Sheriffs Court

Watchester Lan

LC

C4
1 Charlton Cl
2 Highbury Gdns

C5
1 Lancaster Cl
2 Windmill Wk

C3
1 Homeleigh Rd

B5
1 Brandon Rd
2 Brisbane Dr
3 Colombo Sq
4 Denbigh Rd
5 Hamilton Cl

A   B   **32**   C   D   E

Westwood

Saint
Peters

C6
1 Oakfield Ct

1

St Georges
Secondary
School

Lydden

2

C8
1 Hillcrest Gdns

East
Kent
Retail Park

Manston Court Road

Haine
Hospital

3

D2
1 The Silvers

Northwood

Coldswood Road

D4
1 Dorothy Dr
2 Romilly Gdns

Haine

4

Newlands
Farm

The Ramsgate
School

Dame Janet
County
Infant School

Thanet &
District Reform
Synagogue

Old Timber Yard
Industrial Estate

53

Spratling Street

5

Newington

D5
1 E'beth Kemp Ct
2 Lawley Cl
3 Wheatley Rd

Infant School   The Retreat

6

Newington
GM Junior
School

St-Lawrence

Ramsgate
Station

Ramsgate
Swimming Pool

D8
1 Clarence Rd
2 Grosvenor Rd
3 Herbert Rd
4 King Edward Rd
5 Napleton Rd

St Lawrence
Industrial Estate

Park Road

7

E1
1 Canterbury Cl

Canterbury Road East

Lord of
the Manor

Chilton

8

Chilton
CP School

Ramsgate
Athletic &
Football Club

D7, E6, E7, E8
Street names for
these grid squares
are listed at the
back of the index

Pegwell

A   B   C   D   E

E5
1 Larch Cl
2 Willow Av
3 Yew Tree Cl

! grid square represents 500 metres

A **B** 40 **C** **D** **E**

1

2

Court
Lodge

3

Nagden
Marshes

4

61

Ham
Marshes

Ham Farm

5

The
Brents

Upper Brents
Industrial Estate

Davingt **6**

Davington
Primary
School

Abbey
Road

Queen Elizabeths
School

FAVERSHAM

7

Beech
Close

Arthur
Salmon
Cl

Stonebridge

Health
Cen

Arden
Theatre

St Mary of Charity
C of E Junior & Infant
School

Millfield

Faversham
Cottage
Hosp

Fave
Indu

Graveney

Lady Dane Farm

8

Ospringe C of E
School

Ospringe

Ospringe
Place

Faversham
Sports
Centre

Chapel St

Faversham
Station

Preston

Preston
Park

A **B** 81 **C** **CAN** **D** **E**

Faversham Town
Football Club

Windermere

1 grid square represents 500 metres

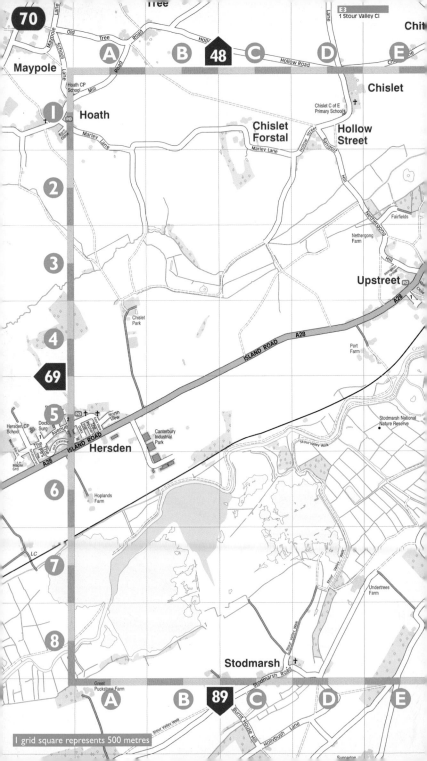

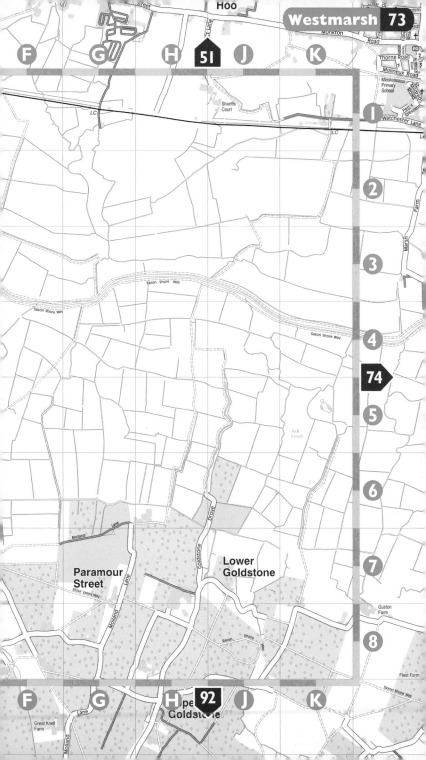

1 Primrose Wy
Thorne Farm
H1

II
1 Greystones Rd

F　　**G**　　**H**　**53**　**J** s End　　　**K**

Clive Road
Cliff View Rd

1

Earlsmead Crescent
Clive Road
Cliffs End
Mount Green Avenue
Meverall Avenue
SANDWICH ROAD
A256

Little Cliffsend

I

Thanet Coastal Path

Sevenscore

Cottington Road

St Augustines Golf Club

Oakland Court
Walmer Gardens

Viking Ship Hugin

LC

Cottington

St Augustines Cross

Nicholas Drive
Cliffs End Grove

2

A256

SANDWICH ROAD

Thanet Coastal Path

Pegwell Bay

3

Ebbsfleet Lane

4

Ebbsfleet House

Shell Ness

Sandwich Bay

5

North Rd
West Road
East Road
South Road

Richborough Port

Stour Valley Walk

Sandwich Flats

6

RAMSGATE ROAD

Stonar Cut

7

Saxon Shore Way

Back Sand Point

8

F　**A256**　**G**　　**H**　**94**　**J**　　　**K**

Prince's Golf Links

Ramsgate Road

Stour Valley Walk

A   B   **59**   C   D   E

Dully Road

nsted

Aymers

The Val

Park Farm

Mill Lane

Ludgate

Ludgate Road

Kingsdown

Lynsted Park

Erriottwood

M2

M2

Little Sharsted Farm

Bistock

Sharsted Court

Sharsted Hill

Down Court Road

Down Court

Newnham

Church Hill

Doddington Place

West End

Doddington

Doddington CP School

Northdown

The Street

The Street

Old Lenham Road

Seed

A   B   **98**   C   D   E

Solomons Temple

Frangbury

Little Frith

I grid square represents 500 metres

1 grid square represents 500 metres

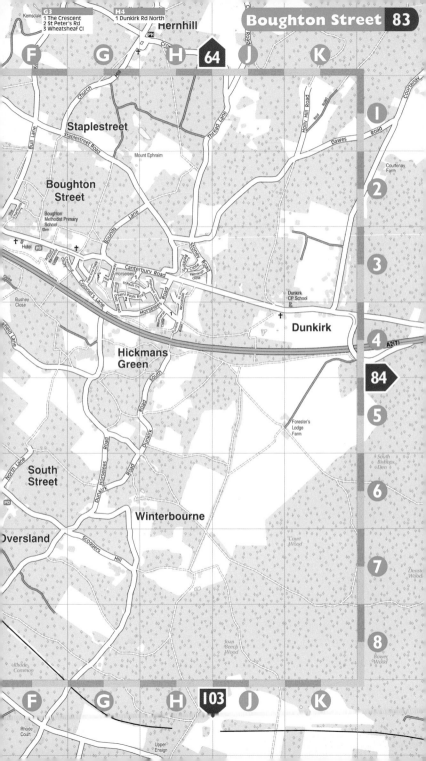

I grid square represents 500 metres

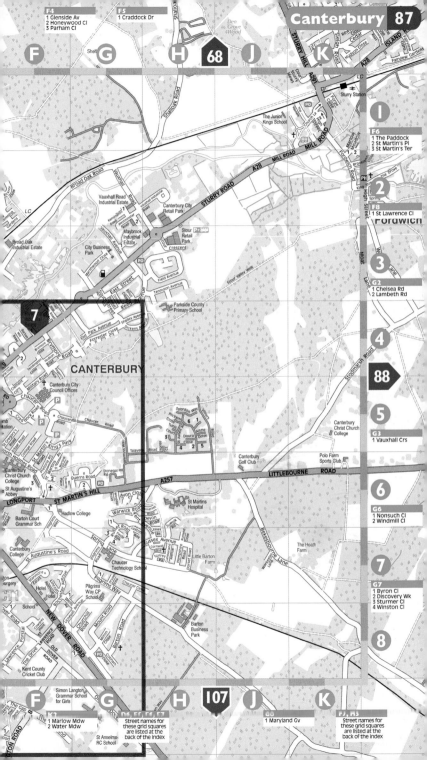

F4
1 Glenside Av
2 Honeywood Cl
3 Parham Cl

F5
1 Craddock Dr

F **G** **H** 68 **J** **K**

Shelf

Sturry Station

I

F6
1 The Paddock
2 St Martin's Pl
3 St Martin's Ter

The Junior
Kings School

Broad Oak Road

MILL ROAD

STURRY ROAD

A28 MILL ROAD

2

Fordwich

F8
1 St Lawrence Cl

Vauxhall Road
Industrial Estate

Canterbury City
Retail Park

Maybrook
Industrial
Estate

Stour
Retail
Park

Broad Oak
Industrial Estate

City Business
Park

Crescent

3

G2
1 Chelsea Rd
2 Lambeth Rd

East Street

Stour Valley Walk

Field Avenue

Tennyson Avenue

Parkside County
Primary School

4

7

Old Park Avenue

Forrester Close

Dickens Road

CANTERBURY

Canterbury City
Council Offices

5

Chaucer Road

Chaucer Road

Chaucer

Douro
Close

Alne
Drive

Canterbury
Christ Church
College

G3
1 Vauxhall Crs

Talavera Road

Canterbury
Golf Club

Polo Farm
Sports Club

Canterbury
Christ Church
College

St Augustine's
Abbey

Queens Road

Donegal Road

A257

LITTLEBOURNE ROAD

6

LONGPORT

ST MARTIN'S HILL

Avon Close

St Martins
Hospital

G6
1 Nonsuch Cl
2 Windmill Cl

Barton Court
Grammar Sch

Hadlow College

Warwick Road

Devon Road

The Hoath
Farm

Canterbury
College

St Augustine's Road

Spring Lane

Sussex Avenue

Little Barton
Farm

Bakesbourne Lane

7

G7
1 Byron Cl
2 Discovery Wk
3 Sturmer Cl
4 Winston Cl

Surgery

Hotel

Pilgrims
Way CP
School

Chaucer
Technology School

NEW DOVER ROAD

Mount Road

Barton Road

Churchill Road

Barton
Business
Park

8

Kent County
Cricket Club

Simon Langton
Grammar School
for Girls

F **G** 107 **H** **J** **K**

St Anselms
RC School

Ware

A   **B**   **73**   **C**   **D**   **E**

1

Great Knell Farm

Overland Farm

2

Upper Goldstone

Cop Street

3

Knell Farm

Weddington

Little Weddington Farm

Brookestreet Farm

A257

4

School Road

Molland Ash

Cartwright & Kelsey Primary School

Chilton Lane

Queens Road

Cop Street Road

Weddington Lane

A257

SANDWICH ROAD

Goss Hall

SANDWICH

91

Guilton

Glebelands

St Faiths at Ash School

The Street

Chilton

1   2

White Boot Gardens

Sandwich Road

New Street

Saunders Lane

New Street

Each Manor Farm

5

Guilton

Poulton Lane

Moat Lane

Ash

Coombe Lane

6

Poulton Farm

Coombe

7

The Rookery

Ringleton Manor

8

Durlock

Fleming Road

Flemings

Woodnesb

Barnsole

Drainless Road

Beacon Lane

A   **B**   **112**   **C**   **D**   **E**

Barnsole Road

Chalk Pit

Drainless Road

1 grid square represents 500 metres

Summerfield

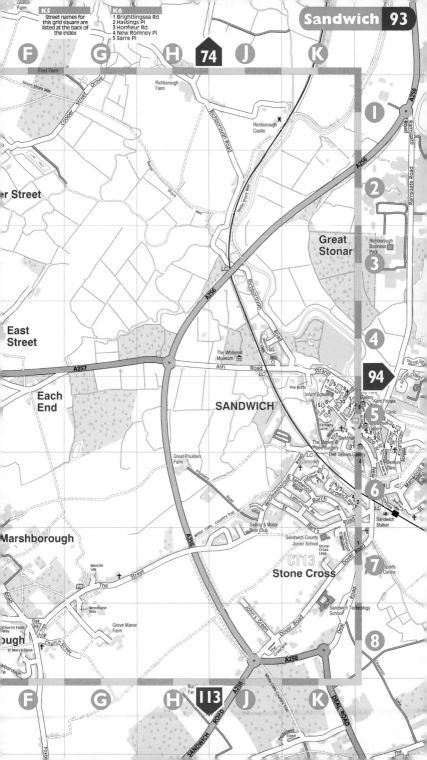

Sandwich
Bay

Sandwich
Bay Estate

Princes Drive

Guilford Road

King's

North Road

Avenue

Waldershare

Av

Princes Drive

Shawdon
Avenue

Francis
Avenue

Cambridge
Avenue

Country Trail

White Cliffs Country Trail

F G H J K

I 2 3 4 5 6 7 8

115

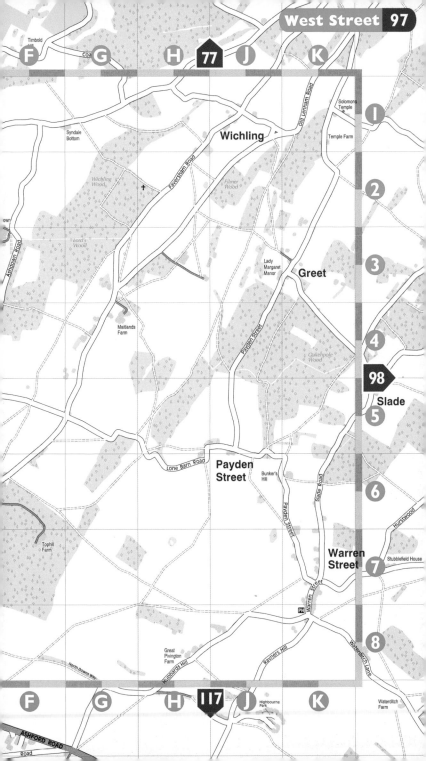

F G H 77 J K

Timbold Hill
Coa

Solomons Temple

1

Syndale Bottom

Temple Farm

Wichling

2

Wichling Wood

Faversham Road

Filmer Wood

3

Lord's Wood

Lady Margaret Manor

Greet

Maitlands Farm

Payden Street

4

Oakenpole Wood

98

Slade

5

Ashdown Road

Lone Barn Road

Payden Street

Bunker's Hill

Slade Road

6

Hurstwood

Tophill Farm

Payden Street

Warren Street

7

Stubblefield House

PH

Warren Street

8

Great Pivington Farm

Hubbards Hill

North Downs Way

Rayners Hill

Highbourne Park

Waterditch Lane

Waterditch Farm

F G H 117 J K

ASHFORD ROAD
Road

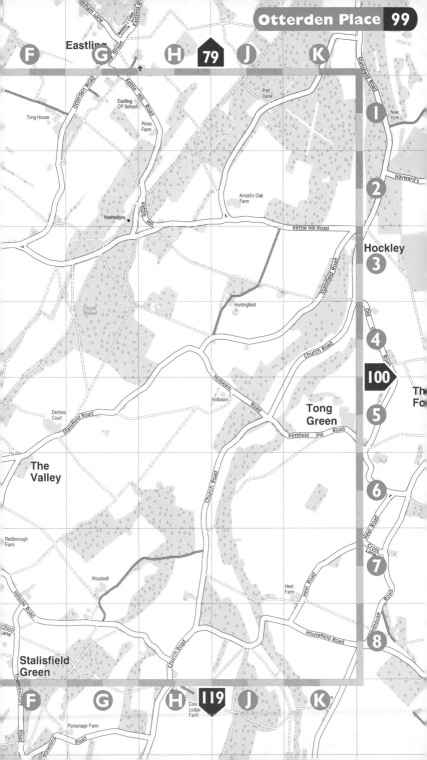

Harefield Farm

Throwley House (Hotel)

Sheldwich

Sheldwich CP School

Cobrahamsole Farm

Sheldwich Lees

Amos Close

Nursery Lane

Morgan Kirby's Garden

Shepherds Hill

Lords Farm

Dayton Road

Badlesmere Court

Woods Court

Fisher Street Road

Stringmans Farm

Bea...

Badlesmere

...eland

A251

ASHFORD ROAD

Shottenden Road

Shottenden Road

Dryland Farm

Pontus

ASHFORD ROAD

FAVERSHAM

...et's Farm

Church Ro...

Coppins Farm

102

A **B** **82** **C** Selling **D** **E**

Harefield
Farm

Church Lane

Selling of E
Primary School

Selling Road

1

Shepherds
Hill

2 Grove Road

Perrywood

3 P11

Conduit Wood

4

The
Mount

Woods
Court

101

Stringmans
Farm

Goldups   Lane

Shottenden

5 Beaney's   Lane

Soleshill

Shottenden Road

Manor   Lane

6

Denne   Lane

7

Wytherling
Court

Denne
Manor
Farm

Great Bower

8

Park
Wood

Young
Manor
Farm

A **B** **122** **C** A252 **D** **E**

Cutlers

1 grid square represents 500 metres

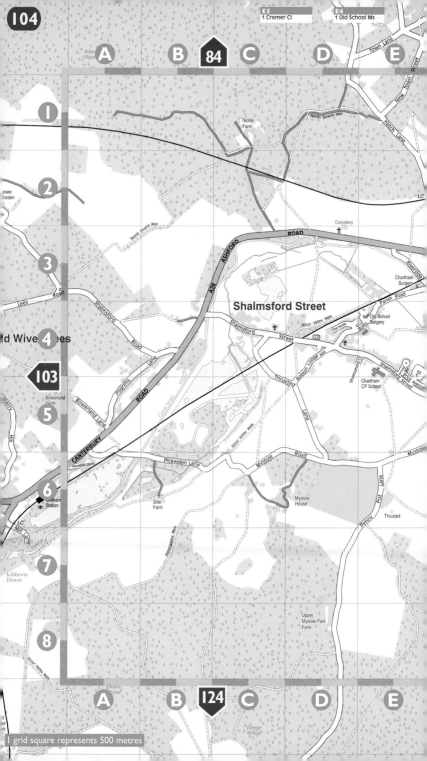

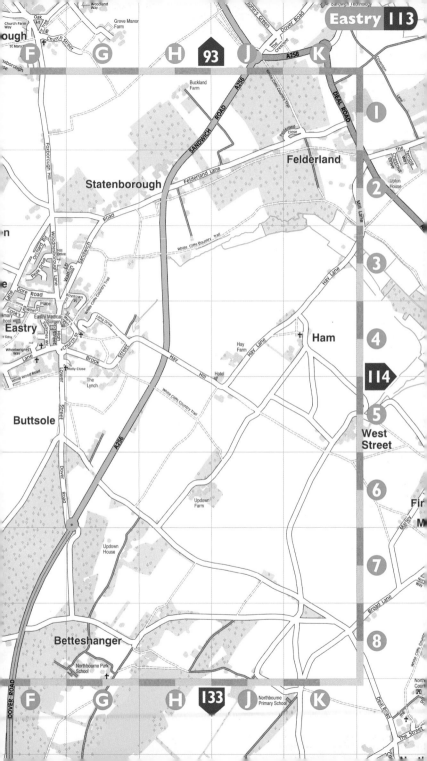

ASHFORD ROAD A20(T)

A **B** 96 **C** **D** **E**

D1
1 Douglas Rd

Cemetery

1

Boldrewood Farm

Maidstone

Ford Road

The Square

Dickley Wood

Ham Lane

Lower Close

Ham Lane

Ham Street

Mitchell Close

Lenham

Malthouse Close

Church Square

Old Ash

Old Ham Lane

Charton Avenue

Honywood Road

Robins Close

Court Gardens

Tanyard Farm

2

Lenham Station

Headcorn Road

3

Sandway Road

Headcorn Road

Leadingcross Green

Sandway

Lenham Heath Road

4

Green Lane

Platt's Heath

M20

Lenham Heath Road

5

Liverton Street

Lewsome Farm

Boughton Road

Chilston Park

Hotel

Chapel Farm

Bowley Lane

M20

6

Greensand Way

Boughton Road

Bowley Farm

7

Church Road

Boughton Malherbe

Greensand Way

Pope's Hall

Bowley Lane

rafty reen

8

Wellham Wood

Field Farm

Coach

Burscombe Road

A **B** 136 **C** **D** **E**

Cold Wood

Foxdene Wood

House

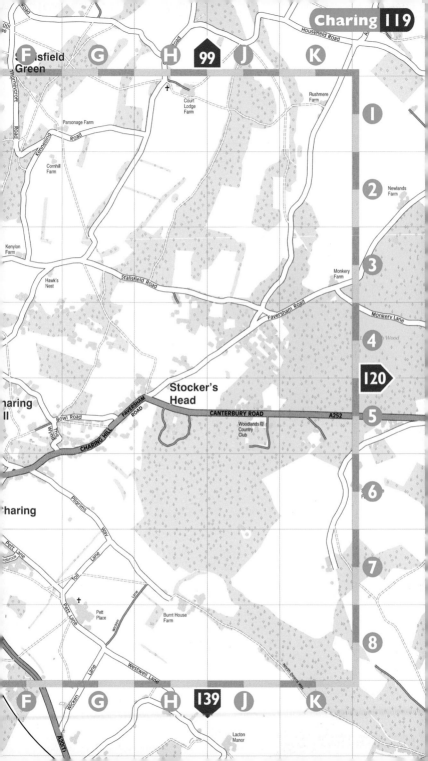

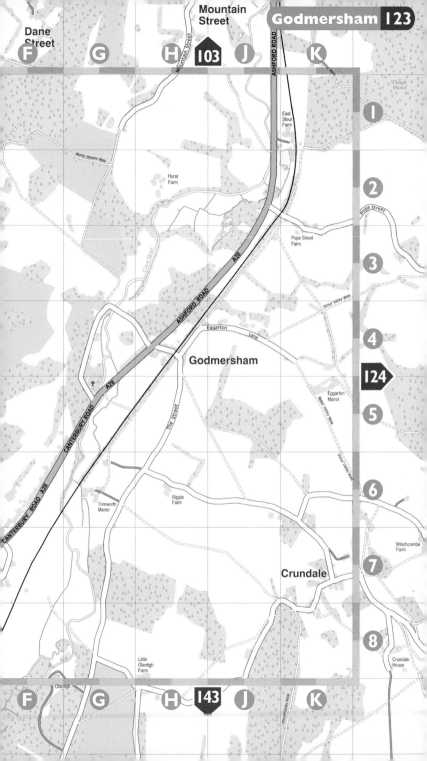

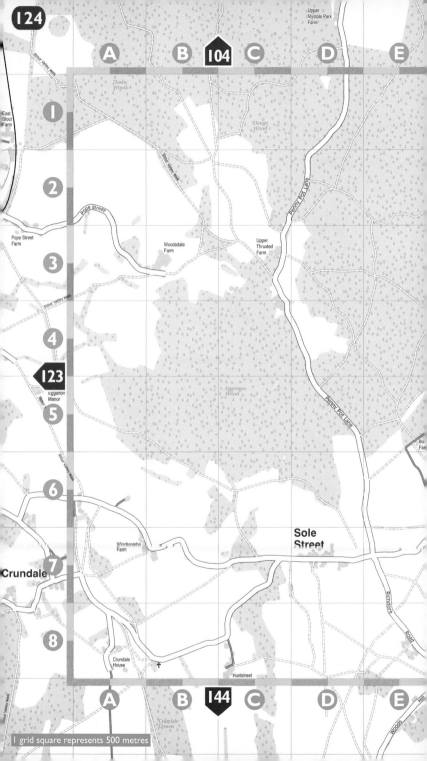

Pett Bottom

Gorsley Wood

Broxhall Farm

Bursted Manor

Bursted Wood

Woodgate

Langham Park Farm

Pheasants' Hall Road

Crows Camp Road

Charlton Wood

Reed Farm

128

The Manor House

Westwood

Lynsore Bottom

Pett Bottom Road

Marley Lane

Covert Lane

Covert Wood

Lynsore Court

Covert Wood

School Lane

ley's Hill

Bursted Hill

F   G   H   107   J   K

F   G   H   147   J   K

Pett Bottom Rd

Palmstead

Dane

Lenhall
Farm

A

B

opp**C**urne

D

E

Frog Lane

Street

DOVER ROAD

Park Lane

Rose Lane

Bonny Bush Hill

Ashf

I

Crows Camp Road

2

Charlton Park

Eltham Valley

Pheasants' Hall Road

Kingston

Nailbourne
Close

Church Lane

3

Charlton
Wood

Greenacre

Whitelocks
Close

Black Robin Lane

Covet Lane

4

The Street

Covet Lane

5

Marley

Jesse's Hill

Marley Lane

Covet Lane

Barham

Bar
Prin

6

Marley Lane

Covet Lane

Duskin
Farm

Heart's
Delight

Green Hills

Eltham Valley Way

7

Railway Hill

Derringstone

Ham Farm

South Barham

8

Covert
Wood

Eltham Valley Way

South

Barham

A

B

C

D

E

South Barham

Breach
Downs

1 grid square represents 500 metres

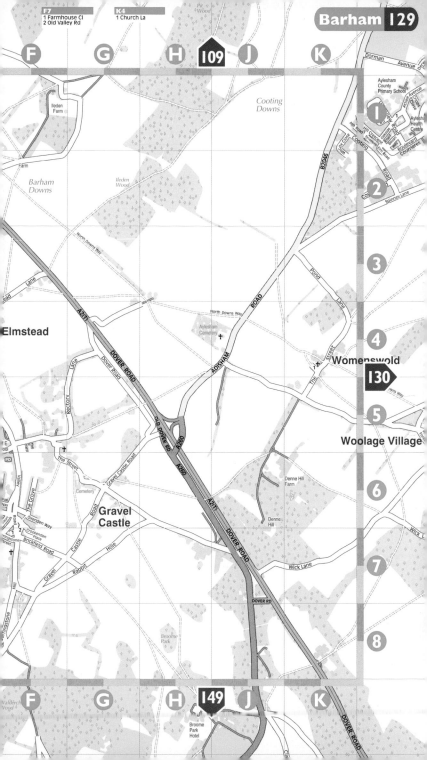

F7
1 Farmhouse Cl
2 Old Valley Rd

K4
1 Church La

F G H **109** J K

Pit Wood

Cooting Downs

Dorman Avenue

Aylesham County Primary School

Attus Avenue

1

Aylesham Health Centre

Cooting

B2046

Courtenars

Boulevard

Spinney Lane

2

Ileden Farm

Farm

Barham Downs

Ileden Wood

3

Pond Lane

North Downs Way

ROAD

Elmstead

A2611

North Downs Way

North Downs Way

DOVER ROAD

Aylesham Cemetery ✝

AYLSHAM

4

Womenswold

130

The Street

Rectory Lane

Lane

OLD DOVER RD

A260

5

Woolage Village

✝

The Grove

The Street

Gravel Castle Road

Cemetery

Denne Hill Farm

6

Oxenden Way

Crookenden

Brickfield Road

Gravel Castle

Castle

Hole

Denne Hill

Wick L

✝

Gravel

Rabbit

A2611

DOVER ROAD

Wick Lane

7

Hill

DOVER RD

8

Broome Park

F G H **149** J K

Waldersh Wood

Broome Park Hotel

DOVER ROAD

A   B   114   C   D   E

Sholden
Downs

Northbourne
Court

The Street

Northbourne

Northbourne Road

CT14

Mongeham
Church Close

Ashton
Close

Willow Road

Great
Mongeham

Cherry Lane

Little Mongeham

Paxwell La.

Stoneheap
Farm

133

White Cliffs Country Trail

White Cliffs Country Trail

Menzies Hill

Church Lane

Mongeham Road

Swingate Road

Sutton Lane

The Ripple
School

Chapel Lane

Ripple Vale
School

Ripple

Sutton Vale
House

Vale Road

Church Hill

Ripple
Farm

Pennieus Lane

Crooked South Road

Sutton

Ripple
Court

A   B   154   C   D   E

Sutton

Ninkland Oaks
Farm

G1, J2
Street names for
these grid squares
are listed at the
back of the index

1 grid square represents 500 metres

1 grid square represents 500 metres

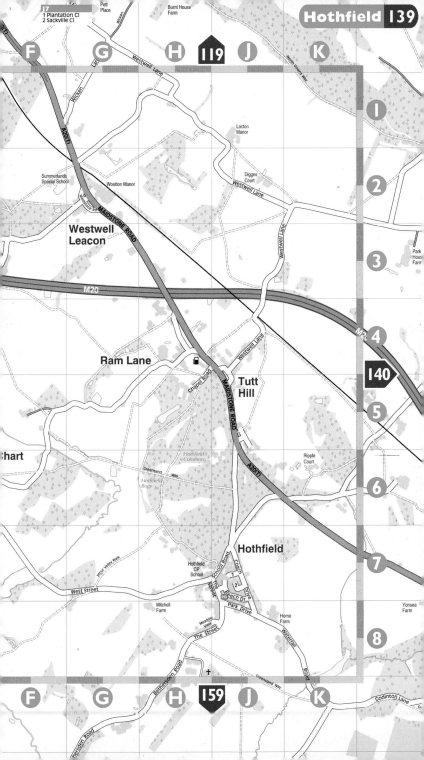

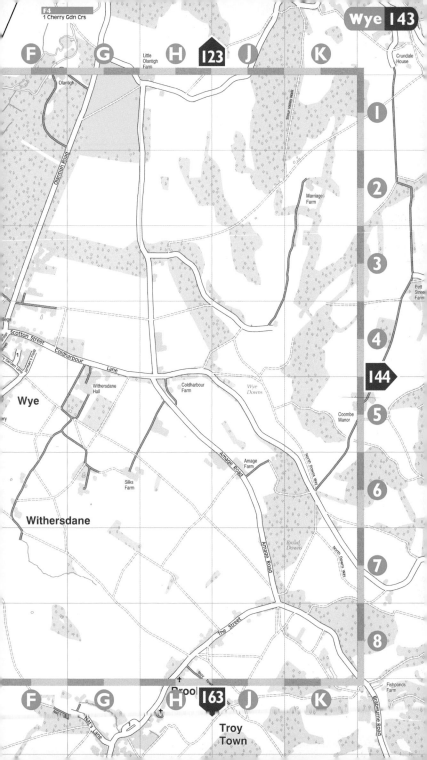

F4
1 Cherry Gdn Crs

F G **H** **123** J **K**

Crundale
House

Little
Olantigh
Farm

Olantigh

Olantigh Road

1

Marriage
Farm

2

3

Pett
Street
Farm

Scotton Street

Coldharbour   Lane

Carter's Lane

Brook's Lane

4

144

Withersdane
Hall

Coldharbour
Farm

Wye
Downs

Wye

Coombe
Manor

5

Amage Road

Amage
Farm

North Downs Way

Silks
Farm

6

Withersdane

Broad
Downs

Amage Road

North Downs Way

7

The Street

8

Brackmire Road

Troy Road

Brook

163

Fishponds
Farm

Nutt's Lane

Troy
Town

D8
1 Becket's Cl
2 Bowl Fld

A ndale B 124 C D E
ouse

Huntstreet

Woods Hill Road

1

Ccundale
Downs

2

Marriage
Farm

3

Ashenfield
Farm

Grandacre
Farm

Pett
Street
Farm

4

Hassell Street

143

Hassell Street

Bavi
Farm

5

nbe
or

6

Lyddendane
Farm

West
Down

North Downs Way

7

North

Cold
Blow

The street

Hastingleigh

8

Fishponds
Farm

Crabtree
Farm

Court Lodge

Tanley Lane

A B 164 C D E

South
Hill
Farm

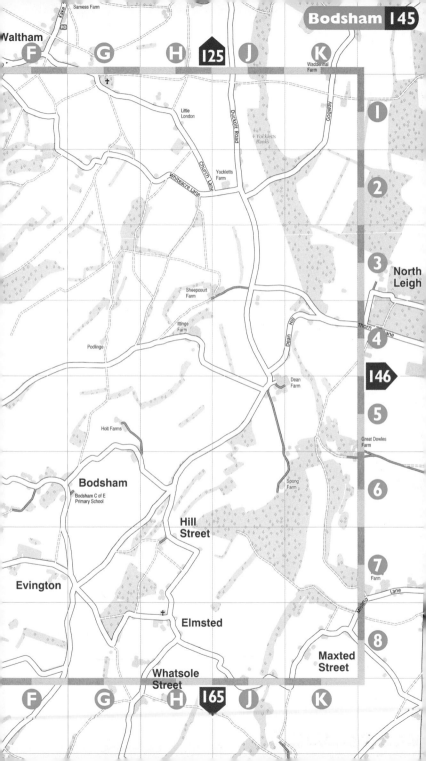

F   G   H   **127**   J   K

I

2

3

4

148

5

6

7

8

Covert Wood

Covert Wood

Atchester Wood

Palmstead

Pett Bottom Rd

Padfield Wood Road

Dane Farm

Red

Fryarne Park

Little Wildage

Bladbean

Farthingsole Farm

Elhampark Wood

Jacques Court

Grimsacre Farm

Hawes Farm

Park Gate

N

E

F   G   E H d   **167**   J   K

Chapel Lane

Park Lane

St Hill High Stre

Elham Valley Way

Elham

Old Hospital

dens

A   B   128   C   D   E

1

2

Redoak

Breach Downs

Breach

3

Lo

Bladbean

4

147

Wingmore

Elham Valley Way

Bunkershill Farm

5

Wingate Farm

6

Hall Downs

Grimsacre Farm

7

Oxroad Farm

8

Dreal's Farm

Henbury

North Elham

A   B   168   C   D   E

Rakeshole Farm

1 grid square represents 500 metres

F G H **129** J K

I

DOVER ROAD
A2(T)

2

Valderchain Wood

Broome Park

Clints Lane

Broome Park Hotel

CANTERBURY ROAD

Shelvin Lane

Shelvin Farm

3

Agester Lane

Denton

e Lees

THE STREET
A260

A260

4

Snodehill Farm

✝

Denton Court

Shelvin Lane

Lane

✝

150

CANTERBURY ROAD

Wootton

Wootton

Lane

5

Gatteridge Farm

Wootton Lane

A260

Hill House Farm

6

CANTERBURY ROAD

7

Wootton Lane

8

Selsted

Selsted C of E Primary School

F G H **169** J K

Newla

Blandred Farm

✝

B4
1 Haslewood Cl

A B **136** C D E

Frith
Wood

I

The
Quarter

Oaklands

Dering
Wood

2

egg Hill
Farm

Berry
Court

TN27

3

New House
Farm

Pluckley Road

Dering
Farm

M
H

Ash
Farm

Mill Lane

4

**Biddenden
Green**

Mainey
Wood

Ashenden

The
Acorns

Glebe

Romden Road

Smarden
CP School

High Street Street Green Lane Bridge Lane

Vesper
Court

PH

PO

5

Smarden

Cage Lane

Vesper Hawk
Farm

Romden Road

Romden
Castle

en Road

Walford
House

6

Bethersden Road

Buckman
Green Farm

Romden
Wood

**Haffenden
Quarter**

7

Luckhurst
Farm

8

Bethersden Road

Hamden

Langley

Tearnden
Farm

A B **177** C D E Bethersden

R

Little

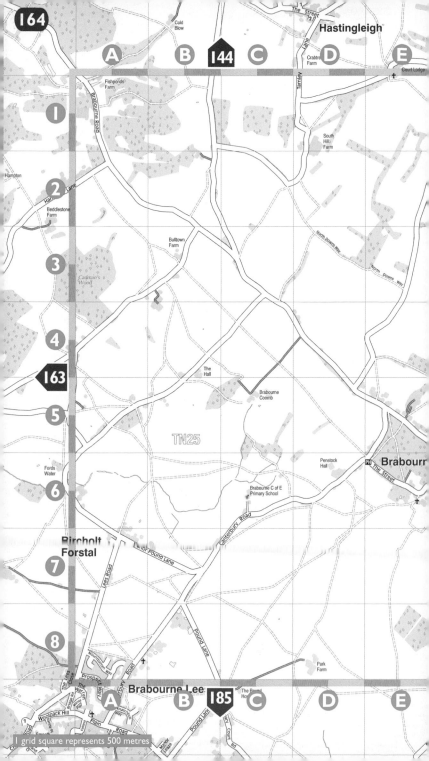

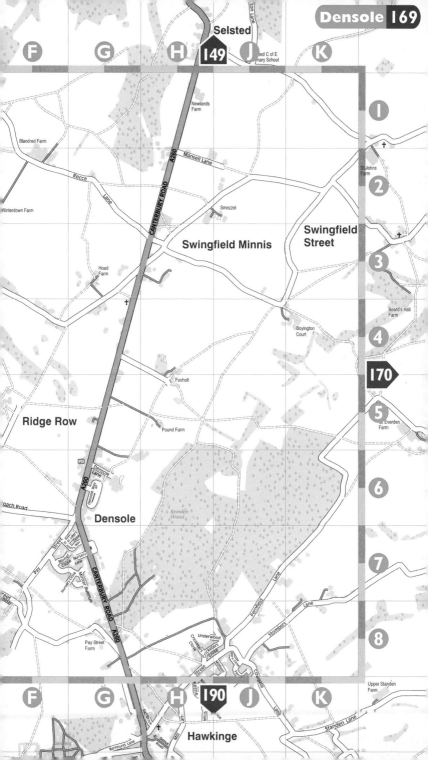

A   B   150   C   D   E

1

St Johns
Farm

2

Swingfield
Street

3

Beard's Hall
Farm

Boyington
Court

4

169

5

Gt Everden
Farm

6

7

8

North
Court

Chalksole

Ellinge

Green Lane

Chalksole

Slip Lane

Slip Lane

Alkh

Alkham Valley Road

South
Alkham

Drellingore

Lower
Standen
Farm

Moss

Lane

Farm

Swanton Court
Farm

Swanton Lane

Fe

Upper Standen
Farm

Lane

A   B   191   C   D   E

Standen Lane

Alkham Va

Hockley
Sole

1 grid square represents 500 metres

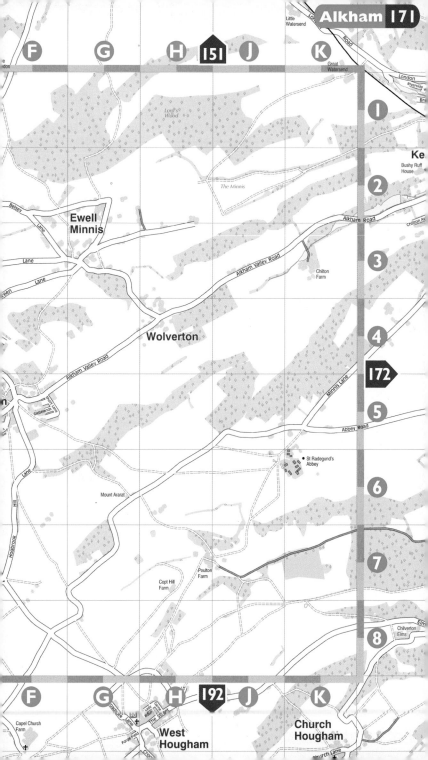

C4
1 The Spinney

C2
1 Courtland Dr

B1
1 Church Hl
2 High St
3 Mill St

Woodville

Great Watersend

A **B** **C** **D** **E**

1

E3
1 Brookfield Rd
2 Dodd's La
3 Mangers Pl
4 Pardoners Wy

Kearsney

Bushy Ruff House

2

E5
1 Beaufoy Ter
2 Coombe Cl
3 Macdonald Rd

3

E8
1 Approach Rd

Chilton Court

River

Badgers Rise

4

Crabble

River Bottom Wood

5

Abbey Road

Abbey Road

St Radegund's Abbey

6

7

Harbour Special Day School

8

Chilverton Elms

Elms Hill

Elms Vale Road

Elms Wood

Church

I grid square represents 500 metres

A **B** **C** **D** **E**

Temple Ewell

1 Temple Ewell C of E Primary School

Brookside

Riverside

London Road

Kearsney Station

The Abbey Practice

Kearsney Abbey

Pavilion Meadow

Sanctuary Close

River Street

Chilton Av

River CP School

Lower Road

Common

Lewisham

Cowper Road

The Ridgeway

Wingrove Hill

Bewsbury Cross Lane

Deanwood Road

Crabble

LONDON ROAD (RIVER) A256

WHITFIELD HILL

Whitfield Hill

A2(T)

A256

Old Park Hill

Friars Way

Pilgrims Way

Weavers Way

Squires Way

Knights Way

Shipmans Way

Crabble Avenue

Crabble Close

Crabble Meadows

CRABB

Hillside Road

St Radigunds CP School

Mayton Close

Beaufoy Road

Primro

Coombe Valley Road

Poulton Business Park

Barwick Road

Poulton Close

Wood Road

Coombes

Buck Hospi

Noah's

Dover Gra School for

Tower Hamlets

Queens Avenue

Queens Road

Elms Vale

Markland Road

Marlborough Road

Brasting Road

St Martins CR School

Eaves Road

Maydman Road Lardwell Lane

Maxton

B2011

Farth loe

B2011 FOLKESTONE ROAD

F4, G5, H6
Street names for these grid squares are listed at the back of the index

Aycliff

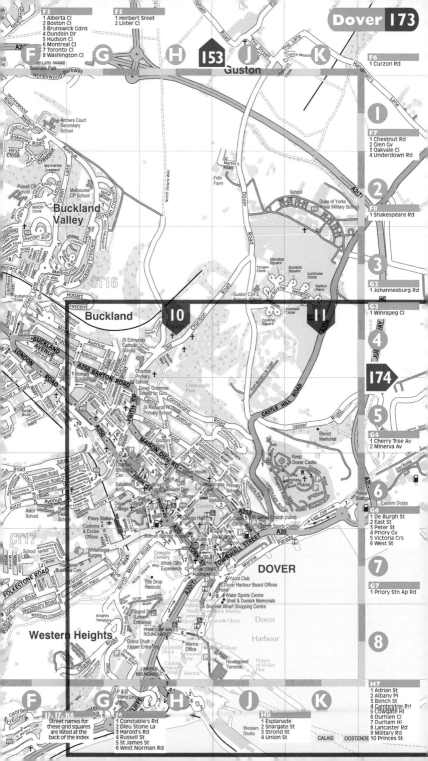

Dover 173

153
Guston

10
Buckland

11

174

Buckland Valley

CT16

CT17

Western Heights

DOVER

Dover Harbour

Prince of Wales Pier

CALAIS   OOSTENDE

Western Docks

Dover Castle

Honeywood Parkway

FOLKESTONE ROAD

LONDON ROAD

A256 BARTON ROAD

MAISON DIEU RD

CASTLE HILL ROAD

TOWNWALL STREET

YORK STREET

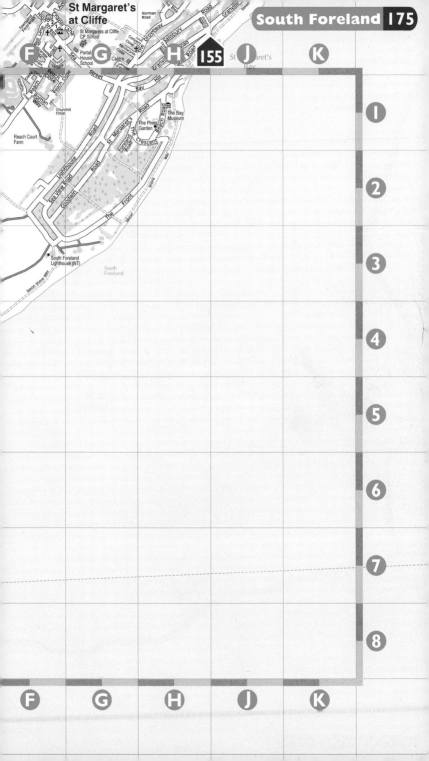

St Margaret's
at Cliffe

Norman
Road

F G H 155 St Margaret's Bay K

St Margaret's at Cliffe
CP School

Portal
House
School

Mill Close

Reach Court
Farm

Churchill
Close

The Pines
Garden

The Bay
Museum

Lighthouse Road

Sea View Road

Goodwin

The Front

South Foreland
Lighthouse (NT)

South
Foreland

I

2

3

4

5

6

7

8

F G H J K

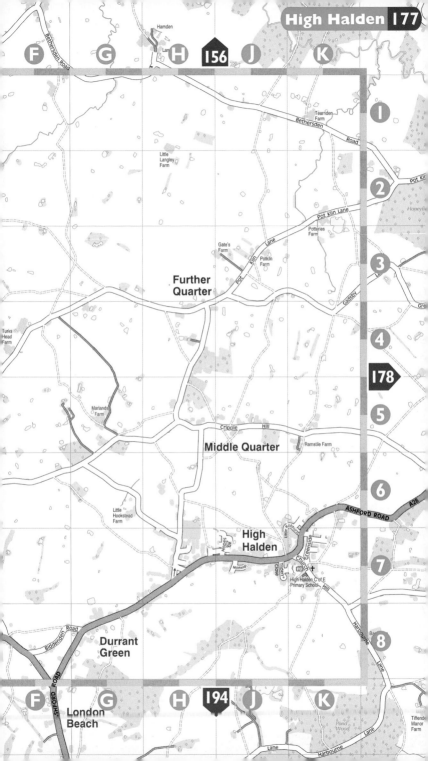

Mill
Farm

Winters Farm

Bethersden

Mill Road

A28 ASHFORD ROAD

Brissenden

Old Surrenden
Manor

Bevenden

A28

ASHFORD ROAD

Brook
Farm

Burntoak

ASHFORD RO

Gable Hook
Farm

**Brissenden
Green**

Vine Hall

180

Bethersden Road

High
Oak
Farm

Harlakenden
Farm

Mayshaves

lurenden
ood

Bethersden Road

Plurenden
Manor

Great
Engeham
Manor

Coleham
Green

Plurenden Road

st Road

Pound
Wood

Engeham Farm

Grove Farm

Hengherst

Redbrook Street

King
Farm

Shirkoak

I
2
3
4
5
6
7
8

Vitters
Oak

Surrenden Manor Road

A B **159** C D E

I

Old Surrenden
Manor

2

Bevenden

Brook
Farm Burntoak

Gable Hook
Farm

3

ASHFORD ROAD

A28

Lodge
Place

4

Bethersden Road

Handcock's
Farm

Criol
Farm

Snailswood
Farm

179

5

Harlakenden
Farm

Mayshaves

Bethersden Road

Criol Lane

Park Farm Close

Shadoxhurst

6

Woodchurst

The Street

7

Shadoxhurst

Coleham

Duck Lane

8

Pound
Wood

Moat Farm

A B **197** C D E

TN26

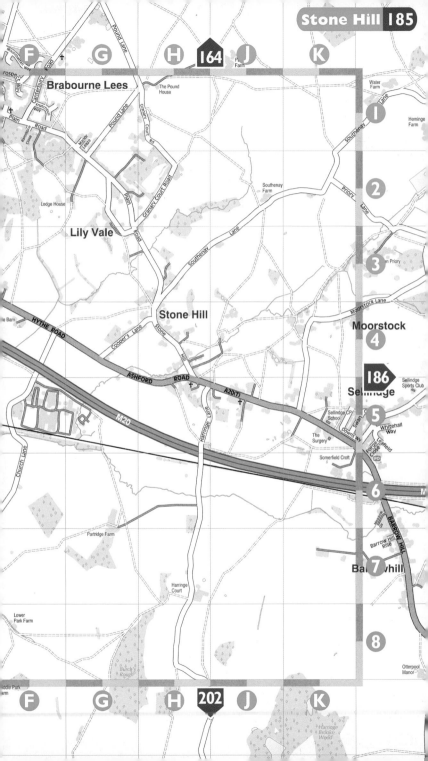

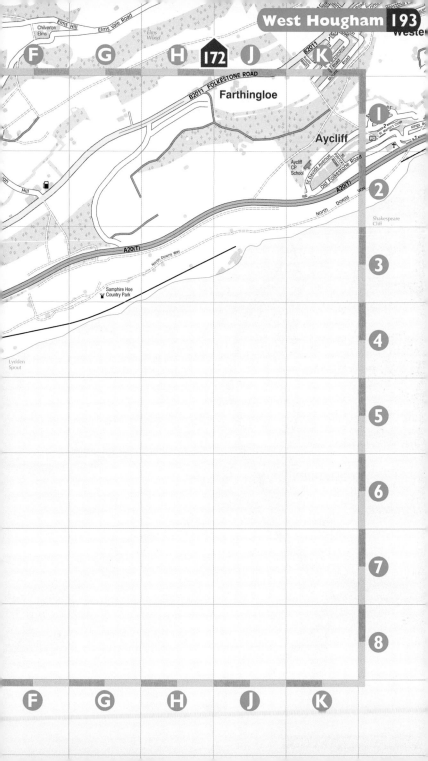

A8
1 Cherry Orch

A7
1 Jacksons La
2 St Mildred's Cl

A6
1 Eastwell Barn Ms
2 Wrights Cl

Durrant Green
177

B3
1 Glenwood Cl

Brook Farm

B4
1 Wayside

B5
1 Goldsmith Ct

B6
1 Green Hedges

C6
1 Mount Pleasant

C7
1 Shrubcote

London Beach

St Michaels

TENTERDEN

Leigh Green

1 grid square represents 500 metres

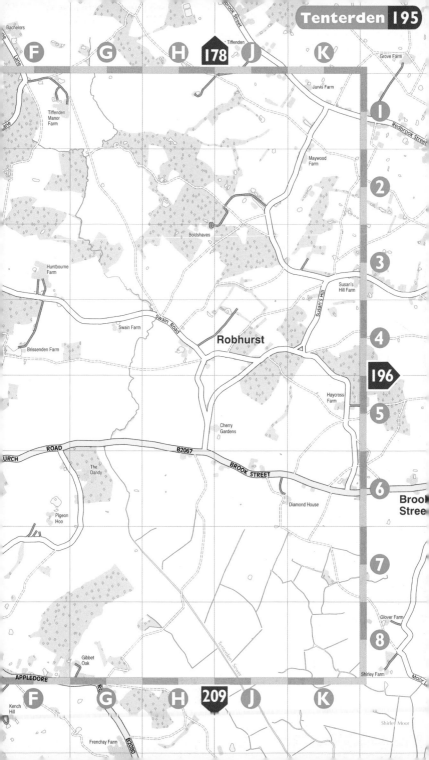

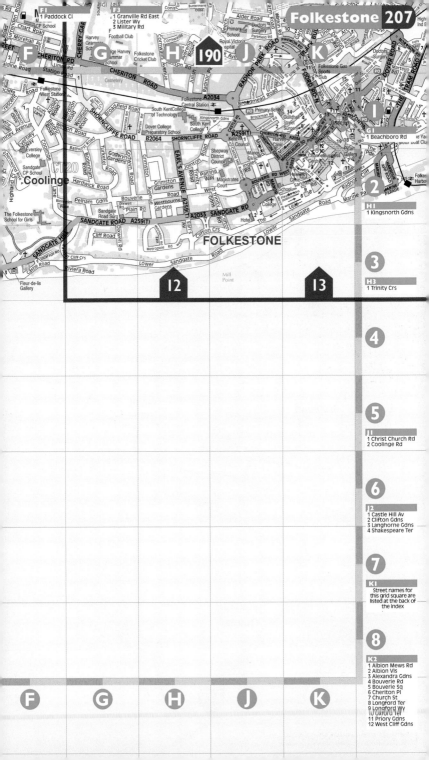

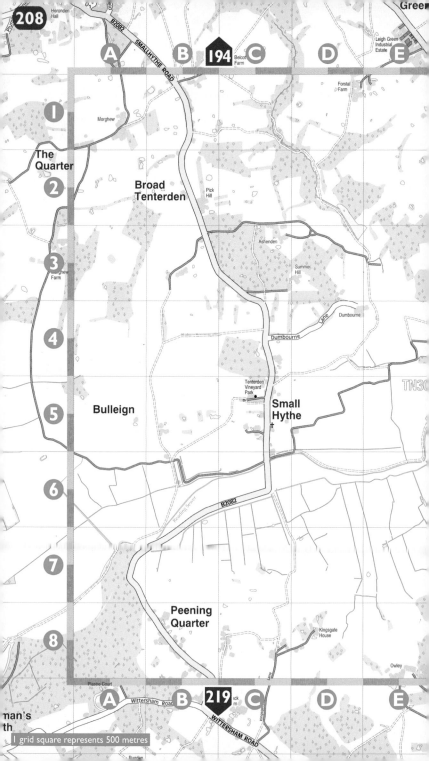

Kenardington

197

F G H J K

Legg Farm

Bench Hill

Beech Hill

Manor Farm

Great Heron Wood

Sly Corner

Kenardington Road

Saxon Shore Way

Church Road

Smith's Farm

Higham Farm

The Firs

Thrift Cottage

Saxon Shore Way

LC

ton Road

Hornes Place

212

Royal Military Canal Path

Appledore Heath

Royal Military Canal Path

Royal Military Canal Path

Hawthorn

The Street

THE STREET

Old Way

B2080

B2080

RHEE WALL

Bridge Farm

e

Road

B2080

B2080

B2080

Appledore Station

B2080

Saxon Shore Way

Saxon Canal Path

I

2

3

4

5

6

7

8

F G H J K

222

Stone Farm

Warehorne

A   **B**   198   **C**   **D**   **E**

Saxon Shore Way

Royal Military Canal Path

1

Royal Military Canal Path

Ham Loes F

2

Bridge Farm

A2070

Higham Farm

Ham Mill Farm

3

Thrift Cottage

LC

The Dowels

Ham Mill Lane

4

211

5

Ham Mill Lane

6

Appledore Station

Ham Farm

Arr...head Lane

Ham

Mill Lane

7

B2080

Whitehall Farm

8

Short Lane

Lane

Codhall

Snargate

Church Lane

A   **B**   223   **C**   **D**   **E**

Snargate Lane

Church Lane

F G H **199** J K

I

2

3

4

214

5

6

7

8

F G H **224** J K

Hans Farm

Lords Farm
Kitsbridge Lane

Wey Street Farm

Wey Street

Kitsbridge Lane

Bainbridge Farm

Wey Street

Stockbridge House

gdon

A2070

Poplar House

Snave

Court-at-Wick

Brenzett Green

Moat House

Newchurch Lane

TN29

New House

Springfarm Rd

2070

Poplar Farm

Melon Farm

A   B   **200**   C   D   E

Pear
Tree Farm

Honeywood
Farm

Kitchbridge

Oak Farm

1

Lords
Farm

Pittsbridge Lane

2

Wey Street
Farm

Wey Street

Will's Farm

Fletchers

Church View

3

Langdon

Brooker
Farm

Norwood Lane

4

Hill's
Farm

213

Millbank

Newchurch Lane

Melon Lane

Norwood
Farm

5

6

Willow Farm

Lodgeland
Farm

7

Littlebern

Melon Lane

8

TN29

A   B   **225**   C   D   E

North Fording
Bungalow

Farm

1 grid square represents 500 metres

G4
1 Hythe Rd

K2
1 Livingstone Cl
2 Stanley Cl

DYMCHURCH ROAD A259

A259 (T)

F G H 203 J K

The Little
Piece

LC

Latne Barn

**Donkey
Street**

I Street

LC

Woodland Way
Crescent
Blackman
Denham Road
Ludeno
Ashford
Crimond Av
Botts

Romney Hythe & Dymchurch Railway

HYTHE ROAD

Marine Av
Wood

A259 (T)

Haguelands
Farm

Dymchurch Wall

Burmarsh Rd

LC

Tower Estate
Lower Sands
Lower Sands
Queensway
Green
Meadow
Crossways
Close
Kingsway

Pear Tree
Lane
Sea Wall

Nurse
Avenue

The Oval

Wychurst

Sea Wall

Dymchurch

I 2 3 4 5 6 7 8

F G H J K

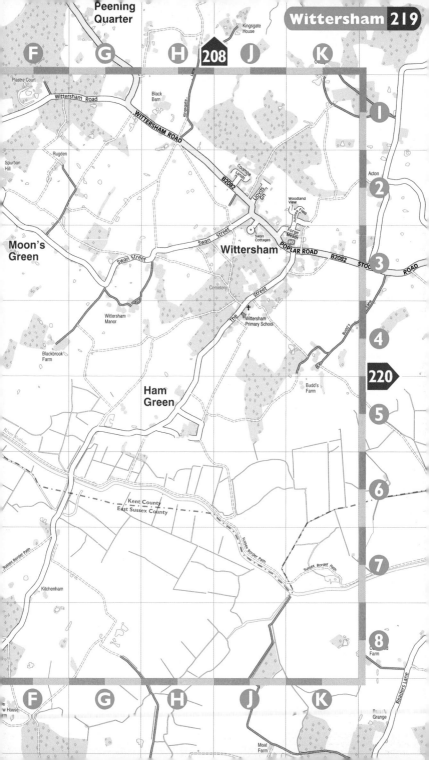

209

219

Owley

I

Odiam Farm

Stone Farm

A

B

C

D

E

Rosehill

Rose Hill

Lower Road

Isle of Oxney

Acton

2

The Stocks

woodland

AR ROAD

3

STOCKS ROAD

B2082

Wittersham Road

Holman's Farm

Tophill Farm

RYE ROAD

4

Budd's Farm

Great Prawls Farm

5

Rother Levels

Newbridge Farm

6

Kent County

East Sussex County

B2082

WITTERSHAM ROAD

Sussex Border

7

Sussex Border Path

River Rother

Thornsdale

8

Corkwood Farm

WITTERSHAM CARDNER'S HILL

Oxenbridge

A

B

C

D

E

Baron's Grange

WITTERSHAM LANE

Bosney Farm

Luckhurst

The Street

Stone
in Oxney

Forge
Meadow

Catt's Hill

Catt
Farm

Top Road

Oxenden

Church Hill

Saxon Shore Way

Mackley
Farm

Knock Hill

Military Road

Royal Military Canal

Highknock Channel

Stone
Bridge

Cliff Farm

Stone
Cliff

Cliff Marsh
Farm

Royal Military Canal Path

Five Watering Sewer

Royal Military Canal

Saxon Shore Way

Military Road

White Kemp Sewer

F G H 210 J K

I

2

3

4

222

5

6

7

8

F G H J K

1 grid square represents 500 metres

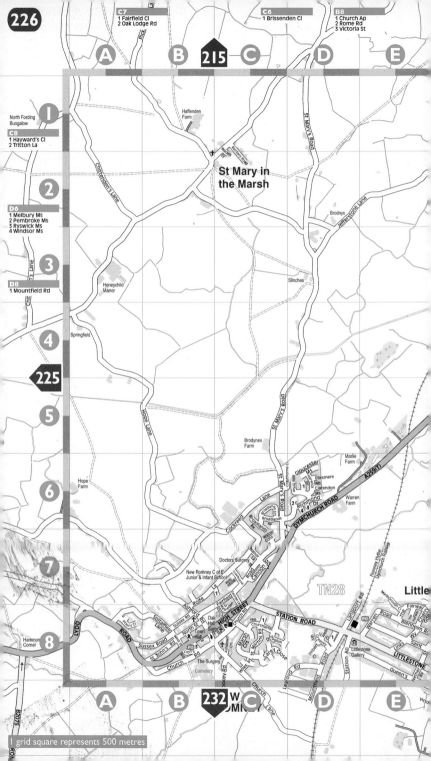

G2
1 Old Bakery Cl

H2
1 Cobsden Cl
2 Highlands Crs
3 Kingsland Hollow

F G H 216 J K

I
2
3
4
5
6
7
8

DYMCHURCH ROAD

Wilton Way
St Mary's Gdns
Brookside

Dunstall Lane
Cobsden Road
Spring Hollow

Cobsden Road

St Mary's Bay

Laurel Avenue
Holly
Maple
Oak Dr
Willow Dr
Hawthorn
Cedar Crs

Coast Drive

Seaway Gdns
Seaway Gdns

Links Crs

Romney Warren Golf Club

St Andrew's Road
Madeira Road
Blenheim Road
Nicholas Road

Littlestone-on-Sea

Coast Road

B2071

F G H 233 J K

White Kemp Sewer

A
B
222
C
D
E

New Buildings
Farm

1

East Sussex County
Kent County

2

FOLKESTONE ROAD

Offen's
Farm

3

Lamb Farm

Guldeford
Lane Corner

4

Collyer's
Farm

5

Vane
Court

6

Barn Farm

7

Kent County
East Sussex County

8

A
B
234
C
D
E

Whitehouse
Farm

GULDEFORD LANE

A259(T)

Kent Ditch

1 grid square represents 500 metres

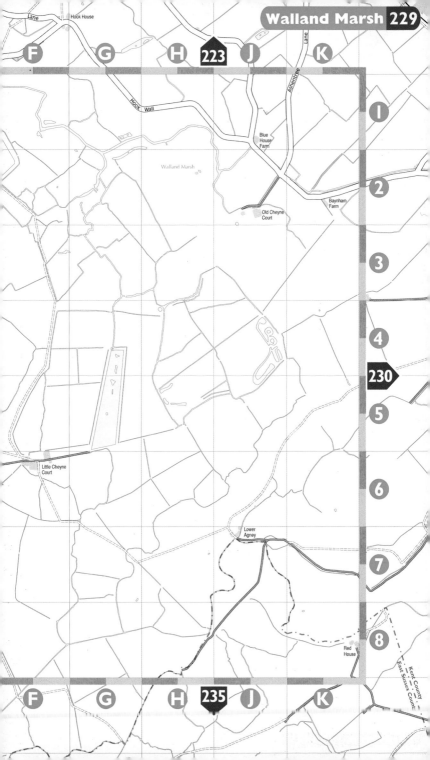

Lane

Hook House

F　　G　　H　223　J　　K

Hook Wall

I

Astentree Lane

Blue House Farm

2

Walland Marsh

Baynham Farm

Old Cheyne Court

3

4

230

5

Little Cheyne Court

6

Lower Agney

7

8

Red House

Kent County
East Sussex County

F　　G　　H　235　J　　K

A　　B　224　C　　D　　E

I

2　Baynham Farm

3

4

229

5

6

7

8　Red House

Coldharbour Lane

LC

Midley Cottages

Wheelsgate

Court Lodge

Hawthorn Corner

LC

Newland Farm

Newland

Little Scotney

Kent County
East Sussex County

A　　B　236　C　　D　　E

1 grid square represents 500 metres

232
Hammonds
Corner

226

NEW
ROMNEY

Kemp's
Hill

Romney
Salls

Belgar
Farm.

Footway
Farm

231

Jack's
Court

Northlade

Airport

LC

238

Denge

1 grid square represents 500 metres

Greatstone
on-Sea

Greatstone
Primary
School

Baldwin

Romney Hythe & Dymchurch Railway

STATION ROAD

HIGH ST

ESTONE

LYDD

ROAD

ROMNEY ROAD

B2075

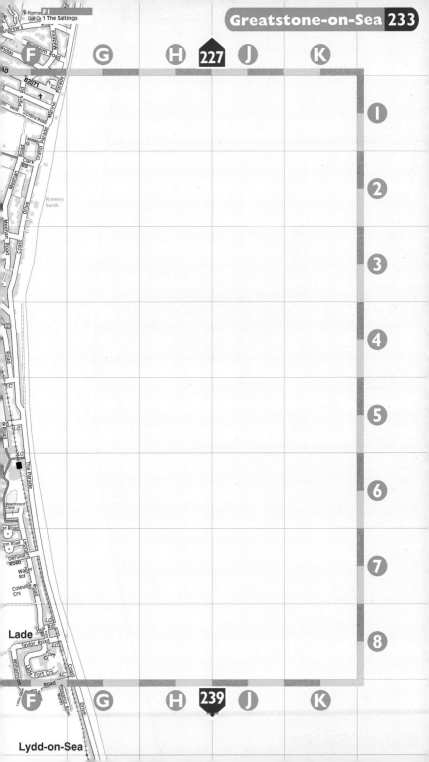

F G H **227** J K

F1 Romney
Golf Ch 1 The Saltings

B2071

Victoria Road

Grand Parade

Marine Parade

Clark Rd

Romney
Sands

Coast Road

Meehan Road

The Parade

Beachmont
Close

Derville
Road

Waller
Rd

Coleville
Crs

Lade

Taylor Road

Fort
Cl

Fort Crs

Williams

Coast Road

I 1
2
3
4
5
6
7
8

F G H **239** J K

Lydd-on-Sea

228

A B C D E

Kent County
East Sussex County

I
2

Point Farm

3

Camber

Camber Road

Farm Lane

Draffin Lane

New Lydd Road

Old Lydd Road

Toenham Way

Lynn Way

South Road

Manchester Drive

Church Lane

First Avenue

Second Avenue

PO

The Suttons

Lydd Road

Broo
Farm

4

5

Camber Sands

6

Rye Bay

7

8

A B C D E

I grid square represents 500 metres

F G H **229** J K Red House

Kent County · East Sussex County

I

2

3

Jury's Gut Sewer

Broomhill Level

4

236

Neath Road

Neath Road

5

Jury's Gap

Midrips

The Wicks

Lydd Road

Broomhill Sands

East Sussex · Ke

6

7

8

F G H J K

Red House

A   B   230   C   D   E

Kent County
East Sussex County

1

Scotney
Court

2

Jury's Gut Sewer

3   The Forelands

Jury's Gap Road

LC   Sandy Brook

Holmstone

4   Neath Road   Ferguson Road   Ferguson Road   LC

Neath Road

235

Midrips

LC   Lydd
Ranges   LC   LC   South
Brooks

5   LC

The
Wicks

East Sussex County
Kent County

6   South Brooks Road

7

8

A   B   C   D   E

I grid square represents 500 metres

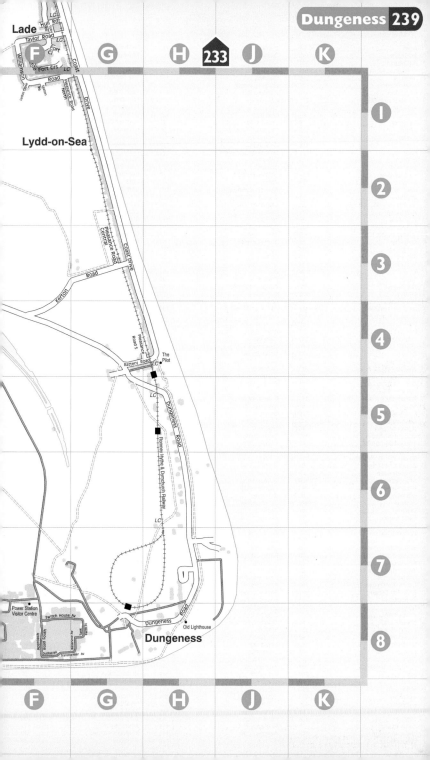

Acol	52	A3
Adisham	109	K6
Aldington	201	J1
Aldington Frith	183	J8
Alkham	170	E5
Anvil Green	125	F7
Appledore	210	E7
Appledore Heath	211	F4
Arpinge	189	H3
Ash	92	C5
Ashford	8	C4
Ashley	132	E8
Aycliff	193	K1
Aylesham	130	B1
Badlesmere	101	G5
Bagham	103	J7
Bapchild	59	F3
Barfrestone	131	G5
Barham	128	E5
Barnfield	137	J2
Barnsole	91	K8
Barrow Green	60	A3
Barrowhill	185	K7
Bay View	24	C4
Bekesbourne	108	D2
Bekesbourne Hill	108	B1
Beltinge	47	J2
Berwick	203	J2
Bethersden	179	F1
Betteshanger	113	F8
Bexon	76	B2
Biddenden Green	156	B4
Bilsington	200	C5
Bilting	122	E6
Birchington	30	B7
Bircholt Forstal	163	K7
Bishopsbourne	108	B8
Bishopstone	48	A1
Blacketts	37	J8
Bladbean	147	K4
Blean	66	C8
Bliby	182	E6
Blue Town	14	A3
Bluetown	77	H5
Bobbing	35	G7
Bockhanger	141	F8
Bodsham	145	G6
Bonnington	201	F3
Borden	57	F4
Bossingham	126	E8
Bossington	109	K3
Bottom Pond	76	D4
Boughton Aluph	142	B1
Boughton Corner	142	C1
Boughton Lees	141	K3
Boughton Malherbe	116	A6
Boughton Street	83	F2
Boyden Gate	48	D6
Brabourne	164	E6
Brabourne Lees	185	F1
Bramling	89	J8
Brattle	196	D6
Bredgar	76	A1
The Brents	62	C5
Brenzett	223	K2
Brenzett Green	213	F8
Bridge	108	A5
Brissenden Green	179	G4
Broad Oak	68	C7
Broad Oak	183	H5
Broadstairs	55	H1
Broad Street	186	C1
Broad Tenterden	208	A2
Bromley Green	181	H8
Bromstone	55	F3
Brook	163	H1
Brookland	223	H6
Brooks End	51	G2
Brook Street	196	A6
Broomfield	47	J4
Broomhill	90	D5
Broom Street	63	J4
Buckland	10	A1
Buckland Valley	173	F2
Bulleign	208	A5
Bullockstone	46	C6
Burmarsh	216	E2
Buttsole	113	F8
Bybrook	161	G1
Calcott	68	D4
Camber	234	C3
Canterbury	7	E1
Capel-le-Ferne	191	J4
Cellarhill	59	K5
Chalksole	170	D2
Chalkwell	57	H2
Challock	121	G5
Chamber's Green	157	J2
Charing	119	F6
Charing Heath	118	A7
Charing Hill	119	F5
Chartham	105	G4
Chartham Hatch	85	F8
Cheriton	189	H8
Chestfield	45	G6
Chestnut Street	56	D2
Chilham	103	H6
Chillenden	111	J6
Chilmington Green	181	F1
Chilton	4	A5
Chislet	70	E1
Chislet Forstal	70	C1
Chitty	48	E8
Church Hougham	192	E1
Church Whitfield	153	F5
Clapham Hill	66	A1
Clap Hill	184	A7
Claypits	110	E2
Cliffs End	53	J8
Cliftonville	32	D4
Cold Harbour	34	E8
Coldred	151	H3
Conyer	38	B8
Coolinge	207	F2
Coombe	92	D6
Cooper Street	92	E2
Coppins Corner	118	C8
Cop Street	92	C2
Copton	81	H4
Court-at-Street	202	C3
Crabble	172	C4
Crouch	82	E5
Crundale	123	K7
Culmers	63	K5
Danaway	56	B4
Dane Street	103	F8
Daniel's Water	159	F6
Dargate	65	F6
Dargate Common	65	F7
Davington	61	K6
Deal	115	K8
Deans Hill	56	C8
Deerton Street	60	D4
Densole	169	G6
Denstroude	65	K6
Denton	149	G3
Derringstone	128	E7
Doddington	78	A7
Donkey Street	217	F1
Dover	10	C4
Drellingore	170	C7
Dumpton	5	E1
Dungate	77	H3
Dungeness	239	H8
Dunkirk	83	K4
Dunn Street	140	C1
Durlock	91	K6
Durrant Green	177	G8
Dymchurch	217	F6
Each End	93	F5
Eastchurch	23	F3
East End	10	A1
East Langdon	154	A5
Eastling	79	G8
Eastry	113	F4
East Stourmouth	72	C5
East Street	93	F4
East Studdal	133	J6
Eastwell Park	141	H3
Eddington	46	D3
Egerton	136	E3
Egerton Forstal	136	D5
Elham	167	J1
Elmsted	145	H8
Elmstone	91	G1
Elvington	132	A5
Erriottwood	78	A3
Etchinghill	188	B3
Evington	145	F7
Ewell Minnis	171	G2
Exted	167	H1
Eythorne	131	K7
Fairfield	222	B5
Farthingloe	193	J1
Faversham	62	D6
Felderland	113	K2
Finglesham	114	A6
Fir Toll	137	J8
Flemings	92	B8
Folkestone	12	B6
Ford	47	K6
Fordwich	88	A2
The Forstal	183	J3
Fostall	64	B7
Four Oaks	61	H5
Frinsted	76	C7
Frogham	130	E5
Frogholt	188	D6
Further Quarter	177	H3
Garlinge	31	F7
Garlinge Green	105	G4
Gibraltar	190	A3
Godmersham	123	H4
Golgotha	131	G8
Goodnestone	63	J7
Goodnestone	111	F5
Gore	112	E3
Gore Street	50	E7
Gosmere	81	H7
Gravel Castle	129	G6
Graveney	63	J4
Great Bower	102	A8
Great Chart	159	K5
Great Mongeham	134	C3
Great Stonar	93	K3
Greatstone-on-Sea	232	E1
Greenhill	46	C4
Greet	97	K3
Grove	71	G6
Grove End	57	H7
Grove Ferry	71	G4
Grove Hill	70	E8
Groves	91	H7
Guilton	92	A5
Gushmere	82	C7
Guston	153	J8
Hacklinge	114	C4
Haffenden Quarter	156	A7
Haine	54	A4
Hale	50	E2
Hales Place	86	E3
Halfway Houses	15	F7
Halfway Street	151	F3
Ham	113	K4
Ham Green	219	H5
Hammill	112	C2
Hampton	46	A1
Hamstreet	199	F6
Harbledown	85	K6
Harman's Corner	57	G4
Hassell Street	144	C4
Hastingleigh	144	C4
Hawkinge	190	C1
Hawthorn Corner	48	B4
Hearts Delight	57	G5
Hemsted	166	B6
Herne	46	E5
Herne Bay	46	E3
Herne Common	46	E7
Hernhill	64	C5
Heronden	112	C5
Hersden	70	A5
Hickmans Green	83	G4
Hicks Forstal	69	F2
High Halden	177	J7
Highstead	49	C5
Highsted	58	A7
Highstreet	65	G4
Hillborough	48	B2
Hill Street	145	H6
Hinxhill	162	D5
Hoaden	91	H2
Hoath	70	A1
Hockley	100	A3
Hogben's Hill	82	A7
Hollow Street	70	D1
Hollybushes	77	G6
Honey Hill	66	B7
Hoo	51	J8
Horn Street	206	B2
Horton	105	H3
Hothfield	139	J2
Howt Green	35	J5
Hunters Forstal	47	G5
Hythe	205	G5
Ickham	89	J5
Ivychurch	224	E3
Iwade	35	J2
Jury's Gap	235	H5
Kearsney	172	A2
Kempe's Corner	142	B4
Kemsley	36	A5

Kenardington 197 H8
Kennington 141 J8
Keycol 34 D8
Key Street 57 F1
Kingsdown 77 K2
Kingsdown 155 H1
Kingsgate 33 H5
Kingsnorth 181 K3
Kingston 128 C3
Knave's Ash 69 H1
Knowlton 112 A7
Lade 233 F8
The Leacon 198 A7
Leadingcross Green 116 C3
Leaveland 100 E6
The Lees 120 E5
Leigh Green 194 E7
Lenham 116 D1
Lenham Forstal 117 H5
Lenham Heath 117 H6
Lewson Street 60 C7
Leysdown-on-Sea 25 G4
Lilyvale 185 G3
Littlebourne 88 E7
Little Chart 138 C5
Little Chart Forstal 138 E6
Little Mongeham 134 A4
Littlestone-on-Sea 226 E7
Lodge Lees 148 E3
London Beach 194 A1
Lower Eythorne 131 K6
Lower Goldstone 73 J7
Lower Halstow 34 B3
Lower Hardres 106 E8
Lower Heppington 106 C6
Lower Herne 46 E5
Lower Island 43 K5
Loyterton 79 F1
Lydd 231 G8
Lydden 53 K2
Lydden 151 G6
Lydd-on-Sea 239 F1
Lymbridge Green 165 K2
Lyminge 167 F8
Lympne 203 J3
Lynsore Bottom 127 G6
Lynsted 59 H8
Maltman's Hill 156 E3
Manston 53 H4
Margate 2 B3
Marine Town 14 A6
Marley 114 A6
Marley 128 B5
Marshborough 93 F7
Marshside 48 E5
Martin 154 B4
Martin Mill 154 C5
Maxted Street 145 K8
Maxton 172 E8
Maypole 47 K8
Mersham 183 K2
Middle Quarter 177 H5
Mile Town 14 B4
Millbank 48 A7
Mill Hill 135 F3
Milstead 76 E4
Milton Regis 57 H1
Minster 15 J7
Minster 52 B8
Molash 121 K2
Monkton 51 G7
Moon's Green 219 F3
Moorstock 185 K4
Morehall 190 A8
Mountain Street 103 H8
Mount Pleasant 52 B6
Mundy Bois 136 D6
Mundy Bois 137 F6
Murston 58 D2
Naccolt 162 E1
Nackington 107 F4
Napchester 153 F3
Neames Forstal 82 D7
Newbarn 188 A2
Newchurch 215 F3
Newingreen 203 J1
Newington 4 A2
Newington 34 B8
Newington 188 E6
Newnham 78 D6
New Romney 232 C1
Nonington 130 E2
Northbourne 134 A2
Northdown 32 E5

North Elham 168 A1
North Leigh 146 A3
North Street 81 H5
Northwood 54 B3
Norton Ash 60 D6
Oad Street 56 D5
Oare 61 K3
Old Romney 225 G2
Old Tree 48 B7
Old Wives Lees 103 J4
Ospringe 61 K8
Otterden Place 98 D5
Ottinge 167 G5
Out Elmstead 128 E4
Overland 83 F7
Paddlesworth 189 H2
Paddock 120 C5
Painter's Forstal 80 C3
Palmarsh 204 A6
Palmstead 147 H1
Paramour Street 73 G7
Patrixbourne 108 B3
Payden Street 97 J6
Pean Hill 66 B4
Pedlinge 204 B2
Peene 189 F6
Peening Quarter 208 B8
Pegwell 4 A6
Pembles Cross 136 C3
Pennypot 204 D5
Perry 90 E3
Perrywood 102 B2
Pested 121 F2
Petham 126 A2
Pett Bottom 127 G1
Pineham 153 H6
Pluckley 137 J7
Pluckley Thorne 137 G8
Plucks Gutter 72 D3
Plumford 80 E4
Postling 187 H4
Potman's Heath 218 D1
Potten Street 50 B2
Potters Corner 140 C8
Potter's Forstal 136 B4
Preston 62 C8
Preston 71 J8
The Quarter 156 B1
Queenborough 20 B1
Radfall 67 F1
Radfield 59 H4
Ram Lane 139 G4
Ramsgate 5 F3
Ratling 110 B6
Reading Street 33 H5
Reading Street 209 J4
Reculver 26 E7
Rhodes Minnis 166 E3
Richborough Port 75 G6
Ridge Row 169 F5
Ridgeway 184 D1
Ringwould 155 G1
Ripper's Cross 159 F2
Ripple 134 D6
River 172 B3
Robhurst 195 J4
Rodmersham 58 E6
Rodmersham Green 58 C7
Rough Common 85 K3
Rowling 111 J4
Rowling Street 182 D8
Ruckinge 199 K6
Rushenden 20 A4
St Lawrence 4 B3
St Margaret's at Cliffe 155 G8
St Mary in the Marsh 226 C2
St Mary's Bay 227 H3
St Michaels 194 B2
St Nicholas at Wade 50 A4
St Peters 54 E1
Saltwood 204 E2
Sandgate 206 E3
Sandway 116 B3
Sandwich 93 J5
Sandwich Bay Estate 95 F6
Sarre 50 A7
Satmar 192 A3
Scrapsgate 15 H5
Seabrook 206 A4
Seasalter 43 H7
Seaton 89 K4
Seed 78 D8
Selgrove 81 G4
Sellindge 185 K5

Selling 82 C8
Selson 112 E3
Selsted 149 H8
Sevington 162 B8
Shadoxhurst 180 D6
Shalmsford Street 104 C4
Shatterling 91 G5
Sheerness 14 D3
Sheldwich 81 G8
Sheldwich Lees 101 H1
Shelvingford 48 B7
Shepherdswell or Sibertswold 151 G1
Shirkoak 196 C1
Sholden 115 F8
Shorncliffe Camp 206 D2
Shottenden 102 D5
Shuttlesfield 168 A8
Silver Street 56 E8
Singleton 160 A7
Sittingbourne 58 B4
Sixmile 166 B1
Skeete 166 B7
Slade 98 A5
Sly Corner 211 H1
Small Hythe 208 C5
Smarden 156 A5
Smeeth 184 D2
Snargate 212 C3
Snave 213 G6
Snipeshill 58 D3
Snowdown 130 B3
Sole Street 124 D7
South Alkham 170 D6
South Ashford 160 D6
South Stour 183 F5
South Street 44 D7
South Street 83 F6
South Willesborough 161 G8
Stalisfield Green 99 F8
Stanford 186 E5
Stanhope 160 D8
Staple 91 J8
Staplestreet 83 F7
Statenborough 113 G2
Stede Quarter 176 D5
Stelling Minnis 146 D4
Stiff Street 56 E7
Stocker's Head 119 H5
The Stocks 208 B2
Stodmarsh 70 C8
Stonebridge Green 137 G1
Stone Cross 93 J7
Stone Cross 182 E8
Stonehall 151 J6
Stone Hill 185 H4
Stone in Oxney 221 G2
Stonestreet Green 184 C7
Stowting 165 J6
Stowting Common 165 J2
Street End 106 D7
Stubb's Cross 181 G4
Studdal 133 G7
Studd Hill 45 K3
Sturry 69 G8
Summerfield 111 K1
Sutton 134 A7
Swalecliffe 45 H3
Swingfield Minnis 169 H3
Swingfield Street 169 K3
Tanden 178 B5
Tankerton 44 D3
Temple Ewell 172 C1
Tenterden 194 A6
Teynham 59 K3
Teynham Street 60 C2
Thanington 105 K1
Throwley 100 C8
Throwley Forstal 100 D3
Tilmanstone 132 E3
Tonge Corner 37 G7
Tong Green 99 K5
Tower Hamlets 172 E6
Townland Green 196 B5
Troy Town 163 J1
Tunstall 57 J6
Tutt Hill 139 J5
Twenties 2 A6
Twitham 91 G8
Tyler Hill 67 H8
Under the Wood 48 C4
Upper Deal 135 F2
Upper Goldstone 92 C1
Upper Harbledown 85 H5
Upper Hardres Court 126 D4

Upper Rodmersham	58 D8	
Upstreet	70 D3	
Upton	55 G2	
The Valley	99 F6	
Wall End	71 H1	
Walmer	135 J4	
Waltham	125 F8	
Warden	24 D2	
Ware	72 E8	
Warehorne	198 B8	
Warren Street	97 K7	
The Warren	160 D1	
Waterham	64 D4	
Way	52 D7	
Weddington	92 B3	
Westbere	69 H7	
Westbrook	31 F4	
West Cliffe	154 D8	
West End	45 K6	
West End	77 K7	
Westenhanger	186 D7	
Western Heights	173 F8	
Westgate on Sea	30 C5	
West Hougham	192 C1	
West Hythe	203 J5	
West Langdon	153 H3	
Westmarsh	72 E6	
West Minster	14 A6	
West Stourmouth	72 A4	
West Street	96 E5	
West Street	114 A5	
Westwell	140 C2	
Westwell Leacon	139 G3	
Westwood	54 C1	
Westwood	127 J6	
Whatsole Street	145 H8	
Wheeelbarrow Town	146 E6	
Whitehill	80 E3	
Whitfield	153 F6	
Whitstable	44 A3	
Wichling	97 J1	
Wickhambreaux	89 G4	
Wilgate Green	80 D8	
Willesborough	9 D5	
Willesborough Lees	162 B4	
Wingham	90 D7	
Wingham Green	90 A7	
Wingham Well	90 A8	
Wingmore	148 B4	
Winterbourne	83 G6	
Wissenden	157 F7	
Withersdane	143 F6	
Wittersham	219 J3	
Wolverton	171 H4	
Womenswold	129 K4	
Woodchurch	196 D5	
Woodland	166 C7	
Woodnesborough	92 E8	
Woodside Green	96 E6	
Woodstock	57 K8	
Woolage Green	130 B7	
Woolage Village	129 K5	
Wootton	149 J5	
Wormshill	76 A7	
Worten	159 J3	
Worth	114 B1	
Wye	143 F5	
Wyebanks	98 B4	
Yardhurst	158 E7	
Yorkletts	65 G3	

USING THE STREET INDEX

Street names are listed alphabetically. Each street name is followed by its postal town or area locality, the Postcode District, the page number, and the reference to the square in which the name is found.

Example: **Abbey Gv** *RAM* CT11 .... 4 B6

Some entries are followed by a number in a blue box. This number indicates the location of the street within the referenced grid square. The full street name is listed at the side of the map page.

GENERAL ABBREVIATIONS

ACC	ACCESS	
ALY	ALLEY	
AP	APPROACH	
AR	ARCADE	
ASS	ASSOCIATION	
AV	AVENUE	
BCH	BEACH	
BLDS	BUILDINGS	
BND	BEND	
BNK	BANK	
BR	BRIDGE	
BRK	BROOK	
BTM	BOTTOM	
BUS	BUSINESS	
BVD	BOULEVARD	
BY	BYPASS	
CATH	CATHEDRAL	
CEM	CEMETERY	
CEN	CENTRE	
CFT	CROFT	
CH	CHURCH	
CHA	CHASE	
CHYD	CHURCHYARD	
CIR	CIRCLE	
CIRC	CIRCUS	
LL		
CLFS	CLIFFS	
CMP	CAMP	
CNR	CORNER	
CO	COUNTY	
COLL	COLLEGE	
COM	COMMON	
COMM	COMMISSION	
CON	CONVENT	
COT	COTTAGE	
COTS	COTTAGES	
CP	CAPE	
CPS	COPSE	
CR	CREEK	
CREM	CREMATORIUM	
CRS	CRESCENT	
CSWY	CAUSEWAY	
CT	COURT	
CTRL	CENTRAL	
CTS	COURTS	
CTYD	COURTYARD	
CUTT	CUTTINGS	
CV	COVE	
CYN	CANYON	
DEPT	DEPARTMENT	
DL	DALE	
DM	DAM	
DR	DRIVE	
DRO	DROVE	
DRY	DRIVEWAY	
DWGS	DWELLINGS	
E	EAST	
EMB	EMBANKMENT	
EMBY	EMBASSY	
ESP	ESPLANADE	
EST	ESTATE	
EX	EXCHANGE	
EXPY	EXPRESSWAY	
EXT	EXTENSION	
F/O	FLYOVER	
FC	FOOTBALL CLUB	
FK	FORK	
FLD	FIELD	
FLDS	FIELDS	
FLS	FALLS	
FLS	FLATS	
FM	FARM	
FT	FORT	
FWY	FREEWAY	
FY	FERRY	
GA	GATE	
GAL	GALLERY	
	GARDEN	
GDNS	GARDENS	
GLD	GLADE	
GLN	GLEN	
GN	GREEN	
GND	GROUND	
GRA	GRANGE	
GRG	GARAGE	
GT	GREAT	
GTWY	GATEWAY	
GV	GROVE	
HGR	HIGHER	
HL	HILL	
HLS	HILLS	
HO	HOUSE	
HOL	HOLLOW	
HOSP	HOSPITAL	
HRB	HARBOUR	
HTH	HEATH	
HTS	HEIGHTS	
HVN	HAVEN	
HWY	HIGHWAY	
IMP	IMPERIAL	
IN	INLET	
IND EST	INDUSTRIAL ESTATE	
INF	INFIRMARY	
INFO	INFORMATION	
INT	INTERCHANGE	
IS	ISLAND	
JCT	JUNCTION	
JTY	JETTY	
KG	KING	
KNL	KNOLL	
L	LAKE	
LA	LANE	
LDG	LODGE	
LGT	LIGHT	
LK	LOCK	
LKS	LAKES	
LNDG	LANDING	
LTL	LITTLE	
LWR	LOWER	
MAG	MAGISTRATE	
MAN	MANSIONS	
MD	MEAD	
MDW	MEADOWS	
MEM	MEMORIAL	
MKT	MARKET	
MKTS	MARKETS	
ML	MALL	
ML	MILL	
MNR	MANOR	
MS	MEWS	
MSN	MISSION	
MT	MOUNT	
MTN	MOUNTAIN	
MTS	MOUNTAINS	
MUS	MUSEUM	
MWY	MOTORWAY	
N	NORTH	
NE	NORTH EAST	
NW	NORTH WEST	
O/P	OVERPASS	
OFF	OFFICE	
ORCH	ORCHARD	
OV	OVAL	
PAL	PALACE	
PAS	PASSAGE	
PAV	PAVILION	
PDE	PARADE	
PH	PUBLIC HOUSE	
PK	PARK	
PKWY	PARKWAY	
PL	PLACE	
PLN	PLAIN	
PLNS	PLAINS	
PLZ	PLAZA	
POL	POLICE STATION	
PR	PRINCE	

PREC......PRECINCT	SCH......SCHOOL	TRL......TRAIL
PREP......PREPARATORY	SE......SOUTH EAST	TWR......TOWER
PRIM......PRIMARY	SER......SERVICE AREA	U/P......UNDERPASS
PROM......PROMENADE	SH......SHORE	UNI......UNIVERSITY
PRS......PRINCESS	SHOP......SHOPPING	UPR......UPPER
PRT......PORT	SKWY......SKYWAY	V......VALE
PT......POINT	SMT......SUMMIT	VA......VALLEY
PTH......PATH	SOC......SOCIETY	VIAD......VIADUCT
PZ......PIAZZA	SP......SPUR	VIL......VILLA
QD......QUADRANT	SPR......SPRING	VIS......VISTA
QU......QUEEN	SQ......SQUARE	VLG......VILLAGE
QY......QUAY	ST......STREET	VLS......VILLAS
R......RIVER	STN......STATION	VW......VIEW
RBT......ROUNDABOUT	STR......STREAM	W......WEST
RD......ROAD	STRD......STRAND	WD......WOOD
RDG......RIDGE	SW......SOUTH WEST	WHF......WHARF
REP......REPUBLIC	TDG......TRADING	WK......WALK
RES......RESERVOIR	TER......TERRACE	WKS......WALKS
RFC......RUGBY FOOTBALL CLUB	THWY......THROUGHWAY	WLS......WELLS
RI......RISE	TNL......TUNNEL	WY......WAY
RP......RAMP	TOLL......TOLLWAY	YD......YARD
RW......ROW	TPK......TURNPIKE	YHA......YOUTH HOSTEL
S......SOUTH	TR......TRACK	

POSTCODE TOWNS AND AREA ABBREVIATIONS

ASH......Ashford (Kent)	HB......Herne Bay	RCANTE......Rural Canterbury east
BRCH......Birchington	HDCN......Headcorn	RCANTW......Rural Canterbury west
BRDST......Broadstairs	HYTHE......Hythe	RDV......Rural Dover
CANT......Canterbury	IOS......Isle of Sheppey	RFOLK......Rural Folkestone
CANTW/ST......Canterbury west/Sturry	KEN/WIL......Kennington/Willesborough	RMAID......Rural Maidstone
CRBK......Cranbrook	LYDD......Lydd	RSIT......Rural Sittingbourne
DEAL......Deal	MARG......Margate	RYE......Rye
DVE/WH......Dover east/Whitfield	MSTR......Minster	SIT......Sittingbourne
DVW......Dover west	NROM......New Romney	SWCH......Sandwich
FAV......Faversham	QBOR......Queenborough	TENT......Tenterden
FOLK......Folkestone	RAM......Ramsgate	WGOS......Westgate on Sea
FOLKN......Folkestone north	RASHE......Rural Ashford east	WSTB......Whitstable
HAWK......Hawkhurst	RASHW......Rural Ashford west	

Index - streets　　　　**Abb - Alm**

A

Abbey Cl DEAL CT14 .... 135 G1
  IOS ME12 .... 16 A8
Abbey Flds FAV ME13 .... 62 E6
Abbey Gdns CANTW/ST CT2 .... 86 E3
Abbey Gv MSTR CT12 .... 74 B1
  RAM CT11 .... 4 B6
Abbey Pl FAV ME13 .... 62 C6
Abbey Rd DVE/WH CT16 .... 172 B2
  FAV ME13 .... 62 C6
  RDV CT15 .... 171 K5
Abbey St FAV ME13 .... 62 C6
Abbeyview Dr IOS ME12 .... 15 J8
Abbey Wy KEN/WIL TN24 .... 162 A4
Abbots Hl FAV ME13 .... 80 C1
  RAM CT11 .... 5 E5
Abbots Pl CANT CT1 .... 6 C2
Abbots Rd FAV ME13 .... 62 D7
The Abbots DVW CT17 .... 10 A3
Abbots Wk RASHE TN25 .... 142 C5
Abbott Rd FOLKN CT19 .... 13 E3
Aberdeen Cl RCANTE CT3 .... 70 E3
Abingdon Gv MARG CT9 .... 3 D3
Ackholt Rd RCANTE CT3 .... 130 C1
Acol Hl BRCH CT7 .... 52 A2
Acorn Cl ASH TN23 .... 182 B3
Acorn St IOS ME12 .... 14 D5
The Acre DVE/WH CT16 .... 152 D6
Acton La TENT TN30 .... 209 G8
Acton Rd WSTB CT5 .... 44 A5
Adams Cl TENT TN30 .... 194 B5
Ada Rd CANT CT1 .... 6 A5
Addelam Cl DEAL CT14 .... 135 G2
Addelam Rd DEAL CT14 .... 135 G2
Addington Rd MARG CT9 .... 3 D3
  SIT ME10 .... 57 K3
Addington Sq MARG CT9 .... 3 D3
Addington St MARG CT9 .... 3 D3
Addiscombe Gdns MARG CT9 .... 3 D4
Addiscombe Rd MARG CT9 .... 3 E4
Adelaide Dr SIT ME10 .... 57 H2
Adelaide Gdns IOS ME12 .... 14 E8
  RAM CT11 .... 5 E5
Adelaide Pl CANT CT1 .... 6 C5
Adelaide Rd RDV CT15 .... 131 K5
Adie Rd NROM TN28 .... 232 E3
Adie Rd North NROM TN28 .... 232 E3
Adisham Downs Rd RCANTE CT3 .... 109 H4
Adisham Gn SIT ME10 .... 36 A6
Adisham Rd RCANTW CT4 .... 108 E3
  RCANTW CT4 .... 129 J4

Adisham Wy MARG CT9 .... 32 D5
Admirals Wk IOS ME12 .... 15 F8
  TENT TN30 .... 194 C5
Admiralty Cl FAV ME13 .... 62 A6
Admiralty Wk WSTB CT5 .... 43 H7
Adrian Sq WGOS CT8 .... 30 D5
Adrian St DVW CT17 .... 10 B4
Aerodrome Rd RCANTW CT4 .... 108 E3
  RFOLK CT18 .... 190 A2
Afghan Rd BRDST CT10 .... 33 G6
Agester La RCANTW CT4 .... 149 G3
Ainsdale Cl FOLKN CT19 .... 12 A2
Airedale Cl MARG CT9 .... 3 E4
Airfield Vw IOS ME12 .... 23 F6
Aisne Dr CANT CT1 .... 87 H5
Albemarle Rd KEN/WIL TN24 .... 9 F5
Alberta Cl DVE/WH CT16 .... 173 F5
Albert La HYTHE CT21 .... 205 F5
Albert Rd BRDST CT10 .... 33 F7
  CANT CT1 .... 7 E3
  DEAL CT14 .... 115 J8
  DVE/WH CT16 .... 10 B2
  FOLKN CT19 .... 13 D3
  HYTHE CT21 .... 205 F5
  KEN/WIL TN24 .... 9 F5
  MARG CT9 .... 2 B3
  RAM CT11 .... 5 F4
  RFOLK CT18 .... 191 K5
Albert St RAM CT11 .... 5 D5
  WSTB CT5 .... 44 A4
Albert Ter MARG CT9 .... 2 C3
Albion Cl HB CT6 .... 47 F6
Albion La HB CT6 .... 47 F6
Albion Ms RAM CT11 .... 5 E5
Albion Mews Rd FOLK CT20 .... 13 D5
Albion Pl CANT CT1 .... 7 D2
  FAV ME13 .... 62 B7
  IOS ME12 .... 14 D4
  KEN/WIL TN24 .... 9 F5
  RAM CT11 .... 5 E5
Albion Rd BRCH CT7 .... 29 K7
  BRDST CT10 .... 33 G8
  DEAL CT14 .... 115 K6
  FOLKN CT19 .... 13 D3
  MARG CT9 .... 2 B2
  RAM CT11 .... 5 F4
  SWCH CT13 .... 112 E4
Albion St BRDST CT10 .... 55 J2
Albion Vls FOLK CT20 .... 13 D5

Albuhera Sq CANT CT1 .... 87 H5
Aldergate La RASHE TN25 .... 202 E5
Alder Rd FOLKN CT19 .... 12 C3
Aldington Rd HYTHE CT21 .... 202 E5
Aldred Rd FAV ME13 .... 62 E8
Aldridge Cl HB CT6 .... 46 A3
Alexander Dr FAV ME13 .... 62 A7
Alexandra Gdns FOLK CT20 .... 13 D5
Alexandra Pl DVE/WH CT16 .... 10 A2
Alexandra Rd BRCH CT7 .... 51 K1
  BRDST CT10 .... 55 J2
  DEAL CT14 .... 135 K4
  DEAL CT14 .... 155 J1
  IOS ME12 .... 14 E4
  MARG CT9 .... 2 C5
  RAM CT11 .... 5 D3
  RFOLK CT18 .... 191 K4
  WSTB CT5 .... 43 K6
Alexandra St FOLKN CT19 .... 13 E3
Alexandria Dr HB CT6 .... 46 B1
Alfred Cl CANT CT1 .... 86 A8
Alfred Cottages RAM CT11 .... 5 E4
Alfred Rd BRCH CT7 .... 29 G6
  CANT CT1 .... 86 A8
  DVE/WH CT16 .... 173 F4
  KEN/WIL TN24 .... 9 D6
  MARG CT9 .... 3 F4
  NROM TN28 .... 232 E3
Alicia Av MARG CT9 .... 31 F6
Alison Cl DVE/WH CT16 .... 152 E8
Alison Crs DVE/WH CT16 .... 152 E8
Alkham Cl MARG CT9 .... 33 G4
Alkham Rd RDV CT15 .... 171 K2
Alkham Valley Rd RFOLK CT18 .... 190 A1
Alland Grange La MSTR CT12 .... 52 D5
Allan Rd WSTB CT5 .... 43 F7
Allen Av WGOS CT8 .... 30 B7
Allenby Av DEAL CT14 .... 135 H1
Allenby Rd MSTR CT12 .... 52 D2
Allendale St FOLKN CT19 .... 13 D5
Allen Fld ASH TN23 .... 160 D6
All Saints' Av MARG CT9 .... 2 A4
All Saints' Cl WSTB CT5 .... 44 B5
All Saints La CANT CT1 .... 6 C3
All Saints Rd SIT ME10 .... 58 D2
Allsworth Cl RSIT ME9 .... 34 A3
Alma Pl CANT CT1 .... 7 D2
  RAM CT11 .... 5 F4
Alma Rd FOLK CT20 .... 206 D1
  HB CT6 .... 47 G1
  IOS ME12 .... 14 D4
  MARG CT9 .... 3 D4

RAM CT11 5 E4
Alma St CANT CT1 7 D2
IOS ME12 14 E4
Almond Cl ASH TN23 160 D1
BRDST CT10 54 D2
WSTB CT5 45 G5
Almond Tree Cl IOS ME12 14 B6
Almshouse Rd FAV ME13 100 A8
Alpha Rd BRCH CT7 29 K7
RAM CT11 5 D5
Alsager Av QBOR ME11 20 A3
Alsops Rd KEN/WIL TN24 9 E6
Alston Cl IOS ME12 15 K7
Alvis Av HB CT6 45 K2
Amage Rd RASHE TN25 143 J6
Amber Cl RSIT ME9 60 A4
Ambleside SIT ME10 58 D3
Amherst Cl MARG CT9 32 D5 1
Amos Cl FAV ME13 101 G1
HB CT6 47 H3
Anchor La IOS ME12 14 B3
Ancress Cl CANTW/ST CT2 86 E2
Anna Pk BRCH CT7 29 J6
Anne Boleyn Cl IOS ME12 23 H3
Anne Cl BRCH CT7 30 A7
Anne Roper Cl NROM TN28 227 F8
Ann's Rd RAM CT11 5 E3
Anselm Cl SIT ME10 57 K2
Anselm Rd DVW CT17 172 E6
Anson Cl BRDST CT10 54 D3
Anstee Rd DVW CT17 10 A2
Anthony Crs WSTB CT5 43 J8
Anvil Cl BRCH CT7 29 K8
Anzio Crs DVE/WH CT16 10 C1
Appledore Av IOS ME12 14 C6
Appledore Crs FOLKN CT19 189 J7 1
Appledore Rd RASHW TN26 196 E6
TENT TN30 194 C7
Appledown Wy CANT CT1 107 H1
Appleford Dr IOS ME12 15 G7
Approach Rd DVW CT17 172 E8 1
MARG CT9 3 E3
RDV CT15 151 F1
Approach Rd South LYDD TN29 239 F8
April Ri WSTB CT5 43 J7 1
Apsley St ASH TN23 8 B3
Aragon Cl ASH TN23 160 C7
Archcliffe Rd DVW CT17 10 A6
Archer Rd FOLKN CT19 13 D3
Archer's Court Rd DVE/WH CT16 153 F7
Archery Sq DEAL CT14 135 K3
Archway Rd IOS ME12 14 B3
Arcon Cl ASH TN23 8 A6
Arcon Rd ASH TN23 8 A6
Arden Dr KEN/WIL TN24 8 C2
Arden Gra RCANTW CT4 103 J6
Arden Rd FAV ME13 62 D7
HB CT6 47 G4
Argent Rd QBOR ME11 20 B4
Argyle Av MARG CT9 2 A4
Argyle Gdns MARG CT9 2 A4 1
Argyle Rd WSTB CT5 44 A5
Argyll Dr RAM CT11 5 F2
Ark La DEAL CT14 115 J7
Arklow Sq RAM CT11 5 F4 1
Arlington ASH TN23 160 D5
Arlington Gdns MARG CT9 32 D6
Armada Cl NROM TN28 233 F1
Armstrong Sq HB CT6 45 K3 1
Arnold Rd MARG CT9 3 D4 3
RCANTW CT4 104 E4
Arolla Rd HB CT6 47 H2
Arrowhead La RASHW TN26 212 B7
Arthur Kennedy Cl FAV ME13 83 F3
Arthur Rd BRCH CT7 29 G6 1
[illegible]
HYTHE CT21 205 G5
MARG CT9 3 E2
Arthur Salmon Cl FAV ME13 62 A7
Arthur St FOLKN CT19 13 E3 1
SIT ME10 57 K2 1
Artillery Gdns CANT CT1 7 D2 3
Artillery Rd RAM CT11 5 F4
Artillery St CANT CT1 7 D2
Arundel Av SIT ME10 57 K5
Arundel Rd MARG CT9 3 F3 1
MSTR CT12 53 J7
Ascot Gdns WGOS CT8 30 D7
Ashbee Gdns HB CT6 47 H1
Ashborne Cl KEN/WIL TN24 141 H8
Ashburnham Rd RAM CT11 4 B4
Ashburton Cl KEN/WIL TN24 9 E3 1
Ash Cl BRDST CT10 54 D2
DVW CT17 172 C3
HB CT6 46 E5
Ash Ct MSTR CT12 75 J2
Ash Crs RCANTE CT3 69 K5
Ashdown Cl HB CT6 47 G4 1
Ashdown Crs NROM TN28 226 C8
Ashdown Rd RSIT ME9 97 F3
Ashenden Cl CANT CT1 106 A1
Ashen Tree La DVE/WH CT16 10 C3
Ashentree La LYDD TN29 229 K1
Ashford Rd ASH TN23 159 K7
ASH TN23 181 K3
FAV ME13 81 G1
HYTHE CT21 187 F8
NROM TN28 226 B8
RASHE TN25 185 G4
RASHW TN26 177 K6
RASHW TN26 180 C1
RASHW TN26 198 D5
RCANTW CT4 104 C3
RMAID ME17 117 F1
TENT TN30 194 B4
Ash Gv LYDD TN29 231 J7
RDV CT15 131 K4
Ashington Cl SIT ME10 57 H1 1
Ashley Av FOLKN CT19 189 K8
Ashley Cl IOS ME12 20 D1
MSTR CT12 4 B1
Ashley Dr WSTB CT5 43 H7
Ash Mdw KEN/WIL TN24 9 F6
Ash Rd RCANTE CT3 129 K1
SWCH CT13 93 J4
Ashtead Dr RSIT ME9 58 E4
Ashton Cl DEAL CT14 134 D2
Ash Tree Cl LYDD TN29 227 G3
Ash Tree Rd FOLKN CT19 13 E3 2
Ashurst Av WSTB CT5 43 K7
Ashurst Gdns MARG CT9 33 F3
Askes Ct ASH TN23 160 B6 1
Aspen Cl LYDD TN29 227 G3
Aspen Rd RCANTW CT4 105 G5
Astley Av DVE/WH CT16 10 A1
Astor Av DVW CT17 173 F6
Astor Dr DEAL CT14 135 J1
Astor Rd BRDST CT10 33 G6
Astrid Rd DEAL CT14 135 G4
Athelstan Pl DEAL CT14 115 J6
Athelstan Rd CANT CT1 106 A1
FAV ME13 62 A8
FOLKN CT19 13 D2
MARG CT9 3 E2
Athol Pl FAV ME13 61 K6 1
Athol Rd ASH TN23 160 D7
WSTB CT5 44 B4
Athol Ter DVE/WH CT16 11 D3 1
Atkinson Wk KEN/WIL TN24 161 K1 1
Attlee Av RCANTE CT3 130 A1
Attlee Wy SIT ME10 35 K7
Auckland Av MSTR CT12 4 A2
Auckland Crs DVE/WH CT16 173 G3
Auckland Dr SIT ME10 57 H3
Audley Av MARG CT9 31 F5
Audley Rd FOLK CT20 207 F1
Augusta Pl RAM CT11 5 F4 2
Augusta Rd RAM CT11 5 F4
Augustine Rd IOS ME12 15 J6
MSTR CT12 52 A8
Austin Av HB CT6 45 J2
Austin Cl SIT ME10 36 B6
Austin Rd ASH TN23 161 F8
Austins La SWCH CT13 94 A5 1
Avebury Av RAM CT11 55 H6
Avenue Gdns MARG CT9 32 D3 1
Avenue of Remembrance
SIT ME10 58 A3
Avenue Rd HB CT6 46 C1
RAM CT11 5 F4
The Avenue DEAL CT14 115 J7 1
DEAL CT14 155 J1
DVE/WH CT16 172 C1
MARG CT9 3 D4
RCANTE CT3 69 K5
RDV CT15 155 F8
Avereng Gdns FOLKN CT19 12 B3
Avereng Rd FOLKN CT19 12 B3
Avon Cl CANT CT1 7 F3
Avondale Cl WSTB CT5 44 D6
[illegible]
Aylesford Pl KEN/WIL TN24 9 E6
Aylesham Rd RCANTE CT3 130 C2
Aylewyn Gn SIT ME10 36 A6
Ayton Rd RAM CT11 4 C5

B

Babs Oak Hl CANTW/ST CT2 69 G8
Back La IOS ME12 16 A8
Back Rd (East) DVE/WH CT16 11 F2
Back St DEAL CT14 155 F1
Baddlesmere Rd WSTB CT5 44 D3
Badgers Cl CANTW/ST CT2 66 D7
Badgers Ri DEAL CT14 135 J6
DVW CT17 172 B3
Badlesmere Cl ASH TN23 160 C8
Bad Munstereifel Rd ASH TN23 182 A1
KEN/WIL TN24 182 C1
Bagham La RCANTW CT4 103 J6
Bagham Rd RCANTW CT4 103 J6
Bagshill Rd FAV ME13 100 C2
Baileys Fld ASH TN23 160 D5
Baird's Hl BRDST CT10 33 G8
Bairdsley Cl BRDST CT10 33 G8
Baker Cl RSIT ME9 59 K3
Baker Rd FOLKN CT19 189 K8
Bakers Cl CANTW/ST CT2 86 A7 1
Baker's La RCANTW CT4 105 F4
Balcomb Crs MARG CT9 32 D6 1
Baldric Rd FOLK CT20 207 F1
Baldwin Rd IOS ME12 16 A7
NROM TN28 232 E5
Baldwin Ter FOLKN CT19 13 D3 3
Balfour Rd DEAL CT14 135 J4
DVE/WH CT16 10 A2
Baliol Rd WSTB CT5 44 B4
Ballard Rd NROM TN28 232 E5
Balliol Rd BRDST CT10 33 G7
Ball La KEN/WIL TN24 141 J7
Balmoral Pl RAM CT11 5 F4 3
Balmoral Rd DEAL CT14 135 J8
MARG CT9 31 G6
Bamford Wy DEAL CT14 135 J2
Bank Rd RASHE TN25 183 J6
Bank Side RASHW TN26 198 D7
Banks Rd ASH TN23 8 A6
The Banks BRDST CT10 33 G8 1
Bank St ASH TN23 8 B3
FAV ME13 62 B7
HYTHE CT21 205 G4 1
Banner Wy IOS ME12 15 F8
Bannister Hl RSIT ME9 57 G4
Barfrestone Rd RDV CT15 131 H5
Bargates ASH TN23 160 C8
Barham's Mill Rd HDCN TN27 136 B4
Barkers Ct SIT ME10 57 J2
Barler Pl QBOR ME11 20 B1
Barley Cl HB CT6 47 J4
RDV CT15 154 C4 1
Barnberry Cl ASH TN23 160 C6 1
Barn Cl RCANTE CT3 69 K1
RSIT ME9 57 F4
WSTB CT5 65 G3
Barn Crs MARG CT9 31 G5
Barnes Av MARG CT9 31 G5
Barnes Cl FAV ME13 61 K6
Barnet's La CANTW/ST CT2 68 C6
Barnett Fld ASH TN23 160 D6
Barnfield HB CT6 46 B4
TENT TN30 194 B4
Barnfield Rd FAV ME13 62 B6
FOLKN CT19 12 C2
Barnhouse La LYDD TN29 223 K7
Barnhurst La RFOLK CT18 190 B1
Barn Platt ASH TN23 8 A5
Barnsley Cl IOS ME12 15 F4
Barnsole Rd RCANTE CT3 111 K1
Barntye Cl RDV CT15 153 J8
Barrack Hl HYTHE CT21 204 E4
Barrey Rd KEN/WIL TN24 162 A8
Barrington Crs BRCH CT7 30 A7
Barrow Gv SIT ME10 57 J3
Barrow Hl ASH TN23 8 A3 1
RASHE TN25 186 A6
Barrowhill Pl ASH TN23 8 B2 1
Barrow Hill Ri RASHE TN25 186 A7
Barrows Cl BRCH CT7 29 K8 1
Bartholomew Cl HYTHE CT21 205 F3
Bartholomew La HYTHE CT21 204 E3
Bartholomew St DVE/WH CT16 10 A2 1
HYTHE CT21 205 F4
Bartlett Dr WSTB CT5 44 D5
Bartletts Cl IOS ME12 20 D1
Barton Fld RFOLK CT18 167 F7
Barton Hill Dr IOS ME12 21 H1
Barton Mill Rd CANT CT1 7 E1
Barton Rd CANT CT1 7 F5
DVE/WH CT16 10 A1
Barton View Ter DVE/WH CT16 10 A2 2
Barville Rd RDV CT15 132 E5
Barwick Rd DVW CT17 172 D5
[illegible]
Baskerville KEN/WIL TN24 8 B2
Bassett Cl HYTHE CT21 205 J2
Bassett Gdns HYTHE CT21 205 H2
Bassett Rd SIT ME10 57 J2
Bastion Rd DVW CT17 10 A4
Bath Pl MARG CT9 3 D3
Bath Rd KEN/WIL TN24 161 J8
MARG CT9 3 D3
Bathurst Cl MSTR CT12 4 B2
Bathurst Rd FOLK CT20 12 A4
Batteries Cl RSIT ME9 59 J6
Battery Point HYTHE CT21 206 B3
Battery Rd LYDD TN29 239 G4
Bawden Cl CANTW/ST CT2 86 E2
Baxendale Ct KEN/WIL TN24 9 D6 1
Baye La RCANTE CT3 89 K5
Bayfield FAV ME13 80 C4
Bayford Rd SIT ME10 58 B2
Bay Hl RDV CT15 175 G1
Bayle St FOLK CT20 13 E4 1
The Bayle FOLK CT20 13 E5
Bay View Gdns IOS ME12 24 C5
Bay View Rd BRDST CT10 5 F1
Bayview Rd DEAL CT14 155 J2
WSTB CT5 44 A7
Beach Ap IOS ME12 24 D3
Beach Av BRCH CT7 29 J6
Beachborough Rd FOLKN CT19 12 A4 1
Beachmont Cl NROM TN28 233 F6

Beach Ri *MARG* CT9 .... **30** E5
Beach Rd *LYDD* TN29 .... **217** J2
   MARG CT9 .... **30** E5
   RDV CT15 .... **175** H1
Beach St *DEAL* CT14 .... **115** K8
   FOLKN CT19 .... **13** E4
   HB CT6 .... **46** E1
   IOS ME12 .... **14** C4
The Beach *DEAL* CT14 .... **135** K3
Beach Wk *WSTB* CT5 .... **44** B3
Beacon Av *HB* CT6 .... **47** G1
Beacon Hl *HB* CT6 .... **47** G1
Beacon La *SWCH* CT13 .... **92** E8
Beacon Oak Rd *TENT* TN30 .... **194** B6
Beacon Rd *BRDST* CT10 .... **33** G7
   HB CT6 .... **47** F2
   RMAID ME17 .... **116** C1
Beaconsfield Av *DVE/WH* CT16 .... **10** A2
Beaconsfield Gdns *BRDST* CT10 .... **55** C1
Beaconsfield Rd *CANTW/ST* CT2 .... **6** C1
   DEAL CT14 .... **135** K1
   DVE/WH CT16 .... **10** A2
   SIT ME10 .... **58** D3
Beacon Wk *HB* CT6 .... **47** F1
Beamont Cl *MSTR* CT12 .... **52** E5
Bean Cl *ASH* TN23 .... **160** A5
Beaney's La *FAV* ME13 .... **102** A5
Bear's La *RASHW* TN26 .... **159** G2
Beatrice Rd *MARG* CT9 .... **2** C5
   RFOLK CT18 .... **191** K4
Beatty Cl *FOLKN* CT19 .... **13** D1
Beatty Rd *FOLKN* CT19 .... **13** D2
Beauchamp Cl *DEAL* CT14 .... **135** G3
Beauchamp Cl *KEN/WIL* TN24 .... **161** J1
Beauchamps La *RDV* CT15 .... **131** F1
Beaufort Av *MSTR* CT12 .... **4** B3
Beaufoy Rd *DVW* CT17 .... **172** E5
Beaufoy Ter *DVW* CT17 .... **172** E5
Beaumanor *HB* CT6 .... **46** E3
Beaumont Davy Cl *FAV* ME13 .... **81** C1
Beaumont St *HB* CT6 .... **46** B3
Beaumont Ter *FAV* ME13 .... **62** C8
Beauvoir Dr *SIT* ME10 .... **36** B6
Beauxfield *DVE/WH* CT16 .... **152** E7
Beaver Ct *ASH* TN23 .... **8** A6
Beaver La *ASH* TN23 .... **8** A6
Beaver Rd *ASH* TN23 .... **8** B5
Beazley Ct *KEN/WIL* TN24 .... **9** D6
Becket Av *CANTW/ST* CT2 .... **6** A2
Becket Cl *DEAL* CT14 .... **115** J6
   RCANTE CT3 .... **92** B4
Becket Ms *CANTW/ST* CT2 .... **6** B2
Becket's Cl *RASHE* TN25 .... **144** D8
Beckett St *KEN/WIL* TN24 .... **62** B7
Becketts Wd *RCANTE* CT3 .... **71** F5
Beckley Pl *RASHE* TN25 .... **186** E6
Beckley Rd *IOS* ME12 .... **15** F4
Beckwith Gn *FOLK* CT20 .... **206** D1
Bedford Wy *BRCH* CT7 .... **50** C5
Bedingfield Wy *RFOLK* CT18 .... **167** F2
Bedlam Court La *MSTR* CT12 .... **74** B1
Beech Av *RCANTW* CT4 .... **105** C5
Beech Cl *FAV* ME13 .... **62** A7
   FOLKN CT19 .... **12** C5
Beech Ct *RASHE* TN25 .... **120** E5
Beechcroft *WSTB* CT5 .... **45** G5
Beechcroft Gdns *RAM* CT11 .... **5** F3
Beech Dr *BRDST* CT10 .... **54** D2
   RASHW TN26 .... **139** J7
   RDV CT15 .... **131** K4
Beech Green Cl *RDV* CT15 .... **132** A7
Beech Gv *MSTR* CT12 .... **75** H1
Beech Hl *RCANTW* CT4 .... **108** B6
Beechmore Dr *KEN/WIL* TN24 .... **161** G1
Beechwood Av *DEAL* CT14 .... **135** J1
   SIT ME10 .... **35** K8
Beechwood Cl *DVE/WH* CT16 .... **152** D5
   LYDD TN29 .... **227** G3
Beecroft Cl *CANTW/ST* CT2 .... **86** E2
Beer Cart La *CANT* CT1 .... **6** C3
Beggarsbush La *LYDD* TN29 .... **224** C7
Bekesbourne Hl *RCANTE* CT4 .... **108** B1
Bekesbourne La *RCANTE* CT3 .... **87** J7
   RCANTE CT3 .... **109** F1
   RCANTW CT4 .... **108** C1
Bekesbourne Rd *RCANTW* CT4 .... **107** K4
Belcaire Cl *HYTHE* CT21 .... **203** J3
Belgrave Cl *RAM* CT11 .... **5** D4
Belgrave Rd *DVW* CT17 .... **173** F7
   IOS ME12 .... **20** D1
   MARG CT9 .... **2** C3
Bell Chapel Cl *ASH* TN23 .... **182** B2
Bell-davies Dr *MSTR* CT12 .... **53** F5
Belle Friday Cl *RSIT* ME9 .... **59** K4
Bellevue Av *RAM* CT11 .... **5** D6
Belle Vue Rd *HB* CT6 .... **47** G1
Bellevue Rd *IOS* ME12 .... **15** K7
   RAM CT11 .... **5** F4
   WSTB CT5 .... **44** C6
Bellevue St *FOLK* CT20 .... **13** D4
Bell Farm La *IOS* ME12 .... **16** C8
Bellflower Av *IOS* ME12 .... **21** H2
Bell Gv *RCANTE* CT3 .... **130** B1
Bell La *SWCH* CT13 .... **94** A5

Bell Rd *SIT* ME10 .... **57** K4
Belmont *DEAL* CT14 .... **135** H5
Belmont Pl *ASH* TN23 .... **8** C6
   KEN/WIL TN24 .... **9** D5
Belmont Rd *BRDST* CT10 .... **55** H2
   FAV ME13 .... **62** B3
   IOS ME12 .... **15** F8
   KEN/WIL TN24 .... **141** H8
   RAM CT11 .... **5** D4
   SIT ME10 .... **57** K3
   WGOS CT8 .... **30** E6
   WSTB CT5 .... **44** A5
Belmont St *RAM* CT11 .... **5** E4
Belmore Pk *KEN/WIL* TN24 .... **8** B2
Belnor Av *RSIT* ME9 .... **34** D5
Belsey La *RDV* CT15 .... **171** F2
Beltinge Rd *HB* CT6 .... **47** G1
Belton Cl *WSTB* CT5 .... **44** B6
Belvedere Rd *BRDST* CT10 .... **55** J2
   IOS ME12 .... **22** C6
Benacre Rd *WSTB* CT5 .... **44** A8
Bench Hl *TENT* TN30 .... **197** F8
Bench St *DVE/WH* CT16 .... **10** A4
Bengal Rd *WSTB* CT12 .... **4** A2
Bennells Av *WSTB* CT5 .... **44** E4
Benson La *RFOLK* CT18 .... **190** A2
Bensted *ASH* TN23 .... **181** J1
Bensted Gv *FAV* ME13 .... **61** K7
Bentley Av *FAV* ME13 .... **62** A2
Bentley Rd *KEN/WIL* TN24 .... **9** F6
Beresford Gap *BRCH* CT7 .... **29** J6
Beresford Gdns *MARG* CT9 .... **32** D3
Beresford Rd *DVW* CT17 .... **172** C3
   RAM CT11 .... **5** D5
   WSTB CT5 .... **44** A5
Berkeley Ct *SIT* ME10 .... **57** J3
Berkeley Rd *BRCH* CT7 .... **29** J6
Bernards Gdns *RDV* CT15 .... **151** G1
Berridge Rd *IOS* ME12 .... **14** D4
Berry St *SIT* ME10 .... **58** A2
Berwick La *HYTHE* CT21 .... **203** J3
Best La *CANT* CT1 .... **6** C3
Bethersden Rd *HDCN* TN27 .... **156** A8
   RASHW TN26 .... **177** K1
Beult Meadow *HDCN* TN27 .... **156** A5
Bevan Wy *RCANTE* CT3 .... **130** A1
Beverley Gdns *LYDD* TN29 .... **217** J2
Beverley Rd *CANTW/ST* CT2 .... **6** B1
Beverley Wy *BRCH* CT12 .... **4** C2
Beverly Rd *BRCH* CT7 .... **30** A6
Bewsbury Crs *DVE/WH* CT16 .... **152** D7
Bewsbury Cross La *DVE/WH* CT16 .... **152** D7
Bhutan Rd *HB* CT6 .... **76** C2
Bicknor Cl *CANTW/ST* CT2 .... **87** F2
Biddenden Rd *HDCN* TN27 .... **176** E8
   RASHW TN26 .... **177** K1
Bifrons Hl *RCANTW* CT4 .... **108** A3
Bifrons Rd *RCANTW* CT4 .... **108** B2
Bigbury Rd *CANTW/ST* CT2 .... **85** G7
Biggin St *DVE/WH* CT16 .... **10** B3
Biggins Wood Rd *FOLKN* CT19 .... **189** K7
Billington Gdns *KEN/WIL* TN24 .... **141** J8
Bindon Blood Rd *DVE/WH* CT16 .... **172** E1
Binnie Cl *BRDST* CT10 .... **5** F1
Birch Cl *BRDST* CT10 .... **54** D3
   IOS TN24 .... **9** E3
Birch Ct *RCANTW* CT4 .... **129** F7
Birchett La *RASHW* TN26 .... **198** B4
Birch Hill Ct *BRCH* CT7 .... **30** A7
Birch Rd *WSTB* CT5 .... **44** D6
Birchwood Ri *DVW* CT17 .... **10** A4
Birds Av *MARG* CT9 .... **31** G7
Birdwood Av *DEAL* CT14 .... **135** J8
Birkdale Dr *FOLKN* CT19 .... **12** A2
Birkdale Gdns *HB* CT6 .... **46** C4
Birling Rd *KEN/WIL* TN24 .... **9** D4
Bishop's Av *BRDST* CT10 .... **33** J8
Bishops Gn *ASH* TN23 .... **160** B7
Bishopstone Dr *HB* CT6 .... **26** A8
Bishopstone La *HB* CT6 .... **48** A1
Bishops Wy *CANTW/ST* CT2 .... **6** A2
Black Bull Rd *FOLKN* CT19 .... **13** D5
Blackburn Rd *HB* CT6 .... **46** A4
Blackhouse Hl *HYTHE* CT21 .... **205** H3
Blackhouse Ri *HYTHE* CT21 .... **205** H3
Blackmanstone Br *LYDD* TN29 .... **215** J2
Black Robin La *RCANTW* CT4 .... **128** C3
Blackwall Rd *KEN/WIL* TN24 .... **162** A4
Blackthorne Rd *IOS* ME12 .... **21** H2
Blake Cl *DEAL* CT14 .... **135** H6
Blake Ct *KEN/WIL* TN24 .... **9** F5
Blandford Gdns *SIT* ME10 .... **57** K5
Blatcher Cl *IOS* ME12 .... **15** J8
Blaxland Cl *FAV* ME13 .... **62** A6
Bleak Rd *LYDD* TN29 .... **221** H9
Blean Cl *CANTW/ST* CT2 .... **85** J1
Blean View Rd *HB* CT6 .... **46** A4
Blenheim Av *CANT* CT1 .... **87** H5
   FAV ME13 .... **81** J1

Blenheim Cl *BRDST* CT10 .... **54** E3
   HB CT6 .... **47** F5
Blenheim Dr *DVE/WH* CT16 .... **173** C3
   RFOLK CT18 .... **190** B2
Blenheim Pl *FOLK* CT20 .... **207** F2
Blenheim Rd *DEAL* CT14 .... **135** J1
   NROM TN28 .... **226** E8
Blindgrooms La *RASHW* TN26 .... **181** F5
Blindhouse La *RASHE* TN25 .... **186** D3
Blind La *RASHE* TN25 .... **121** F5
   RASHE TN25 .... **183** J1
Bloomsbury Rd *RAM* CT11 .... **4** C5
Bloomsbury Wy *KEN/WIL* TN24 .... **141** F8
Bluebell Cl *ASH* TN23 .... **182** A2
Bluebell Rd *ASH* TN23 .... **182** A2
Blue House La *HYTHE* CT21 .... **188** A7
Blue Line La *KEN/WIL* TN24 .... **8** B2
Boarman's La *LYDD* TN29 .... **223** G6
Boat La *RASHE* TN25 .... **201** F2
Bob Amor Cl *FAV* ME13 .... **62** D7
Bobbing Hl *RSIT* ME9 .... **57** F1
Bobbin Lodge Hl *RCANTW* CT4 .... **104** D5
Bockham La *RASHE* TN25 .... **162** E7
Bockhanger La *KEN/WIL* TN24 .... **141** G8
Bodenham Rd *FOLK* CT20 .... **12** A5
Bogle Rd *RSIT* ME9 .... **59** K7
Bognor Dr *HB* CT6 .... **46** C2
Bogshole La *HB* CT6 .... **47** J3
   WSTB CT5 .... **66** A2
Boleyn Av *MARG* CT9 .... **31** F5
Bolton Rd *FOLKN* CT19 .... **13** D3
Bolton St *RAM* CT11 .... **5** D5
Bolts Hl *RCANTW* CT4 .... **104** E4
Bond La *ASH* TN23 .... **181** K4
Bond Rd *ASH* TN23 .... **8** A5
Bonetza Ct *IOS* ME12 .... **14** C6
Bonham Dr *SIT* ME10 .... **58** B1
Bonny Bush Hl *RCANTW* CT4 .... **128** E3
Bonsor Rd *FOLKN* CT19 .... **13** D5
Booth Pl *MARG* CT9 .... **3** D2
Borden La *ASH* TN23 .... **57** G4
Bornefields *ASH* TN23 .... **8** A6
Borough *CANT* CT1 .... **7** D2
Borough Rd *QBOR* ME11 .... **20** C2
Borrowdale Av *RAM* CT11 .... **4** A4
Borstal Hl *WSTB* CT5 .... **44** A8
Boscombe Rd *FOLKN* CT19 .... **12** C3
Bosney Banks *RDV* CT15 .... **151** J7
Bossingham Rd *RCANTW* CT4 .... **146** D4
Bossington Rd *RCANTE* CT3 .... **109** K5
Boston Cl *DVE/WH* CT16 .... **173** F3
Botany Cl *IOS* ME12 .... **14** C5
Botany Rd *BRDST* CT10 .... **33** G4
Botolph's Br *HYTHE* CT21 .... **203** J7
Botolph's Bridge Rd *HYTHE* CT21 .... **203** J7
Bottles La *RSIT* ME9 .... **77** C1
Bottom Pond Rd *RSIT* ME9 .... **76** E2
Boughton Av *BRDST* CT10 .... **55** H5
Boughton Rd *RMAID* ME17 .... **116** B5
Boulevard Courrieres *RCANTE* CT3 .... **130** A2
The Boulevard *KEN/WIL* TN24 .... **161** K8
Boundary Cl *IOS* ME12 .... **16** B8
Boundary Rd *DEAL* CT14 .... **135** K8
   HYTHE CT21 .... **204** E5
   RAM CT11 .... **5** E4
The Boundary *CANT* CT1 .... **6** A5
Bounds La *FAV* ME13 .... **83** G3
Bourne Gv *SIT* ME10 .... **57** H1
Bourne La *RASHW* TN26 .... **198** E6
Bourne Lodge Cl *CANTW/ST* CT2 .... **66** D7
Bournemouth Dr *HB* CT6 .... **46** C1
Bournemouth Gdns *FOLKN* CT19 .... **12** C5
Bournemouth Rd *FOLKN* CT19 .... **12** C5
Bourne Park Rd *RCANTW* CT4 .... **108** B7
Bourne Rd *RASHE* TN25 .... **183** H8
Bournes Cl *CANTW/ST* CT2 .... **68** E7
Bournes Pl *RASHW* TN26 .... **196** D4
Bournewood *RASHW* TN26 .... **198** E6
Bouverie Pl *FOLK* CT20 .... **13** D5
Bouverie Rd *FOLK* CT20 .... **13** D5
Bouverie Rd West *FOLK* CT20 .... **12** A5
Bouverie Sq *FOLK* CT20 .... **13** D5
Bowdell La *LYDD* TN29 .... **223** H2
Bowden Crs *FOLK* CT20 .... **189** H8
Bowen Rd *FOLKN* CT19 .... **189** K8
Bowens Fld *ASH* TN23 .... **8** A4
Bowerland La *RCANTW* CT4 .... **103** J4
Bower Rd *RASHE* TN25 .... **184** A3
Bowes Av *MARG* CT9 .... **31** F5
Bowes La *HB* CT6 .... **47** F3
Bow Hl *RCANTW* CT4 .... **126** D4
Bowland Ct *HB* CT6 .... **47** H4
Bowles Well Gdns *FOLKN* CT19 .... **13** F2
Bowles Wells Gdns *FOLKN* CT19 .... **13** F2
Bowley La *RMAID* ME17 .... **116** E6
Bowl Fld *RASHE* TN25 .... **144** D8
Bowling Green La *DEAL* CT14 .... **135** H1
Bowling St *SWCH* CT13 .... **93** K5
Bowl Rd *HDCN* TN27 .... **118** E3
Bowra Rd *DEAL* CT14 .... **135** J2
Bowyer Rd *WSTB* CT5 .... **43** C7
Box La *FAV* ME13 .... **80** B5
Boxley *ASH* TN23 .... **160** D6
Boxley Cl *IOS* ME12 .... **14** C7

Boyces HI *RSIT* ME9...... **34** C8
Boyden Gate HI *RCANTE* CT3...... **48** C6
Boyes La *RCANTE* CT3...... **111** F4
Boyke La *RCANTW* CT4...... **167** F4
Boyne Rd *RDV* CT15...... **155** G5
Boys Hall *KEN/WIL* TN24...... **9** F6
Boystown Pl *SWCH* CT13...... **113** F3
Brabazon Rd *IOS* ME12...... **23** F6
Brabner Cl *FOLKN* CT19...... **13** E1
Brabourne Cl *CANTW/ST* CT2...... **86** E2
Brabourne Gdns *FOLK* CT20...... **206** E1
Brabourne La *RASHE* TN25...... **165** H4
Brabourne Rd *RASHE* TN25...... **164** A1
Bracken Cl *KEN/WIL* TN24...... **141** G8
Bracken Ct *BRDST* CT10...... **55** F1
Brack La *LYDD* TN29...... **222** E3
Bradbridge Gn *ASH* TN23...... **160** B6
Bradfield Av *MSTR* ME9...... **60** A4
Bradfield Rd *KEN/WIL* TN24...... **161** F1
Bradley Dr *SIT* ME10...... **57** K4
Bradley Rd *FOLK* CT20...... **13** E3
MSTR CT12...... **4** C2
Bradstone Av *FOLKN* CT19...... **13** D3
Bradstone New Rd *FOLK* CT20...... **13** D4
Bradstone Rd *FOLK* CT20...... **13** D4
FOLKN CT19...... **13** D4
Bradstow Wy *BRDST* CT10...... **55** G1
Brady Rd *RFOLK* CT18...... **166** E8
Braggs La *HB* CT6...... **46** C8
Bramble Cl *RASHE* TN25...... **142** D3
Brambledown *FOLKN* CT19...... **13** D3
Bramblefield La *SIT* ME10...... **35** K5
Bramblefields Cl *HB* CT6...... **47** G4
Bramblehill Rd *FAV* ME13...... **62** B6
Bramble La *RASHE* TN25...... **142** C3
Bramley Crs *FOLK* CT20...... **206** E1
Bramley Av *CANT* CT1...... **86** A8
FAV ME13...... **62** D8
Bramley Cl *IOS* ME12...... **23** G5
Bramley Gdns *ASH* TN23...... **160** E8
Bramley Wy *IOS* ME12...... **23** G3
Bramling Rd *RCANTW* CT4...... **109** F4
Bramshaw Rd *CANTW/ST* CT2...... **6** B1
Bramston Rd *IOS* ME12...... **15** K8
Branch Rd *RCANTW* CT4...... **103** J6
Branch St *DVE/WH* CT16...... **10** A2
Brandon Rd *MSTR* CT12...... **4** A2
Brandon Wy *BRCH* CT7...... **30** A8
Brasier Ct *IOS* ME12...... **21** H1
Brassey Av *BRDST* CT10...... **55** G3
Brattle *RASHW* TN26...... **196** D6
Breadlands Cl *KEN/WIL* TN24...... **9** E5
Breadlands Rd *KEN/WIL* TN24...... **9** E5
Brecon Cha *IOS* ME12...... **15** K7
Brecon Ri *KEN/WIL* TN24...... **8** B1
Brecon Sq *MSTR* CT12...... **4** A2
Bredgar Cl *ASH* TN23...... **160** D8
Bredhurst Cl *IOS* ME12...... **14** C7
Bredlands La *RCANTE* CT3...... **69** H5
Brenchley Av *DEAL* CT14...... **135** F2
Brenchley Cl *ASH* TN23...... **160** C8
Brenchley Rd *SIT* ME10...... **58** A4
Brendon Dr *KEN/WIL* TN24...... **8** B2
Brenley La *RASHE* TN25...... **82** C2
Brent HI *FAV* ME13...... **62** B6
Brent Rd *FAV* ME13...... **62** B6
Brentwood *ASH* TN23...... **181** J1
Brewer's Fld *FOLK* CT20...... **206** D3
Brewer St *DEAL* CT14...... **115** K8
Brewery La *RCANTW* CT4...... **108** A5
Brewery Rd *SIT* ME10...... **35** K8
Brewery Sq *RCANTE* CT3...... **72** A4
Brewhouse La *RASHE* TN25...... **141** K2
Briar Cl *DVW* CT17...... **172** D4
KEN/WIL TN24...... **141** G8
RCANTE CT3...... **72** A4
Briars Rd *LYDD* TN29...... **227** G3
Briary Cl *MARG* CT9...... **30** E6
Brice Av *RCANTW* CT4...... **104** E4
Brickfield La *FAV* ME13...... **82** E4
Brickfield Rd *RCANTW* CT4...... **129** F7
Bridewell La *TENT* TN30...... **194** A7
Bridewell Pk *WSTB* CT5...... **44** D5
The Bridge Ap *WSTB* CT5...... **44** B5
Bridge Cl *HYTHE* CT21...... **204** E4
RASHW TN26...... **196** D6
Bridge Down *RCANTW* CT4...... **108** B6
Bridgefield Rd *WSTB* CT5...... **44** E3
Bridgeford Wy *RCANTW* CT4...... **108** A5
Bridge HI *DEAL* CT14...... **114** C6
RCANTW CT4...... **108** B6
Bridge Rd *ASH* TN23...... **160** D4
DEAL CT14...... **115** K7
FAV ME13...... **62** B6
IOS ME12...... **14** C3
MARG CT9...... **31** F5
RASHE TN25...... **184** E1
RCANTW CT4...... **107** J5
Bridges Cl *BRCH* CT7...... **50** B4
Bridgeside *DEAL* CT14...... **115** J8
Bridge St *DVE/WH* CT16...... **10** A2
FOLKN CT19...... **13** E3
RASHE TN25...... **142** D4
Bridgewater Rd *IOS* ME12...... **14** C6
Bridle Wy *HB* CT6...... **46** C3

HYTHE CT21...... **206** A3
Bridleway Gdns *BRDST* CT10...... **54** E3
Bridleway La *ASH* TN23...... **182** A2
Brielle Wy *IOS* ME12...... **14** B5
OBOR ME12...... **14** B8
Brier Rd *SIT* ME10...... **57** F1
Brightlingsea Rd *SWCH* CT13...... **93** K6
Bright's Pl *RAM* CT11...... **5** F4
Brisbane Av *SIT* ME10...... **57** H2
Brisbane Dr *MSTR* CT12...... **4** A2
Brisley La *RASHE* TN25...... **182** C8
Brissenden Cl *NROM* TN28...... **226** C6
Bristol Pl *RAM* CT11...... **5** D4
Bristol Rd *CANT* CT1...... **6** C5
Britannia La *WSTB* CT5...... **43** J7
Britannia Cl *SIT* ME10...... **35** K7
Britannia Rd *DEAL* CT14...... **115** K6
Briton Ct *IOS* ME12...... **14** C5
Briton Rd *FAV* ME13...... **62** B7
Britten Cl *HYTHE* CT21...... **204** E3
Broadacre *RDV* CT15...... **151** H6
RSIT ME9...... **60** A4
Broadfield Crs *FOLK* CT20...... **12** A4
Broadfield Rd *FOLK* CT20...... **12** A4
Broadhurst Dr *KEN/WIL* TN24...... **141** H7
Broadlands *CANTW/ST* CT2...... **68** E8
Broadlands Av *NROM* TN28...... **226** C6
Broadlands Crs *NROM* TN28...... **226** C6
Broad La *DEAL* CT14...... **114** A8
Broadley Av *BRCH* CT7...... **51** J1
Broadmead Rd *FOLKN* CT19...... **11** Q C4
Broadmead Rd *RFOLK* CT19...... **11** Q C4
Broad Oak Rd *CANTW/ST* CT2...... **7** D1
Broadoak Rd *RSIT* ME9...... **57** J7
Broadsole La *RDV* CT15...... **192** B1
Broadstairs Rd *BRDST* CT10...... **55** F1
Broad St *CANT* CT1...... **7** D2
DEAL CT14...... **115** K8
IOS ME12...... **14** C4
MARG CT9...... **2** C2
Broadview *FOLK* CT20...... **189** H8
Broadway *IOS* ME12...... **14** C4
RCANTW CT4...... **125** J4
The Broadway *BRDST* CT10...... **55** G2
HB CT6...... **46** B1
IOS ME12...... **15** J7
Brockenhurst Cl *CANTW/ST* CT2...... **6** B1
Brockenhurst Rd *RAM* CT11...... **5** F3
Brockhill Rd *HYTHE* CT21...... **205** F3
Brockley Rd *MARG* CT9...... **3** D3
Brockman Crs *LYDD* TN29...... **217** K1
Brockman Rd *FOLK* CT20...... **12** C4
Brockman's Cl *MSTR* CT12...... **52** A7
Brogdale Rd *FAV* ME13...... **81** F1
Bromley Green Rd *RASHW* TN26...... **181** H8
Bromstone Rd *BRDST* CT10...... **55** F3
Brook Cl *HB* CT6...... **46** B3
HYTHE CT21...... **206** B3
Brooke Av *MARG* CT9...... **31** G7
Brooke Rd *KEN/WIL* TN24...... **8** B2
Brookes Pl *RSIT* ME9...... **34** A8
Brookfield Pl *DVE/WH* CT16...... **173** F4
Brookfield Rd *ASH* TN23...... **160** C5
DVE/WH CT16...... **172** E3
Brooklands Cl *CANTW/ST* CT2...... **87** K2
Brook La *HB* CT6...... **48** C1
MSTR CT12...... **74** E2
RASHE TN25...... **186** B4
Brook Rd *FAV* ME13...... **62** B6
WSTB CT5...... **45** F3
Brookside *DVE/WH* CT16...... **172** A1
LYDD TN29...... **227** H1
Brook St *RASHW* TN26...... **195** J6
SWCH CT13...... **113** C4
TENT TN30......
Broomfield Crs *MARG* CT9...... **33** C4
Broomfield Ga *WSTB* CT5...... **67** G1
Broomfield Rd *FAV* ME13...... **62** B5
FOLKN CT19...... **189** K8
HB CT6...... **47** G5
Broom Rd *SIT* ME10...... **58** D1
Browning Cl *FOLKN* CT19...... **13** E2
Brownings Orch *RSIT* ME9...... **58** B7
Broxhall Rd *RCANTW* CT4...... **126** E4
Bruce Cl *DEAL* CT14...... **135** H2
Brunswick Fld *RSIT* ME9...... **60** A4
Brunswick Gdns *DVE/WH* CT16...... **173** F3
Brunswick Rd *ASH* TN23...... **160** C4
BRCH CT7...... **51** K1
Brunswick Sq *HB* CT6...... **46** D1
Brunswick St *RAM* CT11...... **5** E4
Brymore Cl *CANT* CT1...... **7** E1
Brymore Rd *CANT* CT1...... **7** E1
Buckhurst Dr *MARG* CT9...... **33** G4
Buckingham Rd *BRDST* CT10...... **55** J2
MARG CT9...... **2** C4
Buckland Av *DVE/WH* CT16...... **173** F4
Buckland La *RCANTE* CT3...... **111** H4
Bucklers Cl *IOS* ME12...... **24** D2
Bucksford La *ASH* TN23...... **160** B6
Buck St *RASHE* TN25...... **121** G4
Buddle Dr *IOS* ME12...... **15** F7
Budd's La *TENT* TN30...... **219** K4
Buenos Ayres *MARG* CT9...... **2** B3

Buffs Av *FOLK* CT20...... **189** G8
Bulleid Pl *ASH* TN23...... **9** D6
Buller's Av *HB* CT6...... **46** D2
Bull HI *RMAID* ME17...... **117** C5
Bull La *FAV* ME13...... **83** F1
RASHW TN26...... **178** C2
Bullockstone Rd *HB* CT6...... **46** C4
Bullwark Rd *DEAL* CT14...... **115** K7
The Bulrushes *ASH* TN23...... **160** A6
Bulwark St *DVW* CT17...... **10** B6
Bunce Court Rd *FAV* ME13...... **98** B7
Bunker's HI *DVW* CT17...... **172** E4
Bunkers Hill *DVW* CT17...... **172** E5
Bunkers Hill Rd *DVW* CT17...... **172** E5
Bunkley Meadow *RASHW* TN26...... **198** E7
Burch Av *SWCH* CT13...... **93** K6
Burgate *CANT* CT1...... **7** D3
Burgate La *CANT* CT1...... **7** D3
Burgess Cl *DVE/WH* CT16...... **153** F7
MSTR CT12...... **52** B7
Burgess Gn *DEAL* CT14...... **114** C6
Burgess Rd *RCANTE* CT3...... **110** B8
Burgoyne Hts *DVE/WH* CT16...... **10** C1
Burkeston Cl *SIT* ME10...... **36** B6
Burleigh Rd *HDCN* TN27...... **118** E7
Burley Rd *SIT* ME10...... **57** K2
Burlington Dr *HB* CT6...... **47** F8
Burlington Gdns *MARG* CT9...... **2** A5
Burma Crs *CANT* CT1...... **87** H5
Burmarsh Rd *LYDD* TN29...... **217** F4
Burman Rd *WSTB* CT5...... **45** F4
Burnham Cl *SIT* ME10...... **35** K6
Burnt House HI *RCANTE* CT3...... **89** H1
Burnt Oast Rd *FAV* ME13...... **83** C3
Burntwick Dr *RSIT* ME9...... **34** C3
Burrow Rd *FOLKN* CT19...... **13** F3
The Burrs *SIT* ME10...... **58** A3
Bursill Crs *MSTR* CT12...... **4** B2
Bursted HI *RCANTW* CT4...... **127** F4
Burton Cl *FOLKN* CT19...... **12** A2
Burton Flds *HB* CT6...... **47** C2
Burton Rd *KEN/WIL* TN24...... **141** H8
Bush Av *MSTR* CT12...... **4** B2
Bushey La *FAV* ME13...... **82** E3
Busheyfields Rd *HB* CT6...... **46** E8
Bushy Hill Rd *CANTW/ST* CT2...... **69** H7
Bushy Royds *KEN/WIL* TN24...... **161** H8
Butchers La *RDV* CT15...... **131** G1
Butchery La *CANT* CT1...... **6** C3
The Butchery *SWCH* CT13...... **94** A5
Butler's HI *FAV* ME13...... **64** E7
Buttermere *FAV* ME13...... **62** D8
Buttermere Cl *FOLKN* CT19...... **12** B3
Buttermere Gdns *RCANTE* CT3...... **110** B8
Butterside Rd *ASH* TN23...... **182** B2
Butter St *RDV* CT15...... **130** D2
Butt Field Rd *ASH* TN23...... **160** C6
The Butts *SIT* ME10...... **58** A2
SWCH CT13...... **93** K5
Buxton Rd *MSTR* CT12...... **4** B1
Bybrook Ct *KEN/WIL* TN24...... **8** C1
Bybrook Fld *FOLK* CT20...... **206** E3
Bybrook Rd *KEN/WIL* TN24...... **161** C1
Bybrook Wy *FOLK* CT20...... **206** E2
Byllan Rd *DVW* CT17...... **172** C3
Byron Av *MARG* CT9...... **30** B5
Byron Cl *CANT* CT1...... **7** F4
Byron Crs *DVE/WH* CT16...... **173** F2
Bysing Wood Rd *FAV* ME13...... **61** K5

Cade Rd *ASH* TN23...... **8** A6
Cadnam Cl *CANTW/ST* CT2...... **86** C7
Caesar's Wy *FOLKN* CT19...... **189** K7
Calais HI *CANTW/ST* CT2...... **67** G8
Caldecot La *LYDD* TN29...... **231** J4
Caldew Gv *SIT* ME10...... **58** B3
Caledon Ter *CANT* CT1...... **7** D4
Calgary Crs *FOLKN* CT19...... **13** E1
Calland *RASHE* TN25...... **185** F1
Callaways La *RSIT* ME9...... **34** A8
Calleywell La *RASHE* TN25...... **184** B7
Callis Court Rd *BRDST* CT10...... **33** G8
Calverden Rd *MSTR* CT12...... **4** A2
Camber Wy *DVE/WH* CT16...... **11** F2
Cambourne Av *WGOS* CT8...... **30** C6
Cambridge Av *SWCH* CT13...... **95** G8
Cambridge Cl *BRCH* CT7...... **30** A7
Cambridge Gdns *FOLK* CT20...... **13** D4
Cambridge Rd *CANT* CT1...... **6** C4
DEAL CT14...... **135** K3
DVW CT17...... **10** B4
FAV ME13...... **62** A8
SIT ME10...... **58** C4
Cambridge Wy *CANT* CT1...... **6** C5
Camden Crs *DVE/WH* CT16...... **10** C4
Camden Rd *BRDST* CT10...... **33** F7
RAM CT11...... **5** E5
Camellia Cl *MARG* CT9...... **31** G6
Campbell Cl *HB* CT6...... **47** H3
Campbell Rd *DEAL* CT14...... **135** K3

Canada Cl *RFOLK* CT18 .... 189 H8
Canada Rd *DEAL* CT14 .... 135 K3 ⚅
Canberra Gdns *SIT* ME10 .... 57 H2
Cannonbury Rd *RAM* CT11 .... 5 D5
Cannongate Av *HYTHE* CT21 .... 205 H3
Cannongate Cl *HYTHE* CT21 .... 205 J4
Cannongate Gdns *HYTHE* CT21 .... 205 H3
Cannon Rd *RAM* CT11 .... 5 D4
Cannon St *DEAL* CT14 .... 115 J7
   LYDD TN29 .... 231 H8
   NROM TN28 .... 226 C7
Canons Gate Rd *DVE/WH* CT16 ..... 10 C3
Canon Woods Wy
   KEN/WIL TN24 .... 141 K8 ⚅
Canterbury Cl *BRDST* CT10 .... 54 E1 ⚅
Canterbury Hl *CANTW/ST* CT2 .... 86 C1
Canterbury La *CANT* CT1 .... 7 D3 ⚅
Canterbury Rd *BRCH* CT7 .... 50 B7
   FAV ME13 .... 81 J1
   FOLKN CT19 .... 13 D3
   HB CT6 .... 46 E7
   KEN/WIL TN24 .... 8 C2
   RASHE TN25 .... 119 J5
   RASHE TN25 .... 185 F1
   RCANTE CT3 .... 88 E6
   RCANTW CT4 .... 104 A6
   RCANTW CT4 .... 149 H2
   RCANTW CT4 .... 167 J3
   RDV CT15 .... 151 G7
   RFOLK CT18 .... 167 G7
   RFOLK CT18 .... 190 C2
   SIT ME10 .... 58 C3
   WSTB CT5 .... 44 A6
Canterbury Road Birchington
   BRCH CT7 .... 29 K3
Canterbury Rd East *RAM* CT11 ...... 54 A7
Canterbury Road Margate
   MARG CT9 .... 31 G5
Canterbury Rd West *MSTR* CT12 ... 53 J7
Canterbury Road Westgate
   WGOS CT8 .... 30 C6
Canute Rd *BRCH* CT7 .... 29 G6
   DEAL CT14 .... 115 J5
   FAV ME13 .... 62 B8
Capel Cl *BRDST* CT10 .... 33 G5
Capel Rd *FAV* ME13 .... 62 A7 ⚅
   RASHW TN26 .... 198 D3
   RCANTW CT4 .... 125 H2
   SIT ME10 .... 57 K1
Capel St *RFOLK* CT18 .... 191 J5
Capstan Rw *DEAL* CT14 .... 115 K7 ⚅
Cardine Cl *SIT* ME10 .... 35 K7
Carey Cl *NROM* TN28 .... 226 C8
Carlsden Cl *DVE/WH* CT16 .... 172 E3
Carlton Av *BRDST* CT10 .... 55 H1
   IOS ME12 .... 14 C5 ⚅
   RAM CT11 .... 5 D5
Carlton Hl *HB* CT6 .... 46 B2
Carlton Ri *WGOS* CT8 .... 30 B6
Carlton Rd *ASH* TN23 .... 8 A3
   DEAL CT14 .... 135 J6
   WSTB CT5 .... 66 A4
Carlton Rd East *WGOS* CT8 .... 30 C6 ⚅
Carlton Rd West *WGOS* CT8 .... 30 B6
Caroland Cl *RASHE* TN25 .... 184 E1
Caroline Cl *WSTB* CT5 .... 43 J8 ⚅
Caroline Crs *BRDST* CT10 .... 33 F8
Carriage Ms *CANTW/ST* CT2 .... 6 C2 ⚅
Carroway's Pl *MARG* CT9 .... 3 D3 ⚅
Carter La *LYDD* TN29 .... 223 H4
Carter's Rd *FOLK* CT20 .... 207 F1
Carter's Wd *RASHW* TN26 .... 198 E7
Caslocke St *FAV* ME13 .... 62 B7 ⚅
Cassino Sq *DVE/WH* CT16 .... 10 C1
Castle Av *BRDST* CT10 .... 33 J8
   DVE/WH CT16 .... 10 B2
   HYTHE CT21 .... 205 F3
Castle Bay *FOLK* CT20 .... 206 C3
Castle Cl *HYTHE* CT21 .... 203 H4
Castle Dr *DVE/WH* CT16 .... 152 D7
Castle Hl *FOLKN* CT19 .... 12 A1
Castle Hill Av *FOLK* CT20 .... 12 C5 ⚅
Castle Hill Rd *DVE/WH* CT16 .... 10 C2
Castle Mayne Av *BRCH* CT7 .... 52 E3
Castlemere Av *QBOR* ME11 .... 20 C1
Castlemount Rd *DVE/WH* CT16 ...... 10 B2
Castle Rd *FOLK* CT20 .... 207 F3
   HYTHE CT21 .... 205 F2
   SIT ME10 .... 58 C1
   WSTB CT5 .... 44 C4
Castle Rough La *SIT* ME10 .... 36 A5
Castle Rw *CANT* CT1 .... 6 C4 ⚅
Castle St *CANT* CT1 .... 6 C4
   DVE/WH CT16 .... 10 C3
   QBOR ME11 .... 20 B1
Catherine Wy *BRDST* CT10 .... 33 H8
Catsole Hl *RCANTE* CT3 .... 111 F4
Cattle Market *SWCH* CT13 .... 93 K5 ⚅
Catt's Hl *TENT* TN30 .... 221 G2
Catt's Wood Rd *RCANTW* CT4 ..... 130 D1
Cauldham Cl *RFOLK* CT18 .... 191 H5
Cauldham La *RFOLK* CT18 .... 191 J2
The Causeway *CANTW/ST* CT2 ...... 6 C2 ⚅
Cave La *RCANTE* CT3 .... 111 F3

Cavell Sq *DEAL* CT14 .... 135 G3
Cavell Wy *SIT* ME10 .... 57 J1
Cavenagh Rd *RDV* CT15 .... 155 H8
Cavendish Rd *HB* CT6 .... 47 F2
Cavour Rd *FAV* ME13 .... 62 B7
   IOS ME12 .... 14 D4
Caxton Rd *MARG* CT9 .... 2 A5
Cecil Av *IOS* ME12 .... 14 C5
Cecil Ct *HB* CT6 .... 47 F2
Cecilia Gv *BRDST* CT10 .... 33 G8
Cecilia Rd *RAM* CT11 .... 5 E3
Cecil Pk *HB* CT6 .... 47 F2
Cecil Rd *DEAL* CT14 .... 135 K7 ⚅
Cecil Sq *MARG* CT9 .... 2 C3 ⚅
Cecil St *MARG* CT9 .... 2 C3 ⚅
Cedar Cl *ASH* TN23 .... 160 C5
   BRDST CT10 .... 33 G7
   MARG CT9 .... 3 F4
   SIT ME10 .... 58 C4 ⚅
Cedar Crs *LYDD* TN29 .... 227 G3
Cedar Rd *CANTW/ST* CT2 .... 68 E8
Cedarview *CANTW/ST* CT2 .... 86 A5 ⚅
Cellar Hl *RSIT* ME9 .... 59 K6
Celt Cl *SIT* ME10 .... 36 A6
Celtic Rd *DEAL* CT14 .... 135 G4
Cemetery La *KEN/WIL* TN24 .... 8 C1
Centenary Gdns *SWCH* CT13 .... 112 E4
Centenary Wk *CANTW/ST* CT2 ...... 85 J6
Centenary Walk Canterbury
   RCANTW CT4 .... 85 G8
Central Av *HB* CT6 .... 46 C1
   SIT ME10 .... 58 A3
Central Pde *HB* CT6 .... 46 D1
Central Rd *RAM* CT11 .... 5 D3
Centre Rd *DVW* CT17 .... 10 A5
Centurion Wk *ASH* TN23 .... 182 A2
Century Rd *FAV* ME13 .... 62 D7
The Chain *SWCH* CT13 .... 94 A6
Chalcroft Rd *FOLK* CT20 .... 206 E2
Chalfont Dr *HB* CT6 .... 47 J4 ⚅
Chalk Av *TENT* TN30 .... 194 B4
Chalk Cl *FOLKN* CT19 .... 12 A2
Chalk Hl *RAM* CT11 .... 54 A8
Chalk Hill Rd *DEAL* CT14 .... 155 J1
Chalkpit Hl *RCANTW* CT4 .... 108 D3
Chalk Pit La *RCANTE* CT3 .... 111 K1
Chalk Rd *QBOR* ME11 .... 20 B1
Chalksole Green La *RDV* CT15 ..... 170 C4
Chalkwell Rd *SIT* ME10 .... 57 J2
Challenger Cl *SIT* ME10 .... 35 K7
Challock Ct *MARG* CT9 .... 33 G4 ⚅
Chamberlain Dr *HB* CT6 .... 46 A2
Chamberlain Rd *DVW* CT17 .... 172 E6
Chance Meadow *RDV* CT15 .... 153 K8
Chanctonbury Cha *WSTB* CT5 .... 43 H8 ⚅
Chandos Sq *BRDST* CT10 .... 55 J2
Channel Cl *FOLKN* CT19 .... 13 D2
Channel Lea *DEAL* CT14 .... 135 J5
Channel View Rd *DVW* CT17 .... 10 A5
Channon Rd *LYDD* TN29 .... 232 E7
Chapel Hl *MARG* CT9 .... 3 E6
   RDV CT15 .... 132 A7
Chapel Hill Cl *MARG* CT9 .... 3 D6 ⚅
Chapel La *CANTW/ST* CT2 .... 66 D7
   CANTW/ST CT2 .... 68 C7
   DEAL CT14 .... 134 D6
   HDCN TN27 .... 136 B3
   LYDD TN29 .... 215 H3
   RCANTE CT3 .... 91 K8
   RCANTW CT4 .... 167 G1
   RDV CT15 .... 133 F8
   RDV CT15 .... 155 F8
Chapel Pl *RAM* CT11 .... 5 D4
Chapel Place La *RAM* CT11 .... 5 D4
Chapel Rd *DEAL* CT14 .... 133 F3 ⚅
   DVE/WH CT16 .... 152 E6 ⚅
   LYDD TN29 .... 216 E6
   RAM CT11 .... 4 C4
   RASHW TN26 .... 139 H5
Chapel St *DEAL* CT14 .... 115 K8 ⚅
   FAV ME13 .... 62 C8
   HYTHE CT21 .... 205 F4
   IOS ME12 .... 14 B3
   IOS ME12 .... 16 A8
Chapmans Cl *RASHE* TN25 .... 121 G4
Chapmans Hl *RCANTE* CT3 .... 130 D1
Chappell Wy *SIT* ME10 .... 35 J8
Charing Cl *MSTR* CT12 .... 4 C3
Charing Crs *WGOS* CT8 .... 30 C7
Charing Heath Rd *HDCN* TN27 .... 118 D3
Charing Hl *HDCN* TN27 .... 119 G5
Charles Cobb Cl *LYDD* TN29 .... 217 H3
Charles Crs *FOLKN* CT19 .... 189 K7
Charles Drayson Ct *FAV* ME13 ...... 62 D7 ⚅
   RAM CT11 .... 5 E3
Charles St *HB* CT6 .... 46 E1
   IOS ME12 .... 14 C5 ⚅
Charlesworth Dr *BRCH* CT7 .... 30 A7
Charlotte Sq *MARG* CT9 .... 3 D4 ⚅
Charlotte St *FOLK* CT20 .... 13 C4 ⚅
   SIT ME10 .... 57 K1
Charlton Av *DVE/WH* CT16 .... 10 A5
Charlton Cl *KEN/WIL* TN24 .... 162 A6
   MSTR CT12 .... 4 B1 ⚅

Charlton Gn *DVE/WH* CT16 .... 10 A2
The Charltons *FAV* ME13 .... 83 F2
Charminster *ASH* TN23 .... 160 C8 ⚅
Charnwood *WSTB* CT5 .... 45 G5
Charnwood Rd *HB* CT6 .... 47 G5
Chart Cl *FAV* ME13 .... 62 A7
Chartham Downs Rd
   RCANTW CT4 .... 105 F5
Chart Rd *ASH* TN23 .... 8 A2
   FOLKN CT19 .... 190 A8
Chartwell Av *HB* CT6 .... 47 J2
Chartwell Gv *SIT* ME10 .... 57 H3 ⚅
Chater Cl *DEAL* CT14 .... 135 J2 ⚅
Chatham Pl *RAM* CT11 .... 5 E4 ⚅
Chatham St *RAM* CT11 .... 5 E4
Chatsworth Dr *SIT* ME10 .... 57 G1
Chaucer Av *WSTB* CT5 .... 44 E5
Chaucer Cl *CANT* CT1 .... 7 F4
Chaucer Crs *DVE/WH* CT16 .... 173 F3
Chaucer Ms *CANTW/ST* CT2 .... 85 H5
Chaucer Rd *BRDST* CT10 .... 55 H3 ⚅
   CANT CT1 .... 7 F2
   RDV CT15 .... 131 K5 ⚅
   SIT ME10 .... 57 J3
Cheddar Cl *KEN/WIL* TN24 .... 8 B2
Cheesmans Cl *MSTR* CT12 .... 74 B1
Chegworth Gdns *SIT* ME10 .... 57 K5
Chelsea Rd *CANT* CT1 .... 87 G2 ⚅
Cheney Hl *RSIT* ME9 .... 77 G2
Cheney Rd *FAV* ME13 .... 62 E7
Chequer La *RCANTW* CT4 .... 92 B4
Chequers Hl *RCANTW* CT4 .... 126 A3
Chequers Pk *RASHE* TN25 .... 142 E5
Chequers Rd *IOS* ME12 .... 16 B8
Cheriton Av *MSTR* CT12 .... 4 B3
Cheriton Court Rd *FOLK* CT20 .... 206 C1
Cheriton Gdns *FOLK* CT20 .... 13 D4
Cheriton High St *FOLKN* CT19 .... 189 K8
   RFOLK CT18 .... 189 G8
Cheriton Int *FOLKN* CT19 .... 189 H8 ⚅
Cheriton Pl *DEAL* CT14 .... 135 K2 ⚅
   FOLK CT20 .... 13 D5 ⚅
Cheriton Rd *DEAL* CT14 .... 135 K2 ⚅
   FOLK CT20 .... 12 C4
   FOLKN CT19 .... 12 A3
Cherry Av *CANTW/ST* CT2 .... 6 A1
Cherrybrook Rd *FOLK* CT20 .... 189 J8 ⚅
Cherry Cl *SIT* ME10 .... 35 J8
Cherry Dr *CANTW/ST* CT2 .... 6 A1
Cherry Flds *SIT* ME10 .... 57 F1
Cherry Garden Av *FOLKN* CT19 ... 12 A2 ⚅
Cherry Garden Crs *RASHE* TN25 . 143 F4 ⚅
Cherry Garden La *FOLKN* CT19 .. 190 A7
   RASHE TN25 .... 142 E4
   RCANTE CT3 .... 92 C5
Cherrygarden La *RCANTE* CT3 .... 111 G6
Cherry Garden Rd *CANTW/ST* CT2 .. 6 A1
Cherry Gdns *BRDST* CT10 .... 54 D3
   HB CT6 .... 46 D2
   NROM TN28 .... 226 E8
   RCANTW CT4 .... 167 K1
   RSIT ME9 .... 59 K4
Cherry Glebe *RASHE* TN25 .... 183 K3
Cherry Gv *RDV* CT15 .... 132 A4
Cherry La *DEAL* CT14 .... 134 D3
Cherry Orch *RASHW* TN26 .... 196 C3
   RCANTW CT4 .... 103 J4
   TENT TN30 .... 194 A8 ⚅
   WSTB CT5 .... 45 F6
Cherry Orchard La *RASHE* TN25 .. 200 E2
Cherry Tree Av *DVE/WH* CT16 ...... 10 A1 ⚅
Cherry Tree Cl *RSIT* ME9 .... 60 A4 ⚅
Cherry Tree Rd *HDCN* TN27 .... 118 A7
Cherry Waye *RDV* CT15 .... 132 A7
Cherrywood Ri *ASH* TN23 .... 160 D2
Cherville La *RCANTE* CT3 .... 89 J7
Chessenden La *HDCN* TN27 .... 156 A5
Chester Av *RASHW* TN26 .... 178 E1
Chester Rd *WGOS* CT8 .... 30 E6 ⚅
Chestfield Rd *WSTB* CT5 .... 45 F7
Chestnut Av *CANTW/ST* CT2 .... 66 D8
   DVE/WH CT16 .... 152 E6 ⚅
   HYTHE CT21 .... 204 C6 ⚅
   TENT TN30 .... 194 C5
Chestnut Cl *FAV* ME13 .... 83 F3
Chestnut Dr *BRDST* CT10 .... 54 E2
   CANTW/ST CT2 .... 69 F8
   DEAL CT14 .... 114 A2
   HB CT6 .... 46 C4
Chestnut La *ASH* TN23 .... 182 B2 ⚅
Chestnut Rd *DVW* CT17 .... 173 F7 ⚅
Chestnuts *RASHE* TN25 .... 184 E1 ⚅
Chestnut St *RSIT* ME9 .... 56 D2
Chestnut Wood La *RSIT* ME9 .... 56 D2
Chevalier Rd *DVW* CT17 .... 172 E7
Cheviot Cl *BRDST* CT10 .... 55 J1 ⚅
Cheviot Wy *KEN/WIL* TN24 .... 8 C1 ⚅
Cheyne Cl *SIT* ME10 .... 56 A6
Cheyne Rd *IOS* ME12 .... 23 G3
Chichester Rd *FOLK* CT20 .... 206 E2 ⚅
   MSTR CT12 .... 4 B2
Chiddingfold Cl *IOS* ME12 .... 16 A8
Chilham Av *WGOS* CT8 .... 30 C7

Chilham Cl *IOS* ME12 .... 14 C6
Chilham Rd *FOLKN* CT19 .... 189 K8
Chilston Rd *RMAID* ME17 .... 116 D1
Chiltern End *KEN/WIL* TN24 .... 8 B2
Chilton Av *RDV* CT15 .... 172 A3
   SIT ME10 .... 58 B3
Chilton Fld *RCANTE* CT3 .... 92 B4
Chilton Gdns *RCANTE* CT3 .... 92 B4
Chilton La *RAM* CT11 .... 4 A5
Chilton Pl *RCANTE* CT3 .... 92 B4
Chilton Sq *RCANTE* CT3 .... 92 B5
Chitton Wy *DVW* CT17 .... 172 C3
The Chimes *KEN/WIL* TN24 .... 8 C2
Chipman's Wy *MSTR* CT12 .... 51 H7
Chislett Cl *RASHE* TN25 .... 186 B4
Chisnall Rd *DVW* CT17 .... 172 C2
Chittenden's La *LYDD* TN29 .... 225 K4
Chitty La *RCANTE* CT3 .... 48 D7
Christchurch Rd *ASH* TN23 .... 8 B4
Christ Church Rd *FOLK* CT20 .... 12 C4
Christchurch Wy *DVE/WH* CT16 ...... 173 F3
Chrysler Av *HB* CT6 .... 45 K2
Church Ap *NROM* TN28 .... 226 B8
Church Cliff *DEAL* CT14 .... 135 K8
Church Cl *RASHE* TN25 .... 183 K3
Church Court Gv *BRDST* CT10 .... 33 F8
Church Farm Wy *SWCH* CT13 .... 93 F8
Church Fld *RASHE* TN25 .... 186 E5
Churchfield Pl *MARG* CT9 .... 2 C5
Churchfields *BRDST* CT10 .... 33 G7
   MARG CT9 .... 3 D4
Churchfield Wy *RASHE* TN25 .... 142 E4
Church Hi *ASH* TN23 .... 181 K3
   CANTW/ST CT2 .... 86 A5
   DVE/WH CT16 .... 172 B1
   FAV ME13 .... 83 C1
   HDCN TN27 .... 117 J6
   RASHW TN26 .... 177 K7
   RASHW TN26 .... 178 E1
   RCANTW CT4 .... 103 H6
   RDV CT15 .... 131 K6
   RDV CT15 .... 134 A6
   RDV CT15 .... 151 F2
   RSIT ME9 .... 78 B7
   TENT TN30 .... 221 G3
Churchill Av *DEAL* CT14 .... 135 J4
   FOLKN CT19 .... 12 C1
   HB CT6 .... 47 J2
Churchill Cl *RCANTW* CT4 .... 107 K5
   RDV CT15 .... 175 F1
Churchill Rd *CANT* CT1 .... 7 F5
   DVW CT17 .... 172 E8
   IOS ME12 .... 16 A7
Churchill St *DVE/WH* CT16 .... 10 A2
Churchill Wy *FAV* ME13 .... 62 A6
The Churchlands *NROM* TN28 .... 226 C8
Church La *CANT* CT1 .... 6 C3
   CANT CT1 .... 7 D2
   CANTW/ST CT2 .... 69 H7
   CANTW/ST CT2 .... 87 K1
   DEAL CT14 .... 134 D5
   DEAL CT14 .... 135 G1
   DEAL CT14 .... 155 F1
   FAV ME13 .... 82 B8
   LYDD TN29 .... 223 K2
   NROM TN28 .... 232 C1
   RASHE TN25 .... 121 F5
   RASHE TN25 .... 142 A1
   RASHE TN25 .... 165 K8
   RASHE TN25 .... 184 E8
   RASHE TN25 .... 186 C2
   RASHW TN26 .... 180 D7
   RCANTE CT3 .... 48 D7
   RCANTE CT3 .... 109 K5
   RCANTW CT4 .... 106 E4
   RCANTW CT4 .... 128 D3
   RCANTW CT4 .... 129 K4
   RCANTW CT4 .... 145 H2
   RDV CT15 .... 151 G6
   RDV CT15 .... 192 E2
   RSIT ME9 .... 34 A8
   WSTB CT5 .... 43 H8
Church Mdw *DEAL* CT14 .... 115 G8
Church Pth *DEAL* CT14 .... 135 H1
Church Rd *ASH* TN23 .... 8 C4
   DVW CT17 .... 172 E7
   FAV ME13 .... 62 C7
   FAV ME13 .... 99 H8
   FOLK CT20 .... 189 H8
   HYTHE CT21 .... 205 G4
   IOS ME12 .... 23 G4
   KEN/WIL TN24 .... 9 F5
   KEN/WIL TN24 .... 162 A3
   KEN/WIL TN24 .... 162 B8
   LYDD TN29 .... 216 A2
   LYDD TN29 .... 231 H7
   MARG CT9 .... 3 D4
   NROM TN28 .... 226 B8
   RAM CT11 .... 5 E4
   RASHE TN25 .... 183 J3
   RASHE TN25 .... 184 E1
   RASHW TN26 .... 197 J8
   RCANTE CT3 .... 69 J1

   RCANTE CT3 .... 89 F6
   RCANTW CT4 .... 121 J1
   RDV CT15 .... 151 J3
   RFOLK CT18 .... 167 G7
   RSIT ME9 .... 37 G7
   RSIT ME9 .... 59 F2
   SIT ME10 .... 58 C1
   TENT TN30 .... 194 A7
Church Sq *RMAID* ME17 .... 116 D1
Church St *BRDST* CT10 .... 33 F8
   CANTW/ST CT2 .... 6 B2
   DEAL CT14 .... 135 H4
   DVE/WH CT16 .... 10 B4
   FAV ME13 .... 62 C6
   FOLK CT20 .... 13 D5
   MARG CT9 .... 3 D4
   MSTR CT12 .... 74 B1
   RASHE TN25 .... 142 E4
   RDV CT15 .... 130 D1
   RSIT ME9 .... 58 D7
   SIT ME10 .... 57 K2
   SWCH CT13 .... 93 F8
   SWCH CT13 .... 93 K5
   SWCH CT13 .... 94 A5
   SWCH CT13 .... 113 F4
   WSTB CT5 .... 44 C5
Church Street (St Pauls)
   CANT CT1 .... 7 D3
Church Vw *HB* CT6 .... 47 H2
   LYDD TN29 .... 214 E3
   RASHE TN25 .... 184 B8
Church Whitfield Rd *RDV* CT15 ...... 153 F5
Church Wood Cl *CANTW/ST* CT2 ..... 85 K4
Churchwood Dr *WSTB* CT5 .... 45 G5
Cinque Ports La *HYTHE* CT21 .... 205 F5
Circular Rd *DEAL* CT14 .... 114 A7
Citadel Crs *DVW* CT17 .... 173 F8
Citadel Rd *DVW* CT17 .... 10 A5
Citroen Cl *HB* CT6 .... 46 A2
City Vw *CANTW/ST* CT2 .... 86 A6
Claire Ct *BRDST* CT10 .... 55 J1
Clanwilliam Rd *DEAL* CT14 .... 135 K1
Clapham Hl *WSTB* CT5 .... 65 K1
Clare Dr *HB* CT6 .... 46 B4
Claremont Gdns *RAM* CT11 .... 4 C4
Claremont Pl *CANT* CT1 .... 6 B4
Claremont Rd *DEAL* CT14 .... 135 H1
   DEAL CT14 .... 135 J8
   FOLK CT20 .... 12 C4
Claremont St *HB* CT6 .... 46 B3
Clarence Av *MARG* CT9 .... 32 E4
Clarence Gdns *IOS* ME12 .... 24 C3
Clarence Pl *DEAL* CT14 .... 115 K7
   DVW CT17 .... 10 B6
Clarence Rd *DEAL* CT14 .... 135 K3
   HB CT6 .... 46 C1
   RAM CT11 .... 4 C5
   RFOLK CT18 .... 191 J5
Clarence St *FOLK* CT20 .... 13 D4
   HB CT6 .... 46 D1
Clarendon Cl *SIT* ME10 .... 58 A5
Clarendon Gdns *RAM* CT11 .... 5 D5
Clarendon Ms *NROM* TN28 .... 226 D6
Clarendon Pl *DVW* CT17 .... 10 A4
Clarendon Rd *BRDST* CT10 .... 55 H2
   DVW CT17 .... 10 A4
   MARG CT9 .... 3 E3
   RCANTE CT3 .... 130 B1
Clarendon St *DVW* CT17 .... 10 A4
   HB CT6 .... 46 B2
Clare Rd *WSTB* CT5 .... 44 B4
Clarke Crs *KEN/WIL* TN24 .... 9 F1
Clarke's Cl *DEAL* CT14 .... 135 F2
Clark Rd *NROM* TN28 .... 233 F2
Claxfield Rd *RSIT* ME9 .... 59 H7

Cliff St *RAM* CT11 .... 5 E5
Clifftown Gdns *HB* CT6 .... 46 A2
Cliff View Gdns *IOS* ME12 .... 24 C4
Cliff View Rd *MSTR* CT12 .... 53 J8
Clifton Crs *FOLK* CT20 .... 12 B6
Clifton Gdns *CANTW/ST* CT2 .... 6 A1
   FOLK CT20 .... 12 C5
   MARG CT9 .... 3 D2
Clifton Lawn *RAM* CT11 .... 5 D6
Clifton Pl *MARG* CT9 .... 3 D2
Clifton Rd *FOLK* CT20 .... 12 C5
   MARG CT9 .... 3 E3
   MSTR CT12 .... 4 B3
   WSTB CT5 .... 44 A6
Clifton St *MARG* CT9 .... 3 D2
Cliftonville Av *MARG* CT9 .... 3 E3
   MSTR CT12 .... 4 B2
Cliftonville Ms *MARG* CT9 .... 3 E2
Clints La *RCANTW* CT4 .... 149 J1
Clive Dennis Ct *KEN/WIL* TN24 .... 9 K2
Clive Rd *MARG* CT9 .... 54 B1
   MSTR CT12 .... 53 J8
   SIT ME10 .... 57 G1
Clockhouse *ASH* TN23 .... 160 C5
Clockhouse Pk *RASHE* TN25 .... 121 F4
The Cloisters *RAM* CT11 .... 5 D6
The Close *ASH* TN23 .... 160 C5
   CANTW/ST CT2 .... 86 D2
   FAV ME13 .... 62 B8
   HYTHE CT21 .... 205 F2
   RASHE TN25 .... 142 E4
   RDV CT15 .... 151 H6
Clovelly Dr *IOS* ME12 .... 15 J6
Clovelly Rd *WSTB* CT5 .... 44 A7
Clover Ri *WSTB* CT5 .... 44 E5
Clubb's La *LYDD* TN29 .... 225 J4
Cluny Rd *FAV* ME13 .... 62 E7
Clyde St *CANT* CT1 .... 7 D2
   IOS ME12 .... 14 E4
Clynton Wy *ASH* TN23 .... 8 A6
Coach Dr *RASHW* TN26 .... 139 J7
Coach Rd *HDCN* TN27 .... 116 E8
   RFOLK CT18 .... 169 F6
Coalpit La *RSIT* ME9 .... 77 G8
Coast Dr *LYDD* TN29 .... 227 G4
   NROM TN28 .... 233 F3
Coast Rd *NROM* TN28 .... 227 G6
Coats Av *IOS* ME12 .... 14 B6
Cobay Cl *HYTHE* CT21 .... 205 H4
Cobblers Bridge Rd *HB* CT6 .... 46 C2
Cobbs Hl *RCANTW* CT4 .... 103 J4
Cobbs Pl *MARG* CT9 .... 2 C2
Cobden Pl *CANT* CT1 .... 7 D2
Cobden Rd *HYTHE* CT21 .... 205 F5
Cobham Av *SIT* ME10 .... 57 K5
Cobham Cha *FAV* ME13 .... 62 A6
Cobham Ct *CANT* CT1 .... 7 F5
Cobsden Cl *LYDD* TN29 .... 227 H2
Cobsden Rd *LYDD* TN29 .... 227 G2
Cockering Rd *RCANTW* CT4 .... 105 F5
Cock La *RASHW* TN26 .... 198 E7
   RCANTW CT4 .... 167 K2
Cockreed La *NROM* TN28 .... 226 C7
Codrington Rd *RAM* CT11 .... 5 D5
Cogans Ter *CANT* CT1 .... 6 B5
Coinston Av *RAM* CT11 .... 4 A4
Colburn Rd *BRDST* CT10 .... 55 H5
Coldblow *DEAL* CT14 .... 135 G5
Coldharbour La *LYDD* TN29 .... 230 B1
   RASHE TN25 .... 143 F4
   RCANTW CT4 .... 108 E7
Cold Harbour La *RSIT* ME9 .... 36 B5
Coldharbour La *SIT* ME10 .... 36 B5
Cold Harbour Rd *FAV* ME13 .... 98 C7
   RMAID ME17 .... 118 B1
Coldred Hl *RDV* CT15 .... 151 J6
Coldred Rd *RDV* CT15 .... 151 J6
Coldswood Rd *MSTR* CT12 .... 53 K4
Colegates Ct *FAV* ME13 .... 61 K4
Colegates Rd *FAV* ME13 .... 61 K4
Coleman Crs *MSTR* CT12 .... 4 C2
Colemans Cl *LYDD* TN29 .... 231 J3
Coleman's Stairs Rd *BRCH* CT7 ...... 29 K6
Coleman's Yd *RAM* CT11 .... 5 E5
Coleridge Gdns *RCANTE* CT3 .... 110 B8
Cole Rd *FAV* ME13 .... 62 D7
Colette Cl *BRDST* CT10 .... 33 H4
Coleville Crs *LYDD* TN29 .... 233 F7
Colewood Rd *WSTB* CT5 .... 45 H3
Colfe Wy *SIT* ME10 .... 36 B6
Colin's Wy *HYTHE* CT21 .... 206 A3
Collard Cl *HB* CT6 .... 47 G2
Collard Rd *KEN/WIL* TN24 .... 162 A7
Collards Cl *MSTR* CT12 .... 51 F7
Collards La *RCANTW* CT4 .... 167 K3
College Rd *CANT* CT1 .... 7 F3
   DEAL CT14 .... 115 K6
   MARG CT9 .... 3 E4
   RAM CT11 .... 5 D3
   SIT ME10 .... 57 J3
College Wy *RCANTE* CT3 .... 90 C7
Collingbourne *ASH* TN23 .... 160 C8
Collingwood Cl *BRDST* CT10 .... 55 F2
   WGOS CT8 .... 30 C7

Collingwood Ri FOLK CT20 .... 206 E1
Collingwood Rd RDV CT15 .... 155 F6
  WSTB CT5 .... 43 K5
Collingwood Rd East RDV CT15 ...... 155 G5
Collins Rd HB CT6 .... 46 B4
Collison Pl TENT TN30 .... 194 D7
Colombo Sq MSTR CT12 .... 4 A2
Colonel's La FAV ME13 .... 83 G3
Colorado Cl DVE/WH CT16 .... 173 F3
Colton Crs DVE/WH CT16 .... 173 F2
Columbia Av WSTB CT5 .... 43 J7
Columbus Av MSTR CT12 .... 55 J2
Common La DVW CT17 .... 172 C5
Commonwealth Cl SIT ME10 .... 58 C3
Conduit St FAV ME13 .... 62 C6
The Conifers DEAL CT14 .... 135 G4
Coniston Dr RCANTE CT3 .... 110 B8
Coniston Rd FOLKN CT19 .... 12 B2
Conker Cl ASH TN23 .... 182 B3
Connaught Gdns MARG CT9 .... 3 D4
Connaught Rd DVE/WH CT16 .... 10 B2
  FOLK CT20 .... 13 D6
  MARG CT9 .... 3 D4
  SIT ME10 .... 57 K3
Conrad Av CANT CT1 .... 87 C3
Constable Rd BRCH CT7 .... 29 K6
Constable's Rd DVE/WH CT16 .... 10 C3
Convent Cl RDV CT15 .... 155 G8
Convent Rd BRDST CT10 .... 33 H5
Conway Cl BRCH CT7 .... 29 H7
Conyer Rd RSIT ME9 .... 38 B8
Conyngham Rd MSTR CT12 .... 4 B1
Conyngham La RCANTW CT4 .... 108 A4
Conyngham Rd MSTR CT12 .... 74 B1
Cooks La SIT ME10 .... 35 K8
Cook's Lea SWCH CT13 .... 113 F4
Coolinge La FOLK CT20 .... 207 F1
Coolinge Rd FOLK CT20 .... 12 C4
Coombe Cl DVW CT17 .... 172 E5
Coombe La SIT ME10 .... 58 D2
Coombe Lands TENT TN30 .... 219 J2
Coombe La RCANTE CT3 .... 92 C5
  TENT TN30 .... 194 A7
Coombe Valley Rd DVW CT17 .... 172 E6
Coombe Wy RFOLK CT18 .... 190 D3
Coombe Wood La RFOLK CT18 ...... 190 C2
Cooper's La RASHE TN25 .... 185 G4
Cooper Street Dro RCANTE CT3 ..... 92 E2
Cooting La RASHE TN25 .... 167 K3
Cooting Rd RCANTE CT3 .... 129 K1
Copinger Cl CANTW/ST CT2 .... 86 E2
Copland Av IOS ME12 .... 15 K8
Copperfield Cl KEN/WIL TN24 .... 161 G1
Copperfields LYDD TN29 .... 231 G8
Coppergate CANTW/ST CT2 .... 6 C1
Coppins La RSIT ME9 .... 57 G4
Coppin St DEAL CT14 .... 115 K8
The Copse ASH TN23 .... 160 C5
Cop Street Rd RCANTE CT3 .... 92 B3
Copt Cl CANTW/ST CT2 .... 68 E3
Copthall Gdns FOLK CT20 .... 13 D4
Cordingham Rd WSTB CT5 .... 43 H8
Cornbrook Rd HYTHE CT21 .... 204 D6
Cornelis Dr MSTR CT12 .... 74 A1
Corner Fld ASH TN23 .... 182 A1
Cornes Cl KEN/WIL TN24 .... 162 A5
Cornford Rd BRCH CT7 .... 29 K8
The Corniche FOLK CT20 .... 206 C3
Cornwall Av RAM CT11 .... 5 F3
Cornwall Gdns CANT CT1 .... 87 H7
  MARG CT9 .... 3 F3
Cornwallis Av FOLKN CT19 .... 12 B3
  HB CT6 .... 47 H5
  RCANTE CT3 .... 130 E1
Cornwallis Cl FOLKN CT19 .... 12 B3
  KEN/WIL TN24 .... 162 B7
Cornwallis Gdns BRDST CT10 .... 33 H8
Cornwall Rd DEAL CT14 .... 135 J3
  HB CT6 .... 46 A4
Coronation Cl BRDST CT10 .... 33 F7
Coronation Crs MARG CT9 .... 31 C6
  QBOR ME11 .... 20 A1
Coronation Dr ASH TN23 .... 160 A5
  IOS ME12 .... 24 C4
Coronation Rd IOS ME12 .... 14 D5
  RAM CT11 .... 5 D5
Corone Cl FOLKN CT19 .... 12 A2
Cortland Cl SIT ME10 .... 35 K8
Cortland Ms SIT ME10 .... 35 K8
Corunna Cl HYTHE CT21 .... 205 F4
Corunna Rd DVE/WH CT16 .... 173 J3
Cossington Rd CANT CT1 .... 7 D4
Cot La HDCN TN27 .... 176 A3
Cotswold Cl KEN/WIL TN24 .... 8 B1
Cottage Rw SWCH CT13 .... 93 F1
Cottington Rd MSTR CT12 .... 75 H1
Cotton Rd CANT CT1 .... 6 A4
Coulson Gv DEAL CT14 .... 134 A1
Coulter Rd HB CT6 .... 46 A4

Countries Fld LYDD TN29 .... 216 E6
Courtenay Rd CANTW/ST CT2 .... 84 A1
  DEAL CT14 .... 115 J6
Court Hall QBOR ME11 .... 20 A1
Court Hl RCANTE CT3 .... 89 F4
Court House Farm RDV CT15 .... 131 G1
Courtland Av DVE/WH CT16 .... 152 E8
Courtland Dr DVE/WH CT16 .... 172 C2
Courtlands DEAL CT14 .... 135 K8
Courtlands Wy WGOS CT8 .... 30 E5
Court La RCANTE CT3 .... 90 C1
Court Lodge Rd RASHW TN26 .... 210 D7
Court Mdw RCANTE CT3 .... 89 F6
Court Rd BRCH CT7 .... 50 B4
  DEAL CT14 .... 135 G5
  SIT ME10 .... 35 K7
The Courts MARG CT9 .... 31 F5
Court St FAV ME13 .... 62 C7
Coventon La DEAL CT14 .... 94 A8
Coventry Gdns HB CT6 .... 47 J1
Covert Rd RCANTE CT3 .... 130 A2
Covet La RCANTW CT4 .... 127 K6
Cowdray Rd DEAL CT14 .... 135 H5
Cowdray Sq DEAL CT14 .... 135 H3
Cowdrey Cl KEN/WIL TN24 .... 162 A7
Cowdrey Pl CANT CT1 .... 7 E5
Cowgate Hl DVW CT17 .... 10 B4
Cowgate La RFOLK CT18 .... 169 J8
Cow La CANT CT1 .... 6 A4
  DVW CT17 .... 172 E7
Cowley Ri MARG CT9 .... 32 D6
Cowper Rd DEAL CT14 .... 135 H1
  DVW CT17 .... 172 C4
  MARG CT9 .... 3 D4
  SIT ME10 .... 58 C2
Coxes Av MSTR CT12 .... 54 C3
Coxes La MSTR CT12 .... 54 C3
Coxett Hl FAV ME13 .... 80 B1
Coxhill RDV CT15 .... 150 D4
Coxhill Crs DVW CT17 .... 172 E4
Coxhill Gdns DVW CT17 .... 172 E3
Crabble Av DVW CT17 .... 172 E4
Crabble Cl DVW CT17 .... 172 D4
Crabble Hl DVW CT17 .... 172 E3
Crabble La DVW CT17 .... 172 C5
Crabble Mdw DVW CT17 .... 172 E4
Crabble Rd DVW CT17 .... 172 C5
Crabtree Av DVW CT17 .... 172 D5
Craddock Dr CANT CT1 .... 7 E2
Craddock Rd CANT CT1 .... 7 E2
Cradle Bridge Dr KEN/WIL TN24 ... 9 E3
Crafford St DVE/WH CT16 .... 10 A3
Cranbourne Cl RAM CT11 .... 5 F3
Cranbrook Cl RAM CT11 .... 5 F3
Cranbrook Dr SIT ME10 .... 57 J5
Cranleigh Dr DVE/WH CT16 .... 152 E7
Cranleigh Gdns WSTB CT5 .... 44 B6
Craufurd Gn FOLK CT20 .... 206 D1
Craven Cl MARG CT9 .... 2 A5
Crawford Gdns MARG CT9 .... 3 F3
Crawford Rd BRDST CT10 .... 55 G1
Craythorne TENT TN30 .... 194 B5
Craythorne La HYTHE CT21 .... 206 B2
  NROM TN28 .... 226 D6
Craythorne La NROM TN28 .... 226 C7
Cremer Cl RCANTW CT4 .... 104 D5
Cremer Pl FAV ME13 .... 61 K6
Cremers Rd SIT ME10 .... 58 C1
Crescent Rd BRCH CT7 .... 29 K7
  BRDST CT10 .... 33 J4
  FAV ME13 .... 62 C7
  MARG CT9 .... 2 B3
  RAM CT11 .... 4 C4
The Crescent CANTW/ST CT2 .... 86 D3
  FAV ME13 .... 83 G3
  FOLK CT20 .... 206 B3
  IOS ME12 .... 15 F8
  RCANTW CT4 .... 105 F5
  RDV CT15 .... 130 C3
  RDV CT15 .... 175 G1
  RSIT ME9 .... 60 A3
  SIT ME10 .... 36 A5
  SWCH CT13 .... 93 J8
Cressfield ASH TN23 .... 160 D5
Cress Wy FAV ME13 .... 61 K7
Crete Rd East RFOLK CT18 .... 190 D5
Crete Rd West RFOLK CT18 .... 189 K5
Creteway Cl FOLKN CT19 .... 13 E1
Cricketers Cl RFOLK CT18 .... 169 H8
  SIT ME10 .... 36 A6
Crimond Av LYDD TN29 .... 217 J2
Criol La RASHW TN26 .... 180 C5
Criol Rd RASHW TN26 .... 180 C8
Cripple Hl RASHW TN26 .... 177 J5
Cripps Cl RCANTE CT3 .... 130 A1
Cripps' La RDV CT15 .... 155 F8
Crispe Park Cl BRCH CT7 .... 30 A7
Crispe Rd BRCH CT7 .... 51 K3
Crispin Pl FAV ME13 .... 62 C6
Crocken Hill Rd HDCN TN27 .... 136 C4
Cresslham La FAV ME13 .... 61 G9
Crockham Rd FAV ME13 .... 64 D8
Crockshard Hl RCANTE CT3 .... 110 D2
Crockshard La RCANTE CT3 .... 110 D2
Crofters Cl HYTHE CT21 .... 204 C6

Croft Gdns RMAID ME17 .... 116 D1
Croft La FOLK CT20 .... 207 F1
Crofton Cl KEN/WIL TN24 .... 141 G8
Crofton Rd WGOS CT8 .... 30 D7
Croft Rd KEN/WIL TN24 .... 9 D3
Croft's Pl BRDST CT10 .... 55 J2
Croftwood ASH TN23 .... 160 B8
Cromer Rd SIT ME10 .... 57 K6
Cromwell Park Pl FOLK CT20 .... 206 D2
Cromwell Rd CANT CT1 .... 7 D5
  IOS ME12 .... 14 A7
  WSTB CT5 .... 44 A4
Crooked S Rd DEAL CT14 .... 134 E7
Crookenden Pl RCANTW CT4 .... 129 F7
Crook's Court La RDV CT15 .... 192 C2
Cross La FAV ME13 .... 100 C7
  SIT ME10 .... 35 K8
Crossley Av HB CT6 .... 45 J2
Cross Rd BRCH CT7 .... 29 K6
  DEAL CT14 .... 135 G5
Cross Stile ASH TN23 .... 160 C6
Cross St CANTW/ST CT2 .... 6 B2
  HB CT6 .... 46 C3
  IOS ME12 .... 14 C4
Crossways CANTW/ST CT2 .... 86 D2
  WSTB CT5 .... 57 K5
Crossways Av MARG CT9 .... 54 B1
Crossways Cl LYDD TN29 .... 217 G4
Crouch Hill Rd RSIT ME9 .... 34 B3
Crouch La FAV ME13 .... 82 E6
Crowbridge Rd KEN/WIL TN24 ...... 9 E6
Crow Hl BRDST CT10 .... 55 J1
Crow Hill Rd MARG CT9 .... 31 G6
Crownfield Rd ASH TN23 .... 160 B6
Crown Gdns CANTW/ST CT2 .... 6 B2
Crown Hill Rd HB CT6 .... 46 B2
Crown La RCANTW CT4 .... 146 C4
Crown Quay La SIT ME10 .... 58 A2
Crown Rd SIT ME10 .... 57 K1
Crows Camp Rd RCANTW CT4 ...... 127 C4
Crundale Cl ASH TN23 .... 160 B8
Crundale Wy MARG CT9 .... 33 F4
Cryalls La RSIT ME9 .... 57 G3
  SIT ME10 .... 57 H2
Cryol Rd ASH TN23 .... 160 D7
Cuckoo La ASH TN23 .... 160 B8
  HYTHE CT21 .... 187 J4
Cudham Gdns MARG CT9 .... 33 F4
Cudworth Rd KEN/WIL TN24 .... 167 J2
Cullens Hl RCANTW CT4 .... 167 J2
Cullet Dr QBOR ME11 .... 20 B3
Culling's Hl RCANTW CT4 .... 167 K2
Culpeper Cl CANTW/ST CT2 .... 68 E2
Culver's La LYDD TN29 .... 237 J1
Cumberland Av BRDST CT10 .... 55 H1
  CANT CT1 .... 87 H7
Cumberland Dr RSIT ME9 .... 34 A3
Cumberland Rd MARG CT9 .... 3 F2
  RAM CT11 .... 5 D5
Cunningham Crs BRCH CT7 .... 29 H6
Curlew Av RSIT ME9 .... 34 A3
Curlinge Ct RAM CT11 .... 4 A5
Curteis Rd TENT TN30 .... 194 B6
Curtis La RCANTW CT4 .... 146 B4
Curtis Rd KEN/WIL TN24 .... 9 E6
Curtis Wood Park Rd HB CT6 .... 47 F6
Curtis Wood Rd HB CT6 .... 46 E7
Curzon Cl DEAL CT14 .... 135 J3
Curzon Rd DVW CT17 .... 173 F6
Cushman Rd CANT CT1 .... 6 B4
Cuthbert Rd WGOS CT8 .... 30 D6
The Cuttings MSTR CT12 .... 4 B2
Cygnet Wy ASH TN23 .... 160 D5
Cylinder Rd HYTHE CT21 .... 205 F2
Cypress Av RSIT ME9 .... 34 A3
Cypress Cl WSTB CT5 .... 43 K7
Cypress Gv RDV CT15 .... 131 K4
Cyprus Rd FAV ME13 .... 62 D7

D

Daglish Cl NROM TN28 .... 226 C8
Daimler Av HB CT6 .... 46 A3
Dalby Rd MARG CT9 .... 3 E2
Dalby Sq MARG CT9 .... 3 E2
Dale Wk KEN/WIL TN24 .... 141 G7
Dalewood SIT ME10 .... 58 B4
Dallas-brett Crs FOLKN CT19 .... 13 E1
Dallinger Rd BRCH CT7 .... 29 J6
Dalmeny Av MARG CT9 .... 32 E5
Damerham Cl CANTW/ST CT2 .... 86 C3
Dan Dr FAV ME13 .... 61 K6
Dane Court Gdns BRDST CT10 ...... 54 E1
Dane Court Rd BRDST CT10 .... 32 D8
Dane Crs RAM CT11 .... 5 E3
Danedale Av IOS ME12 .... 16 C8
Dane End Rd WGOS CT8 .... 30 C6
Dane Gdns MARG CT9 .... 3 E5
Dane Hl MARG CT9 .... 3 E4
Dane Hill Gv MARG CT9 .... 3 D3
Dane Hill Rw MARG CT9 .... 3 D3
Danemore TENT TN30 .... 194 B6
Dane Mt MARG CT9 .... 32 D4

Dane Park Rd *MARG* CT9 .... 3 D3 🔟
 RAM CT11 .... 5 E3
Dane Rd *BRCH* CT7 .... 29 F7
 MARG CT9 .... 3 D3
 RAM CT11 .... 5 E3
Danes Ct *DVE/WH* CT16 .... 10 B1
Danes Dr *IOS* ME12 .... 24 B5
Danes Md *SIT* ME10 .... 35 K4
Danesmead Ter *MARG* CT9 .... 3 D3 🔟
Dane Valley Rd *BRDST* CT10 .... 32 E7
 MARG CT9 .... 3 F4
Daniels Ct *WSTB* CT5 .... 43 K5
Daniel Wy *RYE* TN31 .... 234 C4
Danley Rd *IOS* ME12 .... 15 F7
Danton La *RFOLK* CT18 .... 189 H5
Darby Pl *FOLK* CT20 .... 13 D4 🔟
Darby Rd *FOLKN* CT19 .... 13 D4
Dargate Rd *CANTW/ST* CT2 .... 65 G7
 WSTB CT5 .... 65 G4
Dark HI *FAV* ME13 .... 62 A6
Darlinghurst Rd *FOLKN* CT19 .... 189 K7
Darlington Dr *IOS* ME12 .... 15 E3
Darlington St *FOLK* CT20 .... 13 D4 🔟
Darnley Cl *BRDST* CT10 .... 55 G3
 FOLK CT20 .... 207 F2
Darracott Cl *DEAL* CT14 .... 135 H1 🔟
Darrell Cl *HB* CT6 .... 46 B3
Darren Gdns *BRDST* CT10 .... 55 F1
Darwin Rd *BRCH* CT7 .... 29 J6 🔟
Daryngton Av *BRCH* CT7 .... 29 F7
David Av *MARG* CT9 .... 32 E4
Davids Cl *BRDST* CT10 .... 55 J3
Davie Cl *IOS* ME12 .... 14 C6
Davington HI *FAV* ME13 .... 62 B6
Davis Av *DEAL* CT14 .... 135 G2
Dawes Rd *CANTW/ST* CT2 .... 83 K1
Dawn Ri *IOS* ME12 .... 17 J8
Dawson Rd *CANTW/ST* CT2 .... 83 K1
Daytona Wy *HB* CT6 .... 45 K2
Dayton Rd *FAV* ME13 .... 101 F3
Deal Castle Rd *DEAL* CT14 .... 135 K1
 SWCH CT13 .... 93 K8
Dean Cft *HB* CT6 .... 47 G4
Deane Cl *WSTB* CT5 .... 44 B7
Dean HI *RCANTW* CT4 .... 145 K4
Dean Md *FOLKN* CT19 .... 12 B2
Dean Rd *SIT* ME10 .... 35 K8
Dean's Wk *ASH* TN23 .... 160 D7
Deansway Av *CANTW/ST* CT2 .... 68 D7
Deanwood Rd *DVW* CT17 .... 172 C5
Deborah Cl *WSTB* CT5 .... 44 C7 🔟
De Burgh HI *DVW* CT17 .... 10 A2
De Burgh St *DVW* CT17 .... 10 A3 🔟
Deedes Cl *HYTHE* CT21 .... 205 G3
Deerson La *RCANTE* CT3 .... 90 C2
De Havilland Cl *RFOLK* CT18 .... 190 C2 🔟
De Havillands *RCANTW* CT4 .... 108 E3
Delacourt Cl *MSTR* CT12 .... 75 H1
Delamark Rd *IOS* ME12 .... 14 D4
Delane Rd *DEAL* CT14 .... 135 G1
Delaware Cl *CANTW/ST* CT2 .... 68 E8 🔟
Delfside *SWCH* CT13 .... 94 A6
Delf St *SWCH* CT13 .... 93 K5
Delmaney Cl *BRDST* CT10 .... 55 J7
Demozay Cl *RFOLK* CT18 .... 190 B2
Denbigh Cl *SIT* ME10 .... 35 K7
Denbigh Rd *MSTR* CT12 .... 4 A2 🔟
Dence Cl *HB* CT6 .... 47 G1
Dence Pk *HB* CT6 .... 47 G2
Dencora Wy *ASH* TN23 .... 8 A4
The Dene *CANT* CT1 .... 7 E6
 RASHW TN26 .... 178 E1
Dengemarsh Rd *LYDD* TN29 .... 237 H3
Denham FLAX'PR TN29 .... 217 K7
Denham Wy *RYE* TN31 .... 234 B4
Denmark Rd *RAM* CT11 .... 5 E4
Denmark St *FOLKN* CT19 .... 13 E5
Denne Cl *CANTW/ST* CT2 .... 68 E7
Denne Manor La *RCANTW* CT4 .... 102 C7
Dennes La *LYDD* TN29 .... 231 G5
Dennes Mill Cl *RASHE* TN25 .... 142 D4 🔟
Denness Rd *ASH* TN23 .... 8 B6
Dennis Wy *FOLKN* CT19 .... 189 K7 🔟
Densole La *RFOLK* CT18 .... 169 G6
Densole Wy *RFOLK* CT18 .... 169 G6
Denstead La *RCANTW* CT4 .... 84 E7
Denstroude La *CANTW/ST* CT2 .... 65 K6
Dental St *HYTHE* CT21 .... 205 G4
Dent-de-Lion Ct *MARG* CT9 .... 31 F6
Dent-de-Lion La *MARG* CT9 .... 31 F6
Dent-de-lion Rd *MARG* CT9 .... 31 F6
Denton Wy *MARG* CT9 .... 32 D5
Derby Cl *SIT* ME10 .... 35 J8
Dering Cl *HDCN* TN27 .... 157 J2
 RCANTW CT4 .... 107 K5
Dering Rd *HB* CT6 .... 46 E2
 KEN/WIL TN24 .... 161 J6
 RCANTW CT4 .... 107 K5
Derringstone HI *RCANTW* CT4 .... 129 F8
Derringstone St *RCANTW* CT4 .... 129 F7
Derville Rd *LYDD* TN29 .... 233 F7
Derwent Av *RAM* CT11 .... 4 A4
Derwent Wy *RCANTE* CT3 .... 110 A8

D'este Rd *RAM* CT11 .... 5 F4 🔟
Detling Av *BRDST* CT10 .... 55 H5
Detling Cl *IOS* ME12 .... 14 C7
Devon Av *DEAL* CT14 .... 135 J3
Devon Gdns *BRCH* CT7 .... 29 J8
Devon Rd *CANT* CT1 .... 87 H6
 FOLKN CT19 .... 13 D4 🔟
Devonshire Gdns *MARG* CT9 .... 3 F3
Devonshire Rd *DVW* CT17 .... 173 F6
Diamond Cl *IOS* ME12 .... 14 C5 🔟
Diamond Rd *WSTB* CT5 .... 44 B4
Diana Gdns *DEAL* CT14 .... 135 G1 🔟
Dibdin Rd *DEAL* CT14 .... 115 K7 🔟
Dickens Cl *CANT* CT1 .... 7 F1
Dickens Rd *BRDST* CT10 .... 55 J1
Dickley La *RMAID* ME17 .... 96 A8
Dicksons Bourne *RASHE* TN25 .... 201 F1
Dieu Stone La *DVE/WH* CT16 .... 10 C3 🔟
Digby Rd *DEAL* CT14 .... 206 E1
Diligent Dr *SIT* ME10 .... 36 A7
Dilnot La *BRCH* CT7 .... 52 A3
Discovery Wk *CANT* CT1 .... 7 F4 🔟
Dixwell Rd *FOLK* CT20 .... 12 A6
Dobbie Cl *SIT* ME10 .... 35 K8
Dock Exit Rd *DVE/WH* CT16 .... 11 E3
Dodd's La *DVE/WH* CT16 .... 172 E3 🔟
Dog Kennel La *RFOLK* CT18 .... 166 E8
Dola Av *DEAL* CT14 .... 115 H8
Dolphin Cl *BRDST* CT10 .... 33 H3 🔟
Dolphin La *DVE/WH* CT16 .... 10 C4 🔟
Dolphin Rd *LYDD* TN29 .... 231 H8
 SIT ME10 .... 58 C1
Dolphin St *FOLKN* CT19 .... 12 C2
Dolphin St *DEAL* CT14 .... 115 K7 🔟
 HB CT6 .... 46 D1
Domnena Rd *MSTR* CT12 .... 52 A8 🔟
 WGOS CT8 .... 30 C6
Donald Moor Av *RSIT* ME9 .... 59 K4
Donegal Rd *CANT* CT1 .... 7 F3
Donemowe Dr *SIT* ME10 .... 36 A6
Donkey La *RCANTE* CT3 .... 109 J6
Donkey St *LYDD* TN29 .... 216 E2
Donnahay Rd *MSTR* CT12 .... 54 D3
Dorcas Gdns *BRDST* CT10 .... 33 H8
Doric La *RAM* CT11 .... 4 C6
Dorman Av North *RCANTE* CT3 .... 110 A8
Dorman Av South *RCANTE* CT3 .... 130 B1
Dorothy Dr *MSTR* CT12 .... 4 C1 🔟
Dorset Cl *WSTB* CT5 .... 43 J7
Dorset Gdns *BRCH* CT7 .... 29 J7 🔟
 DEAL CT14 .... 135 J4
Dorset Rd *CANT* CT1 .... 87 H7
 IOS ME12 .... 14 B6
Doubleday Dr *RSIT* ME9 .... 58 E4
Douglas Av *HYTHE* CT21 .... 205 G4 🔟
 WSTB CT5 .... 44 B5
Douglas Cl *BRDST* CT10 .... 55 J7
Douglas Rd *DEAL* CT14 .... 135 G3
 DVW CT17 .... 173 F6
 HB CT6 .... 47 F2
 RMAID ME17 .... 116 D1 🔟
Douro Cl *CANT* CT1 .... 87 H5
Douro Pl *DVE/WH* CT16 .... 10 C4
Dour Side *DVW* CT17 .... 172 D3
Dour St *DVE/WH* CT16 .... 10 B3
Dove Cl *ASH* TN23 .... 182 B3
 HYTHE CT21 .... 204 B6
 WSTB CT5 .... 43 K7
Dovedale *BRCH* CT7 .... 30 A1
Dovedale Cl *BRCH* CT7 .... 30 A7 🔟
Dove Lea Gdns *DVW* CT17 .... 172 C3
Dover HI *FOLKN* CT19 .... 13 F1
Dover Pl *ASH* TN23 .... 8 C4
Dover Rd *DEAL* CT14 .... 133 F2 🔟
Dover St *CANT* CT1 .... 7 D4 🔟
 FOLKN CT19 .... 13 F2
 RCANTW CT4 .... 108 C8
 RDV CT15 .... 154 D8
 SWCH CT13 .... 93 J8
Dover St *CANT* CT1 .... 7 D4
 SIT ME10 .... 57 K2 🔟
Doves Cft *RSIT* ME9 .... 57 H7
Dowle Rd *LYDD* TN29 .... 225 F7
Down Barton Rd *BRCH* CT7 .... 50 A5
Down Court Rd *RSIT* ME9 .... 78 K1
Downhill Cl *DVE/WH* CT16 .... 152 B8 🔟
The Downings *HB* CT6 .... 47 F4
Downland Ct *KEN/WIL* TN24 .... 8 B2
Downlands *DEAL* CT14 .... 135 H6
Downs Av *WSTB* CT5 .... 44 B5
Downs HI *HDCN* TN27 .... 118 C6
 RDV CT15 .... 133 H6
 RFOLK CT18 .... 190 B2 🔟
 SIT ME10 .... 57 J4
Downside *FOLKN* CT19 .... 12 C2
 RDV CT15 .... 155 G8
Downside Rd *DVE/WH* CT16 .... 152 E7
Downs Pk *HB* CT6 .... 47 F2
Downs Rd *CANTW/ST* CT2 .... 86 D2
 DEAL CT14 .... 135 H4
 FOLKN CT19 .... 12 C1
 RAM CT11 .... 4 A5
 RDV CT15 .... 133 J6
The Downs *RCANTE* CT3 .... 71 K8

RCANTW CT4 .... 105 G5
Downs Wy *HDCN* TN27 .... 118 E6
 RASHE TN25 .... 185 K5
Draffin La *RYE* TN31 .... 234 A3
Dragonfly Wy *RFOLK* CT18 .... 190 C2 🔟
Drainless Rd *SWCH* CT13 .... 92 D8
Drake Av *IOS* ME12 .... 22 A1
Drake Rd *KEN/WIL* TN24 .... 162 A1
Drapers Av *MARG* CT9 .... 3 D5
Drapers Cl *MARG* CT9 .... 3 E5
Dray's Fld *RSIT* ME9 .... 76 A7
Dreadnought Av *IOS* ME12 .... 15 H8
Drew La *DEAL* CT14 .... 135 J2
Drill La *RCANTE* CT3 .... 89 H5
The Drive *CANT* CT1 .... 7 E5
 WSTB CT5 .... 45 G6
Drop Redoubt Rd *DVW* CT17 .... 10 A4
Drove Rd *IOS* ME12 .... 15 F6
The Drove *CANTW/ST* CT2 .... 88 A2
 DEAL CT14 .... 134 A1
 DVE/WH CT16 .... 152 E6
 WSTB CT5 .... 45 G6
The Droveway *RDV* CT15 .... 155 H8
Drum La *ASH* TN23 .... 8 B3 🔟
Drury Rd *TENT* TN30 .... 194 A6
Drybeck Av *RAM* CT11 .... 54 A7
Dryden Cl *CANT* CT1 .... 7 F4
Dryden Rd *DVE/WH* CT16 .... 173 F3
Duck La *CANT* CT1 .... 7 D2 🔟
 RASHW TN26 .... 180 C8
Duckpit Rd *RCANTW* CT4 .... 125 K4
Duck St *RCANTW* CT4 .... 167 K2
Duckworth Cl *KEN/WIL* TN24 .... 162 B7 🔟
Dudley Av *WGOS* CT8 .... 30 B6
Dudley Rd *FOLKN* CT19 .... 13 F4
 KEN/WIL TN24 .... 161 J1
Dukes Meadow *RASHW* TN26 .... 198 E2 🔟
Duke St *DEAL* CT14 .... 115 K7
 MARG CT9 .... 2 C2 🔟
Dukeswood *WSTB* CT5 .... 67 G1
Dully Rd *RSIT* ME9 .... 77 K2
Dumbourne La *TENT* TN30 .... 208 C3
Dumergue Av *QBOR* ME11 .... 20 C1
Dumpton Gap Rd *BRDST* CT10 .... 55 H4
Dumpton La *RAM* CT11 .... 5 E2
Dumpton Park Dr *BRDST* CT10 .... 55 H4
Dumpton Park Rd *RAM* CT11 .... 5 E3
Duncan Dr *BRCH* CT7 .... 29 H6
Duncan Rd *RAM* CT11 .... 5 D5
 WSTB CT5 .... 44 A7
Dundein Dr *DVE/WH* CT16 .... 173 F3 🔟
Dundonald Rd *RAM* CT11 .... 4 C4
Dunedin Cl *SIT* ME10 .... 57 H3
Dunedin Rd *MSTR* CT12 .... 54 A5
Dunes Av *RYE* TN31 .... 234 C4
Dunes Rd *NROM* TN28 .... 232 E3
Dungeness Rd *LYDD* TN29 .... 237 K1
Dunkery Ri *KEN/WIL* TN24 .... 8 B1
Dunkirk Rd *FAV* ME13 .... 83 G6
Dunkirk Rd North *FAV* ME13 .... 83 H5
Dunkirk Rd South *FAV* ME13 .... 83 H5
Dunkirk Sq *RDV* CT15 .... 173 K3
Dunnett Rd *FOLKN* CT19 .... 189 K8
Dunstall Cl *LYDD* TN29 .... 227 H1
Dunstall Gdns *LYDD* TN29 .... 227 H1
Dunstall La *LYDD* TN29 .... 227 H1
Dunstan Av *WGOS* CT8 .... 30 C7
Durban Crs *DVE/WH* CT16 .... 173 G2
Durban Rd *MARG* CT9 .... 3 E4
Durham Cl *CANT* CT1 .... 6 C5
 DVW CT17 .... 10 B4 🔟
Durham HI *DVW* CT17 .... 10 B4 🔟
Durlock *MSTR* CT12 .... 74 B1
Durlock Av *RAM* CT11 .... 4 B6
The Durlocks *FOLKN* CT19 .... 13 E4
Durnford Cl *CANTW/ST* CT2 .... 6 B1
Dyke Rd *FOLKN* CT19 .... 13 E4
Dymchurch Rd *HYTHE* CT21 .... 204 C6
 LYDD TN29 .... 216 D7
 NROM TN28 .... 226 D6
Dyngley Cl *SIT* ME10 .... 35 K8 🔟

E

Eagle HI *RAM* CT11 .... 5 D4 🔟
Eagles Cl *SIT* ME10 .... 58 D2
Ealham Cl *CANT* CT1 .... 7 E6 🔟
 KEN/WIL TN24 .... 162 A6 🔟
Earl's Av *FOLK* CT20 .... 12 B5
 KEN/WIL TN24 .... 9 F4
Earlsfield *RASHE* TN25 .... 184 B8
Earlsfield Rd *HYTHE* CT21 .... 205 H4
Earlsmead Crs *MSTR* CT12 .... 75 H1
Earlsworth Rd *KEN/WIL* TN24 .... 161 H8
Easole Hts *RDV* CT15 .... 131 F1 🔟
Easole St *RDV* CT15 .... 131 F1
Eastbridge Rd *LYDD* TN29 .... 216 C6
Eastchurch Rd *IOS* ME12 .... 22 E1
 MARG CT9 .... 33 F4
East Cliff *DVE/WH* CT16 .... 11 D3
 FOLKN CT19 .... 13 E4

East Cliff Gdns FOLKN CT19 .... 13 E4
East Cliff Pde HB CT6 .... 47 F1
East Cliff Pas FOLKN CT19 .... 13 E4
East Cross TENT TN30 .... 194 A7
Eastern Av ASH TN23 .... 8 A3
  IOS ME12 .... 14 E7
  QBOR ME11 .... 20 C2
Eastern Esp BRDST CT10 .... 33 J8
  MARG CT9 .... 33 J8
Eastern Gdns KEN/WIL TN24 .... 9 E5
Eastfield Rd BRCH CT7 .... 29 K7
Eastgate Cl HB CT6 .... 47 G3
Eastgate Rd TENT TN30 .... 194 B5
East Gn SIT ME10 .... 36 B5
East Hall La SIT ME10 .... 58 D1
East Hl ASH TN23 .... 8 C3
  TENT TN30 .... 194 B6
East La IOS ME12 .... 14 B4
East Langdon Rd RDV CT15 .... 153 J8
Eastling Rd FAV ME13 .... 79 G8
East Lodge Rd ASH TN23 .... 160 C3
Eastmead Av ASH TN23 .... 8 C5
East Mountain La
  KEN/WIL TN24 .... 141 K7
East Northdown Cl MARG CT9 .... 33 F5
East Rp DVE/WH CT16 .... 11 E3
East Rd FOLK CT20 .... 206 D3
  MSTR CT12 .... 75 F6
East Roman Ditch DVE/WH CT16 .. 11 D3
Eastry Cl ASH TN23 .... 160 D8
East St ASH TN23 .... 8 B3
  CANT CT1 .... 87 G3
  DVW CT17 .... 10 A3
  FAV ME13 .... 62 C7
  FOLKN CT19 .... 13 E4
  HB CT6 .... 47 F1
  HYTHE CT21 .... 205 H4
  SIT ME10 .... 58 B2
East Vw RCANTE CT3 .... 70 A5
East Weald Dr TENT TN30 .... 194 B5
Eastwell Barn Ms TENT TN30 ...... 194 A6
Eastwell Cl RASHW TN26 .... 180 D5
Eastwell Mdw TENT TN30 .... 194 A6
Eastwood Rd SIT ME10 .... 57 J1
Eaton Hl MARG CT9 .... 2 C3
Eaton Rd DVW CT17 .... 173 F7
  MARG CT9 .... 2 C3
Eaves Rd DVW CT17 .... 172 E7
Ebbsfleet La MSTR CT12 .... 75 F3
Eclipse Dr SIT ME10 .... 35 K6
Eddington La HB CT6 .... 46 C3
Edenbridge Dr IOS ME12 .... 14 C6
Edenfield BRCH CT7 .... 30 A7
Eden Rd WSTB CT5 .... 43 H7
Edgar Cl WSTB CT5 .... 45 G3
Edgar Rd CANT CT1 .... 7 E2
  DVW CT17 .... 173 F5
  MARG CT9 .... 3 E2
  MSTR CT12 .... 52 A8
Edge End Rd BRDST CT10 .... 55 G2
Edgehill Cl FOLK CT20 .... 206 D2
Edinburgh Rd ASH TN23 .... 8 B3
  MARG CT9 .... 31 G6
Edith Rd FAV ME13 .... 62 B8
  RAM CT11 .... 4 C5
  WCOS CT8 .... 30 E5
Edmanson Av MARG CT9 .... 31 F5
Edmund Rd RCANTE CT3 .... 90 C6
Edred Rd DVW CT17 .... 173 F6
Edward Dr BRCH CT7 .... 30 A7
Edward Rd CANT CT1 .... 7 D3
  DEAL CT14 .... 135 J8
  FOLKN CT19 .... 13 D5
  QBOR ME11 .... 20 C1
Edwards Rd DVE/WH CT16 .... 10 B3
Edwina Av IOS ME12 .... 15 H7
Edyngham Cl SIT ME10 .... 36 B6
Effingham Crs DVW CT17 .... 10 B3
Effingham St DVW CT17 .... 10 B3
  RAM CT11 .... 5 E5
Egbert Rd BRCH CT7 .... 29 G6
  FAV ME13 .... 62 A8
  MSTR CT12 .... 52 A8
  WCOS CT8 .... 30 D5
Egerton Dr MARG CT9 .... 33 F4
Egerton House Rd HDCN TN27 ..... 136 E2
Egerton Rd DVE/WH CT16 .... 172 C2
  HDCN TN27 .... 117 J8
Eggarton La RCANTW CT4 .... 123 H4
Eggringe ASH TN23 .... 160 C5
Eighteen Acre La LYDD TN29 ...... 224 B6
The Elders RCANTE CT3 .... 89 F6
Eleanor Dr SIT ME10 .... 35 J6
Elfrida Cl MARG CT9 .... 32 D6
Elgar Pl RAM CT11 .... 5 D4
Elham Rd CANT CT1 .... 6 B5
Elham Valley Wy HYTHE CT21 .... 187 K8
  RCANTW CT4 .... 108 B4
  RFOLK CT18 .... 167 G7
Elham Wy BRDST CT10 .... 55 H4
Elizabeth Carter Av DEAL CT14 ... 135 F2
Elizabeth Dr RFOLK CT18 .... 191 J4
Elizabeth Gdns HYTHE CT21 .... 205 F5
Elizabeth Kemp Ct MSTR CT12 .... 4 C2

Elizabeth Rd DVW CT17 .... 10 B6
Elizabeth Wy HB CT6 .... 47 G3
Ellen Av RAM CT11 .... 5 E2
Ellens Rd DEAL CT14 .... 134 E3
Ellesmere Ms NROM TN28 .... 226 D6
Ellingham Wy ASH TN23 .... 181 K1
Ellington Av MARG CT9 .... 31 G6
Ellington Pl RAM CT11 .... 4 C4
Ellington Rd RAM CT11 .... 4 C4
Elliot Cl CANT CT1 .... 87 G3
Elliots Pl FAV ME13 .... 62 C7
Ellis Dr NROM TN28 .... 226 D6
Ellison Cl WSTB CT5 .... 45 F5
Ellis Rd WSTB CT5 .... 44 D3
Ellis Wy HB CT6 .... 47 H4
Elm Cl HDCN TN27 .... 137 F3
Elmfield TENT TN30 .... 194 B6
Elm Gdns HYTHE CT21 .... 205 J4
Elm Gv SIT ME10 .... 58 C2
  WCOS CT8 .... 30 D6
Elm La IOS ME12 .... 21 K1
Elmleigh Rd RCANTE CT3 .... 89 G6
Elmley Rd IOS ME12 .... 22 A3
Elmley Wy MARG CT9 .... 3 D6
Elm Rd FOLKN CT19 .... 13 E5
  LYDD TN29 .... 227 G3
  RCANTE CT3 .... 130 A1
Elms Hl RDV CT15 .... 172 A8
Elmstead Pl FOLK CT20 .... 13 E4
The Elms MARG CT9 .... 69 K5
Elmstone Gdns MARG CT9 .... 33 F4
Elmstone Rd RAM CT11 .... 5 D4
Elms Vale Rd DVW CT17 .... 172 E7
  RDV CT15 .... 172 B8
Elmton La RDV CT15 .... 132 A5
Elmwood Av BRDST CT10 .... 33 H6
Elmwood Cl BRDST CT10 .... 33 G7
Elm Wd West WSTB CT5 .... 45 F4
Elventon Cl FOLKN CT19 .... 189 K7
Elverland La FAV ME13 .... 79 K4
Elvington La RFOLK CT18 .... 189 K3
Elwick Rd ASH TN23 .... 8 B4
Emerald Vw IOS ME12 .... 24 D2
Emmerson Gdns WSTB CT5 .... 45 F3
Empress Gdns IOS ME12 .... 24 C2
Enbrook Rd FOLK CT20 .... 206 E1
Enbrook Va FOLK CT20 .... 206 E1
Encombe FOLK CT20 .... 206 D3
Enfield Rd DEAL CT14 .... 115 K7
Ennerdale FAV ME13 .... 62 D8
Ennerdale Gdns RCANTE CT3 ...... 110 B8
Enticott Cl WSTB CT5 .... 44 D5
Epping Cl HB CT6 .... 47 J4
Epple Bay Av BRCH CT7 .... 29 K6
Epple Bay Rd BRCH CT7 .... 29 K6
Epple Rd BRCH CT7 .... 30 A6
Epps Rd SIT ME10 .... 57 K3
Eric Rd DVW CT17 .... 173 F4
Erith St DVW CT17 .... 173 F5
Ernwell Rd FOLKN CT19 .... 13 D5
Ersham Rd CANT CT1 .... 7 D4
Eskdale Av RAM CT11 .... 4 A4
Esmonde Dr MSTR CT12 .... 52 E4
Esplanade BRCH CT7 .... 30 B5
  DVW CT17 .... 10 B5
  WCOS CT8 .... 30 D5
Essella Pk KEN/WIL TN24 .... 9 E4
Essella Rd KEN/WIL TN24 .... 9 E4
Essetford Rd ASH TN23 .... 8 A6
Essex Av HB CT6 .... 46 A2
Essex Gdns BRCH CT7 .... 29 J8
Essex Rd CANT CT1 .... 87 H7
  WCOS CT8 .... 30 E6
Essex St WSTB CT5 .... 44 A6
Esther Ct SIT ME10 .... 35 K6
Estuary Rd IOS ME12 .... 14 C5
Etchden Rd RASHW TN26 .... 158 B8
Ethelbert Gdns MARG CT9 .... 3 D2
Ethelbert Rd BRCH CT7 .... 29 G6
  CANT CT1 .... 7 D6
  DEAL CT14 .... 115 J5
  DVW CT17 .... 173 F6
  FAV ME13 .... 62 A8
  FOLKN CT19 .... 13 D2
  MARG CT9 .... 3 D2
  RAM CT11 .... 5 D5
Ethelbert Sq WGOS CT8 .... 30 D5
Ethelbert Ter MARG CT9 .... 3 D2
  WGOS CT8 .... 30 D5
Ethelburga Dr RFOLK CT18 .... 167 F7
Ethelred Ct FAV ME13 .... 62 B8
Ethelred Rd WGOS CT8 .... 30 D5
Ethel Rd BRDST CT10 .... 55 G1
Eurolink Wy SIT ME10 .... 58 B2
Evans Rd KEN/WIL TN24 .... 162 A7
Evenhill Rd RCANTE CT3 .... 88 E6
Everard Wy FAV ME13 .... 62 A6
Evergreen Cl RSIT ME9 .... 35 J2
Eversley Rd HYTHE CT21 .... 206 A3
Eversley Wy FOLK CT20 .... 207 J1
Evison Cl DVE/WH CT16 .... 173 F4
Exchange St DEAL CT14 .... 115 K7
Exeter Cl FOLK CT20 .... 189 J8
Exmoor Ri KEN/WIL TN24 .... 8 B1

Eynsford Cl MARG CT9 .... 33 G4
Eythorne Cl KEN/WIL TN24 .... 161 H1
Eythorne Rd RDV CT15 .... 131 G8

F

Fairacre BRDST CT10 .... 55 F2
Fairacres Cl HB CT6 .... 47 H2
Fairfax Cl FOLK CT20 .... 206 D2
Fairfax Dr HB CT6 .... 48 A1
Fairfield DEAL CT14 .... 115 F8
  RCANTW CT4 .... 167 K1
Fairfield Cl NROM TN28 .... 226 C7
Fairfield Pk BRDST CT10 .... 55 F2
Fairfield Rd BRDST CT10 .... 55 F2
  MSTR CT12 .... 52 A7
  NROM TN28 .... 226 C8
  RAM CT11 .... 5 E2
Fairfield Ter RASHW TN26 .... 198 E7
Fairlawn WSTB CT5 .... 45 G5
Fairlawn Rd MSTR CT12 .... 54 C5
Fairleas SIT ME10 .... 58 C4
Fairlight Av MSTR CT12 .... 4 B3
Fairlight Rd HYTHE CT21 .... 204 E3
Fairoaks HB CT6 .... 47 G2
Fair St BRDST CT10 .... 55 F2
Fairview Cl MARG CT9 .... 3 E3
Fairview Gdns CANTW/ST CT2 ...... 69 F8
  DEAL CT14 .... 135 G4
Fairview Rd RDV CT15 .... 131 K5
  SIT ME10 .... 58 B3
Fairway Av FOLKN CT19 .... 12 A2
Fairway Cl ASH TN23 .... 160 C4
Fairway Crs WSTB CT5 .... 43 H7
The Fairways FAV ME13 .... 61 K8
The Fairways DEAL CT14 .... 115 J6
  HB CT6 .... 46 C4
  HYTHE CT21 .... 205 G5
  LYDD TN29 .... 216 C8
  NROM TN28 .... 226 E8
  SIT ME10 .... 57 K5
Falcon Gdns IOS ME12 .... 16 A7
Falcon Wy ASH TN23 .... 160 C7
Fallowfield SIT ME10 .... 58 B4
Fans La RSIT ME9 .... 35 J2
The Fan DVE/WH CT16 .... 11 E2
Farleigh Rd CANTW/ST CT2 .... 86 E3
Farley Cl RASHW TN26 .... 180 D5
Farley Rd MARG CT9 .... 3 D6
Farm Cl ASH TN23 .... 160 C7
Farm Crs SIT ME10 .... 58 B4
Farmer Cl HYTHE CT21 .... 205 H3
Farmhouse Cl RCANTW CT4 .... 129 F7
Farm House Cl WSTB CT5 .... 44 C6
Farm La DEAL CT14 .... 115 F8
  RYE TN31 .... 234 A3
Farm Rd RASHW TN26 .... 198 E7
Farncombe Wy DVE/WH CT16 .... 153 F7
Farrar Rd BRCH CT7 .... 29 K8
Farrers Wk ASH TN23 .... 182 A2
Farrier Cl ASH TN23 .... 160 D1
Farrier St DEAL CT14 .... 115 K7
Farthinglane Rd DVW CT17 .... 172 E8
Faulkners La CANTW/ST CT2 .... 85 K5
Faussett Hl RCANTW CT4 .... 106 D7
Faversham Reach FAV ME13 .... 62 C6
Faversham Rd FAV ME13 .... 80 A1
  HDCN TN27 .... 119 J4
  KEN/WIL TN24 .... 141 H7
  RASHE TN25 .... 121 H5
  RCANTW CT4 .... 121 F1
  RMAID ME17 .... 96 E7
  RSIT ME9 .... 79 H5
  WSTB CT5 .... 42 D8
Featherbed La FAV ME13 .... 82 A7
  RSIT ME9 .... 35 K4
Felborough Cl RCANTW CT4 .... 103 J6
Felderland Cl DEAL CT14 .... 113 J1
Felderland La SWCH CT13 .... 113 H2
Fenner Cl FOLK CT20 .... 206 E2
Fenton Ct DEAL CT14 .... 115 H8
Ferguson Cl HYTHE CT21 .... 205 K4
Ferguson Rd LYDD TN29 .... 236 B4
Fern Bank Crs FOLKN CT19 .... 13 D3
Fern Cl RFOLK CT18 .... 169 J8
  WSTB CT5 .... 45 F5
Ferndale Cl IOS ME12 .... 14 E8
Ferndale Ct BRCH CT7 .... 29 K8
Ferne La RDV CT15 .... 170 E3
Ferne Wy FOLK CT20 .... 206 E1
Fernfield RFOLK CT18 .... 169 J8
Fernfield La RFOLK CT18 .... 169 J8
Fernlea Av HB CT6 .... 46 D2
Fernleigh Cl FAV ME13 .... 83 H3
Ferry Rd IOS ME12 .... 20 E4
  RSIT ME9 .... 35 K2
Ferry Vw QBOR ME11 .... 20 A3
Fiddling La RASHE TN25 .... 165 C7
Field Av CANT CT1 .... 87 H3
Field End KEN/WIL TN24 .... 162 A5
Field End Pl FAV ME13 .... 83 C3
The Fieldings SIT ME10 .... 57 K4
Fielding St FAV ME13 .... 62 B7

Field Mill Rd *HDCN* TN27 .... 137 G1
Field Vw *ASH* TN23 .... 181 K2
   WSTB CT5 .... 43 J7
Field View Cl *IOS* ME12 .... 14 D8
Fiesta Wk *CANT* CT1 .... 7 F4
Fife Av *HB* CT6 .... 46 A4
Fifth Av *MARG* CT9 .... 3 F2
Fig Tree Rd *BRDST* CT10 .... 33 G7
Filer Rd *IOS* ME12 .... 15 F7
Filmer Rd *RCANTW* CT4 .... 107 K5
The Finches *BRCH* CT7 .... 50 B4
   SIT ME10 .... 58 B3
Finch Gv *HYTHE* CT21 .... 204 B6
Finch Ms *DEAL* CT14 .... 135 J2
Finlay Cl *FAV* ME13 .... 62 A7
Finn Farm Ct *ASH* TN23 .... 182 C5
Finsbury Rd *RAM* CT11 .... 5 E4
Firbank Gdns *MARG* CT9 .... 2 B5
Firbanks *WSTB* CT5 .... 44 C6
Fir Ct *KEN/WIL* TN24 .... 9 F4
Firs Cl *FOLKN* CT19 .... 189 J8
Firs La *FOLKN* CT19 .... 189 J8
Firs Rd *RCANTW* CT4 .... 130 B5
First Av *BRDST* CT10 .... 33 G4
   IOS ME12 .... 14 D5
   IOS ME12 .... 23 H1
   MARG CT9 .... 3 F2 E1
   QBOR ME11 .... 20 A3
   RYE TN31 .... 234 C4
The Firs *RCANTE* CT3 .... 69 K5
Firtree Cl *CANTW/ST* CT2 .... 85 J3
Fir Tree Cl *RAM* CT11 .... 4 C5
Fir Tree Hl *SWCH* CT13 .... 93 F8
Fisher Cl *HYTHE* CT21 .... 205 H5
Fisher Cl *CANTW/ST* CT2 .... 6 A2
Fisher St *SWCH* CT13 .... 94 A5
Fisher Street Rd *FAV* ME13 .... 101 J4
Fishmonger's La *DVE/WH* CT16 .... 10 C4 E1
Fitzgerald Av *HB* CT6 .... 46 B3
Fitzmary Rd *MARG* CT9 .... 31 F5
Fitzroy Av *BRDST* CT10 .... 33 H4
   MARG CT9 .... 3 F4
   MSTR CT12 .... 4 B1
Fitzroy Rd *WSTB* CT5 .... 44 C3
Five Vents La *LYDD* TN29 .... 225 F6
Fiveways Ri *DEAL* CT14 .... 135 F1
Flanders Cl *SIT* ME10 .... 36 A5
Flanders Fld *RASHE* TN25 .... 183 K2 E1
Flax Court La *RDV* CT15 .... 132 A7
Flaxpond Rd *ASH* TN23 .... 160 D7
Fleet Av *IOS* ME12 .... 14 B6 E1
Fleet Rd *RDV* CT15 .... 155 G5
Fleets La *CANTW/ST* CT2 .... 67 G7
Fleetwood Av *HB* CT6 .... 46 C2
Fleetwood Cl *IOS* ME12 .... 15 J8
Fleming Wy *FOLKN* CT19 .... 13 D1
Flete Rd *MARG* CT9 .... 3 J1
Flimwell *ASH* TN23 .... 160 E8 E1
Flint La *MAID* ME17 .... 96 D6
Flood La *FAV* ME13 .... 62 B7
Flood St *RASHE* TN25 .... 183 H5
Flora Rd *RAM* CT11 .... 5 E3
Florence Av *WSTB* CT5 .... 43 H7
Florence Rd *RAM* CT11 .... 5 D5
Florida Cl *DVE/WH* CT16 .... 173 F3
Flying Horse La *DVE/WH* CT16 .... 10 C4 E1
Foads Hl *MSTR* CT12 .... 53 J8
Foads La *MSTR* CT12 .... 75 J1
Foley Cl *KEN/WIL* TN24 .... 162 A7
Folkestone Rd *DVW* CT17 .... 173 F7
   RDV CT15 .... 193 H1
Folly Rd *FOLK* CT20 .... 13 E3
Fonblanque Rd *IOS* ME12 .... 14 D4 E1
Foord Rd *RMAID* ME17 .... 116 D1
Foord Rd South *FOLK* CT20 .... 13 D4 E1
Forbes Rd *FAV* ME13 .... 62 B9
Ford Cl *HB* CT6 .... 45 K2
   RCANTW CT4 .... 107 K5 E1
Ford Hl *RCANTE* CT3 .... 47 K7
Fordoun Rd *BRDST* CT10 .... 55 G1
Ford Wy *ASH* TN23 .... 160 D5
Fordwich Gv *BRDST* CT10 .... 33 F7
Fordwich Pl *SWCH* CT13 .... 93 K6
Fordwich Rd *CANTW/ST* CT2 .... 87 K2
Foreland Av *FOLKN* CT19 .... 13 F5
   MARG CT9 .... 32 A2
Foreland Rd *RDV* CT15 .... 175 G2
Forelands Sq *DEAL* CT14 .... 135 H5
The Foreland *CANT* CT1 .... 7 E6
Foreness Cl *BRDST* CT10 .... 33 H3 E1
Forestall Meadow *ASH* TN23 ...... 181 K2
Foresters Wy *FOLK* CT20 .... 13 D4
Forge Cl *CANTW/ST* CT2 .... 87 K1
   RASHE TN25 .... 186 A6
   RDV CT15 .... 132 A7 E1
Forgefield *RASHW* TN26 .... 178 E1
Forge Fld *RDV* CT15 .... 192 B1
Forgefields *HB* CT6 .... 47 F6
Forge Hl *RASHE* TN25 .... 201 J1
   RASHW TN26 .... 179 F1
Forge La *DVE/WH* CT16 .... 152 E6 E1
   HDCN TN27 .... 136 C5
   RCANTE CT3 .... 48 D6

RDV CT15.................................. 154 A1
Forge Meadow *TENT* TN30 .... 221 H2
Forge Meads *TENT* TN30 .... 219 K3
Forge Pth *DVE/WH* CT16 .... 152 E6
Forge La *SIT* ME10 .... 35 K8
Forrester Cl *CANT* CT1 .... 7 F1
Forson Cl *TENT* TN30 .... 194 B6
Forstal Rd *HDCN* TN27 .... 136 C5
   RCANTW CT4 .... 130 A5
The Forstal *RASHE* TN25 .... 142 E4 E1
   RCANTE CT3 .... 71 J8
Fort Burgoyne Rd *DVE/WH* CT16.. 10 C2
Fort Cl *LYDD* TN29 .... 233 F8
Fort Crs *MARG* CT9 .... 3 D2
Fort Hl *MARG* CT9 .... 2 C2
Fort Lower Prom *MARG* CT9 .... 3 D2
Fort Paragon *MARG* CT9 .... 3 D2 E1
Fort Rd *BRDST* CT10 .... 55 J2
   HYTHE CT21 .... 204 E4
   MARG CT9 .... 2 C2
Fortuna Ct *RAM* CT11 .... 5 D4 E1
Forty Acres Hl *IOS* ME12 .... 21 J2
Forty Acres Rd *CANTW/ST* CT2 ..... 6 B2
Fostall Rd *FAV* ME13 .... 62 B5
Foster Cl *FOLKN* CT19 .... 189 K7
Foster Rd *KEN/WIL* TN24 .... 162 A8
Foster's Av *BRDST* CT10 .... 33 F7
Foster's Ct *SWCH* CT13 .... 94 A7 E1
Foster Wy *DEAL* CT14 .... 135 H1
Fougeres Wy *KEN/WIL* TN24 .... 8 A1
Fountains Cl *KEN/WIL* TN24 ...... 162 A5 E1
Fountain St *SIT* ME10 .... 57 K2 E1
Fourth Av *IOS* ME12 .... 17 J8
Foxborough Cl *SWCH* CT13 .... 93 F8
Foxborough Hl *SWCH* CT13 ...... 113 F1
Foxborough La *MSTR* CT12 .... 52 B6
Fox Cl *RFOLK* CT18...................... 171 F7
Foxdown Cl *CANTW/ST* CT2 .... 6 A1
Foxglove Cl *KEN/WIL* TN24 .... 9 F3 E1
Foxglove Gn *KEN/WIL* TN24 .... 9 F3 E1
Foxglove Rd *KEN/WIL* TN24 .... 9 E4
Foxgrove *SIT* ME10...................... 35 K7
Foxgrove Rd *WSTB* CT5 .... 44 D5
Fox Hl *SIT* ME10 .... 58 E3
Foxley Rd *QBOR* ME11 .... 20 B1
Fox's Cross Hl *WSTB* CT5 .... 65 H3
Fox's Cross Rd *WSTB* CT5 .... 65 J3
Fox Wy *RCANTW* CT4 .... 129 F6
Frampton Rd *HYTHE* CT21 .... 204 E4
France Rd *DVE/WH* CT16 .... 172 E1
Frances Gdns *RAM* CT11 .... 5 F3 E1
Francis Av *SWCH* CT13 .... 95 C7
Francis Rd *ASH* TN23 .... 8 B5
   BRDST CT10 .... 33 J7
Frankapps Cl *RSIT* ME9 .... 34 A8 E1
Franklyn Rd *CANTW/ST* CT2 .... 86 A7
Freda Cl *BRDST* CT10 .... 55 F2
Frederick Rd *DEAL* CT14 .... 135 J5
Frederick St *SIT* ME10 .... 57 K2
The Freedown *RDV* CT15 .... 155 G7
Freeman's Cl *WSTB* CT5 .... 43 H8
Freeman's Rd *MSTR* CT12 .... 52 A8
Freemen's Wy *DEAL* CT14 .... 135 H3
Fremantle Rd *FOLK* CT20 .... 206 E1
Frencham Cl *CANTW/ST* CT2 .... 86 E2
Frensham Cl *SIT* ME10 .... 58 C2
Freshfield La *HYTHE* CT21 .... 204 E2
Freshlands *HB* CT6 .... 47 K1 E1
Freshwater Cl *HB* CT6 .... 46 A3
Friars Cl *WSTB* CT5 .... 44 C5
The Friars *CANT* CT1 .... 6 C2 E1
Friars Wy *DVE/WH* CT16............. 172 E5
Friary Wy *CANTW/ST* CT2............. 6 A1
Friendly Cl *MARG* CT9 .... 32 E5
Friends Av *MARG* CT9 .... 32 E6
Friesian Wy *KEN/WIL* TN24 ...... 141 G6
Frith Rd *DVE/WH* CT16............. 172 D4
   RASHE TN25 .... 182 E8
Frittenden Cl *ASH* TN23 .... 160 C8
Frobisher Cl *SIT* ME10 .... 35 K8 E1
Frog La *RCANTW* CT4 .... 108 B8
Frognal Gdns *RSIT* ME9 .... 59 J4
Frognal Rd *RSIT* ME9 .... 59 J4
Frognal La *RSIT* ME9 .... 59 J4
Front Brents *FAV* ME13 .... 62 C6
Front Rd *RASHW* TN26 .... 196 C5
Front St *DEAL* CT14 .... 155 F1
The Front *RDV* CT15 .... 175 G2
Fruiterer's Cl *RSIT* ME9 .... 58 B7
Fulbert Rd *DVE/WH* CT16 .... 173 F1
Fulham Av *MARG* CT9 .... 31 G7
Fulsam Pl *MARG* CT9.................... 2 B5
Fulston Pl *SIT* ME10 .... 58 B3
Furze Hill Crs *IOS* ME12 .... 14 E8
Fusilier Av *FOLK* CT20 .... 206 B1

G

Gadby Rd *SIT* ME10 .... 57 H1
Gadsby La *RASHW* TN26 .... 177 K4
Gainsboro Rd *BRCH* CT7 .... 29 J6 E1
Gainsborough Cl *FOLKN* CT19 ..... 12 A2 E1

Gainsborough Dr *HB* CT6............. 47 K1
Galliard St *SWCH* CT13 .... 94 A6 E1
Galloways Rd *LYDD* TN29 .... 237 H5
Gallwey Av *BRCH* CT7 .... 29 H7
Galway Rd *IOS* ME12 .... 14 D4
Gammon's Farm La *LYDD* TN29 .. 215 G2
Gann Rd *WSTB* CT5 .... 44 C4
The Gap *CANT* CT1 .... 7 E6
   CANTW/ST CT2 .... 66 D7
Garden Cl *CANTW/ST* CT2 .... 85 J4
Garden Pl *KEN/WIL* TN24 .... 141 J8
Garden Rd *FOLKN* CT19 .... 13 D8
Gardner's Hl *RYE* TN31 .... 227 J7
Garfield Pl *FAV* ME13 .... 62 C7 E1
Garfield Rd *MARG* CT9 .... 2 B5 E1
Garlinge Green Rd *RCANTW* CT4.. 105 G8
Garrard Av *MARG* CT9................. 31 G6
Gas Rd *SIT* ME10 .... 36 C8
Gas St *CANT* CT1 .... 6 C4 E1
Gasworks La *ASH* TN23................ 8 B4
Gateacre Rd *WSTB* CT5 .... 43 H8 E1
Gaunt's Cl *DEAL* CT14 .... 135 G2
Gayhurst Dr *SIT* ME10................. 57 H1
Gazedown *LYDD* TN29 .... 227 G3
Gaze Hill Av *SIT* ME10 .... 58 B3
Genesta Av *WSTB* CT5 .... 43 J7
Genesta Cl *SIT* ME10 .... 35 K7
George Gurr Crs *FOLKN* CT19 ..... 13 D1
George Hill Rd *BRDST* CT10 .... 33 G5
   MARG CT9 .... 33 F5
George La *NROM* TN28 .... 226 C7
George Roche Rd *CANT* CT1 .... 7 D5 E1
George's Av *WSTB* CT5 .... 43 H7
George St *ASH* TN23 .... 8 B4
   DEAL CT14 .... 115 K7 E1
   DVW CT17 .... 173 F5
   RAM CT11 .... 5 E5
   SIT ME10 .... 58 C3 E1
George V Av *MARG* CT9 .... 31 G6
George Williams Wy
   KEN/WIL TN24 .... 161 J1 E1
George Wood Cl *LYDD* TN29 ...... 231 H8 E1
Geraldine Rd *FOLKN* CT19 .... 190 A8
Gerrards Dr *SIT* ME10 .... 58 A4
Gibbons Rd *SIT* ME10 .... 57 G1
Gibraltar La *RFOLK* CT18............ 190 A3
Gibraltar Sq *RDV* CT15 .... 173 J3
Gibson St *SIT* ME10 .... 57 K2
Gigger's Green Rd *RASHE* TN25 .. 201 J3
Gilbert Rd *RAM* CT11.................... 5 D3
Gilchrist Av *HB* CT6 .... 46 B4
Giles Gdns *MARG* CT9 .... 3 D5
Giles La *CANTW/ST* CT2 .... 86 A3
Gilford Rd *DEAL* CT14 .... 135 J1
Gilham Gv *DEAL* CT14 .... 135 H2
Gillett Rd *LYDD* TN29 .... 231 J7
Gill La *RASHE* TN25 .... 183 F6
   RASHW TN26 .... 199 G4
Gillman Cl *RFOLK* CT18 .... 189 K2
Giraud Dr *FAV* ME13 .... 62 A6
Glack Rd *DEAL* CT14 .... 135 F2
The Glade *DEAL* CT14 .... 115 F8
Gladstone Dr *SIT* ME10 .... 58 D3
Gladstone Rd *BRDST* CT10 .... 55 C3
   DEAL CT14 .... 135 J2
   FOLKN CT19 .... 13 E3
   KEN/WIL TN24 .... 161 J8
   MARG CT9 .... 2 C4
Glebe Cl *HDCN* TN27 .... 156 B4
   RDV CT15 .... 175 F1
Glebe Gdns *MARG* CT9 .... 31 G6 E1
   RMAID ME17 .... 116 E1
Glebeland *HDCN* TN27 .... 137 F2
Glebelands *RCANTE* CT3 .... 92 A4
   RDV CT15 .... 174 A7 E1
Glebe La *SIT* ME10 .... 57 H2
Glebe Rd *MARG* CT9 .... 31 G6
The Glebe *HDCN* TN27 .... 118 E7
Glebe Wy *KEN/WIL* TN24 .... 141 H7
   WSTB CT5 .... 44 A6
Glen Av *HB* CT6 .... 47 H1
Glenbervie Dr *HB* CT6................. 47 K1
Glenbrook Gv *SIT* ME10............... 35 K7
Glencoe Rd *MARG* CT9 .... 3 E4
Glendale Rd *IOS* ME12 .... 15 J7
Glenfield Rd *DVE/WH* CT16 .... 173 F3
Glen Gv *DVW* CT17 .... 173 F7 E1
Glen Iris Av *CANTW/ST* CT2 .... 86 A4
Glen Iris Cl *CANTW/ST* CT2 .... 86 A4
Glen Rd *DEAL* CT14 .... 135 J7
Glenside *WSTB* CT5 .... 44 D6
Glenside Av *CANT* CT1 .... 7 E1 E1
The Glen *IOS* ME12 .... 15 K7
   SIT ME10 .... 151 F1
Glenwood Cl *TENT* TN30 .... 194 B3 E1
Glenwood Dr *IOS* ME12 .... 15 J7
Gloster Cl *RFOLK* CT18 .... 190 C3
Gloster Rd *RFOLK* CT18 .... 190 C3
Gloster Ropewalk *DVW* CT17 ...... 10 A6
Gloster Wy *DVW* CT17 .... 10 A6 E1
Gloucester Av *BRDST* CT10 .... 55 C3
   MARG CT9 .... 32 E4
Gloucester Ms *NROM* TN28 .... 226 D6
Gloucester Pl *FOLK* CT20 .... 13 D4 E1
Gloucester Rd *WSTB* CT5 .... 44 C4

Glover Rd *KEN/WIL* TN24 .... 9 E4
Goat Lees La *KEN/WIL* TN24 ...... 141 H7
Godden Rd *CANTW/ST* CT2 .... 86 E2
Godfrey Wk *ASH* TN23 .... 8 B5
Godinton La *RASHW* TN26 .... 160 A1
Godinton Rd *ASH* TN23 .... 8 B3
Godinton Wy *ASH* TN23 .... 8 A3
Godwin Cl *SIT* ME10 .... 36 A5
Godwin Rd *CANT* CT1 .... 86 A8
   DVE/WH CT16 .... 11 D3
   MARG CT9 .... 3 E3
Godwyne Cl *DVE/WH* CT16 .... 10 B3
Godwyne Pth *DVE/WH* CT16 ..... 10 C2
Godwyne Rd *DVE/WH* CT16 ...... 10 B3
Godwyn Gdns *FOLK* CT20 .... 12 A5
Godwyn Rd *DEAL* CT14 .... 115 J6
   FOLK CT20 .... 12 A5
Gogway *RCANTW* CT4 .... 145 K1
Golden Acre La *WGOS* CT8 .... 30 C7
Golden Cl *WGOS* CT8 .... 30 C7
Golden Hl *WSTB* CT5 .... 66 C1
Golden Sq *TENT* TN30 .... 194 B6
Golden St *DEAL* CT14 .... 115 K7 ⑩
Goldfinch Cl *FAV* ME13 .... 62 B5
   HB CT6 .... 47 H4 ②
Gold Hl *RASHE* TN25 .... 140 B3
Goldsmith Ct *TENT* TN30 ...... 194 B5 ⑪
Goldstone Dro *RCANTE* CT3 ...... 73 H7
Goldups La *FAV* ME13 .... 102 B5
Goldwell Cl *RASHE* TN25 .... 184 B8
Goldwell La *RASHE* TN25 .... 184 B8
   RASHW TN26 .... 159 G4
Golf Rd *DEAL* CT14 .... 115 J5
Golf Road Pl *DEAL* CT14 .... 115 J6
Goodban Sq *RCANTE* CT3 ..... 92 B5 ⑥
Goodcheap La *KEN/WIL* TN24 .. 162 D3
Goodfellow Wy *DVE/WH* CT16 .. 10 B5 ③
Goodnestone Hl *RCANTE* CT3 .. 111 F3
Goodnestone Rd *RCANTE* CT3 ... 90 D8
   SIT ME10 .... 58 C3
Goodwin Av *WSTB* CT5 .... 45 C4
Goodwin Rd *RAM* CT11 .... 4 B6
   RDV CT15 .... 175 F2
Goosefields *FAV* ME13 .... 63 J5
Gordon Av *OBOR* ME11 .... 20 B2
Gordon Cl *SIT* ME10 .... 58 D2 ①
Gordon Gv *WGOS* CT8 .... 30 D5
Gordon Rd *CANT* CT1 .... 6 C4 ⑥
   DVE/WH CT16 .... 172 E1
   FAV ME13 .... 62 D6
   FOLK CT20 .... 206 D1
   HB CT6 .... 46 E2
   MARG CT9 .... 3 E2 ③
   MARG CT9 .... 54 B1
   RAM CT11 .... 5 D3 ③
   WSTB CT5 .... 44 A7
Gordon Sq *BRCH* CT7 .... 29 J7
   FAV ME13 .... 62 D7
Gore Court Rd *SIT* ME10 .... 57 K4
Gore End Cl *BRCH* CT7 .... 29 J7 ②
Gore La *SWCH* CT13 .... 112 E4
Gore Rd *SWCH* CT13 .... 113 F3
Goretop La *DEAL* CT14 .... 114 C1
Gorrell Rd *WSTB* CT5 .... 44 B6
Gorse La *HB* CT6 .... 47 H4
Gorse Rd *SIT* ME10 .... 58 D1
Goschen Rd *DVW* CT17 .... 173 F6
Gosfield Rd *HB* CT6 .... 47 F2
Gosselin St *WSTB* CT5 .... 44 B6
Goss Hall La *SWCH* CT13 .... 92 E4
Goteley Mere *KEN/WIL* TN24 .. 141 G7
Gothic Cl *DEAL* CT14 .... 135 H5 ①
Goudhurst Cl *CANTW/ST* CT2 ... 86 E2
Gough Rd *FOLK* CT20 .... 206 E3 ③
Grace Hl *FOLK* CT20 .... 13 D4 ③
Grace Meadow *DVE/WH* CT16 .. 152 E7
Grace Rd *IOS* ME12 .... 14 B5
Grafton Ri *HB* CT6 .... 46 B3
Grafton Rd *BRDST* CT10 .... 33 F6
   SIT ME10 .... 58 A2
Grampion Cl *KEN/WIL* TN24 .... 8 C2
Gram's Rd *DEAL* CT14 .... 135 J6
Granary Court Rd *RASHE* TN25 . 185 H2
Grand Dr *HB* CT6 .... 46 B2
Grand Pde *NROM* TN28 .... 233 F2
Grange Crs *TENT* TN30 .... 194 A3
Grange Rd *BRDST* CT10 .... 33 C8
   DEAL CT14 .... 135 H1
   FOLKN CT19 .... 189 K8 ⑪
   HB CT6 .... 47 G2
   HYTHE CT21 .... 205 F2
   RAM CT11 .... 4 C4
The Grange *FAV* CT15 .... 151 F1
   WSTB CT5 .... 43 H8
Grange Wy *BRDST* CT10 .... 5 F1
Grant Cl *BRDST* CT10 .... 33 F8
Grantham Av *DEAL* CT14 .... 135 G1
Grantley Cl *ASH* TN23 .... 8 A6
Granville Av *BRDST* CT10 ..... 55 J3 ③
   MSTR CT12 .... 4 B2
Granville Cl *FAV* ME13 .... 62 R7
Granville Dr *HB* CT6 .... 46 A4
Granville Pde *FOLK* CT20 .... 206 E3
Granville Pl *IOS* ME12 .... 14 D4 ③
Granville Rd *BRDST* CT10 .... 55 J3

DEAL CT14 .... 135 J4
IOS ME12 .... 14 C4
RDV CT15 .... 155 H8
Granville Rd East *FOLK* CT20 . 207 F3 ②
Granville St *DEAL* CT14 .... 135 K1
   DVE/WH CT16 .... 10 A2
Grasmere Av *RAM* CT11 .... 4 A4
Grasmere Gdns *FOLKN* CT19 ... 12 B2
Grasmere Rd *KEN/WIL* TN24 .. 141 G8
   WSTB CT5 .... 44 D6
Grasmere Wy *RCANTW* CT3 ... 110 B8
Grassmere *LYDD* TN29 .... 227 F5
Gravel Castle Rd *RCANTW* CT4 129 F7
Gravel Hl *FAV* ME13 .... 98 E6
Gravel La *RDV* CT15 .... 192 C2
Gravel Wk *ASH* TN23 .... 8 B2 ②
   CANT CT1 .... 6 C3 ⑥
Graveney Rd *FAV* ME13 .... 62 E7
Gray Cl *RFOLK* CT18 .... 190 D1
Graylings Cl *SIT* ME10 .... 57 H4
Grayshott Cl *SIT* ME10 .... 58 A3
Graystone Rd *WSTB* CT5 .... 44 D3
Grays Wy *CANT* CT1 .... 85 K8
Great Conduit St *HYTHE* CT21 205 G4 ③
Grebe Cl *RFOLK* CT18 .... 190 B2
Grebe Crs *HYTHE* CT21 .... 204 A6
Greenacre *RCANTW* CT4 .... 128 D3
Greenacre Dr *DEAL* CT14 .... 135 J5
Greenbank *KEN/WIL* TN24 ..... 141 H8
Greenbanks *RFOLK* CT18 .... 167 G8
Green Cl *RFOLK* CT18 .... 190 C2
Green Ct *RCANTW* CT4 .... 108 A5 ③
Greencroft *ASH* TN23 .... 160 B8
Green Dell *CANTW/ST* CT2 ...... 86 D2
Greenfield Rd *FOLKN* CT19 ...... 13 E2
   MSTR CT12 .... 4 C1
Greenfields *RASHE* TN25 .... 186 B4
Green Hedges *TENT* TN30 .... 194 B6 ⑪
Greenhill Cl *MSTR* CT12 .... 52 A7 ①
Greenhill Gdns *HB* CT6 .... 46 C3
   MSTR CT12 .... 52 A7
Greenhill La *HDCN* TN27 .... 136 E7
Greenhill Rd *HB* CT6 .... 46 B4
Green Hills *RCANTW* CT4 .... 128 E6
Green La *ASH* TN23 .... 181 H1
   BRDST CT10 .... 55 F1
   DEAL CT14 .... 135 H5
   DVE/WH CT16 .... 172 C1
   FOLK CT19 .... 13 E2
   HDCN TN27 .... 156 A5
   HYTHE CT21 .... 204 E4
   RASHE TN25 .... 120 E4
   RASHW TN26 .... 178 A4
   RCANTE CT3 .... 111 K3
   RCANTW CT4 .... 103 J4
   RDV CT15 .... 132 B7
   RDV CT15 .... 155 F5
   RDV CT15 .... 171 F4
   RFOLK CT18 .... 166 B5
   RFOLK CT18 .... 191 J3
   RSIT ME9 .... 58 C7
   WSTB CT5 .... 44 A4
Green Lane Av *HYTHE* CT21 .... 204 D4
Green Leas *WSTB* CT5 .... 45 G5
Greenly Wy *NROM* TN28 .... 226 D8
Green Mdw *LYDD* TN29 .... 217 F4
Green Porch Cl *SIT* ME10 .... 36 A7
Green Rd *BRCH* CT7 .... 29 J6
Greensand Wy *HDCN* TN27 .... 137 F4
   RASHE TN25 .... 196 D2
Greenside *RASHW* TN26 .... 177 K7
Greensland Wy *ASH* TN23 ...... 181 G2
   RASHW TN26 .... 139 J8
Greensole La *MSTR* CT12 .... 53 K6
The Green *CANTW/ST* CT2 .... 66 D8
   CANTW/ST CT2 .... 85 G5 ①
   HYTHE CT21 .... 205 F2 ②
   LYDD TN29 .... 216 E2
   MSTR CT12 .... 53 J5 ③
   RASHE TN25 .... 142 E4 ③
   RCANTE CT3 .... 91 F3
   RCANTW CT4 .... 105 F3
   RCANTW CT4 .... 130 A5 ③
   RSIT ME9 .... 34 A3 ①
Greenway *FAV* ME13 .... 62 A6
Green Wy *LYDD* TN29 .... 231 G8
Greenways *SIT* ME10 .... 58 C3
Gregory Cl *SIT* ME10 .... 36 B6
Grenham Bay Av *BRCH* CT7 ...... 29 H7
Grenham Rd *BRCH* CT7 .... 29 H6
Grenville Gdns *BRCH* CT7 .... 29 H6
Grenville Wy *BRDST* CT10 .... 55 F2
Gresham Av *MARG* CT9 .... 31 F5
Greystones Rd *MSTR* CT12 .... 75 J1 ①
Grey Willow Gdns *ASH* TN23 .. 160 B6
Griffin St *DEAL* CT14 .... 115 K7
Grimshill Rd *WSTB* CT5 .... 44 A6
Grimston Av *FOLK* CT20 .... 12 B5
Grimston Gdns *FOLK* CT20 .... 12 D6
Grimthorpe Av *WSTB* CT5 .... 43 K7
Grinsell Hl *MSTR* CT12 .... 52 D8
Grisbrook Farm Cl *LYDD* TN29 231 J8 ②
Grosvenor Gdns *MARG* CT9 ..... 2 C4 ②

Grosvenor Hl *MARG* CT9 .... 2 C3 ②
Grosvenor Pl *MARG* CT9 .... 2 C3
Grosvenor Rd *BRDST* CT10 ...... 55 H2
   KEN/WIL TN24 .... 141 G7
   RAM CT11 .... 4 C5 ②
   WSTB CT5 .... 44 A7
Grotto Gdns *MARG* CT9 .... 3 D3
Grotto Hl *MARG* CT9 .... 3 D3
Grotto Rd *MARG* CT9 .... 3 D3
Grove Av *IOS* ME12 .... 25 F4
Grove Cl *FAV* ME13 .... 61 K8
Grove Ferry Hl *RCANTE* CT3 .... 71 F5
Grove Ferry Rd *RCANTE* CT3 ... 71 G3
Grove Gdns *MARG* CT9 .... 2 A4
Grovehurst Av *SIT* ME10 .... 36 A5
Grovehurst Rd *RSIT* ME9 .... 35 K3
   SIT ME10 .... 35 K5
Grovelands *RMAID* ME17 .... 116 E1
Grove La *LYDD* TN29 .... 223 G8
Grove Park Av *SIT* ME10 .... 57 F1
Grove Pl *FAV* ME13 .... 61 K8 ③
Grove Rd *DEAL* CT14 .... 135 K3
   FAV ME13 .... 102 A2
   FOLK CT20 .... 13 E3
   RAM CT11 .... 5 D5
   RCANTE CT3 .... 71 G6
   RCANTE CT3 .... 89 J3
   RCANTE CT3 .... 91 H8
Grove Ter *CANT* CT1 .... 6 B4 ③
The Grove *DEAL* CT14 .... 115 J8
   DVE/WH CT16 .... 10 A2
   HB CT6 .... 46 B4
   KEN/WIL TN24 .... 141 J8
   RCANTW CT4 .... 129 F6
   WGOS CT8 .... 30 E5 ①
   WGOS CT8 .... 30 E6 ②
Groveway *IOS* ME12 .... 24 E4
Grummock Av *RAM* CT11 .... 4 B4
Guildcount La *SWCH* CT13 .... 93 K5 ③
Guildford Lawn *RAM* CT11 .... 5 E5 ③
Guildford Rd *CANT* CT1 .... 6 C4
Guildhall St *CANT* CT1 .... 6 C3 ⑥
Guildhall St North *FOLKN* CT19 . 13 D4
Guilford Av *DVE/WH* CT16 ..... 152 E6
Guilford Rd *SWCH* CT13 .... 95 F6
Guilton *RCANTE* CT3 .... 91 K5
Guldeford La *RYE* TN31 .... 228 C3
Gurling Rd *RDV* CT15 .... 155 F5
Guy Cl *BRDST* CT10 .... 33 J7
Gwyn Rd *MSTR* CT12 .... 4 C1

H

Hackfield *ASH* TN23 .... 160 D5
Hackington Cl *CANTW/ST* CT2 ... 86 C2
Hackington Rd *CANTW/ST* CT2 . 67 C5
Hacklinge Hl *DEAL* CT14 .... 114 B4
Hadleigh Gdns *HB* CT6 .... 47 G1
Hadlow Dr *MARG* CT9 .... 33 F4 ②
Haffenden Rd *TENT* TN30 ...... 194 A5
Haine Rd *MSTR* CT12 .... 54 A4
Hales Cl *TENT* TN30 .... 194 B6
Hales Dr *CANTW/ST* CT2 .... 86 D3
Hales Rd *SIT* ME10 .... 57 J5
Halfmile Ride *MARG* CT9 .... 31 K8
Halford Cl *HB* CT6 .... 47 G4 ③
Halfway Rd *IOS* ME12 .... 14 E6
Hall Av *KEN/WIL* TN24 .... 161 K8
Hall Cl *SIT* ME10 .... 35 K8
Hall Crs *DEAL* CT14 .... 135 F1
Hallcroft Ct *RAM* CT11 .... 4 C4 ③
Halstatt Rd *DEAL* CT14 .... 135 G3
Halstead Cl *CANTW/ST* CT2 ..... 86 E2 ②
Halstead Gdns *MARG* CT9 ..... 33 G3 ①
Halstow Wy *ASH* TN23 .... 160 D6
The Halt *RCANTW* CT4 .... 167 K2
   WSTB CT5 .... 44 C7
Hambrook Cl *RCANTW* CT4 .... 103 H6 ①
Hambrook La *RCANTW* CT4 .... 103 H7
Hambrook Wk *SIT* ME10 .... 36 A6
The Hamele *CANTW/ST* CT2 ..... 87 K1
Hamilton Cl *MSTR* CT12 .... 4 A2 ③
Hamilton Crs *SIT* ME10 .... 57 H3
Hamilton Rd *DEAL* CT14 .... 135 H2
   DVW CT17 .... 172 E6
   KEN/WIL TN24 .... 161 H8
   LYDD TN29 .... 231 H8
   WSTB CT5 .... 44 A5
Ham La *RMAID* ME17 .... 116 B1
Ham Mill La *LYDD* TN29 .... 212 E5
Hammond Cl *RDV* CT15 .... 131 G1
Hammond's Pl *FOLK* CT20 ..... 206 E1 ③
Hampden La *ASH* TN23 .... 8 A6 ③
Hampden Ms *ASH* TN23 .... 160 E8
Hampden Rd *ASH* TN23 .... 160 E8
Hampshire Rd *CANT* CT1 .... 87 H7
Hampton Cl *HB* CT6 .... 45 K3
Hampton Gdns *HB* CT6 .... 45 K3
Hampton La *RASHE* TN25 .... 163 H4
Hampton Pier Av *HB* CT6 .... 46 A2
Hampton V *HYTHE* CT21 .... 206 A2
Ham Rd *FAV* ME13 .... 62 B5
Ham Shades La *WSTB* CT5 ...... 44 D5

Hamstreet Rd *RASHW* TN26 .... 198 C2
Hancocks Fld *DEAL* CT14 .... 135 G1
Hangman's La *DEAL* CT14 .... 154 D1
   RDV CT15 .... 153 K8
Hanover Cl *DEAL* CT14 .... 135 J5 ⑤
   MARG CT9 .... 33 F4 ⑥
   SIT ME10 .... 57 K4
Hanover Pl *CANTW/ST* CT2 .... 6 C1
Hanover Sq *HB* CT6 .... 46 E1
Hanover St *HB* CT6 .... 46 E1
Hanslett's La *FAV* ME13 .... 80 A3
Harbledown Gdns *MARG* CT9 .... 33 F3
Harble Down Pk *CANTW/ST* CT2 .... 86 A5 ⑨
Harbour Approach Rd *FOLK* CT20 .... 13 E5
Harbourne La *RASHW* TN26 .... 194 E2
   TENT TN30 .... 194 D2
Harbour Pde *RAM* CT11 .... 5 E5
Harbour St *BRDST* CT10 .... 13 E4 ⑤
   FOLK CT20 .... 13 E4 ⑥
   WSTB CT5 .... 44 A4
Harbour Wy *FOLK* CT20 .... 13 E4
Harcourt Dr *CANTW/ST* CT2 .... 6 A1
   HB CT6 .... 46 A2
Harcourt Rd *FOLKN* CT19 .... 190 A7
Harden Rd *LYDD* TN29 .... 231 J7
Hardinge Rd *KEN/WIL* TN24 .... 8 C2
Hardres Court Rd *RCANTW* CT4 .... 126 E5
Hardres Rd *RAM* CT11 .... 5 E4
Hardres St *RAM* CT11 .... 5 E4
Hardwicke Rd *DVW* CT17 .... 173 F8
Hardwick Rd *FOLK* CT20 .... 12 A5
Hardy Cl *CANTW/ST* CT2 .... 86 A5 ⑥
   KEN/WIL TN24 .... 162 A7
Hardy Rd *NROM* TN28 .... 232 E3
   RDV CT15 .... 154 E6
Harkness Dr *CANTW/ST* CT2 .... 6 A1
Harman Av *HYTHE* CT21 .... 203 H3
Harmers Wy *HDCN* TN27 .... 137 F3
Harmsworth Gdns *BRDST* CT10 .... 55 H1 ①
Harnet St *SWCH* CT13 .... 93 K5
Harold Av *WGOS* CT8 .... 30 D6
Harold Ct *FAV* ME13 .... 62 B8
Harold Rd *BRCH* CT7 .... 29 G6
   DEAL CT14 .... 115 J6
   MARG CT9 .... 3 F5
   SIT ME10 .... 58 C2
Harold's Rd *DVE/WH* CT16 .... 10 C3 ⑤
Harold St *DVE/WH* CT16 .... 10 B3
   QBOR ME11 .... 20 B2
Harps Av *IOS* ME12 .... 15 J8
Harpswood La *HYTHE* CT21 .... 204 E3
Harrier Dr *SIT* ME10 .... 58 B4
Harringe La *RASHE* TN25 .... 202 D1
Harriot Cl *FOLKN* CT19 .... 12 B2
Harrison Rd *RAM* CT11 .... 5 E4
Harris Rd *IOS* ME12 .... 14 D4
Harris's Aly *RCANTE* CT3 .... 90 C7
Harrow Dene *BRDST* CT10 .... 55 F1
Harriets Cnr *WSTB* CT5 .... 65 H2
Harrys Rd *RSIT* ME9 .... 59 K3
Harry Wells Rd *HB* CT6 .... 46 A3
Hart Cl *RFOLK* CT18 .... 190 B2
Hart Hl *HDCN* TN27 .... 118 D3
Hartlip Cl *IOS* ME12 .... 14 C7
Hartsdown Rd *MARG* CT9 .... 2 A3 ⑥
Harty Ferry Rd *IOS* ME12 .... 24 A5
Harvest Wy *ASH* TN23 .... 160 B7
Harvey Dr *SIT* ME10 .... 58 B4
Harvey Pl *FOLK* CT20 .... 13 E4 ⑥
Harvey Rd *KEN/WIL* TN24 .... 9 F5
Harvey St *FOLK* CT20 .... 13 E4
Harville Rd *RASHE* TN25 .... 142 C4
Harwich St *WSTB* CT5 .... 44 A6
Harwick Dr *FOLKN* CT19 .... 13 F5
Haslemere Av *FOLKN* CT19 .... 190 D7 ⑥
Haslewood Cl *HDCN* TN27 .... 156 B4 ⑤
Hassall Reach *CANT* CT1 .... 85 K8
Hassell St *RASHE* TN25 .... 144 C5
Hasted Rd *RSIT* ME9 .... 34 A7
Hastings Av *MARG* CT9 .... 5 D4
Hastings Pl *SWCH* CT13 .... 93 K6 ⑤
Hatch La *RCANTW* CT4 .... 104 E1
Hatch Rd *RMAID* ME17 .... 116 C1
Hatch St *FAV* ME13 .... 62 B7
Hatfield Rd *MARG* CT9 .... 2 A3 ⑥
   RAM CT11 .... 5 D4
Havelock Rd *DEAL* CT14 .... 135 J3 ⑤
Havelock St *CANT* CT1 .... 7 D3
Haven Dr *HB* CT6 .... 26 A8
   RFOLK CT18 .... 190 B2
The Haven *HYTHE* CT21 .... 204 A6 ⑤
Haventhorpe *KEN/WIL* TN24 .... 8 C2 ⑤
Hawe Cl *CANTW/ST* CT2 .... 86 E2
Hawe Farm Wy *HB* CT6 .... 47 G4
Hawe La *CANTW/ST* CT2 .... 69 F7
Hawes Av *RAM* CT11 .... 4 B4
Hawkesbury St *DVW* CT17 .... 10 B6 ⑤
Hawkhurst Cl *BRCH* CT7 .... 30 A6 ⑥
Hawkhurst Wy *BRDST* CT10 .... 55 H4
Hawkins Cl *SIT* ME10 .... 35 K8
Hawkins Rd *FOLKN* CT19 .... 189 J8
Hawksdown *DEAL* CT14 .... 135 H6
Hawksdown Rd *DEAL* CT14 .... 135 J6
Hawkshill Rd *DEAL* CT14 .... 135 K6

Hawk's La *CANT* CT1 .... 6 C3 ⑩
Hawks Wy *ASH* TN23 .... 160 C7
Hawley Sq *MARG* CT9 .... 2 C3 ⑦
   MARG CT9 .... 3 D3 ⑤
Hawley St *MARG* CT9 .... 2 C5
Hawthorn *RASHW* TN26 .... 211 F6
Hawthorn Av *CANTW/ST* CT2 .... 7 D1
   IOS ME12 .... 14 B6
Hawthorn Cl *DVW* CT17 .... 172 C4
   HYTHE CT21 .... 204 C6 ⑥
   LYDD TN29 .... 227 G3
   RAM CT11 .... 5 E2 ⑥
Hawthorn Cnr *HB* CT6 .... 48 B3
Hawthorne Cl *RDV* CT15 .... 132 B7 ⑤
Hawthorn Rd *ASH* TN23 .... 182 A2
   SIT ME10 .... 57 K2
The Hawthorns *BRDST* CT10 .... 54 D2
Hay Hl *SWCH* CT13 .... 113 H4
Hay La *DEAL* CT14 .... 113 J4
Haymakers La *ASH* TN23 .... 160 B6
Haysel *SIT* ME10 .... 58 B4
Hayton Rd *RASHE* TN25 .... 186 D5
Hayward Cl *DEAL* CT14 .... 135 G2
   KEN/WIL TN24 .... 162 A6
Hayward's Cl *NROM* TN28 .... 226 C8 ⑥
Hayward's Hl *FAV* ME13 .... 100 A2
Hazebrouck Rd *FAV* ME13 .... 61 K7
Hazel Cl *RDV* CT15 .... 132 A7
Hazeldown Cl *DVW* CT17 .... 172 C4
Hazel Dr *HB* CT6 .... 47 J1
Hazelwood Meadow *SWCH* CT13 .... 93 K7
Hazlemere Rd *WSTB* CT5 .... 43 H7
Hazling Dane *RDV* CT15 .... 151 H1
Headcorn Dr *CANTW/ST* CT2 .... 86 E2
Headcorn Gdns *MARG* CT9 .... 33 F4
Headcorn Rd *RMAID* ME17 .... 116 B3
Head Hl *FAV* ME13 .... 63 J8
Head Hill Rd *FAV* ME13 .... 63 J6
Heights Ter *DVW* CT17 .... 58 C1
Heart In Hand Rd *HB* CT6 .... 48 A4
Hearts Delight Rd *RSIT* ME9 .... 57 G5
Heath Cl *CANTW/ST* CT2 .... 68 E7
Heather Cl *MARG* CT9 .... 2 A5
   SIT ME10 .... 58 B3
Heather Dr *TENT* TN30 .... 194 B3
Heathfield Av *DVE/WH* CT16 .... 173 F4
Heathfield Rd *KEN/WIL* TN24 .... 8 C2
Heathfield Wy *RCANTW* CT4 .... 129 F6
Heathside *RASHW* TN26 .... 210 E5
Heathwood Dr *RAM* CT11 .... 5 E2 ⑥
Heaton Rd *CANT* CT1 .... 6 B5
Hedgerows *ASH* TN23 .... 160 B7
Heel La *CANTW/ST* CT2 .... 68 B6
Heel Rd *FAV* ME13 .... 99 K7
Heights Ter *DVW* CT17 .... 10 A5
The Heights *WSTB* CT5 .... 44 B3
Helding Cl *HB* CT6 .... 47 G4
Helena Av *MARG* CT9 .... 2 C5
Helena Corniche *FOLK* CT20 .... 206 C3
Helena Rd *RFOLK* CT18 .... 191 K4
Helen Thompson Cl *RSIT* ME9 .... 35 K2
Helmdon Cl *MSTR* CT12 .... 4 C1
Helvellyn Av *RAM* CT11 .... 4 B4
Hempstead La *RSIT* ME9 .... 59 F3
Hempsted St *ASH* TN23 .... 8 B3 ⑤
Hengest Rd *DEAL* CT14 .... 115 K7 ⑪
Hengist Av *MARG* CT9 .... 3 F4
Hengist Rd *BRCH* CT7 .... 29 F7
   WGOS CT8 .... 30 C6
Henley Flds *TENT* TN30 .... 194 B4
Henley Mdw *TENT* TN30 .... 194 A3
Henwood *KEN/WIL* TN24 .... 9 D2
Herbert Rd *KEN/WIL* TN24 .... 161 H8
   RAM CT11 .... 4 C5 ⑤
Herbert Sreet *DVW* CT17 .... 173 F5 ⑤
Hereford Gdns *BRCH* CT7 .... 29 J7
Hereson Rd *RAM* CT11 .... 5 F3
Hereward Av *BRCH* CT7 .... 29 G6
Heritage Cl *WSTB* CT5 .... 43 H8 ②
Heritage Rd *FOLK* CT20 .... 189 J8
Hermitage Cl *HYTHE* CT21 .... 205 F4
Herne Av *HB* CT6 .... 47 F2
Herne Bay Rd *CANTW/ST* CT2 .... 68 D7
   RCANTE CT3 .... 68 D5
   WSTB CT5 .... 45 F3
Herne Dr *HB* CT6 .... 46 B4
Herne St *HB* CT6 .... 47 F5
Herneville Gdns *HB* CT6 .... 47 G2
Heron Cl *RSIT* ME9 .... 34 A3
Heronden Rd *SWCH* CT13 .... 112 E5
Heron Dr *IOS* ME12 .... 21 J1
Heron Forstal Av *RFOLK* CT18 .... 190 C2
Heron's Brook *RASHE* TN25 .... 142 D8
Herons Cl *RCANTW* CT4 .... 103 J6
Heron's Wy *HYTHE* CT21 .... 204 A6
Herschel Rd *BRCH* CT7 .... 29 J6
Herschell Rd East *DEAL* CT14 .... 135 J3 ⑥
Herschell Rd West *DEAL* CT14 .... 135 J3 ⑥
Herschell Sq *DEAL* CT14 .... 135 J3 ⑥
Hertford Rd *MARG* CT9 .... 3 F5
Hertford St *RAM* CT11 .... 5 D5
Hever Pl *CANTW/ST* CT2 .... 86 E3
   SIT ME10 .... 57 H3
Hewitt Rd *DVE/WH* CT16 .... 10 B3

Hewitts Pl *KEN/WIL* TN24 .... 9 F4 ⑤
Hextable Cl *ASH* TN23 .... 160 D8 ②
Heyford Cl *RFOLK* CT18 .... 190 C2 ⑥
Hibernia St *RAM* CT11 .... 5 E5
Hicks Forstal Rd *RCANTE* CT3 .... 68 E2
Higham La *RCANTW* CT4 .... 108 B6
Highbourne Pk *RMAID* ME17 .... 117 J1
Highbury Gdns *MSTR* CT12 .... 4 B1 ⑥
Highbury La *TENT* TN30 .... 194 A7
Highfield Cl *CANTW/ST* CT2 .... 85 K3
   HYTHE CT21 .... 204 E2
   MSTR CT12 .... 54 C3
Highfield Gdns *MARG* CT9 .... 2 A4
Highfield La *KEN/WIL* TN24 .... 162 C8
Highfield Rd *IOS* ME12 .... 15 F8
   KEN/WIL TN24 .... 162 A6
   MSTR CT12 .... 54 C3
Highfields Av *HB* CT6 .... 47 H2
Highfields Vw *HB* CT6 .... 47 H2
Highgate Rd *WSTB* CT5 .... 44 E5
Highland Cl *FOLK* CT20 .... 207 F2
Highland Rd *RCANTW* CT4 .... 104 E5
Highlands Crs *LYDD* TN29 .... 227 H2 ⑥
High Minnis *RCANTW* CT4 .... 146 D7
High Oak Hl *RSIT* ME9 .... 34 D6
Highridge *HYTHE* CT21 .... 206 A3
High Snoad Wd *RASHE* TN25 .... 120 E4
Highsted Rd *RSIT* ME9 .... 58 A7
High St *ASH* TN23 .... 8 C3
   BRDST CT10 .... 55 F1
   CANT CT1 .... 6 C3 ⑥
   CANT CT1 .... 7 D2 ⑥
   CANTW/ST CT2 .... 87 K1
   DEAL CT14 .... 115 K7
   DVE/WH CT16 .... 10 A3
   DVE/WH CT16 .... 172 B1 ⑥
   HB CT6 .... 46 E1
   HDCN TN27 .... 156 A5
   HYTHE CT21 .... 205 G4
   IOS ME12 .... 14 B3
   IOS ME12 .... 16 A8
   IOS ME12 .... 23 G3
   LYDD TN29 .... 216 E7
   LYDD TN29 .... 223 G6
   LYDD TN29 .... 231 G8
   LYDD TN29 .... 237 G1
   MARG CT9 .... 2 C3 ⑥
   MARG CT9 .... 3 D4
   MSTR CT12 .... 52 B8
   MSTR CT12 .... 53 H6
   NROM TN28 .... 226 C8
   QBOR ME11 .... 20 A1
   RAM CT11 .... 5 E4
   RASHE TN25 .... 142 C4
   RCANTE CT3 .... 89 F6
   RCANTE CT3 .... 90 C7
   RCANTW CT4 .... 107 K4
   RCANTW CT4 .... 167 K1
   RDV CT15 .... 155 F8
   RFOLK CT18 .... 167 F8
   RMAID ME17 .... 116 D2
   RSIT ME9 .... 34 A8
   SIT ME10 .... 35 K8
   SIT ME10 .... 58 A2
   SWCH CT13 .... 94 A5
   SWCH CT13 .... 113 F4
   TENT TN30 .... 194 A7
   WSTB CT5 .... 44 A4
Highstreet Rd *FAV* ME13 .... 64 D3
High Street St Lawrence *RAM* CT11 .... 4 B4
The High St *HDCN* TN27 .... 118 E7
High Trees Cl *KEN/WIL* TN24 .... 162 A6 ⑥
High View Av *HB* CT6 .... 46 A1
Highview Cl *KEN/WIL* TN24 .... 83 H3
Highview Rd *IOS* ME12 .... 15 K7
Hilbury Cl *HB* CT6 .... 47 F1
Hilda Av *IOS* ME12 .... 14 C8
Hildersham Cl *BRDST* CT10 .... 33 F8
Hill Av *RDV* CT15 .... 151 G1
Hillborough Dr *HB* CT6 .... 26 A8
Hill Brow *SIT* ME10 .... 57 J4
Hillbrow Av *CANTW/ST* CT2 .... 68 E7
   HB CT6 .... 47 G4
Hillbrow La *ASH* TN23 .... 160 D5
Hillbrow Rd *ASH* TN23 .... 8 A5
   RAM CT11 .... 5 D3
Hill Crs *RCANTE* CT3 .... 130 A1
Hillcrest *ASH* TN23 .... 159 K6
Hillcrest Cl *KEN/WIL* TN24 .... 141 J8
Hillcrest Gdns *DEAL* CT14 .... 135 G4
   RAM CT11 .... 4 B5 ⑥
Hillcrest Rd *DEAL* CT14 .... 155 J2
   HYTHE CT21 .... 205 F3
   RCANTE CT3 .... 88 E6 ⑥
Hillcroft Rd *HB* CT6 .... 47 G3
Hill Dr *SWCH* CT13 .... 113 F5
Hiller Cl *BRDST* CT10 .... 33 H8
Hill House Dr *MSTR* CT12 .... 52 B7
Hill La *RFOLK* CT18 .... 189 G5
Hillman Av *HB* CT6 .... 45 K2
Hill Pk *KEN/WIL* TN24 .... 162 C7
Hill Rd *FOLKN* CT19 .... 13 E1
Hillside Av *CANTW/ST* CT2 .... 86 A5
   QBOR ME11 .... 20 A3
Hillside Rd *DVW* CT17 .... 172 E4

FAV ME13 .... 99 F7
IOS ME12 .... 15 J7
WSTB CT5 .... 44 D5
Hillside St HYTHE CT21 .... 205 F4
The Hill HDCN TN27 .... 118 E6
RCANTE CT3 .... 88 C6
Hilltop Rd IOS ME12 .... 21 H1
Hill Vw KEN/WIL TN24 .... 8 C2
Hillview Rd CANTW/ST CT2 .... 86 A4
WSTB CT5 .... 44 A6
Hillyfield Rd ASH TN23 .... 8 A5
Hillyfields Ri ASH TN23 .... 160 D5
Hilton Dr SIT ME10 .... 35 G8
Hilton Rd ASH TN23 .... 160 D4
Hinchliffe Wy MARG CT9 .... 32 E6
Hind Cl LYDD TN29 .... 216 E6
Hinde Cl SIT ME10 .... 36 A7
Hinxhill Rd KEN/WIL TN24 .... 162 C6
Hirst Cl DVE/WH CT16 .... 173 F2
Hither Fld RCANTW TN27 .... 118 D7
Hoades Wood Rd CANTW/ST CT2 .. 69 F7
Hoads Wood Gdns KEN/WIL TN24 .. 140 C8
Hoath Rd RCANTE CT3 .... 69 G7
Hobart Crs DVE/WH CT16 .... 173 F3
Hobart Gdns SIT ME10 .... 57 H2
Hobart Rd MSTR CT12 .... 4 A2
Hobbs La RYE TN31 .... 218 C8
Hockeredge Gdns WGOS CT8 .... 30 E6
Hodge's Gap MARG CT9 .... 32 D3
Hodgson Rd WSTB CT5 .... 43 F7
Hogarth Cl HB CT6 .... 47 K1
Hogben Cl RFOLK CT18 .... 167 F7
Holbrook Hill La RDV CT15 .... 171 F7
Hogg La RCANTW CT4 .... 126 C4
Hog Gn RCANTW CT4 .... 167 K2
Holbeam Rd FAV ME13 .... 99 J5
Holbourn Cl HB CT6 .... 47 G6
Holbrook Dr MSTR CT12 .... 4 B2
Holdenhurst ASH TN23 .... 160 C8
Holland Cl BRDST CT10 .... 33 H4
IOS ME12 .... 14 C5
Hollands Av FOLKN CT19 .... 13 F2
Hollicondane Rd RAM CT11 .... 5 D3
Hollington Pl KEN/WIL TN24 .... 8 C3
Hollow La CANT CT1 .... 6 B5
Hollowmede CANT CT1 .... 6 B5
Hollow Rd RCANTE CT3 .... 48 B8
Hollow St RCANTE CT3 .... 70 D2
Hollow Wood Rd DVW CT17 .... 172 C6
RDV CT15 .... 172 C6
Hollybush La RCANTE CT3 .... 89 H1
Holly Cl BRDST CT10 .... 54 D5
FOLKN CT19 .... 13 E2
SWCH CT13 .... 113 G4
Holly Gdns MARG CT9 .... 32 D4
Holly Hill Rd FAV ME13 .... 83 K1
Holly La MARG CT9 .... 32 D4
Holly Rd LYDD TN29 .... 227 G2
RAM CT11 .... 5 E3
Holme Oak Cl CANT CT1 .... 6 C5
Holmestone Rd RDV CT15 .... 172 C5
Holmlea Cl KEN/WIL TN24 .... 9 F4
Holm Oak Gdns BRDST CT10 .... 55 C2
Holmscroft Rd HB CT6 .... 47 J1
Holmside Av IOS ME12 .... 14 E8
Holmwood Rd ASH TN23 .... 160 C7
Holness Rd RCANTE CT3 .... 92 B4
Holton Cl BRCH CT7 .... 29 K8
Holt St RDV CT15 .... 130 E2
Holyrood Dr IOS ME12 .... 21 H1
Holywell Av FOLKN CT19 .... 12 C1
Homefield Av DEAL CT14 .... 115 H8
Homeleigh Rd MSTR CT12 .... 54 C3
Homestall La FAV ME13 .... 82 B1
Homestead ASH TN23 .... 160 B6
Homestead Cl MARG CT9 .... 3 D4
Homestead Ct DEAL CT14 .... 135 G2
Homestead La RDV CT15 .... 133 G7
Homestead Vw RSIT ME9 .... 57 G4
Homeview SIT ME10 .... 58 C2
Homewood Av SIT ME10 .... 57 J3
Homewood Rd CANTW/ST CT2 .... 69 H5
TENT TN30 .... 194 B5
Honeyball Wk RSIT ME9 .... 59 K4
Honey Hl CANTW/ST CT2 .... 66 C6
Honeysuckle Cl MARG CT9 .... 2 A5
Honeysuckle Rd RAM CT11 .... 5 F3
Honeysuckle Wy HB CT6 .... 47 J4
Honeywood Cl CANT CT1 .... 7 E1
HYTHE CT21 .... 203 H2
Honeywood Pkwy RDV CT15 .... 173 F1
Honeywood Rd DVE/WH CT16 .... 152 E9
RDV CT15 .... 173 F1
Honfleur Rd SWCH CT13 .... 93 K6
Honywood Rd RMAID ME17 .... 116 C1
Hook Cl FOLK CT20 .... 207 F1
Hook La HDCN TN27 .... 118 C7
LYDD TN29 .... 222 E8
Hook St RMAID ME17 .... 117 F6
Hook Wall LYDD TN29 .... 229 D1
Hoopers La HB CT6 .... 47 J5
Hope La NROM TN28 .... 226 A5
Hope Rd DEAL CT14 .... 135 K1
Hopes Gv RASHW TN26 .... 177 J7
Hope's La MSTR CT12 .... 54 D3
Hope St IOS ME12 .... 14 C4
Hopeville Av BRDST CT10 .... 32 E8
Hoppers Wy ASH TN23 .... 160 B6
Hopsons Pl IOS ME12 .... 21 K1
Hornash La RASHW TN26 .... 180 E6
Hornbeam Cl ASH TN23 .... 160 D3
Hornbrook La TENT TN30 .... 196 E7
Horn Hl RSIT ME9 .... 76 E4
Horn St HYTHE CT21 .... 206 B3
Horsa Rd BRCH CT7 .... 29 G7
DEAL CT14 .... 115 H8
Horsebridge Rd WSTB CT5 .... 43 K4
Horselees Rd FAV ME13 .... 85 G6
The Horshams HB CT6 .... 47 J1
Horsley Cl RFOLK CT18 .... 190 B3
Hoser Gdns BRCH CT7 .... 29 K7
Hospital Hl HYTHE CT21 .... 206 C3
Hospital La CANT CT1 .... 6 C3
Hotel Rd RDV CT15 .... 155 H8
Hougham Court La RDV CT15 ..... 192 D3
House Fld KEN/WIL TN24 .... 9 F4
Housefield Rd FAV ME13 .... 99 K8
Hovenden Cl CANTW/ST CT2 .... 86 E2
Howard Av SIT ME10 .... 35 J8
Howard Cl IOS ME12 .... 15 K7
Howard Rd BRDST CT10 .... 55 H3
Howfield La RCANTW CT4 .... 105 G1
Hoxton Cl ASH TN23 .... 160 B6
The Hoystings Cl CANT CT1 .... 7 D4
Hubbards Hl RMAID ME17 .... 117 H1
Hubert Wy BRDST CT10 .... 33 F8
Hudson Cl CANTW/ST CT2 .... 68 E8
DVE/WH CT16 .... 175 F5
Hudson Rd CANT CT1 .... 7 E1
Hugh Price Cl SIT ME10 .... 58 D1
Hugin Av BRDST CT10 .... 33 F7
Hull Rd LYDD TN29 .... 233 F8
Humber Av HB CT6 .... 45 J2
Hundreds Cl WGOS CT8 .... 30 C7
Hunger Hatch La HDCN TN27 ..... 138 B2
Hunt Cl RFOLK CT18 .... 190 B2
Hunter Av KEN/WIL TN24 .... 9 E5
Hunter Cl KEN/WIL TN24 .... 9 E5
Hunter Rd KEN/WIL TN24 .... 9 E5
Hunters Bank RCANTW CT4 .... 167 K2
Hunters Cha HB CT6 .... 47 H4
WSTB CT5 .... 44 B7
Hunters Forstal Rd HB CT6 .... 47 G4
Hunters Wy FAV ME13 .... 101 G1
Hunting Ga BRCH CT7 .... 29 J6
Hunting Rd BRCH CT7 .... 29 J6
Hunton Gdns CANTW/ST CT2 ...... 86 E2
Hurstford La RASHW TN26 .... 138 D4
Hurst Gv MSTR CT12 .... 4 C2
Hurst La HDCN TN27 .... 118 A8
RFOLK CT18 .... 191 J2
SIT ME10 .... 36 A5
Hurst Rd KEN/WIL TN24 .... 141 G7
Hurstwood Rd FAV ME13 .... 98 A6
Hyde Pl RCANTE CT3 .... 130 B1
The Hyde RCANTW CT4 .... 104 D3
Hythe Cl FOLK CT20 .... 207 F1
Hythe Pl SWCH CT13 .... 94 A6
Hythe Rd HYTHE CT21 .... 204 A2
KEN/WIL TN24 .... 9 E4
KEN/WIL TN24 .... 162 C2
LYDD TN29 .... 216 E6
LYDD TN29 .... 217 G4
RASHE TN25 .... 184 C2
SIT ME10 .... 57 J1

Ian's Wk HYTHE CT21 .... 206 A3
Iden La HDCN TN27 .... 137 H2
Iffin La RCANTW CT4 .... 106 C4
Ilex Rd FOLKN CT19 .... 190 A8
Imbert Cl NROM TN28 .... 226 D8
Imperial Av IOS ME12 .... 16 A7
Imperial Dr IOS ME12 .... 21 D2
Ince Rd CANTW/ST CT2 .... 68 E7
Ingle Cl BRCH CT7 .... 30 A7
Ingleden Cl SIT ME10 .... 36 A6
Ingleden Park Rd TENT TN30 ...... 194 B5
Ingles La FOLK CT20 .... 13 C4
Ingles Rd FOLK CT20 .... 12 C5
Ingoldsby Rd BRCH CT7 .... 29 G7
CANT CT1 .... 6 A5
FOLKN CT19 .... 13 E2
Institute Rd FAV ME13 .... 62 C7
Inverness Ter BRDST CT10 .... 55 H3
Invicta Ct SIT ME10 .... 36 A7
Invicta Rd FOLKN CT19 .... 13 D2
IOS ME12 .... 14 D4
LYDD TN29 .... 237 F4
MARG CT9 .... 3 F2
WSTB CT5 .... 44 B4
Irchester St RAM CT11 .... 5 F4
Iron Bar La CANT CT1 .... 7 D3
Irvine Dr MARG CT9 .... 32 D6
Isis Cl HYTHE CT21 .... 203 J3

Island Rd CANTW/ST CT2 .... 69 F8
RCANTE CT3 .... 69 K6
Island Wall WSTB CT5 .... 43 K5
Ivanhoe Rd HB CT6 .... 47 F2
WGOS CT8 .... 30 D5
Ivory Cl FAV ME13 .... 61 K5
Ivychurch Gdns MARG CT9 .... 33 F4
Ivychurch Rd LYDD TN29 .... 224 A3
Ivy Cl RFOLK CT18 .... 188 B3
Ivy Cottage Hl MSTR CT12 .... 52 D7
Ivy Ct CANTW/ST CT2 .... 67 H8
Ivy House Rd WSTB CT5 .... 44 C5
Ivy La CANT CT1 .... 7 D3
RAM CT11 .... 5 D5
Ivy Pl CANT CT1 .... 6 B4
Ivy Wy FOLKN CT19 .... 13 E2

Jaarlen Rd LYDD TN29 .... 231 G8
Jackson Rd CANT CT1 .... 6 B4
Jacksons La TENT TN30 .... 194 A7
Jacob Cl MARG CT9 .... 2 C6
James Allchin Gdns KEN/WIL TN24 .. 9 F1
James Cl RCANTE CT3 .... 92 B4
RFOLK CT18 .... 167 F7
James Hall Gdns DEAL CT14 ...... 135 J3
James Haney Dr KEN/WIL TN24 .. 161 K1
James St ASH TN23 .... 8 A3
FOLKN CT19 .... 13 D3
IOS ME12 .... 14 E4
RAM CT11 .... 5 D5
Jarman's Fld RASHE TN25 .... 143 F4
Jarvis Dr KEN/WIL TN24 .... 162 A7
Jarvis Pl TENT TN30 .... 194 B3
Jarvist Pl DEAL CT14 .... 135 K8
Jasmine Cl RCANTW CT4 .... 105 F5
Jayne Wk WSTB CT5 .... 43 J8
Jefferson Rd IOS ME12 .... 14 E5
Jefferstone La LYDD TN29 .... 227 F2
Jefferstone La LYDD TN29 .... 226 D3
Jellicoe Cl KEN/WIL TN24 .... 162 A7
Jemmett La RASHE TN25 .... 183 J2
Jemmett Rd ASH TN23 .... 8 A5
Jenner's Wy LYDD TN29 .... 227 F3
Jennifer Gdns MARG CT9 .... 32 D6
Jersey Cl KEN/WIL TN24 .... 141 G6
Jersey La RCANTW CT4 .... 106 A8
Jesmond St FOLKN CT19 .... 13 D3
Jesse's Hl RCANTW CT4 .... 128 A5
Jessica Ms SIT ME10 .... 35 K7
Jesuit Cl CANTW/ST CT2 .... 86 E2
Jetty Rd IOS ME12 .... 24 D2
Jewry La CANT CT1 .... 6 C3
Johannesburg Rd
   DVE/WH CT16 .... 173 C2
John Hall Cl FAV ME13 .... 62 A4
John Newington Cl
   KEN/WIL TN24 .... 161 K1
John's Gn SWCH CT13 .... 93 J8
Johnson Cl KEN/WIL TN24 .... 162 A7
Johnson Ct FAV ME13 .... 62 A5
Johnson Rd SIT ME10 .... 57 J2
Johnson Wy IOS ME12 .... 15 H7
John St BRDST CT10 .... 55 J2
John Tapping Cl DEAL CT14 .... 135 H5
Jointon Rd FOLK CT20 .... 12 B5
Joss Gap Rd BRDST CT10 .... 33 J5
Joyes Cl DVE/WH CT16 .... 153 F7
   FOLKN CT19 .... 13 E2
Joyes Rd DVE/WH CT16 .... 152 E7
   FOLKN CT19 .... 13 E2
Joy La WSTB CT5 .... 43 H7
Jubilee Cl HYTHE CT21 .... 204 B6
Jubilee Crs QBOR ME11 .... 20 A1
Jubilee Fld TENT TN30 .... 219 K2
Jubilee Rd DEAL CT14 .... 114 B3
   RCANTE CT3 .... 89 F6
   SWCH CT13 .... 93 K6
Jubilee St SIT ME10 .... 57 K1
Jubilee Wy DVE/WH CT16 .... 11 E1
   DVE/WH CT16 .... 11 E3
Judd Rd FAV ME13 .... 61 K7
Julian Rd FOLKN CT19 .... 12 B4
Julie Cl BRDST CT10 .... 33 H8
Julien Pl KEN/WIL TN24 .... 162 A6
Juniper Cl ASH TN23 .... 160 C4
   CANT CT1 .... 7 D5
Jury's Gap Rd LYDD TN29 .... 236 D2

Kake St RCANTW CT4 .... 125 F8
Keat Farm Cl HB CT6 .... 48 A1
Keddow's Cl HYTHE CT21 .... 204 B6
Keeper's Hl RCANTW CT4 .... 108 D4
Keith Av MSTR CT12 .... 4 A3
Kelvedon Rd DEAL CT14 .... 135 J4
Kemp Rd WSTB CT5 .... 45 F4
Kemsdale Rd FAV ME13 .... 64 A8

Kemsing Gdns *CANTW/ST* CT2 .... 87 F2
Kenardington Rd *RASHW* TN26 ...... 210 E4
Kenbrook *KEN/WIL* TN24 .... 141 G7 ⑩
Kendal Cl *RAM* CT11 .... 4 B5
Kendal Ri *BRDST* CT10 .... 55 H1
Kenfield Rd *RCANTW* CT4 .... 105 J8
Kenilworth Cl *RDV* CT15 .... 155 G8
Kenilworth Ct *SIT* ME10 .... 57 H1
Kennedy Cl *FAV* ME13 .... 62 C5
Kennedy Dr *DEAL* CT14 .... 135 H4
Kennel Hl *RDV* CT15 .... 132 C8
Kennelling Rd *FAV* ME13 .... 119 F2
Kennett Dr *DEAL* CT14 .... 135 G4 ⑩
Kennett La *RASHE* TN25 .... 186 D5
Kennington Pl *KEN/WIL* TN24 ..... 141 H7 ⑩
Kennington Rd *KEN/WIL* TN24 ..... 162 A4
Kensington Rd *CANT* CT1 .... 87 G2
Kent Cl *RCANTW* CT1 .... 7 F3
　IOS ME12 .... 15 J8
　KEN/WIL TN24 .... 8 B2
　SIT ME10 .... 57 J3
Kent Gdns *BRCH* CT7 .... 29 J7
Kentmere Av *RAM* CT11 .... 54 A7
Kenton Gdns *MSTR* CT12 .... 52 A8
Kent Rd *FOLKN* CT19 .... 189 K7
　IOS ME12 .... 14 C5
　MARG CT9 .... 3 F5 ⑩
Kent St *WSTB* CT5 .... 44 A6
Kent Ter *RAM* CT11 .... 5 F5 ⑩
Kent View Dr *IOS* ME12 .... 23 G5
Kerton Rd *LYDD* TN29 .... 239 F4
Kestrel Cl *SIT* ME10 .... 58 B4
Keswick Rd *SIT* ME10 .... 58 D3
Kettle Dr *RFOLK* CT18 .... 190 C1
Kettle Hl *FAV* ME13 .... 99 H2
Kettle Hill Rd *FAV* ME13 .... 99 G1
Kevin Dr *RAM* CT11 .... 4 A5
Keycol Hl *RSIT* ME9 .... 56 D1
Keyes Pl *FOLKN* CT19 .... 13 E2
Key St *SIT* ME10 .... 57 F1
Khartoum Sq *DVE/WH* CT16 ..... 172 E1
Kiln Cl *RASHE* TN25 .... 121 F5
　SIT ME10 .... 58 B3
Kilndown Cl *ASH* TN23 .... 160 C6
Kilndown Gdns *CANTW/ST* CT2 ..... 86 E2
　MARG CT9 .... 33 F4
Kiln Fld *TENT* TN30 .... 194 C7
Kiln La *RASHW* TN26 .... 179 G2
Kiln Rd *RASHE* TN25 .... 201 F2 ⑩
Kimberley Cl *DVE/WH* CT16 ..... 173 G3
Kimberley Gv *WSTB* CT5 .... 43 G8
Kimberley Rd *MSTR* CT12 .... 4 A2
King Arthur Rd *MSTR* CT12 .... 53 J7
King Edward Av *BRDST* CT10 ..... 55 H1
　HB CT6 .... 47 G2
King Edward Rd *BRCH* CT7 .... 51 K1
　DEAL CT14 .... 115 K6
　RAM CT11 .... 4 C5 ⑩
King Edward St *WSTB* CT5 .... 44 A5
Kingfisher Av *HYTHE* CT21 .... 204 B6
Kingfisher Cl *KEN/WIL* TN24 ..... 162 A1
　MARG CT9 .... 31 G6 ⑩
　RSIT ME9 .... 35 K2
　WSTB CT5 .... 43 K7
Kingfisher Ct *HB* CT6 .... 46 C3
King's Av *ASH* TN23 .... 8 A3
　BRCH CT7 .... 29 G6
　BRDST CT10 .... 55 J1
　MSTR CT12 .... 4 B2
　SWCH CT13 .... 95 F7
　WSTB CT5 .... 44 B5
King's Cl *DEAL* CT14 .... 155 J1
Kingsdown Hl *DEAL* CT14 .... 155 J2
Kingsdown Pk *WSTB* CT5 .... 44 C4
Kingsdown Rd *DEAL* CT14 .... 135 K4
　RSIT ME9 .... 77 J3
Kingsferry Br *RSIT* ME9 .... 20 B7
Kingsfield Rd *HB* CT6 .... 47 G4
Kingsford St *KEN/WIL* TN24 ..... 162 D8
　RASHE TN25 .... 183 K2
Kingsgate Av *BRDST* CT10 .... 33 G5
Kingsgate Bay Rd *BRDST* CT10 ..... 33 H4
Kingsgate Cl *TENT* TN30 .... 219 H1
King's Head Aly *IOS* ME12 .... 14 B4 ⑩
Kingsland Gdns *DEAL* CT14 ..... 135 H6 ⑩
Kingsland Hollow *LYDD* TN29 ..... 227 H2 ⑩
Kingsland La *HDCN* TN27 .... 136 E5
　RASHE TN25 .... 140 D7
Kingsley Rd *WSTB* CT5 .... 44 B6 ⑩
Kingsmarsh La *LYDD* TN29 .... 231 H2
Kings Meadow *KEN/WIL* TN24 ... 141 J7 ⑩
Kingsmead *CANTW/ST* CT2 .... 7 D1
Kings Mill Cl *SIT* ME10 .... 57 K1 ⑩
Kingsnorth Gdns *FOLK* CT20 ..... 12 B4 ⑩
Kingsnorth Rd *ASH* TN23 .... 160 E8
　FAV ME13 .... 62 B8
King's Pk *CANT* CT1 .... 7 E2
King's Rd *BRCH* CT7 .... 29 K8
　DVV CT17 .... 172 E5
　FAV ME13 .... 62 B7
　FOLK CT20 .... 189 J8
　HB CT6 .... 46 D2
　IOS ME12 .... 16 A7

RAM CT11 .... 5 D3
RCANTE CT3 .... 130 B1
Kingston Av *MARG* CT9 .... 31 G7
Kingston Cl *DVV* CT17 .... 172 D5
　HB CT6 .... 47 K1
　MSTR CT12 .... 4 B2
King St *CANT* CT1 .... 6 C2 ⑩
　CANTW/ST CT2 .... 87 K2
　DEAL CT14 .... 115 K8
　DVE/WH CT16 .... 10 B4
　IOS ME12 .... 14 B4 ⑩
　LYDD TN29 .... 223 K3
　MARG CT9 .... 2 C2 ⑩
　RAM CT11 .... 5 E4
　SIT ME10 .... 57 K1
　SWCH CT13 .... 94 A5
Kingsway *LYDD* TN29 .... 217 G4
Kingswood *KEN/WIL* TN24 ..... 161 H1 ⑩
Kipling Rd *ASH* TN23 .... 8 B3
Kipping Cl *RFOLK* CT18 .... 190 B2
Kirby's La *CANTW/ST* CT2 .... 6 C2
Kirkstone Av *RAM* CT11 .... 54 A7
Kirkwood Av *RASHW* TN26 ..... 196 C5 ⑩
Kitchener Cl *RCANTW* CT4 .... 128 E6
Kitchener Dr *DVV* CT17 .... 172 A7
Kitchener Sq *FOLKN* CT19 .... 13 E1 ⑩
Kite Farm *WSTB* CT5 .... 45 G3
Kitewell La *LYDD* TN29 .... 231 J6
Kither Rd *ASH* TN23 .... 8 A6
Kit Hl *FAV* ME13 .... 82 D6
Kitsbridge La *RASHW* TN26 ..... 213 K1
Knatchbull Wy *RASHE* TN25 ..... 185 F1
Knight Av *CANTW/ST* CT2 .... 86 E3
Knightrider St *SWCH* CT13 .... 94 A6
Knight's Av *BRDST* CT10 .... 33 J8
Knightsfield Rd *SIT* ME10 .... 35 J8
Knight's Rd *DVE/WH* CT16 .... 10 C3
Knights Templars *DVV* CT17 ..... 10 A5
Knights Wy *DVE/WH* CT16 ..... 172 E3
Knock Hl *TENT* TN30 .... 221 H4
Knockholt Rd *MARG* CT9 .... 33 F3
Knock Rd *ASH* TN23 .... 8 A6
Knockwood Rd *TENT* TN30 ..... 194 C5
Knold Pk *MARG* CT9 .... 2 C5 ⑩
The Knole *FAV* ME13 .... 62 A7
Knoll Hl *RASHE* TN25 .... 201 J3
Knoll La *ASH* TN23 .... 160 C7
Knoll Pl *DEAL* CT14 .... 135 J5
Knoll Wy *IOS* ME12 .... 24 C2
Knott Crs *KEN/WIL* TN24 .... 162 A7 ⑩
Knott's La *CANT* CT1 .... 6 C2 ⑩
　RDV CT15 .... 155 F8 ⑩
Knowler Wy *HB* CT6 .... 47 H1
Kohima Pl *DVE/WH* CT16 .... 11 D1
Kymbeline Ct *DEAL* CT14 ..... 135 H2 ⑩

L

Laburnum Av *SWCH* CT13 .... 93 K6
Laburnum Cl *DVE/WH* CT16 ..... 172 C2
Laburnum La *CANTW/ST* CT2 ..... 69 G7
Laburnum Pl *SIT* ME10 .... 57 K2 ⑩
Labworth Cl *IOS* ME12 .... 15 F8 ⑩
Lacton Oast *KEN/WIL* TN24 ..... 162 B6
Lacton Wy *KEN/WIL* TN24 ..... 162 A6 ⑩
Lade Fort Crs *LYDD* TN29 ..... 233 F8
Ladyfields *HB* CT6 .... 47 J4
Ladyfields Cl *RSIT* ME9 .... 56 E1
Lady Garne Rd *RDV* CT15 ..... 192 C1
Ladysmith Gv *WSTB* CT5 .... 43 G8
Ladysmith Rd *WSTB* CT5 .... 65 J1
Ladywell *DVE/WH* CT16 .... 10 B3
Ladywood Rd *CANTW/ST* CT2 ..... 68 E7
Lagos Av *MSTR* CT12 .... 4 A2
Lakemead *ASH* TN23 .... 160 C6
Laking Av *BRDST* CT10 .... 33 H7
Laleham Gdns *MARG* CT9 .... 3 F3
Laleham Rd *MARG* CT9 .... 3 F4
Lambeth Rd *CANT* CT1 .... 87 G2 ⑩
Lamberhurst Wy *MARG* CT9 ..... 33 G3 ⑩
Lamb's Wk *WSTB* CT5 .... 43 K8
Lambton Rd *DVV* CT17 .... 172 E5
Laming Rd *BRCH* CT7 .... 30 A8
Lammas Dr *SIT* ME10 .... 35 K8
Lammas Ga *FAV* ME13 .... 62 C6 ⑩
Lancaster Av *RFOLK* CT18 ..... 191 J4
Lancaster Cl *MSTR* CT12 .... 4 B2 ⑩
　RASHW TN26 .... 198 E6
Lancaster Gdns *BRCH* CT7 .... 29 J8
　HB CT6 .... 47 J1
Lancaster Rd *CANT* CT1 .... 6 C4
　DVV CT17 .... 10 A1
Lance Cl *SIT* ME10 .... 36 A6 ⑩
Lanchester Cl *HB* CT6 .... 45 K3
Landbury Wk *ASH* TN23 .... 160 D2
Landon Rd *HB* CT6 .... 47 H1
Landrail Rd *SIT* ME9 .... 34 A3
Lane End *HB* CT6 .... 46 C1
The Lanes *MSTR* CT12 .... 52 C8
The Lane *RDV* CT15 .... 153 K8

Lanfranc Gdns *CANTW/ST* CT2 ..... 86 A5
Lanfranc Rd *DEAL* CT14 .... 115 J6
Lang Ct *WSTB* CT5 .... 45 F3
Langdale *ASH* TN23 .... 160 C6
Langdale Av *RAM* CT11 .... 4 A4
Langdon Av *RCANTE* CT3 .... 92 C5
Langdon Cl *RDV* CT15 .... 175 F1
Langdon Rd *FOLKN* CT19 ..... 189 J7
Langham Cl *MARG* CT9 .... 31 G5
Langington Rd *ASH* TN23 .... 8 A6 ⑩
Langhorne Gdns *FOLK* CT20 ..... 12 C5 ⑩
Langley Gdns *MARG* CT9 .... 33 F3 ⑩
Langley Rd *SIT* ME10 .... 36 A8
Langney Dr *ASH* TN23 .... 160 C8
Langport Rd *NROM* TN28 ..... 226 D8
Langton La *CANT* CT1 .... 106 E2
Lansdown Rd *CANT* CT1 .... 7 D4
　SIT ME10 .... 58 D2
Lanthorne Rd *BRDST* CT10 .... 33 H7
Lapwing Cl *IOS* ME12 .... 21 K1
Lapwing Dr *RSIT* ME9 .... 34 A3
Larch Cl *BRDST* CT10 .... 54 E2 ⑩
The Larches *FAV* ME13 .... 61 K6
　WSTB CT5 .... 43 K6 ⑩
Larch Rd *RDV* CT15 .... 131 K5
Larch Wk *KEN/WIL* TN24 .... 141 G8
Larkey Vw *RCANTW* CT4 .... 105 G5 ⑩
Larkfield Av *SIT* ME10 .... 35 K8
Larkfield Rd *FAV* ME13 .... 62 B5
Lascelles Rd *DVV* CT17 .... 172 E8
La-tene *DEAL* CT14 .... 135 H4
Latimer Cl *HB* CT6 .... 46 A4
Laundry Rd *MSTR* CT12 .... 52 C7
Laureate Cl *MARG* CT9 .... 3 F3 ⑩
Laurel Av *LYDD* TN29 .... 227 G3
Laurel Cl *FOLK* CT20 .... 189 K8
Laurel Wy *RCANTW* CT4 .... 105 C5
Laureston Pl *DVE/WH* CT16 ..... 10 C3
Lauriston Cl *RAM* CT11 .... 4 A6
Lauriston Mt *BRDST* CT10 .... 55 H1
Lausanne Rd *MARG* CT9 ..... 3 D3 ⑩⑩
Lavender Cl *MARG* CT9 .... 2 A5
Lavender Ct *SIT* ME10 .... 58 B3
Lawley Cl *MSTR* CT12 .... 4 C2 ⑩
Lawn Rd *BRDST* CT10 .... 55 H2
　DEAL CT14 .... 135 J5
Lawrence Cl *FOLKN* CT19 ..... 190 A3 ⑩
Lawrence Ct *FOLKN* CT19 .... 13 E3
Lawrence Gdns *HB* CT6 .... 47 H2
Laws La *RASHE* TN25 .... 183 H7
Laxton Wy *CANT* CT1 .... 7 F4
　FAV ME13 .... 81 J8
　SIT ME10 .... 35 J8
　WSTB CT5 .... 45 F5
Laylam Cl *BRDST* CT10 .... 54 E1
Lea Cl *HYTHE* CT21 .... 205 F2
Leacon Rd *ASH* TN23 .... 160 C5
Leafield *RASHE* TN25 .... 186 A5
Learoyd Rd *NROM* TN28 ..... 232 C1
Leas Gn *BRDST* CT10 .... 54 E2
Leas Rd *DEAL* CT14 .... 135 H1
The Leas *DEAL* CT14 .... 155 K3
　FAV ME13 .... 62 A6
　FOLK CT20 .... 12 C5
　IOS ME12 .... 15 J5
　WSTB CT5 .... 45 F5
Leatt Cl *BRDST* CT10 .... 55 G2
Leaveland Cl *ASH* TN23 .... 160 D8
The Lees *RASHE* TN25 .... 184 E1
Lees Court Rd *FAV* ME13 .... 81 G8
Lees Rd *KEN/WIL* TN24 ..... 162 A5
　RASHE TN25 .... 164 A7
The Lees *HB* CT6 .... 47 H1
Leicester Av *MARG* CT9 .... 32 D4
Leicester Gdns *IOS* ME12 ..... 24 C3
Leigh Rd *IOS* ME12 .... 21 G1
Leighton Rd *DVE/WH* CT16 ..... 10 A2 ⑩
Leighville Dr *HB* CT6 .... 46 C2
Leivers Rd *DEAL* CT14 .... 135 G3
Lenacre Av *DVE/WH* CT16 ..... 152 D7
Lenacre La *DVE/WH* CT16 ..... 152 D6
Lenacre St *RASHE* TN25 .... 140 E4
The Length *BRCH* CT7 .... 50 C4
Lenham Cl *BRDST* CT10 .... 55 H4 ⑩
Lenham Gdns *MARG* CT9 .... 31 G6 ⑩
Lenham Forstal Rd *RMAID* ME17 .. 117 G5
Lenham Heath Rd *RMAID* ME17 .. 116 B3
Lennard Rd *FOLK* CT20 .... 13 E4
Leonard Rd *LYDD* TN29 ..... 233 F7
Leonard's Av *RAM* CT11 .... 5 E3
Leopold Rd *RAM* CT11 .... 5 E3
Leopold St *RAM* CT11 .... 5 E5 ⑩
Le Roux Cl *RFOLK* CT18 ..... 190 A2
Lerryn Gdns *BRDST* CT10 .... 33 G6
Lesley Av *CANT* CT1 .... 7 D5
Leslie Av *MARG* CT9 .... 31 G7
Leslie Crs *TENT* TN30 .... 194 B4
Leslie Rd *BRCH* CT7 .... 29 K6 ⑩
Leslie Smith Dr *FAV* ME13 .... 62 B7
Lewd La *HDCN* TN27 .... 156 A2
Lewis Cl *FAV* ME13 .... 61 K7
Lewis Crs *MARG* CT9 .... 3 F2
Lewisham Rd *DVV* CT17 .... 172 C3
Lewson Street Rd *RSIT* ME9 .... 60 B6

Leybourne Dr *MARG* CT9 .... 31 G6
Leybourn Rd *BRDST* CT10 .... 55 J4
Leyburne Rd *DVE/WH* CT16 .... 10 B2
Leycroft Cl *CANTW/ST* CT2 .... 86 C3
Leysdown Rd *IOS* ME12 .... 23 H3
Lichfield Av *CANT* CT1 .... 7 E5
Liege Cl *SIT* ME10 .... 36 A5
Lighthouse Rd *RDV* CT15 .... 175 F2
Lillian Rd *RAM* CT11 .... 5 F3 🔲
Lime Cl *ASH* TN23 .... 160 D3
Lime Gv *IOS* ME12 .... 20 E1 🔲
    SIT ME10 .... 58 B2
Lime Kiln Rd *CANT* CT1 .... 6 C4
Limekiln Rbt *DVW* CT17 .... 10 B5
Limes Cl *TENT* TN30 .... 194 C7
    FOLKN CT19 .... 190 A8
The Limes *ASH* TN23 .... 181 K1
The Limes *DVE/WH* CT16 .... 173 F2
Lincoln Av *CANT* CT1 .... 7 E4 🔲
Lincoln Gdns *BRCH* CT7 .... 29 J7
Linden Av *BRDST* CT10 .... 55 J1
    HB CT6 .... 46 D2
    WSTB CT5 .... 44 C6
Linden Cha *CANTW/ST* CT2 .... 6 B2 🔲
Linden Cl *SIT* ME10 .... 57 J3
    WGOS CT8 .... 30 D7
Linden Crs *FOLKN* CT19 .... 13 D3
Linden Dr *IOS* ME12 .... 14 A7
Linden Gv *CANTW/ST* CT2 .... 6 C2 🔲
Linden Rd *KEN/WIL* TN24 .... 9 D3
    RCANTW CT4 .... 105 C5
    WGOS CT8 .... 30 E6
Lindenthorpe Rd *BRDST* CT10 ...... 33 G8
Lindridge Cl *HB* CT6 .... 47 F6
Linington Rd *BRCH* CT7 .... 29 K7
Link Hill La *HDCN* TN27 .... 136 C4
Link La *CANT* CT1 .... 7 D3 🔲
Link Rd *CANTW/ST* CT2 .... 67 G8
Links Crs *LYDD* TN29 .... 227 H2
Linksfield Rd *WGOS* CT8 .... 30 C6
Links Rd *DEAL* CT14 .... 115 J6 🔲
Linksway *FOLKN* CT19 .... 12 A2
    RYE TN31 .... 234 B4
Linksway Cl *FOLKN* CT19 .... 12 B1 🔲
Linkway *RSIT* ME9 .... 35 J2
Linley Rd *BRDST* CT10 .... 33 F7
Linnet Av *WSTB* CT5 .... 43 J8
Lion Fld *FAV* ME13 .... 61 K7
Lion's Rd *NROM* TN28 .... 226 B8
Lion Yd *FAV* ME13 .... 61 K8 🔲
Lismore Rd *HB* CT6 .... 47 J1
    WSTB CT5 .... 44 E6
Liss Rd *SWCH* CT13 .... 112 E5
Lister Cl *DEAL* CT14 .... 135 J1
    DVW CT17 .... 173 F5 🔲
Lister Rd *MARG* CT9 .... 3 E5
Lister Wy *FOLK* CT20 .... 207 F3 🔲
The List *RCANTE* CT3 .... 89 J4
Little Av *DEAL* CT14 .... 135 F3
Littlebourne Rd *RCANTE* CT3 .... 87 J6
Littlebrook Cl *ASH* TN23 .... 8 A2
Little Brook Rd *ASH* TN23 .... 8 A2 🔲
Little Chequers *RASHE* TN25 ..... 142 E4
Little Glovers *SIT* ME10 .... 58 A3
Little Meadow *CANTW/ST* CT2 ..... 85 C5
Little Paddocks *WSTB* CT5 .... 45 C7
Little Robhurst *RASHW* TN26 ..... 177 J7
Littlestone Rd *NROM* TN28 .... 226 E8
Little Walton *SWCH* CT13 .... 113 C3
Liverpool Lawn *RAM* CT11 .... 5 E5 🔲
Liverpool Rd *DEAL* CT14 .... 135 J5
Livingstone Cl *LYDD* TN29 .... 217 K2 🔲
Livingstone Rd *BRDST* CT10 .... 33 F8
Lloyds Gn *TENT* TN30 .... 219 J2
Lockholt Cl *ASH* TN23 .... 160 C3
Loder Cl *RMAID* ME17 .... 116 B1
Lodge Wood Dr *ASH* TN23 .... 160 C1
Lomas Rd *SIT* ME10 .... 58 E2
Lombard St *FAV* ME13 .... 2 C5 🔲
London Rd *CANTW/ST* CT2 .... 6 A2
    DEAL CT14 .... 135 H1
    DVE/WH CT16 .... 172 C2
    DVW CT17 .... 173 F4
    FAV ME13 .... 61 K8
    HYTHE CT21 .... 204 D3
    RAM CT11 .... 4 B5
    RDV CT15 .... 151 K8
    RSIT ME9 .... 34 A8
    SIT ME10 .... 57 H1
London Road Temple Ewell
    DVE/WH CT16 .... 172 A1
London St *FOLK* CT20 .... 13 E4 🔲
Lone Barn Rd *RMAID* ME17 .... 97 H6
Lonefield *RASHW* TN26 .... 180 E5
Longacre *WSTB* CT5 .... 45 C5
Long Acre La *CANTW/ST* CT2 .... 6 B1
Longacre Rd *ASH* TN23 .... 160 B7
Longage Hl *RCANTW* CT4 .... 166 E4
The Long Barrow *KEN/WIL* TN24 .. 108 D1
Long Beech *ASH* TN23 .... 160 C5
Longbridge *KEN/WIL* TN24 .... 162 B5 🔲
Long Dr *SWCH* CT13 .... 113 G4
Longfield *TENT* TN30 .... 194 A7

Longfield Cl *WSTB* CT5 .... 45 G4
Longfield Rd *DVW* CT17 .... 173 F8
Longford Ter *FOLK* CT20 .... 13 D5 🔲
Longford Wy *FOLK* CT20 .... 13 D5 🔲
Long Hl *RCANTW* CT4 .... 103 J4
Long La *RDV* CT15 .... 130 E7
Long Length *ASH* TN23 .... 181 G3
Long Market *CANT* CT1 .... 7 D3 🔲
Longmead Cl *HB* CT6 .... 46 B3
Long Meadow Wy *CANTW/ST* CT2 . 86 D2
Longmete Rd *RCANTE* CT3 .... 90 E1
Longmore Dr *IOS* ME12 .... 23 F5
Longport *CANT* CT1 .... 7 D3 🔲🔲
Long Reach Cl *WSTB* CT5 .... 43 K8
Longridge *SIT* ME10 .... 58 C4
Long Rock *WSTB* CT5 .... 45 F5
Longsfield *RASHE* TN25 .... 184 D8
Longtye Dr *WSTB* CT5 .... 45 F7
Long Wk *ASH* TN23 .... 160 C2
Lonsdale Av *MARG* CT9 .... 32 D3
Lonsdale Dr *SIT* ME10 .... 57 H1
Lookers La *HYTHE* CT21 .... 205 F3
Loop Court Ms *SWCH* CT13 .... 93 K5 🔲
Loop St *SWCH* CT13 .... 93 K5
Loose Down Rd *FAV* ME13 .... 100 C7
Lords Cl *RSIT* ME9 .... 59 F4
Lord Warden Av *DEAL* CT14 ...... 135 K4
Lord Warden Sq *DVW* CT17 .... 10 B6 🔲
Lorina Rd *MSTR* CT12 .... 4 C3
Lorne Rd *DVE/WH* CT16 .... 173 F5
    RAM CT11 .... 4 C5
Loudon Ct *ASH* TN23 .... 160 C3
Loudon Wy *ASH* TN23 .... 160 C3
Lovelace Ct *RASHW* TN26 .... 178 D1
Love La *CANT* CT1 .... 7 D3 🔲🔲
    FAV ME13 .... 62 E6 🔲
    IOS ME12 .... 16 A7
    MARG CT9 .... 2 C2 🔲
    RCANTE CT3 .... 110 A4
Lovell Rd *CANTW/ST* CT2 .... 85 K3
    IOS ME12 .... 21 H1
Lower Blackhouse Hl *HYTHE* CT21.. 205 H4
Lower Bridge St *CANT* CT1 .... 7 D3
Lower Chantry La *CANT* CT1 .... 7 D4
Lower Denmark Rd *ASH* TN23 .... 8 B5 🔲
Lower Ensden Rd *RCANTW* CT4 .. 103 J2
Lower Herne Rd *HB* CT6 .... 46 D6
Lower Lees Rd *RCANTW* CT4 ..... 103 J4
Lower Mill La *DEAL* CT14 .... 135 J1
Lower Northdown Av *MARG* CT9 .... 3 F3 🔲
Lower Rd *DVE/WH* CT16 .... 172 B1
    DVW CT17 .... 172 C2
    FAV ME13 .... 61 K7
    IOS ME12 .... 21 F2
    RASHW TN26 .... 196 D5
    RCANTE CT3 .... 91 J8
    RSIT ME9 .... 59 C3
    TENT TN30 .... 209 J8
Lower Sandgate Rd *FOLK* CT20 ... 13 E5 🔲
Lower Sands *LYDD* TN29 .... 217 G4
Lower Santon La *RCANTE* CT3 ..... 72 A7
Lower St *DEAL* CT14 .... 132 E4
    SWCH CT13 .... 113 F4
Lower Vicarage Rd *KEN/WIL* TN24.. 141 G7
Lower Wall Rd *HYTHE* CT21 .... 203 F7
    RASHE TN25 .... 201 J7
Lowfield Rd *IOS* ME12 .... 15 F8 🔲
Lowslip Hl *RDV* CT15 .... 192 C1
Lowther Rd *DVW* CT17 .... 175 F6
Loxwood Cl *DVE/WH* CT16 .... 153 F7 🔲
Lucerne Dr *WSTB* CT5 .... 43 G8
Lucerne La *RDV* CT15 .... 154 C4
Luckhurst Gdns *MARG* CT9 .... 33 F3 🔲
Luckhurst Rd *DVW* CT17 .... 172 C3
    KEN/WIL TN24 .... 162 A7
Lucknow Cl *RDV* CT15 .... 175 K3
Lucy Av *FOLKN* CT19 .... 12 A2
Lucy's Hl *HYTHE* CT21 .... 205 F4
Luddenham Cl *ASH* TN23 .... 160 D8
Ludgate Rd *RSIT* ME9 .... 78 A2
Lukes Cl *DVW* CT17 .... 172 E5
Luton Av *BRDST* CT10 .... 55 C3
Luton Ct *BRDST* CT10 .... 55 G3 🔲
Luton Rd *FAV* ME13 .... 62 D7
Lybrook Cl *SIT* ME10 .... 57 H2
Lydden Hl *RDV* CT15 .... 151 F6
Lydd Rd *NROM* TN28 .... 226 A8
    RYE TN31 .... 234 B4
Lydd Town Crossing *LYDD* TN29 .. 231 K6
Lydia Rd *DEAL* CT14 .... 135 G4
Lydos Cl *LYDD* TN29 .... 239 F1
Lyell Cl *HYTHE* CT21 .... 204 E5
Lyell Rd *BRCH* CT7 .... 29 J6 🔲
Lyminge Wy *MARG* CT9 .... 32 D5
Lymington Rd *WGOS* CT8 .... 30 C7
Lympne Hl *HYTHE* CT21 .... 203 J4
Lyndhurst Av *MARG* CT9 .... 3 F3 🔲
Lyndhurst Cl *CANTW/ST* CT2 ...... 86 C3
Lyndhurst Gv *SIT* ME10 .... 57 K4
Lyndhurst Rd *BRDST* CT10 .... 33 H8
    DVW CT17 .... 170 D1
    LYDD TN29 .... 216 E6
    RAM CT11 .... 5 F3
Lyndon Wy *RFOLK* CT18 .... 167 G7
Lyngate Ct *MARG* CT9 .... 32 E4 🔲

Lynmouth Dr *IOS* ME12 .... 15 K7
Lynsted Cl *ASH* TN23 .... 160 D8
Lynsted La *RSIT* ME9 .... 59 J7
Lynsted Rd *IOS* ME12 .... 15 F7
Lynton Rd *HYTHE* CT21 .... 205 G5
Lynwood *FOLKN* CT19 .... 12 C3
Lysander Cl *BRDST* CT10 .... 54 D3
    RCANTW CT4 .... 108 E2 🔲
Lysander Wk *RFOLK* CT18 .... 190 B2 🔲
Lytham Aveune *HB* CT6 .... 46 C5 🔲

M

Mabledon Av *KEN/WIL* TN24 .... 9 D4
Mabledon Cl *NROM* TN28 .... 226 C8
Macdonald Pde *WSTB* CT5 .... 43 H7
Macdonald Rd *DVW* CT17 .... 172 E5 🔲
Mace La *ASH* TN23 .... 8 C3
Mackenzie Dr *FOLK* CT20 .... 206 E1
Madeira Rd *MARG* CT9 .... 3 E3
    NROM TN28 .... 227 F8
Magazine Rd *KEN/WIL* TN24 .... 8 B2
Magdala Rd *BRDST* CT10 .... 33 F8
    DVW CT17 .... 173 F5
Magdalen Cl *BRDST* CT10 .... 55 H1
    CANT CT1 .... 7 E4 🔲
Magness Rd *DEAL* CT14 .... 135 G4
Magnolia Av *MARG* CT9 .... 32 E4
Magpie Ct *IOS* ME12 .... 15 H8 🔲
Magpie Hall Rd *RASHW* TN26 ... 181 G4
Magpie La *RCANTW* CT4 .... 167 F3
Maiden La *CANT* CT1 .... 6 A5
Maidstone Rd *ASH* TN23 .... 8 A2
    HDCN TN27 .... 139 G2
    RMAID ME17 .... 116 C1
    RSIT ME9 .... 56 C3
    SIT ME10 .... 35 F8
Maine Cl *DVE/WH* CT16 .... 173 F3
Main Rd *IOS* ME12 .... 14 B3
    QBOR ME11 .... 20 B1
Maison Dieu Pl *DVE/WH* CT16 .... 10 B3 🔲
Maison Dieu Rd *DVE/WH* CT16 ... 10 A2
Maitland Ct *FAV* ME13 .... 62 A5 🔲
Makenade Av *FAV* ME13 .... 81 H1
Malcolm Sargent Rd *ASH* TN23 .. 161 F8
Malham Dr *MARG* CT9 .... 3 E4 🔲
Mallard Ct *SIT* ME10 .... 15 H8 🔲
Mallards *KEN/WIL* TN24 .... 9 D6 🔲
Mallory Cl *MSTR* CT12 .... 4 C1
The Mall *FAV* ME13 .... 62 B8
Malmains Rd *DVW* CT17 .... 172 E7
Malthouse Hl *HYTHE* CT21 .... 205 F4 🔲
Malthouse La *RASHE* TN25 .... 141 J5
    RASHW TN26 .... 198 B6
Malt House La *TENT* TN30 .... 194 A7
Malthouse Rd *CANTW/ST* CT2 ...... 6 C1
The Maltings *RCANTE* CT3 .... 89 F7
Malvern Meadow *DVE/WH* CT16 .. 172 C1
Malvern Pk *HB* CT6 .... 47 J2
Malvern Rd *DVE/WH* CT16 .... 152 E7 🔲
    KEN/WIL TN24 .... 8 B1
Manciple Cl *CANTW/ST* CT2 .... 86 A6 🔲
Mandeville Rd *CANTW/ST* CT2 ..... 6 B1
Mangers La *DVE/WH* CT16 .... 172 E4
Mangers Pl *DVE/WH* CT16 .... 172 E3 🔲
Manley Cl *DVE/WH* CT16 .... 152 E7 🔲
Mannering Cl *DVW* CT17 .... 172 D3
Manns Hl *RCANTW* CT4 .... 126 E8
Manor Av *DEAL* CT14 .... 135 H2
Manor Cl *CANT* CT1 .... 106 A1
    DEAL CT14 .... 135 G2 🔲
    HB CT6 .... 26 A8
    QBOR ME11 .... 20 A3
Manor Dr *BRCH* CT7 .... 29 J8
Manorfield Rd *ASH* TN23 .... 160 C6
Manor Gv *SIT* ME10 .... 57 K3
Manor House Dr *ASH* TN23 .... 182 B3
Manor Lea *BRCH* CT7 .... 50 C5 🔲
Manor Leaze *RASHE* TN25 .... 185 G1
Manor Ms *DEAL* CT14 .... 155 F1
Manor Pound La *RASHE* TN25 ... 164 A7
Manor Ri *DVW* CT17 .... 172 E8
Manor Rd *BRCH* CT7 .... 50 C5
    DEAL CT14 .... 135 G2
    DVW CT17 .... 172 E8
    FOLK CT20 .... 12 C4
    HB CT6 .... 26 A8
    LYDD TN29 .... 237 H1
    QBOR ME11 .... 20 A3
    RSIT ME9 .... 77 F5
    WSTB CT5 .... 44 D3
Manor Wy *ASH* TN23 .... 8 A2
    IOS ME12 .... 25 F4
Manse Fld *RASHE* TN25 .... 184 E1
Mansell La *RDV* CT15 .... 169 H2
Mansion Gdns *DVE/WH* CT16 ..... 172 E2
Manston Court Rd *MARG* CT9 ...... 33 K7
    MSTR CT12 .... 53 H6
Manston Rd *MSTR* CT12 .... 52 D4
Mantles Hl *DEAL* CT14 .... 134 D5
Manwood Av *CANTW/ST* CT2 ...... 86 D3
Manwood Cl *SIT* ME10 .... 58 A4

Manwood Rd *SWCH* CT13 .... 94 A6
Maple Cl *ASH* TN23 .... 160 B4
   CANTW/ST CT2 .... 85 J4
Maple Ct *RCANTE* CT3 .... 69 K5
Maple Dr *LYDD* TN29 .... 227 G3
Maple Gdns *RCANTE* CT3 .... 69 K6
The Maples *BRDST* CT10 .... 54 D2
   IOS ME12 .... 15 J8 🔟
Maple St *IOS* ME12 .... 14 D5
Marchants Dr *RYE* TN31 .... 234 B4
Marden Av *MSTR* CT12 .... 4 B3
Mardol Rd *KEN/WIL* TN24.. .... 161 G1
Maresfield Cl *DVE/WH* CT16 .... 173 F4 🔟
Margarets Rd *RDV* CT15.. .... 155 G4
Margaret St *FOLK* CT20 .... 13 E4 🔟
Margate Hl *BRCH* CT7 .... 52 A5
Margate Rd *BRDST* CT10 .... 54 C2
   HB CT6 .... 47 K4
Marian Av *IOS* ME12 .... 15 H7
Marilyn Crs *BRCH* CT7 .... 30 A7
Marina Dr *IOS* ME12 .... 15 H7
Marina Rd *RAM* CT11 .... 5 F4
The Marina *DEAL* CT14 .... 115 K3
Marine Av *LYDD* TN29 .... 217 H3
Marine Crs *WSTB* CT5 .... 44 E3
Marine Dr *BRDST* CT10 .... 33 H3
   MARG CT9 .... 2 C3
Marine Gap *WSTB* CT5 .... 43 K5
Marine Gdns *MARG* CT9 .... 2 C3
Marine Pde *DVE/WH* CT16 .... 10 C4
   FOLK CT20 .... 13 D5
   IOS ME12 .... 14 E4
   NROM TN28 .... 233 F1
   WSTB CT5 .... 44 C3
Marine Rd *DEAL* CT14 .... 135 K2
Mariners Lea *BRDST* CT10 .... 54 E2
Marine Ter *FOLK* CT20 .... 13 E5
   MARG CT9 .... 2 B3
Marine Walk St *HYTHE* CT21 .... 205 G4 🔟
Maritime Av *HB* CT6 .... 47 H2
Marjan Cl *DVW* CT17 .... 172 E5
Mark Av *RAM* CT11 .... 4 B6
Market Hl *HYTHE* CT21 .... 205 G4 🔟
   RCANTE CT3 .... 130 B1 🔟
Market St *DEAL* CT14 .... 115 K8
   FAV ME13 .... 62 C7
   HB CT6 .... 46 E1
   MARG CT9 .... 2 C2 🔟
   SWCH CT13 .... 94 A5
Market Vw *RCANTE* CT3 .... 130 B1
Market Wy *CANTW/ST* CT2 .... 7 D1
Markland Rd *DVW* CT17 .... 172 E7
   RDV CT15 .... 172 E7
Marlborough Rd *BRDST* CT10 .... 55 F3 🔟
   NROM TN28 .... 226 E7
Marlborough Rd *DEAL* CT14 .... 135 G4
   DVW CT17 .... 172 D7
   MARG CT9 .... 2 C4
   RAM CT11 .... 5 D5
   RDV CT15 .... 172 E7
   WSTB CT5 .... 66 A1
Marlborough Wy *KEN/WIL* TN24 .... 141 K7
Marler Rd *FOLKN* CT19 .... 189 K8 🔟
Marley La *DEAL* CT14 .... 114 A7
   RCANTE CT3 .... 70 A1
   RCANTW CT4 .... 127 K6
Marlow Cl *WSTB* CT5 .... 44 E5 🔟
Marlowe Av *CANT* CT1 .... 6 C4 🔟
Marlowe Rd *ASH* TN23 .... 8 B3 🔟
   DVE/WH CT16 .... 173 F3 🔟
   MARG CT9 .... 3 F5
Marlow Mdw *CANTW/ST* CT2 .... 87 K2 🔟
Marr Cl *IOS* ME12 .... 15 G7
Marrose Av *MSTR* CT12 .... 54 C3
Marshalls Land *TENT* TN30 .... 194 A3
Marshall St *FOLKN* CT19 .... 13 K2
Marshborough Rd *SWCH* CT13 .... 92 E7
Marsh Crs *NROM* TN28 .... 226 C8
Marsh Farm Rd *MSTR* CT12 .... 74 A3
Marshlands *LYDD* TN29 .... 216 D8
Marshlands Cl *LYDD* TN29 .... 216 D7 🔟
Marsh La *DEAL* CT14 .... 115 G8
Marsh Vw *HYTHE* CT21.. .... 204 A6
Marshwood Cl *CANT* CT1 .... 87 G3
Martello Dr *HYTHE* CT21.. .... 204 C5
Martello Rd *FOLK* CT20 .... 13 E3
Marten Rd *FOLK* CT20 .... 12 B4
Martha Cl *FOLKN* CT19 .... 12 B2 🔟
Martin Dale Crs *RDV* CT15 .... 154 C4 🔟
Martindown Rd *WSTB* CT5 .... 43 K7
Martin's Cl *WSTB* CT5 .... 4 C1
   TENT TN30 .... 194 C6
The Martins *RASHW* TN26 .... 178 B5
Martin's Wy *HYTHE* CT21.. .... 204 B6
Martyrs' Field Rd *CANT* CT1 .... 6 B5
Maryland Gv *CANT* CT1 .... 7 F5 🔟
Mary Rd *DEAL* CT14.. .... 135 G3
Mason's Ri *BRDST* CT10 .... 55 H1
Masons Ct *DVW* CT17 .... 172 E5
Matthews Cl *DEAL* CT14 .... 115 J8
Matthew's Pl *DVE/WH* CT16 .... 10 A2 🔟

Matthews Rd *HB* CT6 .... 46 B4
Maugham Ct *WSTB* CT5 .... 44 A6
Maunsell Rd *KEN/WIL* TN24.. .... 9 D6
Maxine Gdns *BRDST* CT10 .... 55 C1
Maxton Rd *DVW* CT17.. .... 172 E8
Maxwell Pl *DEAL* CT14 .... 135 J2 🔟
Maydowns Rd *WSTB* CT5 .... 45 G4
Mayers Rd *DEAL* CT14.. .... 135 G5
Mayfield Av *DVE/WH* CT16 .... 173 F4
Mayfield Gdns *DVE/WH* CT16 .... 10 A1
Mayfield Rd *DVE/WH* CT16 .... 152 E7
   HB CT6 .... 47 F3
   RFOLK CT18 .... 167 G8
Mayfly Dr *RFOLK* CT18 .... 190 B2
Mayforth Gdns *RAM* CT11 .... 4 B5
Mayhew Cl *ASH* TN23 .... 8 A5 🔟
Maynard Av *MARG* CT9 .... 31 C6
Maynard Rd *CANT* CT1 .... 6 A4
Maypits *ASH* TN23 .... 160 D6
Maypole La *RCANTE* CT3 .... 47 K8
Maypole Rd *RCANTE* CT3 .... 69 J1
Mays Rd *RAM* CT11 .... 4 C5
Maystreet *HB* CT6 .... 48 A2
Mayton La *CANTW/ST* CT2 .... 68 A5
Mayville Rd *BRDST* CT10 .... 33 F8
Mccarthy Av *CANTW/ST* CT2 .... 68 E7
Mcclean Wk *IOS* ME12 .... 22 E6
The Meade *RFOLK* CT18 .... 190 A2
Meadowbrook Cl
   KEN/WIL TN24 .... 141 H8 🔟
Meadowbrook Rd *KEN/WIL* TN24.. .... 141 H8
Meadow Cl *HB* CT6 .... 47 H2
   RCANTW CT4 .... 104 A6
   RCANTW CT4 .... 107 G8
   RSIT ME9 .... 35 J2
Meadow Ct *RASHE* TN25 .... 186 E8
Meadow Gv *RASHE* TN25 .... 186 A6
Meadow Ri *RSIT* ME9 .... 35 J2
Meadow Rd *ASH* TN23 .... 8 A1
   CANTW/ST CT2 .... 68 E8
   MARG CT9 .... 31 G5
The Meadows *HB* CT6 .... 47 H4
   SIT ME10 .... 58 A4
Meadow Vw *RASHW* TN26 .... 139 H8
Meadow View Rd *RDV* CT15 .... 131 G8
Meadow Wk *WSTB* CT5 .... 43 K7
Meadow Wy *HYTHE* CT21.. .... 204 B6
Mead Rd *FOLKN* CT19 .... 13 D3
   KEN/WIL TN24.. .... 9 E6
The Meads Av *SIT* ME10 .... 35 J7
Meads Wy *LYDD* TN29 .... 227 F3
Mead Wy *CANTW/ST* CT2 .... 6 B2
Meadway *DVW* CT17.. .... 172 B5
Medina Av *WSTB* CT5 .... 43 J7
Medlar Cl *RSIT* ME9 .... 57 F8
Medway Cl *SIT* ME10 .... 57 J2
Medway Rd *IOS* ME12 .... 14 C5
Meehan Rd *NROM* TN28 .... 233 F2
Meehan Rd South *NROM* TN28 .... 232 E3
Meeres Court La *SIT* ME10 .... 36 D8
Meeson's Cl *FAV* ME13 .... 79 G8
Meeting St *RAM* CT11 .... 5 E4 🔟
Meggett La *RDV* CT15.. .... 170 E7
Megone Cl *RFOLK* CT18 .... 190 B2
Melbourne Av *DVE/WH* CT16 .... 173 F1
   MSTR CT12 .... 4 A3
Melbury Ms *NROM* TN28 .... 226 D6 🔟
Mellanby Cl *BRCH* CT7 .... 29 K8
Mellor Rw *SIT* ME10 .... 36 A5 🔟
Melody Cl *IOS* ME12 .... 24 D2
Melon La *LYDD* TN29 .... 224 E2
   RASHW TN26 .... 214 B5
Melsetter Cl *SWCH* CT13 .... 30 A7 🔟
Melville Lea *SWCH* CT13 .... 93 G7
Mendip Ri *KEN/WIL* TN24.. .... 8 B1
Menin Rd *SIT* ME10 .... 36 A5
Mentmore Rd *MSTR* CT12 .... 54 C3
Menzies Av *DEAL* CT14 .... 135 H5
Menzies Ct *IOS* ME12 .... 21 H1 🔟
Mercery La *CANT* CT1 .... 6 C3 🔟🔟
Merchants Wy *CANTW/ST* CT2 .... 86 A7
Mere Ga *MARG* CT9 .... 2 C4
Merleburgh Dr *SIT* ME10 .... 36 A6 🔟
Merlin Cl *SIT* ME10 .... 58 B3
Merritt Rd *NROM* TN28 .... 232 E4
Merrivale Hts *BRDST* CT10 .... 55 H3
Merton La *CANT* CT1 .... 106 D3
Meryl Gdns *DEAL* CT14 .... 135 J5
Meteor Av *WSTB* CT5 .... 43 J7
Meteor Cl *SIT* ME10 .... 35 K6
Metropole Rd East *FOLK* CT20 .... 12 B6
Metropole Rd West *FOLK* CT20 .... 12 B6
Meverall Av *MSTR* CT12 .... 75 J1
The Mews *SIT* ME10 .... 58 A3
Michael Av *RAM* CT11 .... 55 H6
Michelle Gdns *MARG* CT9 .... 31 F6
Mickleburgh Av *HB* CT6 .... 47 F3
Mickleburgh Hl *HB* CT6 .... 47 G2
Middelburg Sq *FOLK* CT20 .... 13 D5
Middle Cl *ASH* TN23 .... 160 A5 🔟
Middle Deal Rd *DEAL* CT14.. .... 135 H1
Middle Md *FOLKN* CT19.. .... 12 B2

Middle Rw *FAV* ME13 .... 62 C7
Middle St *ASH* TN23 .... 8 B3 🔟
   DEAL CT14 .... 115 K8 🔟
Middletune Av *SIT* ME10 .... 35 K7
Middle Wall *WSTB* CT5 .... 44 A4
Middle Wy *SIT* ME10 .... 58 C3
Midsummer Hl *KEN/WIL* TN24 .... 141 H8 🔟
Milbourne Gv *SIT* ME10 .... 35 K7
Mile Rd *CANT* CT1 .... 50 C8
Miles Ct *RCANTE* CT3 .... 90 C6 🔟
Milestone Cl *FOLKN* CT19.. .... 12 A2
Milestone Rd *DEAL* CT14 .... 135 H1 🔟
Miles Wy *BRCH* CT7 .... 29 J7
Military Rd *CANT* CT1 .... 7 E2
   DVW CT17 .... 10 B4 🔟
   FOLK CT20 .... 207 F3 🔟
   HYTHE CT21 .... 204 E4
Millais Rd *DVE/WH* CT16.. .... 10 A2
Millbank La *LYDD* TN29 .... 224 E7
Millbank Rd *ASH* TN23 .... 181 J1
Mill Bay *FOLK* CT20 .... 13 D4
Millbrook Meadow *ASH* TN23 .... 160 C5
Mill Cl *DVW* CT17 .... 172 D4
   RMAID ME17 .... 116 C2
   SWCH CT13 .... 93 J4
Mill Cottages *RAM* CT11 .... 4 C5
Mill Ct *KEN/WIL* TN24.. .... 9 D3
Milldale Cl *DEAL* CT14 .... 135 H2
Millennium Wy *BRDST* CT10 .... 54 D2
Mill Rd *SIT* ME10 .... 57 K1
Miller Av *CANTW/ST* CT2 .... 6 A3
Miller Cl *KEN/WIL* TN24.. .... 9 D5
   SIT ME10 .... 36 B6
Miller Ct *IOS* ME12 .... 21 H1 🔟
Millers Ct *WSTB* CT5 .... 44 A7
Millers La *MSTR* CT12 .... 51 F7
Millfield *ASH* TN23 .... 160 B5
Mill Fld *BRDST* CT10 .... 55 G1
Millfield *FOLK* CT20 .... 12 C5
   RASHW TN26 .... 177 J7
Mill Fld *RCANTE* CT3 .... 92 C5
Millfield *RDV* CT15 .... 155 F8
   RFOLK CT18 .... 169 J8
   SIT ME10 .... 58 A3
Millfield Cl *RFOLK* CT18 .... 190 C1
Millfield Mnr *WSTB* CT5 .... 44 B5 🔟
Millfield Rd *FAV* ME13 .... 62 D7
   MSTR CT12 .... 54 C3
Millfields *RDV* CT15 .... 151 G2
Mill Fields Rd *HYTHE* CT21 .... 204 D4
Mill Gn *SWCH* CT13 .... 112 E4
Mill Hl *DEAL* CT14.. .... 135 G3
Mill La *BRCH* CT7 .... 29 J8
   CANT CT1 .... 6 C2 🔟
   CANTW/ST CT2 .... 86 A6
   DEAL CT14 .... 113 K2
   DEAL CT14 .... 133 K2
   DVE/WH CT16 .... 10 C4 🔟
   DVE/WH CT16 .... 152 E6
   HB CT6 .... 47 G3
   KEN/WIL TN24.. .... 162 K5
   LYDD TN29 .... 231 H7
   MARG CT9 .... 2 C3
   RASHE TN25 .... 200 E1
   RCANTE CT3 .... 71 K8
   RCANTE CT3 .... 103 K7
   RCANTW CT4 .... 107 K5
   RCANTW CT4 .... 146 D4
   RDV CT15 .... 131 G2
   RDV CT15 .... 151 H1
   RFOLK CT18 .... 169 H6
   RSIT ME9 .... 78 D1
   SWCH CT13 .... 112 E4
   TENT TN30 .... 194 B5
Millmead Av *MARG* CT9 .... 32 E5
Millmead Rd *MARG* CT9 .... 3 F4
Mill Ms *DEAL* CT14 .... 135 H2 🔟
Mill Rd *CANTW/ST* CT2 .... 87 J2
   DEAL CT14 .... 135 H2
   HYTHE CT21 .... 205 H4
   LYDD TN29 .... 216 D7
   LYDD TN29 .... 231 J8
   RASHW TN26 .... 179 F1 .
   RCANTE CT3 .... 70 A1
   RCANTE CT3 .... 90 A8
   RCANTE CT3 .... 91 J8
Mill Rw *BRCH* CT7 .... 29 J8
Mills Cl *IOS* ME12 .... 15 G8
Millstream Cl *FAV* ME13 .... 62 B7 🔟
   WSTB CT5 .... 44 B5
Mill St *DVE/WH* CT16 .... 172 B1 🔟
   SIT ME10 .... 57 K1
Millstrood Rd *WSTB* CT5.. .... 44 B6
Mill Vw *KEN/WIL* TN24 .... 9 F5
   RASHW TN26.. .... 196 C3
Mill View Rd *HB* CT6 .... 47 F5
Mill Wall Pl *SWCH* CT13.. .... 94 A6
Mill Wy *SIT* ME10 .... 36 A8
Milner Crs *RCANTE* CT3 .... 130 A1
Milne Rd *KEN/WIL* TN24 .... 9 F5
Milner Rd *RDV* CT15 .... 131 K5
   WSTB CT5 .... 43 H8
Milstead Cl *IOS* ME12 .... 14 C6 🔟

Milton Av *MARG* CT9 .... 3 D4
Milton Cl *CANT* CT1 .... 7 F5
  DVE/WH CT16 .... 173 F2
Milton Rd *ASH* TN23 .... 8 A3
  CANT CT1 .... 7 D5
  DVE/WH CT16 .... 173 F2
  SIT ME10 .... 57 K2
Minerva Av *DVE/WH* CT16 .... 10 A1 ²
Minnis La *RDV* CT15 .... 171 K5
Minnis Rd *BRCH* CT7 .... 29 G6
Minnis Wy *DEAL* CT14 .... 114 B1
Minster Dr *HB* CT6 .... 46 C2
  IOS ME12 .... 15 J5
Minster Rd *BRCH* CT7 .... 52 A4
  FAV ME13 .... 62 D7 ²
  IOS ME12 .... 15 J8
  MSTR CT12 .... 52 B6
  RAM CT11 .... 5 B3
  WGOS CT8 .... 30 E7
Mintching Wood La *RSIT* ME9 .... 77 F4
Minter Av *RFOLK* CT18 .... 169 G7
Minter Cl *RFOLK* CT18 .... 169 F7
Minterne Av *SIT* ME10 .... 57 H4
Miranda Ct *IOS* ME12 .... 14 C5
Misling La *RCANTW* CT4 .... 146 A8
Mitcham Rd *LYDD* TN29 .... 216 C6
Mitchell Av *RFOLK* CT18 .... 190 C1
Mitchell Cl *RMAID* ME17 .... 116 C1
Mitchell St *FOLKN* CT20 .... 189 J8 ²
Moat Farm Cl *FOLKN* CT19 .... 12 C2
Moat Farm Rd *FOLKN* CT19 .... 12 C2
Moatfield Meadow *ASH* TN23 ...... 182 A2
Moat La *CANTW/ST* CT2 .... 85 K2
  CANTW/ST CT2 .... 87 K3
  RCANTE CT3 .... 92 B5
Moat Sole *SWCH* CT13 .... 93 K5
The Moat *HDCN* TN27 .... 118 C2 ¹
Moat Wy *OBOR* ME11 .... 20 B1
Mockett Dr *BRST* CT10 .... 33 G7 ¹
Mock La *ASH* TN23 .... 159 K8
Molehill Rd *WSTB* CT5 .... 45 C7
Molineux Rd *MSTR* CT12 .... 52 A8
Molland Cl *RCANTE* CT3 .... 92 A4
Molland La *RCANTE* CT3 .... 92 B1
Molland Lea *RCANTE* CT3 .... 92 A4
Molloy Rd *RASHW* TN26 .... 180 E5
Monastery Av *DVE/WH* CT16 .... 10 C2
Monastery St *CANT* CT1 .... 7 D3 ¹¹
Mongeham Church Cl *DEAL* CT14 .. 134 D2
Mongeham Rd *DEAL* CT14 .... 134 D4
Monica Cl *FAV* ME13 .... 82 E8
Monins Rd *DVW* CT17 .... 173 F7
Monkery La *RASHE* TN25 .... 120 A4
Monks Cl *CANTW/ST* CT2 .... 7 D1
  FAV ME13 .... 62 A6
Monkshill Rd *FAV* ME13 .... 64 B4
Monks Wk *HDCN* TN27 .... 118 C2 ²
Monks Wy *DVE/WH* CT16 .... 172 E3
Monkton Court La *RDV* CT15 .... 132 B7
Monkton Gdns *MARG* CT9 .... 33 F3 ²
Monkton Pl *RAM* CT11 .... 5 D4
Monkton Rd *MSTR* CT12 .... 51 K8
Monkton St *MSTR* CT12 .... 51 F7
Mons Ct *SIT* ME10 .... 36 A5
Montague Cl *IOS* ME12 .... 14 C5
Montague Rd *RAM* CT11 .... 5 E3
Montague St *HB* CT6 .... 46 C1
Montefiore Av *RAM* CT11 .... 55 H5
Montefiore Cottages *RAM* CT11 .... 5 F3 ¹
Montfort Cl *ASH* TN23 .... 160 D7
  CANTW/ST CT2 .... 86 E2
Montgomery Rd *FOLKN* CT19 .... 13 D1
Montpelier Av *WSTB* CT5 .... 44 A8
Montreal Cl *DVE/WH* CT16 .... 173 F3 ²
Monument Wy *KEN/WIL* TN24 ...... 182 E1
Moon Hl *RDV* CT15 .... 151 G2
Moore Cl *LYDD* TN29 .... 223 K3
Moorfield *CANTW/ST* CT2 .... 86 D2
The Moorings *RSIT* ME9 .... 58 B7
Moorland Rd *RDV* CT15 .... 151 F2
Moor La *LYDD* TN29 .... 224 C3
  RASHW TN26 .... 196 B7
Moorstock La *RASHE* TN25 .... 185 K4
Moorwell Dr *RDV* CT15 .... 151 F1
Moray Av *BRCH* CT7 .... 29 J6
Mordaunt Av *WGOS* CT8 .... 30 D6
Morehall Av *FOLKN* CT19 .... 190 A8
Morello Cl *RSIT* ME9 .... 59 K4 ¹
Morgan Kirby's Gdn *FAV* ME13 .... 101 H1
Morris Av *HB* CT6 .... 45 J2
Morris Court Cl *RSIT* ME9 .... 58 E4
Morrison Rd *FOLK* CT20 .... 13 E3
Mortimer Cl *ASH* TN23 .... 8 B6 ²
Mortimer Rd *DVE/WH* CT16 .... 10 C3
Mortimer St *HB* CT6 .... 46 E1
Mossend Ms *RAM* CT11 .... 5 E1
Mountain St *RCANTW* CT4 .... 103 H8
Mountbatten Wy *RASHE* TN25 .... 164 A8
Mount Castle La *RMAID* ME17 .... 117 F5
Mount Fld *FAV* ME13 .... 62 A7
  OBOR ME11 .... 10 D1 ¹
Mountfield Rd *NROM* TN28 .... 226 D8 ¹
Mountfield Wy *WGOS* CT8 .... 30 C8
Mount Green Av *MSTR* CT12 .... 75 J1
Mount Pleasant *CANTW/ST* CT2 ... 66 D8

TENT TN30 .... 194 C6 ¹
Mountpleasant Cl *RFOLK* CT18 .... 167 G7
Mount Pleasant Rd *FOLK* CT20 .... 13 D4 ¹
Mount Rd *CANT* CT1 .... 7 F5
  DVW CT17 .... 193 K1
Mounts Cl *DEAL* CT14 .... 135 G1
Mount St *HYTHE* CT21 .... 205 G4 ¹
Mountview *RSIT* ME9 .... 57 G4
Mount View Rd *HB* CT6 .... 47 F4
Moyes Cl *MSTR* CT12 .... 75 J1
Muir Rd *RAM* CT11 .... 5 F3
Mulberry Cl *RAM* CT11 .... 5 F3 ²
Mulberry Ct *CANT* CT1 .... 6 C3 ¹⁵
Mulberry Fld *SWCH* CT13 .... 93 K5 ²
Mulberry Hl *RCANTW* CT4 .... 103 K5
Munday Bois Rd *HDCN* TN27 .... 136 E5
Munsgore La *RSIT* ME9 .... 58 C2
Murston Rd *SIT* ME10 .... 58 C3
Murthwaite Ct *IOS* ME12 .... 21 H1 ²
Murton Pl *FAV* ME13 .... 63 K5
Musgrave Ct *MSTR* CT12 .... 52 E4 ¹
Musgrave Rd *SIT* ME10 .... 36 A8
Musgrove *ASH* TN23 .... 8 A5
Mustards Rd *IOS* ME12 .... 24 C4
Mutrix Gdns *MARG* CT9 .... 31 F5
Mutrix Rd *MARG* CT9 .... 31 F6
Mutton La *FAV* ME13 .... 80 E1
Mymms Cl *WSTB* CT5 .... 45 F6
Myrtle Rd *FOLKN* CT19 .... 13 E3 ¹
Mystole La *RCANTW* CT4 .... 104 E6
Mystole Rd *RCANTW* CT4 .... 104 C6

N

Nackington Rd *RCANTW* CT4 .... 106 E5
Nailbourne Cl *RCANTW* CT4 .... 128 D3
Nailldown Cl *HYTHE* CT21 .... 206 A3
Nailldown Rd *HYTHE* CT21 .... 206 A3
Nairne Cl *RASHW* TN26 .... 180 D6
Namur Pl *RDV* CT15 .... 173 K3
Napchester Rd *DVE/WH* CT16 ...... 152 E6
Napier Cl *SIT* ME10 .... 57 H2
Napier Gdns *HYTHE* CT21 .... 205 G5
Napier Rd *BRDST* CT10 .... 33 F8 ¹
  DVE/WH CT16 .... 173 F3
Napleton Rd *FAV* ME13 .... 62 B7
  RAM CT11 .... 4 C5 ¹³
Nargate St *RCANTE* CT3 .... 89 G6
Narrabeen Rd *FOLKN* CT19 .... 189 K8
Narrowbush La *LYDD* TN29 .... 223 K7
Naseby Av *FOLK* CT20 .... 206 D1
Nash Court Gdns *MARG* CT9 .... 2 C5
Nash Court Rd *MARG* CT9 .... 3 D5
Nash Gdns *BRDST* CT10 .... 55 J2 ¹
Nash Hl *RFOLK* CT18 .... 167 G8
Nash La *MARG* CT9 .... 3 D6
Nash Rd *MARG* CT9 .... 2 C5
Nasmyth Rd *BRCH* CT7 .... 29 K6 ¹
Natal Rd *DVE/WH* CT16 .... 173 K2
Nativity Cl *SIT* ME10 .... 57 K2
Nat's La *RASHE* TN25 .... 163 F1
Nautilus Cl *IOS* ME12 .... 21 H1 ¹
Nautilus Dr *IOS* ME12 .... 21 H1 ¹
Naylands *MARG* CT9 .... 2 B4
Neal's Place Rd *CANTW/ST* CT2 ... 86 A4
Neame Rd *BRCH* CT7 .... 29 K7
Neason Wy *FOLKN* CT19 .... 13 F3 ¹
Neath Rd *LYDD* TN29 .... 235 K4
Nelson Av *IOS* ME12 .... 16 A8
Nelson Cl *IOS* ME12 .... 14 B6
  KEN/WIL TN24 .... 162 B6 ¹
Nelson Ct *BRCH* CT7 .... 29 H6
Nelson Crs *RAM* CT11 .... 5 E5
Nelson Park Rd *RDV* CT15 .... 154 E6
Nelson Pl *BRDST* CT10 .... 55 J1
Nelson Rd *WSTB* CT5 .... 43 K5
Nelson St *DEAL* CT14 .... 115 K7
  FAV ME13 .... 62 B8
Nesbit Rd *LYDD* TN29 .... 227 G2
Ness Rd *LYDD* TN29 .... 231 H8
The Ness *CANT* CT1 .... 7 D6
Nether Av *NROM* TN28 .... 232 E1
Nethercourt Farm Rd *RAM* CT11 ..... 4 B3
Nethercourt Gdns *RAM* CT11 .... 4 B5
Nethercourt Hl *RAM* CT11 .... 4 B5
Nethergong Hl *RCANTE* CT3 .... 70 E2
Netherhale Farm Rd *BRCH* CT7 ..... 50 E2
Nethersole Rd *RCANTW* CT4 .... 130 A5
Nettlefield *KEN/WIL* TN24 .... 161 J1
Nettlepole La *HDCN* TN27 .... 138 A5
Nevill Gdns *DEAL* CT14 .... 135 H5
Newbridge Av *SIT* ME10 .... 35 K7
Newbury Cl *BRCH* CT7 .... 30 A3 ¹
  FOLK CT20 .... 206 D1
Newcastle Hl *RAM* CT11 .... 5 E4 ¹
Newchurch La *LYDD* TN29 .... 213 J8
Newcomen Rd *IOS* ME12 .... 14 D4 ¹
New Cross St *MARG* CT9 .... 2 C3 ¹⁰
New Cut Rd *FAV* ME13 .... 103 G2
New Dover Rd *CANT* CT1 .... 7 E5
  RFOLK CT18 .... 191 J1
Newenden Cl *ASH* TN23 .... 160 D8

New Forest La *RCANTW* CT4 .... 103 J2
New Gardens Rd *RSIT* ME9 .... 59 K4
Newgate Gap *MARG* CT9 .... 3 E2
Newgate Lower Prom *MARG* CT9 ..... 3 E2
New Hall Cl *LYDD* TN29 .... 216 E6
New House Cl *CANT* CT1 .... 106 B2
Newhouse La *RAM* ME13 .... 81 C7
New House La *RCANTW* CT4 .... 106 A4
Newing Cl *RCANTE* CT3 .... 88 E6
Newington Rd *MSTR* CT12 .... 4 B1
  RFOLK CT18 .... 189 F6
Newland Green La *HDCN* TN27 .... 136 D6
Newland Rd *IOS* ME12 .... 14 A7 ²
Newlands *ASH* TN23 .... 160 B8
  DVE/WH CT16 .... 153 F8
  LYDD TN29 .... 227 C3
Newlands Av *SIT* ME10 .... 57 G2
Newlands Dr *DEAL* CT14 .... 135 H6
Newlands La *MSTR* CT12 .... 5 D1
Newlands Rd *HDCN* TN27 .... 138 B1
  MSTR CT12 .... 5 D2
New La *LYDD* TN29 .... 231 H8
Newlyn's Meadow *RDV* CT15 ...... 170 E5
Newman Dr *SIT* ME10 .... 36 A6
Newman Rd *RCANTE* CT3 .... 130 A1
Newnham La *FAV* ME13 .... 79 G7
New Rectory La *ASH* TN23 .... 182 A2
New Rd *CANT* CT1 .... 67 J3
  CANTW/ST CT2 .... 84 E3
  HDCN TN27 .... 137 G4
  HYTHE CT21 .... 205 F2
  IOS ME12 .... 14 B6
  IOS ME12 .... 15 K8
  RCANTW CT4 .... 167 K2
  RDV CT15 .... 132 A7
New Road Hl *RASHE* TN25 .... 201 F2
New Romney Pl *SWCH* CT13 .... 93 K6 ¹
New Ruttington La *CANT* CT1 .... 7 D2
New St *CANT* CT1 .... 6 B4
  CANTW/ST CT2 .... 86 E2 ¹
  DEAL CT14 .... 115 K7 ¹
  DVE/WH CT16 .... 10 B3
  FOLK CT20 .... 13 D4 ¹
  IOS ME12 .... 14 C5
  KEN/WIL TN24 .... 8 B2
  LYDD TN29 .... 231 H8
  MARG CT9 .... 2 C3
  RCANTE CT3 .... 92 C5
  SWCH CT13 .... 94 A6
Newton Rd *FAV* ME13 .... 62 C7
  WSTB CT5 .... 44 E4
New Town Gn *KEN/WIL* TN24 .... 9 D5
Newtown Rd *ASH* TN23 .... 8 C5
New Town Rd *KEN/WIL* TN24 .... 9 D5
New Town St *CANT* CT1 .... 7 D1
  RCANTW CT4 .... 104 E1
Nicholas Dr *MSTR* CT12 .... 75 J1
Nicholas Rd *KEN/WIL* TN24 .... 140 E7
Nicholls Av *BRDST* CT10 .... 55 F1
Nickley Wood Rd *RASHW* TN26 ... 180 B4
Nightingale Av *HYTHE* CT21 .... 204 B6
  WSTB CT5 .... 43 J8
Nightingale Cl *KEN/WIL* TN24 .... 162 B7 ¹
  RCANTW CT4 .... 84 E8
Nightingale La *RDV* CT15 .... 130 E3
Nightingale Pl *MARG* CT9 .... 3 E3 ¹
Nightingale Rd *DVE/WH* CT16 ...... 10 A1
  FAV ME13 .... 62 B7
Nine Acres *KEN/WIL* TN24 .... 161 G1
Nine Ash La *FAV* ME13 .... 82 C3
Ninn La *ASH* TN23 .... 159 J4
Nixon Av *MSTR* CT12 .... 4 C2
Noah's Ark Rd *DVW* CT17 .... 172 E6
Noakes Meadow *ASH* TN23 .... 160 D6
Nobel Cl *RSIT* ME9 .... 59 K4
Nobel Ct *FAV* ME13 .... 62 A7
Noble Cl *MARG* CT9 .... 31 F6 ¹
Noble Gdns *MARG* CT9 .... 31 F6
Nonsuch Cl *CANT* CT1 .... 7 F3 ¹
Noreen Av *IOS* ME12 .... 15 H8
Norfolk Dr *ASH* TN23 .... 8 A3
Norfolk Rd *CANT* CT1 .... 6 B5
  MARG CT9 .... 3 F3
Norman Rd *ASH* TN23 .... 8 B6
  BRDST CT10 .... 33 F8
  CANT CT1 .... 6 C4
  FAV ME13 .... 62 B7
  MARG CT9 .... 30 E5
  RAM CT11 .... 4 B5
  RDV CT15 .... 155 H8
  WGOS CT8 .... 30 E5 ¹
  WSTB CT5 .... 44 A6
Norman St *DVW* CT17 .... 10 B3 ¹
Norrie Rd *BRCH* CT7 .... 29 K8
Norrington Md *FOLKN* CT19 .... 12 A2 ¹
North Barrack Rd *DEAL* CT14 ...... 135 K2
Northbourne Av *DVW* CT17 .... 173 F6
Northbourne Rd *DEAL* CT14 .... 133 J5
Northbrook La *KEN/WIL* TN24 .... 9 D5
Northbrooke La *KEN/WIL* TN24 ...... 8 C2
Northcliffe Gdns *BRDST* CT10 ...... 33 H7
North Cl *FOLK* CT20 .... 206 D2
Northcote Rd *DEAL* CT14 .... 135 K1 ¹

North Court Cl *RCANTE* CT3 .... 90 C6
North Court La *DEAL* CT14 .... 132 E2
Northdown *KEN/WIL* TN24 .... 8 C1 ◩
  RSIT ME9 .... 78 B7
Northdown Av *MARG* CT9 .... 3 F3
Northdown Hl *BRDST* CT10 .... 32 E7
Northdown Park Rd *MARG* CT9 ...... 3 F4
Northdown Rd *BRDST* CT10 .... 33 F7
  MARG CT9 .... 3 E2
North Downs Cl *RCANTW* CT4 ...... 103 H4
Northdowns Cl *RDV* CT15 .... 133 F8
North Downs Wy *CANTW/ST* CT2 .... 85 J6
  DVE/WH CT16 .... 10 B1
  DVW CT17 .... 193 K2
  HYTHE CT21 .... 187 G2
  RASHE TN25 .... 141 F2
  RASHE TN25 .... 143 K6
  RCANTW CT4 .... 108 B5
  RCANTW CT4 .... 122 D5
  RDV CT15 .... 152 E1
  RFOLK CT18 .... 191 K5
  RMAID ME17 .... 96 D7
  RMAID ME17 .... 117 K2
North Downs Wy
& Saxon Shore Wy *FOLKN* CT19... 189 H5
Northdown Wy *MARG* CT9 .... 32 D5 ◩
North Eastling Rd *RSIT* ME9 ...... 79 G5
Northern By-pass *HDCN* TN27 .. 118 E6
North Foreland Av *BRDST* CT10 .. 33 J7
North Foreland Rd *BRDST* CT10 .. 33 J7
Northgate *CANT* CT1 .... 7 D2
Northgate Borough *CANT* CT1 ..... 7 D2 ◩
North Holmes Rd *CANT* CT1 .... 7 E2
North La *CANTW/ST* CT2 .... 6 C2 ◩
  FAV ME13 .... 62 B7
  FAV ME13 .... 83 F6
North Lea *DEAL* CT14 .... 115 J7
North Lyminge La *RFOLK* CT18 .. 167 G7
North Military Rd *DVW* CT17 ...... 10 A4
North Pends *KEN/WIL* TN24 ...... 161 J1 ◩
North Rd *DEAL* CT14 .... 135 K8
  DVW CT17 .... 10 A1
  FOLK CT20 .... 206 E2
  HYTHE CT21 .... 205 G4
  MSTR CT12 .... 75 F5
  QBOR ME11 .... 20 A1
  SWCH CT13 .... 95 G6
North Rd West *HYTHE* CT21 ...... 204 E3
North St *DEAL* CT14 .... 115 K7
  DVW CT17 .... 173 F7
  FOLKN CT19 .... 13 E4
  HB CT6 .... 46 E1
  KEN/WIL TN24 .... 8 C2
  NROM TN28 .... 226 B8
  SIT ME10 .... 35 K7
Northumberland Av
  KEN/WIL TN24 .... 161 H1
  MARG CT9 .... 32 D5
North Vw *RCANTE* CT3 .... 70 A5
Northwall Ms *DEAL* CT14 .... 115 J7
Northwall Rd *DEAL* CT14 .... 115 J7
North Wy *DEAL* CT14 .... 114 A7
Northwood Dr *SIT* ME10 .... 58 A5
Northwood Rd *BRDST* CT10 .... 54 D3
  WSTB CT5 .... 44 B4
Norton Av *HB* CT6 .... 46 D3
Norton Dr *MSTR* CT12 .... 52 A8 ◩
Norton La *RASHW* TN26 .... 178 E1
Norton Rd *RSIT* ME9 .... 60 B8
Norview Rd *WSTB* CT5 .... 43 J7
Norway Dro *RDV* CT15 .... 155 G5
Norwood Gdns *ASH* TN23 .... 8 B3
Norwood Ri *LYDD* TN29 .... 214 D3
Norwood Ri *IOS* ME12 .... 15 K7
Norwood St *ASH* TN23 .... 8 B3
Nottingham Rd *BRCH* CT7 .... 51 J1 ◩
Nouds La *RSIT* ME9 .... 60 A7
Nouds Rd *RSIT* ME9 .... 60 A7
Nunnery Flds *CANT* CT1 .... 7 D5
Nunnery Rd *CANT* CT1 .... 6 C4
Nursery Cl *IOS* ME12 .... 14 E5
  RAM CT11 .... 4 C4 ◩
  RFOLK CT18 .... 169 F7 ◩
  WSTB CT5 .... 44 D5
Nursery Flds *BRCH* CT7 .... 52 A3
  HYTHE CT21 .... 204 D4
Nurserylands *HB* CT6 .... 46 E3
Nursery La *DVE/WH* CT16 .... 152 D7
  FAV ME13 .... 101 G1
  RFOLK CT18 .... 169 G7
Nutberry Cl *RSIT* ME9 .... 60 A4
Nutfields *SIT* ME10 .... 58 C3
Nutley Cl *KEN/WIL* TN24 .... 8 C2
Nutts Av *IOS* ME12 .... 25 F4

Oak Av *IOS* ME12 .... 16 B8
  RDV CT15 .... 152 B1
Oak Caer *RASHE* TN25 .... 201 F2 ◩
Oakdale Rd *HB* CT6 .... 47 F2

Oakdene Rd *MSTR* CT12 .... 4 C2
Oak Dr *LYDD* TN29 .... 227 G3
  RFOLK CT18 .... 190 C1
Oakenpole *ASH* TN23 .... 160 C5 ◩
Oakfield Ct *MSTR* CT12 .... 4 B3 ◩
Oakfield La *KEN/WIL* TN24 .... 9 D1
Oakfields *SIT* ME10 .... 57 H3 ◩
Oak Gv *RDV* CT15 .... 131 K4 ◩
Oak Hl *SWCH* CT13 .... 93 F8
Oakland Ct *MSTR* CT12 .... 75 H1
Oaklands *ASH* TN23 .... 160 D5
  RASHE TN25 .... 183 K2
Oaklands Av *BRDST* CT10 .... 55 F1
Oaklands Wy *CANTW/ST* CT2 ..... 69 G7
Oak La *IOS* ME12 .... 16 B8
  LYDD TN29 .... 231 C8 ◩
Oakleigh La *RCANTW* CT4 .... 108 B1
Oak Lodge Rd *NROM* TN28 .... 226 C7 ◩
Oakridge *BRDST* CT10 .... 33 H5
Oak Rdg *RASHE* TN25 .... 199 K6
Oak Rd *SIT* ME10 .... 58 D1
Oaks Av *HB* CT6 .... 46 C4
Oakside Rd *RCANTE* CT3 .... 130 A1
Oaks Pk *CANTW/ST* CT2 .... 85 K3
Oaks Rd *FOLK* CT20 .... 189 J8
  TENT TN30 .... 194 B7
The Oaks *BRCH* CT7 .... 50 C4
  BRDST CT10 .... 33 G7
  RCANTE CT3 .... 70 A5
Oak St *DEAL* CT14 .... 115 K8
Oaks Vw *HYTHE* CT21 .... 204 A6
Oak Tree Gv *MARG* CT9 .... 31 F6
Oak Tree Rd *ASH* TN23 .... 160 D6
Oakvale Cl *DVW* CT17 .... 173 F7 ◩
Oakwood Dr *WSTB* CT5 .... 44 D5
Oakwood Rd *CANTW/ST* CT2 ...... 68 F5
Oare Rd *FAV* ME13 .... 62 A5
Oast Ct *MARG* CT9 .... 3 D5 ◩
  SIT ME10 .... 57 K4
Oasthouse Fld *LYDD* TN29 ...... 224 E2
Oast La *FAV* ME13 .... 100 C8
Oast Meadow *KEN/WIL* TN24 ...... 9 F4
Oaten Hl *CANT* CT1 .... 7 D4
Oaten Hill Pl *CANT* CT1 .... 7 D4 ◩
Ocean Cl *BRCH* CT7 .... 30 A6
Ocean Vw *BRDST* CT10 .... 55 H5
Octavian Dr *HYTHE* CT21 .... 203 J3
Odo Rd *DVW* CT17 .... 173 F6
Offley Cl *MARG* CT9 .... 32 D5
Okehampton Cl *KEN/WIL* TN24 .. 141 K7 ◩
Olantigh Rd *RASHE* TN25 .... 143 J3
Olave Rd *MARG* CT9 .... 32 D5
Old Ash Cl *KEN/WIL* TN24 .... 161 G1 ◩
Old Ashford Rd *HDCN* TN27 .... 118 E7
  RMAID ME17 .... 116 A7
Old Badgins Rd *FAV* ME13 .... 80 E5
Old Bakery Cl *LYDD* TN29 .... 227 G2 ◩
Old Billet La *IOS* ME12 .... 17 F8
Old Boundary Rd *MARG* CT9 ...... 30 E5
Old Bridge Rd *WSTB* CT5 .... 44 B5
Old Charlton Rd *DVE/WH* CT16 .. 10 B1
Old Court Hl *RDV* CT15 .... 110 D8
Old Crossing Rd *MARG* CT9 ...... 31 G5
Old Dover Rd *CANT* CT1 .... 7 D4
  RCANTW CT4 .... 129 H5
  RFOLK CT18 .... 191 K5
Old Farm Rd *BRCH* CT7 .... 29 G7
Old Ferry Rd *RSIT* ME9 .... 19 K8
Old Fold *WSTB* CT5 .... 45 F6
Old Folkestone Rd *DVW* CT17 .. 193 K6
Old Gate Rd *FAV* ME13 .... 62 A7
Old Green Rd *BRDST* CT10 .... 33 G7
  MARG CT9 .... 32 D5
Old Hall Dr *MSTR* CT12 .... 75 H1
Oldhawe Hl *HB* CT6 .... 110 U6
The Old High St *FOLK* CT20 ...... 13 D4
Old Hockley Rd *FAV* ME13 .... 100 H4
Old Hook Rd *IOS* ME12 .... 22 C5
Oldhouse La *LYDD* TN29 .... 223 H5
Old Kingsdown Cl *BRDST* CT10 . 55 F3 ◩
Old Lenham Rd *RSIT* ME9 .... 97 K1
Old London Rd *HYTHE* CT21 ..... 204 C4
Old Lydd Rd *RYE* TN31 .... 234 B4
Old Md *FOLKN* CT19 .... 12 A2
Old Orch *ASH* TN23 .... 160 B6
Old Park Av *CANT* CT1 .... 7 F1
Old Park Cl *DVE/WH* CT16 ...... 172 E2
Old Park Hl *DVE/WH* CT16 ...... 172 E2
Old Park Rd *DVE/WH* CT16 ...... 173 F4
Old Pond Rd *ASH* TN23 .... 160 D5
Old Rectory Cl *RASHE* TN25 ..... 183 K2
  RFOLK CT18 .... 190 C2
Old Rd *BRCH* CT7 .... 49 K8
  RCANTW CT4 .... 167 K2
Old Roman Rd *RDV* CT15 .... 154 C5
Old Ruttington La *CANT* CT1 ...... 7 D2 ◩
Old School Cl *RMAID* ME17 ...... 116 D2
Old School Ct *HDCN* TN27 .... 137 F3
Old School Gdns *MARG* CT9 .... 3 E4 ◩
Old School Ms *RCANTW* CT4 .... 104 E4 ◩
Oldstairs Rd *DEAL* CT14 .... 155 J3
Old Surrenden Manor Rd
  RASHW TN26 .... 158 D8

Old Tree Rd *RCANTE* CT3 .... 47 K8
Old Valley Rd *RCANTW* CT4 ...... 129 F7 ◩
Old Vicarage Gdns *RASHE* TN25 .. 142 E4 ◩
Old Wy *RASHW* TN26 .... 211 F7
Omer Av *MARG* CT9 .... 32 B7
Orange St *CANT* CT1 .... 6 C3 ◩
Orchard Av *DEAL* CT14 .... 135 H1
Orchard Cl *CANTW/ST* CT2 .... 86 D2
  DVE/WH CT16 .... 152 E6
  MSTR CT12 .... 52 A7
  MSTR CT12 .... 54 C3
  RASHE TN25 .... 183 K3
  RCANTE CT3 .... 89 F7
  WSTB CT5 .... 44 C3 ◩
Orchard Dr *ASH* TN23 .... 160 D2
  DVW CT17 .... 172 C3
  NROM TN28 .... 227 F8
  RASHE TN25 .... 142 E5
Orchard Fld *RASHW* TN26 .... 178 E2
Orchard Gdns *MARG* CT9 .... 31 F5
Orchard Gv *IOS* ME12 .... 15 H8
Orchard La *KEN/WIL* TN24 ...... 141 K8
  RASHE TN25 .... 121 F4
Orchard Pl *FAV* ME13 .... 62 C7
  SIT ME10 .... 58 B3
Orchard Rd *HB* CT6 .... 46 E3
  LYDD TN29 .... 227 H2
  MARG CT9 .... 31 F5
  SWCH CT13 .... 113 F3
  TENT TN30 .... 194 A3
The Orchards *RCANTW* CT4 ...... 167 K2 ◩
Orchard St *CANTW/ST* CT2 .... 6 B2
Orchard Va *HYTHE* CT21 .... 204 E4
Orchard Vw *RCANTE* CT3 .... 92 D5
  RSIT ME9 .... 51 K8
  TENT TN30 .... 194 C7
Orchid Cl *IOS* ME12 .... 23 G5
Orchid Cl *IOS* ME12 .... 21 H2
The Orchids *RASHE* TN25 .... 183 K2
  RFOLK CT18 .... 188 C3
Orgarswick Av *LYDD* TN29 ...... 216 D7
Orgarswick Wy *LYDD* TN29 ..... 216 E7 ◩
Orient Pl *CANTW/ST* CT2 .... 6 C2 ◩
Orion Wy *KEN/WIL* TN24 .... 9 E5
Ormonde Rd *FOLK* CT20 .... 13 E5 ◩
  HYTHE CT21 .... 205 G5
Osborne Gdns *HB* CT6 .... 47 K1
Osborne Rd *DEAL* CT14 .... 135 J8
  KEN/WIL TN24 .... 9 E4
Osborne Ter *MARG* CT9 .... 3 D4 ◩
Osbourn Av *WGOS* CT8 .... 30 D6 ◩
Osbourne Rd *BRDST* CT10 .... 55 J2
Oscar Rd *BRDST* CT10 .... 55 J2
Osier Fld *KEN/WIL* TN24 .... 141 J7
Osier Rd *RSIT* ME9 .... 60 B5
Osprey Cl *WSTB* CT5 .... 43 K7
Osprey Ct *SIT* ME10 .... 58 B3
Ospringe Pl *FAV* ME13 .... 62 A8
Ospringe Rd *FAV* ME13 .... 62 A8
Ospringe St *FAV* ME13 .... 61 K8
Ostlers La *BRCH* CT7 .... 50 B1 ◩
Oswald Pl *DVW* CT17 .... 173 F7
Oswald Rd *DVW* CT17 .... 173 F4
Otham Cl *CANTW/ST* CT2 .... 86 E2 ◩
Ottawa Crs *DVE/WH* CT16 .... 173 G3
Otterden Cl *ASH* TN23 .... 160 D8
Otterden Rd *FAV* ME13 .... 98 E4
Otterpool La *HYTHE* CT21 .... 203 G2
Out Elmstead La *RCANTW* CT4 . 128 E4
Outfall Av *LYDD* TN29 .... 239 F8
The Oval *LYDD* TN29 .... 217 F5
Overland La *RCANTE* CT3 .... 91 J3
Owen's Cl *HYTHE* CT21 .... 206 B3 ◩
Owen Sq *DEAL* CT14 .... 135 H4
Owl's Hatch Rd *HB* CT6 .... 46 B5
Oxenden Park Dr *HB* CT6 .... 46 D2
Oxenden Rd *FOLK* CT20 .... 206 E2
Oxenden Wy *RCANTW* CT4 ...... 129 F6
Oxen Lease *ASH* TN23 .... 160 C6
Oxenturn Rd *RASHE* TN25 ...... 142 E7
Oxford Cl *CANT* CT1 .... 6 C4
Oxford St *MARG* CT9 .... 3 D4 ◩
Oxford Ter *FOLK* CT20 .... 13 D5 ◩
Ox La *TENT* TN30 .... 194 B4
Oxney Cl *BRCH* CT7 .... 29 J7 ◩
Oyster Cl *HB* CT6 .... 46 A3
  SIT ME10 .... 35 K8 ◩

Packer's La *RAM* CT11 .... 5 E4 ◩
Padbrook La *RCANTE* CT3 .... 91 F7
Paddock Cl *DEAL* CT14 .... 135 F1
  FOLK CT20 .... 207 F1 ◩
  LYDD TN29 .... 231 G8
Paddock Rd *BRCH* CT7 .... 29 K7 ◩
The Paddocks *ASH* TN23 .... 160 A5
  BRDST CT10 .... 33 G7
  HB CT6 .... 48 A1 ◩
  MARG CT9 .... 32 D5 ◩
The Paddock *CANT* CT1 .... 7 E3 ◩

Paddock Vw *WSTB* CT5 ...... 44 A7
Padwell La *ASH* TN23 ...... 160 A6
Paffard Cl *CANTW/ST* CT2 ...... 68 E8
Page Pl *FOLKN* CT19 ...... 13 D1
Paine Av *FOLK* CT20 ...... 231 H8
Painesfield Cl *LYDD* TN29 ...... 216 E2
Painter's Forstal Rd *FAV* ME13 ...... 80 C3
Palace Cl *WSTB* CT5 ...... 44 E4
Palace St *CANT* CT1 ...... 6 C2 □
Palm Bay Av *MARG* CT9 ...... 32 D3
Palm Bay Gdns *MARG* CT9 ...... 32 D5 □
Palmbeach Av *HYTHE* CT21 ...... 204 D6
Palmer Cl *HB* CT6 ...... 47 C6
Palmer Crs *MARG* CT9 ...... 32 D6
Palmer Rd *RCANTE* CT3 ...... 90 C6
Palmers Cross HI *CANTW/ST* CT2 ...... 85 J5
    DEAL CT14 ...... 135 J3
Palmerston Av *BRDST* CT10 ...... 55 J3
Palmerston St *FOLKN* CT19 ...... 13 D3 □
Palm Tree Cl *RDV* CT15 ...... 132 B7
Palm Tree Wy *RFOLK* CT18 ...... 167 F7
Palting Wy *FOLK* CT20 ...... 231 H7
Pannell Dr *RFOLK* CT18 ...... 190 A2
Panteny La *RSIT* ME9 ...... 59 F4
Papworth Cl *FOLKN* CT19 ...... 12 A2 □
Parade *CANT* CT1 ...... 6 C3 □
Parade Rd *FOLK* CT20 ...... 206 E3 □
The Parade *BRCH* CT7 ...... 29 F7
    FOLK CT20 ...... 13 E4
    KEN/WIL TN24 ...... 182 E1
    MARG 2 C2
    NROM TN28 ...... 233 F6
Paradise *CANT* CT1 ...... 5 D4
Paradise Rw *SWCH* CT13 ...... 93 K5 □
Paragon *CANT* CT1 ...... 5 D6
Paragon St *RAM* CT11 ...... 5 D6
Paraker Wy *HYTHE* CT21 ...... 206 B3
Pardoner Cl *CANTW/ST* CT2 ...... 86 A7
Pardoners Wy *DVE/WH* CT16 ...... 172 E5 □
Parfitt Wy *DVE/WH* CT16 ...... 173 F4
Parham Cl *CANT* CT1 ...... 7 E1 □
Parham Rd *CANT* CT1 ...... 7 E1 □
Parish Rd *IOS* ME12 ...... 21 H1
    RCANTW CT4 ...... 104 E4
Park Av *BRCH* CT7 ...... 29 K8
    BRDST CT10 ...... 5 E1
    DEAL CT14 ...... 135 H1
    DVE/WH CT16 ...... 10 B2
    IOS ME12 ...... 25 F5
    QBOR ME11 ...... 20 C2
    SIT ME10 ...... 57 K4
    WSTB CT5 ...... 44 C3
Park Cha *BRDST* CT10 ...... 5 E1 □
Park Crescent Rd *MARG* CT9 ...... 3 F3 □
Park Dr *RASHW* TN26 ...... 139 J8
    SIT ME10 ...... 57 J5
Park Farm Cl *CANTW/ST* CT2 ...... 67 H8
    RASHW TN26 ...... 180 D5
Park Farm Rd *FOLKN* CT19 ...... 12 A1
Parkfield Rd *FOLKN* CT19 ...... 12 C3
Park Ga *BRDST* CT10 ...... 5 F1
Parkland Ct *BRDST* CT10 ...... 33 G8
Park La *BRCH* CT7 ...... 29 K8
    MARG CT9 ...... 3 D3 □
    RASHW TN26 ...... 158 E2
    RCANTW CT4 ...... 128 B1
    RCANTW CT4 ...... 167 K1
Park Pl *ASH* TN23 ...... 8 B6
    KEN/WIL TN24 ...... 9 F5
    MARG CT9 ...... 2 C4 □
Park Rd *BRCH* CT7 ...... 29 K7
    BRDST CT10 ...... 33 J8
    DVE/WH CT16 ...... 172 B1
    FAV ME13 ...... 62 C8
    FOLK CT20 ...... 189 K8
    HB CT6 ...... 46 E2
    HYTHE CT21 ...... 205 F5
    IOS ME12 ...... 14 E5
    KEN/WIL TN24 ...... 141 H8
    MARG CT9 ...... 3 E3
    NROM TN28 ...... 233 F1
    QBOR ME11 ...... 20 A1 □
    RAM CT11 ...... 4 C4
    RCANTE CT3 ...... 72 A7
    SIT ME10 ...... 57 K3
Park Rd North *KEN/WIL* TN24 ...... 8 B2 □
Park St *ASH* TN23 ...... 8 C3
    DEAL CT14 ...... 115 K8
    LYDD TN29 ...... 231 G8
Park V *KEN/WIL* TN24 ...... 141 H8
Park Vw *CANTW/ST* CT2 ...... 68 E8
    FOLKN CT19 ...... 12 C3
Park View Cl *RCANTE* CT3 ...... 111 F4
Park View Ri *RDV* CT15 ...... 131 F2
The Parkway *BRCH* CT7 ...... 30 A7
Park Wood Cl *ASH* TN23 ...... 182 A1
Parkwood Cl *BRDST* CT10 ...... 5 E1
Parsonage Cha *IOS* ME12 ...... 21 G1
Parsonage Flds *MSTR* CT12 ...... 51 F7
Parsonage La *RSIT* ME9 ...... 35 F6
Parsonage Rd *HB* CT6 ...... 47 F3
Parsonage Stocks Rd *FAV* ME13 ...... 100 E1
Partridge La *FAV* ME13 ...... 62 B1
Pastime Cl *SIT* ME10 ...... 35 K6 □
The Pasture *KEN/WIL* TN24 ...... 141 H8

Patchways *LYDD* TN29 ...... 214 E3
Patricia Wy *BRDST* CT10 ...... 54 E3
Patrixbourne Rd *RCANTW* CT4 ...... 108 B4
Patterson Cl *DEAL* CT14 ...... 135 G2
Paul's Pl *DVE/WH* CT16 ...... 10 A2 □
The Pavement *TENT* TN30 ...... 194 A3
Pavilion Dr *SIT* ME10 ...... 36 A5
Pavilion Meadow *DVW* CT17 ...... 172 B2
Pavilion Rd *FOLKN* CT19 ...... 12 C3
Payden St *RMAID* ME17 ...... 97 K6
    RSIT ME9 ...... 97 J4
Payers Pk *FOLK* CT20 ...... 13 D4 □
Pays La *RASHE* TN25 ...... 120 B5
Pay St *RFOLK* CT18 ...... 168 E7
    RFOLK CT18 ...... 169 F7
Payton Cl *MARG* CT9 ...... 32 A8
Peafield Wood Rd *RCANTW* CT4 ...... 147 J2
Peak Dr *SWCH* CT13 ...... 113 F3
Pean Court Rd *WSTB* CT5 ...... 66 A3
Pean HI *WSTB* CT5 ...... 66 A3
Pearson's Wy *BRDST* CT10 ...... 33 F7 □
Pear Tree Cl *BRDST* CT10 ...... 54 D2
Pear Tree La *LYDD* TN29 ...... 217 F5
Peartree Rd *HB* CT6 ...... 47 G3
Pedding HI *RCANTE* CT3 ...... 91 H5
Pedding La *RCANTE* CT3 ...... 91 H5
Peel Dr *SIT* ME10 ...... 58 D2
Pegwell Av *RAM* CT11 ...... 4 A6
Pegwell Cl *RAM* CT11 ...... 4 A6
Pegwell Rd *RAM* CT11 ...... 4 A6
Pelham Gdns *FOLK* CT20 ...... 12 A5
Pelwood Rd *RYE* TN31 ...... 234 D4
Pemberton Rd *KEN/WIL* TN24 ...... 9 D3 □
Pembroke Av *MARG* CT9 ...... 31 G5
Pembroke Ms *NROM* TN28 ...... 226 D6 □
Pembury St *SIT* ME10 ...... 57 K2 □
Pencester Rd *DVE/WH* CT16 ...... 10 B3
Penderel Ms *TENT* TN30 ...... 194 B6
Penfield La *RSIT* ME9 ...... 77 G2
Penfold Gdns *RDV* CT15 ...... 151 F1
Penfold Rd *FOLKN* CT19 ...... 13 E3
Penn Cl *SIT* ME10 ...... 58 C4
Penn HI *ASH* TN23 ...... 160 C8
Pennine Wy *KEN/WIL* TN24 ...... 8 B1 □
Pennington Cl *CANTW/ST* CT2 ...... 69 H7
Penny Pot La *RCANTW* CT4 ...... 104 E6
    RCANTW CT4 ...... 124 D5
Penshurst Cl *CANTW/ST* CT2 ...... 86 E3 □
Penshurst Gdns *MARG* CT9 ...... 33 G4 □
Penshurst Ri *FAV* ME13 ...... 62 A6
Penshurst Rd *RAM* CT11 ...... 5 F4
Pent Vale Cl *FOLKN* CT19 ...... 12 A3
Pepys Av *IOS* ME12 ...... 14 C4
Percy Av *BRDST* CT10 ...... 33 G5
Percy Rd *BRDST* CT10 ...... 55 G1
    MARG CT9 ...... 3 E2 □
    RAM CT11 ...... 5 D3
Peregrine Cl *HYTHE* CT21 ...... 204 B6
Peregrine Dr *SIT* ME10 ...... 58 B3
Peri Ct *CANT* CT1 ...... 6 B5 □
Periwinkle Cl *SIT* ME10 ...... 57 K1
Perkins Av *MARG* CT9 ...... 3 D5
Perries Md *FOLKN* CT19 ...... 12 A2
Perry Rd *RCANTE* CT3 ...... 90 E3
Pested La *RASHE* TN25 ...... 121 F3
Peter James Cl *RYE* TN31 ...... 234 B4 □
Peter St *DEAL* CT14 ...... 115 K7
    DVE/WH CT16 ...... 10 A3 □
    FOLK CT20 ...... 13 D4
Petfield Cl *IOS* ME12 ...... 15 K8 □
Petta La *RCANTW* CT4 ...... 90 C5
Pett Bottom Rd *RCANTW* CT4 ...... 107 H7
    RCANTW CT4 ...... 127 G4
    RCANTW CT4 ...... 147 G2
Pettfield Hill Rd *FAV* ME13 ...... 99 K5
Pett HI *RCANTW* CT4 ...... 107 K5
Pett La *HDCN* TN27 ...... 119 F7
Pettman Cl *HB* CT6 ...... 46 E3
Pett's Crs *MSTR* CT12 ...... 74 A1
Peverell Rd *DVE/WH* CT16 ...... 173 F1
Pheasants' Hall Rd *RCANTW* CT4 ...... 127 K5
Phillippa Ct *SIT* ME10 ...... 35 K7
Phillip Rd *FOLKN* CT19 ...... 13 E3
Phillips Rd *BRCH* CT7 ...... 29 K8
Pickelden La *RCANTW* CT4 ...... 106 B6
Pickneybush La *LYDD* TN29 ...... 215 F8
Picton Rd *RAM* CT11 ...... 4 C5
Pie Factory Rd *RDV* CT15 ...... 131 G5
Pier Av *HB* CT6 ...... 46 D1
    WSTB CT5 ...... 44 A4
Pierpoint Rd *WSTB* CT5 ...... 44 A7
Pierremont Av *BRDST* CT10 ...... 55 H2
The Pier *DVE/WH* CT16 ...... 152 D6
Pigeon La *HB* CT6 ...... 47 F4
Pike Cl *FOLKN* CT19 ...... 12 A2
Pike Rd *RDV* CT15 ...... 132 C3
Pilckem Cl *CANT* CT1 ...... 87 H5
Pilgrims La *RCANTW* CT4 ...... 104 A5
    WSTB CT5 ...... 65 J2
Pilgrims Spring *FOLKN* CT19 ...... 12 C1
Pilgrims Rd *CANT* CT1 ...... 7 F4
Pilgrims Wy *CANT* CT1 ...... 7 E4
    DVE/WH CT16 ...... 172 E3
    HDCN TN27 ...... 119 G6

    RASHE TN25 ...... 140 B1
    RASHE TN25 ...... 165 J7
Pilots Av *DEAL* CT14 ...... 135 G2
Pilot's Farm Rd *RCANTW* CT4 ...... 126 E2
Pineham Rd *RDV* CT15 ...... 153 H7
Pineside Rd *RCANTE* CT3 ...... 88 E6 □
The Pines *BRDST* CT10 ...... 54 D2
Pine Tree Av *CANTW/ST* CT2 ...... 6 B1
Pinetree Cl *WSTB* CT5 ...... 44 C3 □
Pine Wk *HB* CT6 ...... 47 K1 □
Pine Wy *FOLKN* CT19 ...... 189 J7 □
Pinewood Cl *MSTR* CT12 ...... 4 C2
Pin HI *CANT* CT1 ...... 6 C4
Pinners HI *RDV* CT15 ...... 110 E8
Pinners La *RDV* CT15 ...... 130 E1
Pintail Wy *HB* CT6 ...... 47 H4 □
Pioneer Rd *DVE/WH* CT16 ...... 172 E3
Pippin Av *RCANTW* CT4 ...... 108 B6
Pippin Cl *SIT* ME10 ...... 35 J8 □
Pitstock Rd *RSIT* ME9 ...... 77 H2
Pittlesden *TENT* TN30 ...... 194 A7
Pivington La *HDCN* TN27 ...... 137 H4
Pixwell La *DEAL* CT14 ...... 134 D3
Place La *RASHW* TN26 ...... 196 D4
The Place *RCANTW* CT4 ...... 130 B5 □
Plain Rd *FOLK* CT20 ...... 12 A5
    RASHE TN25 ...... 185 G2
Plains of Waterloo *RAM* CT11 ...... 5 E4
Plantation Cl *RASHW* TN26 ...... 139 J7 □
Plantation Rd *FAV* ME13 ...... 62 B7
    WSTB CT5 ...... 45 G4
Playstool Cl *RSIT* ME9 ...... 34 A8
Pleasance Road Central
    LYDD TN29 ...... 239 G1
Pleasance Rd North *LYDD* TN29 ...... 239 F1
Pleasance Rd South *LYDD* TN29 ...... 239 G4
Pleasent Pl *IOS* ME12 ...... 15 F8 □
Pleydell Gdns *FOLK* CT20 ...... 12 C5
Plimsoll Av *FOLKN* CT19 ...... 13 D1
Plough Cl *HB* CT6 ...... 47 J4 □
Plough HI *RDV* CT15 ...... 192 E2
Plough La *WSTB* CT5 ...... 45 G3
Plough Rd *IOS* ME12 ...... 22 D1
Plover Rd *IOS* ME12 ...... 21 H1
Pluckley Gdns *MARG* CT9 ...... 33 F4
Pluckley Rd *HDCN* TN27 ...... 138 D1
    HDCN TN27 ...... 156 B4
    HDCN TN27 ...... 157 F2
    HDCN TN27 ...... 157 J7
    RASHW TN26 ...... 158 C1
Plumford Rd *FAV* ME13 ...... 80 E4
Plumpudding La *FAV* ME13 ...... 64 E6
Plumstone Rd *BRCH* CT7 ...... 51 K4
Plum Tree Gdns *RASHW* TN26 ...... 196 D5 □
Plurenden Rd *RASHW* TN26 ...... 179 F7
Poets Cnr *MARG* CT9 ...... 3 D4
Poets Wk *DEAL* CT14 ...... 135 H5
Pollard Cl *ASH* TN23 ...... 160 D6 □
Polo Wy *WSTB* CT5 ...... 45 F5
Pomfret Rd *RCANTW* CT4 ...... 105 F5
Pommeus La *DEAL* CT14 ...... 134 C3
Poncia Rd *ASH* TN23 ...... 8 A6 □
Pond Dr *SIT* ME10 ...... 58 B4
Pond Farm Rd *RSIT* ME9 ...... 56 E5
Pond HI *RCANTE* CT3 ...... 109 K5
Pond Hill Rd *FOLK* CT20 ...... 206 C1
Pond La *RCANTE* CT3 ...... 129 K3
    RDV CT15 ...... 154 D7
Ponycart La *RCANTW* CT4 ...... 146 C3
Pook La *HDCN* TN27 ...... 176 A1
Poorhole La *BRDST* CT10 ...... 54 B1
Pope House La *TENT* TN30 ...... 194 B2
Popes La *CANTW/ST* CT2 ...... 68 D7
Pope St *RCANTW* CT4 ...... 124 A2
Poplar Cl *ASH* TN23 ...... 160 D3
Poplar Dr *HB* CT6 ...... 46 B4
    RDV CT15 ...... 131 K4 □
Poplar La *LYDD* TN29 ...... 231 H3 □
Poplar Rd *BRDST* CT10 ...... 33 F8
    RAM CT11 ...... 5 D4
    TENT TN30 ...... 219 J3
The Poplars *RCANTE* CT3 ...... 70 A5
Popsal La *RCANTE* CT3 ...... 90 D8
Porter Cl *IOS* ME12 ...... 15 H8
Porter's La *FAV* ME13 ...... 81 F4
Portland Av *SIT* ME10 ...... 58 D2
Portland Cl *HYTHE* CT21 ...... 205 F4
    KEN/WIL TN24 ...... 141 F7
Portland Ct *RAM* CT11 ...... 5 E4 □
Portland Rd *HYTHE* CT21 ...... 205 F4
    RASHE TN25 ...... 160 C5 □
Postling Rd *FOLKN* CT19 ...... 189 K7
Pot Kiln La *RASHW* TN26 ...... 177 J3
Potten Street Rd *BRCH* CT7 ...... 50 E3
Potters Cl *KEN/WIL* TN24 ...... 140 C8
Potter St *SWCH* CT13 ...... 94 A5 □
Poulders La *SWCH* CT13 ...... 93 H6
Poulton Cl *DVW* CT17 ...... 172 D6
Poulton La *RCANTE* CT3 ...... 92 A5
Pound Ct *ASH* TN23 ...... 181 K3
Poundhurst Rd *RASHW* TN26 ...... 199 F2
Pound La *ASH* TN23 ...... 181 J2
    CANTW/ST CT2 ...... 6 C2
    RASHE TN25 ...... 185 G1
    RCANTW CT4 ...... 121 K2

RCANTW CT4	**167** K2	
Power Station Rd *IOS* ME12	**15** F7	
Prentis Cl *SIT* ME10	**57** H1	
Prentis Quay *SIT* ME10	**57** K1	
Prescott Rd *RDV* CT15	**173** J1	
Prestedge Av *RAM* CT11	**5** E1	
Preston Av *FAV* ME13	**81** J1	
Preston Gv *FAV* ME13	**62** B8	
Preston Hall Gdns *IOS* ME12	**24** C2	
Preston La *FAV* ME13	**62** B8	
RCANTE CT3	**90** D2	
Preston Pde CT5	**43** G7	
Preston Pk *FAV* ME13	**62** C8	
Preston Rd *MSTR* CT12	**53** J3	
RCANTE CT3	**90** D2	
Preston St *FAV* ME13	**62** C8	
Pretoria Rd *CANT* CT1	**7** E3	
Price's Av *MARG* CT9	**3** G5	
RAM CT11	**4** C5	
Priest Av *CANTW/ST* CT2	**86** A6	
Priest Flds *HB* CT6	**48** A1	
Priest Wk *WSTB* CT5	**44** E3	
Primrose Rd *ASH* TN23	**182** A3	
Primrose Hl *RCANTW* CT4	**84** C7	
Primrose La *RSIT* ME9	**57** F8	
Primrose Rd *DVW* CT17	**172** E5	
Primrose Wy *MSTR* CT12	**75** H1	
WSTB CT5	**45** F5	
Prince Andrew Rd *BRDST* CT10	**33** F7	
Prince Charles Av *IOS* ME12	**15** K8	
SIT ME10	**58** C4	
Prince Charles Rd *BRDST* CT10	**33** F7	
Prince of Wales Rbt *DVW* CT17	**10** B5	
Prince of Wales Ter *DEAL* CT14	**135** K1	
Princes Av *IOS* ME12	**16** A7	
MSTR CT12	**4** B2	
Princes Cl *BRCH* CT7	**29** G7	
Princes Crs *MARG* CT9	**3** D3	
Princes Dr *SWCH* CT13	**95** G5	
Prince's Gdns *MARG* CT9	**32** D4	
Princes Pde *HYTHE* CT21	**205** K4	
Prince's Rd *RAM* CT11	**5** D1	
Princess Anne Rd *BRDST* CT10	**33** F7	
Princess Cl *WSTB* CT5	**45** F5	
Princess Margaret Av *MARG* CT9	**32** E4	
MSTR CT12	**4** A2	
Princess Rd *WSTB* CT5	**45** F5	
Princess St *FOLKN* CT19	**13** E3	
Princes St *DEAL* CT14	**115** K5	
DVW CT17	**10** B3	
MARG CT9	**3** D3	
Prince's Wk *MARG* CT9	**32** D3	
Princes Wy *CANTW/ST* CT2	**6** A2	
Prioress Rd *CANTW/ST* CT2	**6** A3	
Prior Rd *LYDD* TN29	**232** E2	
Priory Cl *NROM* TN28	**226** A8	
Priory Gdns *FOLK* CT20	**13** D5	
Priory Gate Rd *DVW* CT17	**10** A3	
Priory Gv *DVW* CT17	**10** A3	
Priory Hl *DVW* CT17	**10** A3	
Priory La *RASHE* TN25	**185** K2	
Priory of St Jacob *CANT* CT1	**6** B5	
Priory Rd *DVE/WH* CT16	**10** B3	
FAV ME13	**62** A6	
RAM CT11	**5** D5	
RASHE TN25	**183** H8	
Priory Rw *FAV* ME13	**62** B5	
Priory Station Approach Rd		
DVW CT17	**10** A4	
Priory St *DVE/WH* CT16	**10** B3	
Priory Wy *TENT* TN30	**194** C7	
Promenade *BRCH* CT7	**29** J5	
DEAL CT14	**135** K3	
The Promenade *IOS* ME12	**25** H4	
Prospect Gdns *MSTR* CT12	**52** A7	
Prospect Pl *BRDST* CT10	**55** J2	
CANT CT1	**7** D4	
DVW CT17	**173** F5	
Prospect Rd *BRCH* CT7	**29** J7	
BRDST CT10	**55** J2	
FOLK CT20	**206** D3	
HYTHE CT21	**205** G4	
MSTR CT12	**52** A8	
Prospect Wy *RASHE* TN25	**164** A8	
Provender Rd *FAV* ME13	**60** C8	
Providence St *ASH* TN23	**8** C5	
Puckle La *CANT* CT1	**7** D5	
Pudding La *RCANTE* CT3	**92** B5	
Pullman Cl *MSTR* CT12	**4** C1	
Pump La *MARG* CT9	**2** C3	
Purchase La *RASHW* TN26	**159** G7	
Puttney Dr *SIT* ME10	**36** B6	
Pye Alley La *WSTB* CT5	**65** J3	
Pyson's Rd *MSTR* CT12	**4** C1	

Q

Quantock Dr *KEN/WIL* TN24	**8** B2	
Quantock Gdns *MSTR* CT12	**54** C3	
Quarrington La *RASHE* TN25	**163** F6	

Quarry Rd *HYTHE* CT21	**205** F3	
Quarry Vw *ASH* TN23	**160** B7	
Quarry Wk *HYTHE* CT21	**205** F3	
Quarry Wd *RASHE* TN25	**184** B8	
Quay La *SWCH* CT13	**94** A5	
Queen Bertha Rd *RAM* CT11	**4** C5	
Queen Bertha's Av *BRCH* CT7	**30** B6	
Queenborough Dr *IOS* ME12	**15** J7	
Queenborough Rd *IOS* ME12	**14** D8	
IOS ME12	**20** D2	
Queendown Rd *BRCH* CT7	**52** E2	
Queen Elizabeth Av *MARG* CT9	**32** E5	
Queen Elizabeth Rd *DVE/WH* CT16	**11** G3	
Queen's Av *BRCH* CT7	**29** G7	
BRDST CT10	**33** J8	
CANTW/ST CT2	**6** A2	
DVW CT17	**172** E7	
FOLK CT20	**189** G8	
HB CT6	**47** J1	
MARG CT9	**2** C4	
MSTR CT12	**4** B2	
Queensbridge Dr *HB* CT6	**46** B1	
Queens Ct *MARG* CT9	**3** E2	
Queensdown Rd *DEAL* CT14	**155** J2	
Queen's Gdns *DVE/WH* CT16	**10** B3	
HB CT6	**46** E1	
Queen's Gate Rd *RAM* CT11	**4** C4	
Queens Ms *DEAL* CT14	**115** K8	
Queens Pde *MARG* CT9	**3** E2	
Queen's Prom *MARG* CT9	**3** F2	
Queen's Ri *DEAL* CT14	**155** F1	
Queen's Rd *BRDST* CT10	**55** J2	
FAV ME13	**62** A7	
IOS ME12	**16** A7	
KEN/WIL TN24	**8** B2	
KEN/WIL TN24	**162** A5	
LYDD TN29	**231** H8	
NROM TN28	**226** E8	
RAM CT11	**4** A7	
RCANTE CT3	**92** B4	
RCANTE CT3	**130** B1	
WGOS CT8	**30** E6	
WSTB CT5	**44** C4	
Queen St *ASH* TN23	**8** B3	
DEAL CT14	**115** J8	
DVE/WH CT16	**10** B4	
FOLK CT20	**13** E4	
HB CT6	**46** E1	
MARG CT9	**2** C3	
Queen's Wy *IOS* ME12	**14** B6	
Queensway *LYDD* TN29	**217** F4	
LYDD TN29	**231** H8	
Quern Rd *DEAL* CT14	**135** G4	
Querns Pl *CANT* CT1	**7** E3	
Querns Rd *CANT* CT1	**7** E3	
Quested Rd *FOLKN* CT19	**189** K8	
Quetta Rd *MSTR* CT12	**54** A5	
Quex Rd *WGOS* CT8	**30** E6	
Quex View Rd *BRCH* CT7	**51** K1	
Quince Orch *RASHW* TN26	**198** B6	
Quinton Rd *RSIT* ME9	**35** H7	

R

Rabbit Hole *RCANTW* CT4	**129** C3	
Radfall Ride *WSTB* CT5	**67** F1	
Radfall Rd *WSTB* CT5	**45** F8	
Radley Cl *BRDST* CT10	**33** H8	
Radnor Bridge Rd *FOLK* CT20	**13** G4	
Radnor Cliff *FOLK* CT20	**13** D5	
Radnor Cliff Crs *FOLK* CT20	**207** F5	
Radnor Cl *HB* CT6	**47** G5	
Radnor Park Av *FOLKN* CT19	**13** D4	
Radnor Park Gdns *FOLKN* CT19	**12** C3	
Radnor Park Rd *FOLKN* CT19	**12** C4	
Radnor Pk West *FOLKN* CT19	**12** B4	
Radnor St *FOLKN* CT19	**13** E4	
Ragstone Hollow *RASHE* TN25	**184** B8	
Railway Av *WSTB* CT5	**44** B5	
Railway Hl *RCANTW* CT4	**128** C6	
Railway Rd *IOS* ME12	**14** C4	
Railway Ter *QBOR* ME11	**20** B3	
Raleigh Cl *KEN/WIL* TN24	**162** A6	
Raleigh Wy *IOS* ME12	**15** F8	
Ram La *RASHW* TN26	**138** E6	
Rampart Rd *HYTHE* CT21	**205** F3	
Ramsey Cl *CANTW/ST* CT2	**6** B2	
Ramsgate Rd *BRDST* CT10	**5** F1	
BRDST CT10	**55** G3	
MARG CT9	**3** D4	
SWCH CT13	**75** F7	
SWCH CT13	**94** A1	
Ramstone Cl *RASHE* TN25	**185** F1	
Rancorn Rd *MARG* CT9	**2** A4	
Randolph Cl *CANT* CT1	**7** D5	
Randolph Gdns *KEN/WIL* TN24	**161** J1	
Randolph Rd *DVW* CT17	**173** F5	
Ranelagh Gdns *BRDST* CT10	**55** F1	
Ranelagh Gv *BRDST* CT10	**55** F1	
Ranelagh Rd *DEAL* CT14	**135** K1	
IOS ME12	**14** D4	

Range Rd *HYTHE* CT21	**205** F6	
IOS ME12	**23** G5	
Raspberry Hill La *RSIT* ME9	**19** H8	
Ratling Rd *RCANTE* CT3	**110** C3	
Rattington St *RCANTW* CT4	**105** F4	
Ravenlea Rd *FOLK* CT20	**12** A4	
Ravenscourt Rd *CANTW/ST* CT2	**85** K3	
DEAL CT14	**135** J1	
Rawdon Rd *RAM* CT11	**4** C5	
Rawling St *RSIT* ME9	**77** F2	
Rayham Rd *WSTB* CT5	**44** D6	
Raymond Av *CANT* CT1	**7** D4	
Raymond Fuller Wy *KEN/WIL* TN24	**9** E1	
Raymoor Av *LYDD* TN29	**227** H2	
Rayners Hl *RMAID* ME17	**97** J8	
Reach Cl *RDV* CT15	**155** F8	
Reachfields *HYTHE* CT21	**204** E5	
Reach Rd *HYTHE* CT21	**205** F4	
RDV CT15	**175** F1	
Reading Cl *DEAL* CT14	**135** H5	
Reading Rd *DVW* CT17	**172** D7	
Reading St *BRDST* CT10	**33** G6	
TENT TN30	**209** H3	
Reading Street Rd *MARG* CT9	**33** F5	
Recce La *RFOLK* CT18	**169** G2	
Recreation Ground Rd *TENT* TN30	**194** B7	
Rectory Cl *RASHW* TN26	**196** C4	
Rectory Gdns *WSTB* CT5	**45** G4	
Rectory La *HYTHE* CT21	**205** F2	
RCANTW CT4	**129** G5	
RFOLK CT18	**167** G8	
Rectory Rd *BRDST* CT10	**55** J1	
DEAL CT14	**135** F2	
LYDD TN29	**226** C1	
SIT ME10	**58** C3	
Recutver Wy *KEN/WIL* TN24	**161** G1	
Reculver Av *BRCH* CT7	**29** H1	
Reculver Cl *HB* CT6	**26** A8	
Reculver Dr *HB* CT6	**47** K1	
Reculver La *HB* CT6	**48** B1	
Reculver Rd *HB* CT6	**47** K1	
Reculvers Rd *WGOS* CT8	**30** E7	
Redberry Rd *ASH* TN23	**182** A1	
Redbrook St *RASHW* TN26	**178** C5	
Redbrooks Wy *HYTHE* CT21	**204** D3	
Redcot La *RCANTE* CT3	**69** C7	
Redhill Rd *WGOS* CT8	**30** C6	
Redhouse La *RCANTW* CT4	**106** C6	
Redhouse Wall *DEAL* CT14	**115** H5	
Redmill Cl *FOLK* CT20	**206** E1	
Redoubt Wy *LYDD* TN29	**217** J2	
Red Rd *FAV* ME13	**83** K1	
Redsull Av *DEAL* CT14	**135** G3	
Red Tree Orch *ASH* TN23	**160** C7	
Redwood Cl *CANTW/ST* CT2	**6** B1	
Reed Av *CANT* CT1	**7** F1	
Reedland Crs *FAV* ME13	**62** B6	
Reedmace Cl *ASH* TN23	**160** B6	
Reeds Cl *HB* CT6	**47** G2	
Reeves Wy *WSTB* CT5	**45** F5	
Regency Ct *SIT* ME10	**57** J2	
Regency Pl *CANT* CT1	**7** E1	
Regents Pl *ASH* TN23	**8** B3	
Regent St *WSTB* CT5	**44** A4	
Regis Crs *SIT* ME10	**36** A7	
Rendezvous St *FOLK* CT20	**13** D4	
The Rendezvous *MARG* CT9	**2** C2	
Rentain Rd *RCANTW* CT4	**105** F4	
Repton Cl *BRDST* CT10	**33** G8	
Repton Manor Rd *ASH* TN23	**8** A2	
Reservoir Av *LYDD* TN29	**239** C8	
Reservoir Rd *WSTB* CT5	**44** B4	
Rest Harrow *FAV* ME13	**101** G1	
The Retreat *BRCH* CT7	**30** A6	
MSTR CT12	**4** B3	
Rhee Wall *RASHW* TN26	**211** F7	
Rheims Ct *CANTW/ST* CT2	**6** A2	
Rheims Wy *CANT* CT1	**6** B3	
Rhodaus Cl *CANT* CT1	**6** C4	
Rhodaus Town *CANT* CT1	**6** C4	
Rhodes Gdns *BRDST* CT10	**33** G8	
Richardson Wy *MSTR* CT12	**53** J8	
Richborough Rd *SWCH* CT13	**93** J1	
WGOS CT8	**30** E7	
Richbourgh Rd *SWCH* CT13	**93** J3	
Richdore Rd *RCANTW* CT4	**124** E7	
Richmond Av *MARG* CT9	**3** F4	
Richmond Dr *HB* CT6	**47** K2	
NROM TN28	**226** D6	
SIT ME10	**35** K7	
Richmond Gdns *CANTW/ST* CT2	**86** A4	
Richmond Rd *RAM* CT11	**5** D5	
WSTB CT5	**44** E5	
Richmond St *FOLKN* CT19	**189** J8	
HB CT6	**46** E1	
IOS ME12	**14** E4	
Riddles Rd *SIT* ME10	**57** H3	
The Ridge *KEN/WIL* TN24	**161** J1	
Ridgeway *HYTHE* CT21	**203** J3	
WSTB CT5	**45** F5	
Ridgeway Cliff *HB* CT6	**46** B1	
Ridgeway Rd *HB* CT6	**47** F7	
The Ridgeway *BRDST* CT10	**55** F3	
DVW CT17	**172** C4	

FAV ME13 .... 83 G3
MARG CT9 .... 3 F4
RASHE TN25 .... 184 C1
Ridgeway Wk HB CT6 .... 47 F7
Ridham Av SIT ME10 .... 36 B5
Riding Gate Rbt CANT CT1 .... 6 C4 ⑧
Riding HI KEN/WIL TN24 .... 141 G8 ⑧
The Ridings MARG CT9 .... 33 F3
WSTB CT5 .... 45 G5
Ridley Cl HB CT6 .... 47 F6
Rigden Rd ASH TN23 .... 8 B6
Rigshill Rd FAV ME13 .... 118 D1
Riley Av HB CT6 .... 45 J2
Ringold Av MSTR CT12 .... 4 A3
Ring Wall DEAL CT14 .... 114 E4
Ringwood Cl CANTW/ST CT2 .... 86 C5
Ringwould Rd DEAL CT14 .... 155 H1
RDV CT15 .... 154 D2
Ripley Rd KEN/WIL TN24 .... 162 A6
Ripple Rd DEAL CT14 .... 135 F8
Risborough La FOLK CT20 .... 206 D1
Risborough Wy FOLK CT20 .... 189 K8
Risdon Cl CANTW/ST CT2 .... 68 E3
The Rise TN23 .... 160 C7
DEAL CT14 .... 155 J1
IOS ME12 .... 20 D1
RDV CT15 .... 155 H8
RSIT ME9 .... 57 G4
Rising Rd ASH TN23 .... 8 A4
River Ct RCANTW CT4 .... 105 F3
River Dl DVW CT17 .... 172 D3
Riverdale Rd CANT CT1 .... 87 E3
River Dr DVW CT17 .... 172 D4
Riverhead Cl MARG CT9 .... 3 F4 ⑧
SIT ME10 .... 57 H3
River Meadow DVW CT17 .... 172 D5
Riversdale Rd ASH TN23 .... 4 A2
MSTR CT12 .... 4 A2
Riverside RCANTW CT4 .... 104 E3
Riverside Cl ASH TN23 .... 181 K3
RCANTW CT4 .... 108 A5
Riverside Ms RCANTW CT4 .... 108 A5 ⑧
Riverside Rd MSTR CT12 .... 75 F5
Rivers Rd RSIT ME9 .... 60 A4
River St DVW CT17 .... 172 C3
Riverview ASH TN23 .... 160 C5 ⑧
River Vw CANTW/ST CT2 .... 68 E7
QBOR ME11 .... 20 A3
Riviera Rd FOLK CT20 .... 207 F3
Riverslade DVE/WH CT16 .... 172 A1
Road of Remembrance FOLK CT20 .. 13 D5
Roberts Cl IOS ME12 .... 35 J7
Roberts Rd NROM TN28 .... 233 F5
WSTB CT5 .... 43 G8
Robert St DEAL CT14 .... 115 K7
Robin Hood La LYDD TN29 .... 237 H1
Robin La LYDD TN29 .... 231 H8
Robins Av RMAID ME17 .... 116 C1
Robin's Cl HYTHE CT21 .... 204 A6
RMAID ME17 .... 116 C2
Robus Cl RFOLK CT18 .... 167 G7
Rochester Av CANT CT1 .... 7 E5
Rock Hill Rd HDCN TN27 .... 136 E4
Rockingham Pl HB CT6 .... 47 G4
Rock Rd SIT ME10 .... 57 K2
Rockstone Wy MSTR CT12 .... 54 A5
Rocky Bourne Rd RASHE TN25 ..... 183 J8
RASHE TN25 .... 200 D1
Rodmer Cl IOS ME12 .... 15 K6
Rodney St RAM CT11 .... 5 D5
Roebuck Rd FAV ME13 .... 61 K7
Rokesley Rd DVE/WH CT16 .... 173 F1
Rolfe La NROM TN28 .... 226 B8
Roll's Av IOS ME12 .... 23 C5 ⑧
Rolvenden Dr SIT ME10 .... 57 G1
Roman Cl DEAL CT14 .... 115 H8
Roman Rd FAV ME13 .... 62 B7
MSTR CT12 .... 4 B7
RDV CT15 .... 153 C1
RDV CT15 .... 153 H5
Roman Sq SIT ME10 .... 58 A3
Roman Wy ASH TN23 .... 182 A2
FOLKN CT19 .... 189 H8
RDV CT15 .... 131 K4
RDV CT15 .... 175 F1
Romden Rd HDCN TN27 .... 156 E4
Rome Rd NROM TN28 .... 226 B8 ⑧
Romilly Gdns MSTR CT12 .... 4 C1 ⑧
Romney Av FOLK CT20 .... 207 F1
Romney Cl SIT ME10 .... 57 J1
Romney Marsh Rd ASH TN23 .... 8 C4
ASH TN23 .... 182 A1
Romney Rd KEN/WIL TN24 .... 9 E4
LYDD TN29 .... 231 K1
RASHW TN26 .... 198 E7
Romney Wy HYTHE CT21 .... 204 C5
Romsey Cl KEN/WIL TN24 .... 162 A4 ⑧
Rookery Cl KEN/WIL TN24 .... 141 J7 ⑧
RSIT ME9 .... 57 F8
Rook La ASH TN23 .... 34 E8
Roonagh Ct SIT ME10 .... 57 K4
Roosevelt Av DVE/WH CT16 .... 173 F3
Roper Cl CANTW/ST CT2 .... 6 B2
Roper Rd CANTW/ST CT2 .... 6 C1 ⑧
RSIT ME9 .... 60 A3

Roseacre Cl CANTW/ST CT2 .... 6 B2
Roseacre Ct MARG CT9 .... 33 F4 ⑧
Rose Acre Rd RCANTW CT3 .... 89 F7
Rosebery Av HB CT6 .... 47 K1
RAM CT11 .... 5 F2
Rosebery Cl SIT ME10 .... 58 E2
Rosedale Rd MARG CT9 .... 3 E1
Rose Gdns BRCH CT7 .... 29 J8 ⑧
HB CT6 .... 47 H2
MSTR CT12 .... 52 A8
RDV CT15 .... 132 B7
Rose HI TENT TN30 .... 220 C1
Roselands DEAL CT14 .... 135 H5
Roselands Gdns CANTW/ST CT2 ...... 6 A1 ⑧
Rose La CANT CT1 .... 6 C5
RCANTW CT4 .... 128 C1
RMAID ME17 .... 117 H5
Roselawn Gdns MARG CT9 .... 31 G6
Roselea Av HB CT6 .... 46 E3
Roseleigh Rd SIT ME10 .... 57 J5
Rosemary Av BRDST CT10 .... 5 F1
IOS ME12 .... 14 E8
Rosemary Gdns BRDST CT10 .... 5 F1
IOS ME12 .... 14 C4
Rosemary La CANT CT1 .... 6 C3 ⑪
Rose St IOS ME12 .... 14 C4
Rosetower Ct BRDST CT10 .... 33 G5
Rose Wk RFOLK CT18 .... 190 B2
Rossendale Gdns FOLK CT20 .... 13 E5 ⑧
Rossendale Rd FOLK CT20 .... 13 E5
Rossetti Rd BRCH CT7 .... 29 J6
Ross Gdns CANTW/ST CT2 .... 85 J3
Rossland Rd MSTR CT12 .... 4 A3
Ross Wy FOLK CT20 .... 206 E2
Rothbrook Dr KEN/WIL TN24 .... 141 G7
Rothley Cl TENT TN30 .... 194 B6
Rough Common Rd CANTW/ST CT2 .. 85 J4
Roundel Cl RSIT ME9 .... 60 A4
The Roundel SIT ME10 .... 57 K4
Rowan Cl ASH TN23 .... 160 C4
CANTW/ST CT2 .... 68 E8
RCANTE CT3 .... 91 J8 ⑧
Rowe Cl RMAID ME17 .... 3 D6
Rowena Av WGOS CT8 .... 30 D5
Rowetts Wy IOS ME12 .... 23 F3
Rowland Crs HB CT6 .... 47 K1 ⑧
Rowland Dr HB CT6 .... 46 B4
The Row RCANTW CT4 .... 167 K2
Roxburgh Rd WGOS CT8 .... 30 E5
Royal Av WSTB CT5 .... 65 K1
Royal Cl BRDST CT10 .... 55 F2
Royal Esp MARG CT9 .... 31 F5
RAM CT11 .... 4 B6
Royal Military Av FOLK CT20 .... 206 D1
Royal Military Canal Pth
RASHE TN25 .... 200 A6
RASHW TN26 .... 211 G5
TENT TN30 .... 221 H6
Royal Military Rd HYTHE CT21 ..... 205 F5
Royal Pde RAM CT11 .... 5 F5
Royal Rd IOS ME12 .... 14 D4 ⑧
RAM CT11 .... 5 D5
Royds Rd KEN/WIL TN24 .... 161 H8
Royston Gdns RDV CT15 .... 155 F8
Royton Av RMAID ME17 .... 116 D1
Rubery Dro RCANTE CT3 .... 74 B8
Ruckinge Rd RASHW TN26 .... 198 E7
Rugby Cl BRDST CT10 .... 55 G1
Rugby Gdns ASH TN23 .... 8 C5 ⑧
Rugby Rd DVW CT17 .... 172 E8
Ruins Barn Rd RSIT ME9 .... 76 C2
SIT ME10 .... 57 K6
Rumfields Rd BRDST CT10 .... 54 E2
Runnymede Ms FAV ME13 .... 62 B7 ⑧
Rush Cl LYDD TN29 .... 216 D8
Rushenden Rd QBOR ME11 .... 20 B2
Rushmead Cl CANTW/ST CT2 .... 6 A1
Russell Cl SIT ME10 .... 57 H3
Russell Dr WSTB CT5 .... 45 G3
Russell Pl FAV ME13 .... 62 A3
Russell Rd FOLKN CT19 .... 13 D3 ⑩
IOS ME12 .... 14 C4
Russell St DVE/WH CT16 .... 10 C3 ⑧
Russet Av FAV ME13 .... 81 J1
Russet Cl CANT CT1 .... 7 F4
The Russets WSTB CT5 .... 45 G5
Rutherford Rd KEN/WIL TN24 ...... 161 F1
Rutland Av MARG CT9 .... 32 D4 ⑧
Rutland Cl CANT CT1 .... 87 F2
Rutland Gdns BRCH CT7 .... 29 J7
MARG CT9 .... 32 D4
Rutland Rd DVE/WH CT16 .... 173 F3 ⑧
Rydal Av RAM CT11 .... 4 A4
Ryder's Av WGOS CT8 .... 30 C6
Ryde St CANTW/ST CT2 .... 6 B2
Rye Rd LYDD TN29 .... 223 G6
TENT TN30 .... 220 B4
Rye Wk HB CT6 .... 47 H4
Ryland Pl FOLK CT20 .... 13 E4 ⑧
Rylands Rd KEN/WIL TN24 .... 9 D1
Rype Cl LYDD TN29 .... 237 H1
Ryswick Ms NROM TN28 .... 226 D6 ⑧

S

Sackett's Gap MARG CT9 .... 32 D3 ⑧
Sacketts HI BRDST CT10 .... 32 C8
Sackville Cl RASHW TN26 .... 139 J7 ⑧
Sackville Crs ASH TN23 .... 8 A3 ⑧
Saddlers HI RCANTE CT3 .... 111 F4
Saddlers Ms WSTB CT5 .... 45 G5 ⑧
Saddler's Wall La LYDD TN29 ...... 222 E5
Saddlers Wy ASH TN23 .... 182 A2
Saddleton Rd WSTB CT5 .... 44 A6
Saffron's Pl FOLK CT20 .... 13 E4 ⑧
Saffron Wy SIT ME10 .... 36 A7
St Agnes Gdns IOS ME12 .... 14 D5
St Alban's Rd RCANTE CT3 .... 69 K5
St Alphege Cl WSTB CT5 .... 43 J7 ⑧
St Alphege La CANT CT1 .... 6 C2 ⑬
St Alphege Rd DVE/WH CT16 .... 10 A2 ⑧
St Ambrose Gn RASHE TN25 .... 142 E4 ⑧
St Andrews Cl CANT CT1 .... 6 B4 ⑧
FOLKN CT19 .... 12 B2
HB CT6 .... 46 E2
MARG CT9 .... 3 D6
WSTB CT5 .... 44 B7
St Andrews Gdns DVW CT17 .... 173 F4 ⑧
RDV CT15 .... 151 G1
St Andrew's Lees SWCH CT13 ...... 94 A6
St Andrew's Rd DEAL CT14 .... 115 J8
NROM TN28 .... 226 E8
RAM CT11 .... 5 F3
St Andrews Wy DEAL CT14 .... 132 E3
St Anne's Dr HB CT6 .... 46 C2
St Anne's Gdns MARG CT9 .... 3 D5
St Anne's Rd ASH TN23 .... 160 D7
WSTB CT5 .... 44 C3
St Ann's Rd FAV ME13 .... 62 A8
LYDD TN29 .... 216 D7
St Anthony's Wy MARG CT9 .... 32 D5
St Augustine's Av MARG CT9 .... 3 D5 ⑧
St Augustine's Crs WSTB CT5 .... 45 G3
St Augustine's Pk RAM CT11 .... 4 C6 ⑧
St Augustine's Rd CANT CT1 .... 7 E4
DEAL CT14 .... 135 F2 ⑧
RAM CT11 .... 5 D6
St Bart's Rd SWCH CT13 .... 93 J6
St Benedict's Lawn RAM CT11 .... 5 D6 ⑧
St Benet's Rd WGOS CT8 .... 30 D7
St Benets Wy TENT TN30 .... 194 B6
St Catherine's Dr FAV ME13 .... 62 C8
St Catherine's Gv MSTR CT12 .... 53 J5
St Christopher Cl MARG CT9 .... 32 E6 ⑧
St Christophers Gn BRDST CT10 .... 55 G1 ⑧
St Clare Rd DEAL CT14 .... 135 J1
St Clements SWCH CT13 .... 94 A5 ⑧
St Clements Cl IOS ME12 .... 24 C4
St Clements Ct BRDST CT10 .... 55 F1 ⑧
St Clements Rd IOS ME12 .... 24 D3 ⑧
WGOS CT8 .... 30 D5
St Cosmus Cl RASHE TN25 .... 121 F5
St Crispin's Rd WGOS CT8 .... 30 D6
St Davids Av DVW CT17 .... 193 K2
St David's Cl BRCH CT7 .... 30 A6
WSTB CT5 .... 44 B7
St David's Rd DEAL CT14 .... 115 J8 ⑧
RAM CT11 .... 5 F2
St Denys Rd RFOLK CT18 .... 190 C1
St Dunstan's Cl CANTW/ST CT2 ...... 6 B2
St Dunstan's Rd MARG CT9 .... 3 E5 ⑧
St Dunstan's St CANTW/ST CT2 ...... 6 B2
St Dunstan's Ter CANTW/ST CT2 .... 6 B2
St Eanswythe Wy FOLK CT20 .... 13 D4 ⑧
St Edmunds Rd CANT CT1 .... 6 C5 ⑧
DEAL CT14 .... 134 E2
St Francis Cl DEAL CT14 .... 134 E2
MARG CT9 .... 32 E6 ⑧
St Francis Rd FOLKN CT19 .... 190 C1
St George's Av IOS ME12 .... 14 C6
IOS ME12 .... 23 F4
St George's Cl WSTB CT5 .... 44 B7
St Georges La CANT CT1 .... 7 D3 ⑬
St George's Lees SWCH CT13 .... 94 A6 ⑧
St George's Pl CANT CT1 .... 7 D3
HYTHE CT21 .... 204 B6
RDV CT15 .... 155 F8
SWCH CT13 .... 94 B6
St George's Rd BRDST CT10 .... 55 H2
DEAL CT14 .... 115 K8 ⑧
FOLKN CT19 .... 190 A3
RAM CT11 .... 5 F3
SWCH CT13 .... 94 A6
St Georges Sq CANT CT1 .... 7 D3 ⑬
St Georges Ter HB CT6 .... 46 E2
St Gregory's CANT CT1 .... 7 D2 ⑮
St Gregory's Cl DEAL CT14 .... 135 F2 ⑧
St Gregory's Rd CANT CT1 .... 7 E2
St Helen's Rd IOS ME12 .... 14 E5
St Hilda Rd FOLKN CT19 .... 189 K8 ⑧
St Hilda's Rd HYTHE CT21 .... 205 F5
St Jacob's Pl CANT CT1 .... 6 A5 ⑧
St James' Av BRDST CT10 .... 55 F7 ⑧
MSTR CT12 .... 4 B2
St James Cl IOS ME12 .... 24 C2
St James' Gdns WSTB CT5 .... 44 A6 ⑧

St James La *DVE/WH* CT16 .... 10 C4 ③
St James' Park Rd *MARG* CT9 .... 31 F6 ②
St James Rd *DEAL* CT14 .... 155 J1
St James's Terreace *BRCH* CT7 .... 30 A6
St James St *DVE/WH* CT16 .... 10 C3 ⑦
  DVE/WH CT16 .... 10 C3 ②
St Jean's Rd *WGOS* CT8 .... 30 D7
St John's Av *MSTR* CT12 .... 4 A2
  SIT ME10 .... 58 C3
St John's Church Rd *FOLKN* CT19 .. 12 C3 ③
St John's Cl *RFOLK* CT18 .... 169 G7
St Johns Crs *CANTW/ST* CT2 .... 67 G7
St John's La *ASH* TN23 .... 9 A3 ⑥
  CANT CT1 .... 6 C3 ②⓪
St John's Pl *CANT* CT1 .... 7 D2
St John's Rd *DVW* CT17 .... 10 A4
  FAV ME13 .... 62 C7
  HYTHE CT21 .... 204 E3
  MARG CT9 .... 3 D5
  NROM TN28 .... 226 B8
  RDV CT15 .... 131 K4
  WSTB CT5 .... 45 G3
St John's St *FOLK* CT20 .... 13 E4 ①①
  MARG CT9 .... 3 D5
St John's Wy *RFOLK* CT18 .... 169 F7
St Julien Av *RAM* CT11 .... 87 H5
St Katherine Rd *IOS* ME12 .... 15 F7
St Laurence Cl *RSIT* ME9 .... 58 E4
St Lawrence Av *RAM* CT11 .... 4 B6
St Lawrence Cl *CANT* CT1 .... 7 E5 ③
St Lawrence Forstal *CANT* CT1 .... 7 E5
St Lawrence Rd *CANT* CT1 .... 7 E5
St Leonard's Rd *DEAL* CT14 .... 135 H2 ③
  HYTHE CT21 .... 205 F5
St Louis Gv *HB* CT6 .... 46 B2
St Luke's Av *RAM* CT11 .... 5 D3
St Luke's Cl *WGOS* CT8 .... 30 D6
  WSTB CT5 .... 44 B7
St Luke's Rd *RAM* CT11 .... 5 D3
St Luke's Wk *RFOLK* CT18 .... 189 K2
St Margaret's Cl *WSTB* CT5 .... 43 H8 ③
St Margarets Dr *DEAL* CT14 .... 135 H6 ②
St Margarets Rd *BRCH* CT7 .... 52 E3
  RDV CT15 .... 175 G1
  WGOS CT8 .... 30 D7
St Margaret's St *CANT* CT1 .... 6 C3 ③①
St Mark's Cl *FOLK* CT20 .... 206 D1
  WSTB CT5 .... 44 B6
St Martins Av *CANT* CT1 .... 7 E3
St Martins Cl *CANT* CT1 .... 7 E3
St Martin's Hl *CANT* CT1 .... 7 E3 ③
St Martin's Pl *CANT* CT1 .... 7 E3 ②
St Martin's Rd *CANT* CT1 .... 7 E3 ③
  DEAL CT14 .... 135 F2
  FOLK CT20 .... 189 J8
  NROM TN28 .... 226 C8
  RDV CT15 .... 173 J2
St Martin's Ter *CANT* CT1 .... 7 E3 ③
St Martin's Vw *HB* CT6 .... 47 F6
St Mary's Av *SWCH* CT13 .... 93 K5 ③
St Mary's Cl *MARG* CT9 .... 32 E5
St Mary's Cl *RASHW* TN26 .... 198 E6
  RDV CT15 .... 130 E1
  SWCH CT13 .... 93 F8
  SWCH CT13 .... 113 F4
St Mary's Gdns *LYDD* TN29 .... 227 H1
  RCANTE CT3 .... 71 F3 ③
St Marys Gv *KEN/WIL* TN24 .... 141 J7 ②
St Mary's Gv *DEAL* CT14 .... 132 E2
  WSTB CT5 .... 43 G8
St Mary's Meadow *RCANTE* CT3 ... 90 C6
St Marys Ms *KEN/WIL* TN24 .... 9 F5 ①
St Mary's Rd *BRDST* CT10 .... 55 J2 ⑦
  DEAL CT14 .... 135 J5
  FAV ME13 .... 62 C8
  MSTR CT12 .... 52 A8
  NROM TN28 .... 226 C6
  RCANTW CT4 .... 108 B3
St Mary's Ster *CANT* CT1 .... 6 C3 ③⑦
St Mary's Vw *RSIT* ME9 .... 34 B8
St Michaels Av *MARG* CT9 .... 32 E6
St Michaels Cl *CANTW/ST* CT2 ..... 85 J5
St Michael's Pl *CANTW/ST* CT2 ..... 6 B1
St Michael's Rd *CANTW/ST* CT2 ..... 6 B1
  SIT ME10 .... 57 K2
  SIT ME10 .... 58 A2
St Michael's St *FOLK* CT20 .... 13 D4
St Michael's Wk *RFOLK* CT18 .... 190 A2 ①
St Mildred's Av *BRCH* CT7 .... 29 H7
  BRDST CT10 .... 55 H2
  RAM CT11 .... 4 C5
St Mildred's Cl *TENT* TN30 .... 194 A7 ②
St Mildreds Ct *DEAL* CT14 .... 135 J5 ①
St Mildred's Gdns *WGOS* CT8 ...... 30 E5 ③
St Mildreds Pl *CANT* CT1 .... 6 B4 ④
St Mildred's Rd *MARG* CT9 .... 3 E5 ③
  MSTR CT12 .... 74 A1
  RAM CT11 .... 4 C5
St Monicas Rd *DEAL* CT14 .... 135 K8
St Nicholas Cl *CANTW/ST* CT2 ..... 68 E7
  DEAL CT14 .... 135 F2
St Nicholas Rd *CANT* CT1 .... 86 A8
  FAV ME13 .... 61 K7
  HYTHE CT21 .... 205 F4

  NROM TN28 .... 226 E8
St Patrick's Cl *DEAL* CT14 .... 115 J8 ③
  WSTB CT5 .... 44 B7
St Patrick's Rd *DEAL* CT14 .... 115 J8
  DVW CT17 .... 193 K2
  RAM CT11 .... 5 F3
St Paul's Av *FAV* ME13 .... 61 K7
St Pauls Crs *FAV* ME13 .... 83 G3
St Pauls Rd *FAV* ME13 .... 83 G3
  MARG CT9 .... 3 E2
St Paul's St *SIT* ME10 .... 57 K1 ③
St Pauls Ter *CANT* CT1 .... 7 D3 ①⑤
St Paul's Wy *FOLK* CT20 .... 206 E2
St Peter's Cl *IOS* ME12 .... 14 D8
St Peter's Ct *BRDST* CT10 .... 55 G1
  FAV ME13 .... 61 K7
St Peter's Footpath *MARG* CT9 ...... 3 D4
St Peter's Gv *CANT* CT1 .... 6 C3 ②③
St Peter's La *CANTW/ST* CT2 .... 6 C2 ②①
St Peter's Park Rd *BRDST* CT10 ... 55 G1
  FAV ME13 .... 6 B3
St Peter's Rd *BRDST* CT10 .... 55 F1
  FAV ME13 .... 83 G3 ②
  MARG CT9 .... 3 E5
  WSTB CT5 .... 44 A4
St Peter's St *CANT* CT1 .... 6 C3 ②④
  SWCH CT13 .... 94 A5 ③
St Radigund's Pl *CANT* CT1 .... 7 D2 ①②
St Radigund's Rd *DVW* CT17 ...... 172 F5
St Radigunds St *CANT* CT1 .... 6 C2
St Richard's Rd *DEAL* CT14 .... 135 F2
St Saviour's Cl *FAV* ME13 .... 62 D7
  FOLKN CT19 .... 13 D2 ①
St Stephen's Cl *CANTW/ST* CT2 .... 6 C1 ③
St Stephen's Ct *CANTW/ST* CT2 ..... 6 C1
St Stephen's Flds *CANTW/ST* CT2 .. 6 C2 ③
St Stephen's Gn *CANTW/ST* CT2 ... 86 D3
St Stephen's Hl *CANTW/ST* CT2 .... 86 C2
St Stephen's Pth *CANTW/ST* CT2 ... 86 D3
St Stephen's Wk *ASH* TN23 .... 160 E8
St Swithin's Rd *WSTB* CT5 .... 44 E4
St Theresa's Cl *KEN/WIL* TN24 ..... 8 B2 ③
St Thomas Hl *CANTW/ST* CT2 ...... 86 A3
St Vincent Rd *RDV* CT15 .... 154 E7
St Vincent's Cl *RCANTE* CT3 .... 89 F6
  WSTB CT5 .... 44 B7
St Winifred Rd *FOLKN* CT19 .... 190 A8 ③
Salisbury Av *BRDST* CT10 .... 55 G3
  RAM CT11 .... 5 F3
Salisbury Cl *SIT* ME10 .... 58 D2
Salisbury Rd *CANTW/ST* CT2 .... 6 B1
  DEAL CT14 .... 135 H4
  DVE/WH CT16 .... 10 B2
  FOLKN CT19 .... 189 K7
  HB CT6 .... 47 G1 ③
  RDV CT15 .... 155 H8
  WSTB CT5 .... 44 A4 ⑦
Salmestone Ri *MARG* CT9 .... 2 C5
Salmestone Rd *MARG* CT9 .... 2 C5
Salmon Crs *IOS* ME12 .... 15 G8
Salters La *FAV* ME13 .... 81 H1
  LYDD TN29 .... 223 F6
Salthouse Cl *LYDD* TN29 .... 223 G6
The Saltings *NROM* TN28 .... 233 F1 ③
Salts Cl *WSTB* CT5 .... 44 A5
Salt's Dr *BRDST* CT10 .... 55 F1
Saltwood Gdns *MARG* CT9 .... 33 F4
Samian Crs *FOLKN* CT19 .... 189 H8
Sancroft Av *CANTW/ST* CT2 .... 86 A5
Sanctuary Cl *BRDST* CT10 .... 5 F1
  DVW CT17 .... 172 B2
Sandbanks Rd *FAV* ME13 .... 63 C4
Sandford Rd *SIT* ME10 .... 57 G1
Sandgate Esp *FOLK* CT20 .... 206 C4
Sandgate Hl *FOLK* CT20 .... 207 F3
  FOLK CT20 .... 13 D5
Sandhurst Cl *CANTW/ST* CT2 ...... 86 E2 ③
Sandhurst Rd *MARG* CT9 .... 33 G4
Sandilands *KEN/WIL* TN24 .... 9 E4
Sandle's Rd *BRCH* CT7 .... 29 J7 ③
Sandlewood Dr *BRCH* CT7 .... 50 C5 ③
Sandling Rd *HYTHE* CT21 .... 187 J8
Sandown Cl *DEAL* CT14 .... 115 K5 ③
Sandown Dr *HB* CT6 .... 46 C2
Sandown Lees *SWCH* CT13 .... 94 C7
Sandown Rd *DEAL* CT14 .... 115 K5
  SWCH CT13 .... 94 C6
Sandpiper Rd *WSTB* CT5 .... 43 J8
Sandpit Hl *RCANTE* CT3 .... 70 D1
Sandstone Dr *SIT* ME10 .... 35 K6
Sandway Rd *RMAID* ME17 .... 116 A3
Sandwich Cl *FOLK* CT20 .... 207 F1
Sandwich Hl *RCANTE* CT3 .... 90 D6
Sandwich Rd *DVE/WH* CT16 ...... 152 E7
  MSTR CT12 .... 75 G3
  RCANTE CT3 .... 92 E5
  RDV CT15 .... 131 G1
  RDV CT15 .... 152 E4
  SWCH CT13 .... 113 G3
Sandwood Rd *BRDST* CT10 .... 5 F2
  SWCH CT13 .... 93 H8
Sandyhurst La *KEN/WIL* TN24 ... 140 E6
Sandy La *HYTHE* CT21 .... 206 B5
  KEN/WIL TN24 .... 162 B5

Sangro Pl *CANT* CT1 .... 87 H5 ③
Sanspareil Av *IOS* ME12 .... 15 G8
Santon La *RCANTE* CT3 .... 72 A6
Sark Cl *LYDD* TN29 .... 216 E6
Sarre Pl *SWCH* CT13 .... 93 K6 ②
Satis Av *SIT* ME10 .... 35 K7
Satmar Rd *RFOLK* CT18 .... 192 A3
Satmore La *RFOLK* CT18 .... 191 K2
Saunders La *RCANTE* CT3 .... 92 D5
Saunders Wy *RYE* TN31 .... 234 D4 ③
Savernake Dr *HB* CT6 .... 47 G4
Saw Lodge Fld *ASH* TN23 .... 182 B2
Sawpit Rd *RSIT* ME9 .... 77 C3
Saxon Av *IOS* ME12 .... 15 J8
Saxon Cl *HYTHE* CT21 .... 205 J4
Saxon Rd *FAV* ME13 .... 62 B8
  RAM CT11 .... 4 B5
  RCANTW CT4 .... 108 A5
  WGOS CT8 .... 30 E5
Saxon Shore Wy *DEAL* CT14 ..... 135 K6
  FAV ME13 .... 62 E5
  HB CT6 .... 26 A8
  HYTHE CT21 .... 202 E5
  RASHE TN25 .... 199 H4
  RASHW TN26 .... 198 A8
  RASHW TN26 .... 211 G4
  RCANTE CT3 .... 48 D3
  RCANTE CT3 .... 71 F2
  RCANTE CT3 .... 73 J8
  RCANTE CT3 .... 73 K4
  RCANTE CT3 .... 93 F1
  RDV CT15 .... 155 J8
  RDV CT15 .... 155 Q2
  RFOLK CT18 .... 188 B2
  RSIT ME9 .... 19 H5
  RSIT ME9 .... 36 C1
  SWCH CT13 .... 93 H2
  WSTB CT5 .... 44 E3
Saxon St *DVW* CT17 .... 10 B3
Saxton Rd *LYDD* TN29 .... 239 F1
Sayer Rd *HDCN* TN27 .... 118 E6
Scanlons Bridge Rd *HYTHE* CT21 .. 204 E4
Scarborough Dr *IOS* ME12 .... 15 J3
Sceales Dr *MSTR* CT12 .... 53 J8 ③
Sceptre Wy *WSTB* CT5 .... 43 J7 ③
The School Cl *WGOS* CT8 .... 30 D5 ③
School Hl *RCANTW* CT4 .... 103 H7
School La *CANTW/ST* CT2 .... 66 D7
  FAV ME13 .... 99 F8
  HB CT6 .... 47 F6
  RAM CT11 .... 5 E4
  RCANTE CT3 .... 47 K8
  RCANTE CT3 .... 72 B4
  RCANTE CT3 .... 89 J6
  RCANTE CT3 .... 90 C3
  RCANTE CT3 .... 91 J8
  RCANTE CT3 .... 110 E4
  RCANTW CT4 .... 108 B2
  RCANTW CT4 .... 127 F1
  RFOLK CT18 .... 189 F7
  RSIT ME9 .... 34 A4
  RSIT ME9 .... 34 A7
  RSIT ME9 .... 35 H3
  RSIT ME9 .... 56 E3
  RSIT ME9 .... 58 E4
School Rd *DEAL* CT14 .... 132 E3
  FAV ME13 .... 62 A8
  HDCN TN27 .... 118 E6
  HYTHE CT21 .... 205 F2
  RASHW TN26 .... 139 J7
  RASHW TN26 .... 210 D5
  RCANTE CT3 .... 92 A4
  RFOLK CT18 .... 168 C7
  SIT ME10 .... 58 C3
  SWCH CT13 .... 93 K5
Scocles Rd *IOS* ME12 .... 21 J2
Scoggers Hl *FAV* ME13 .... 83 G7
Scot's La *RASHE* TN25 .... 165 F6
Scotton St *RASHE* TN25 .... 143 F4
Scotts Acre *RYE* TN31 .... 234 B3
Scrapsgate Rd *IOS* ME12 .... 15 H7
Scraps Hl *RSIT* ME9 .... 59 F2
Sea Ap *IOS* ME12 .... 24 C2
Seabourne Wy *LYDD* TN29 .... 216 D7
Seabrook Ct *HYTHE* CT21 .... 206 B3
Seabrook Gdns *HYTHE* CT21 ...... 206 A4
Seabrook Gv *HYTHE* CT21 .... 206 A4
Seabrook Rd *HYTHE* CT21 .... 205 J4
Seabrook V *HYTHE* CT21 .... 206 B2
Seacroft Rd *BRDST* CT10 .... 55 H5
Seadown Cl *HYTHE* CT21 .... 206 A2 ③
Seafield Rd *BRDST* CT10 .... 55 G2
  RAM CT11 .... 4 C4
  WSTB CT5 .... 43 J8
Seagar Rd *FAV* ME13 .... 62 A5
Seager Rd *IOS* ME12 .... 15 F4
Seagrave Crs *FOLKN* CT19 .... 13 F3
Seamark Cl *MSTR* CT12 .... 51 G8
Seamark Rd *MSTR* CT12 .... 51 G6

Seapoint Rd *BRDST* CT10 ...... 55 J3
Sea Rd *BRCH* CT7 ...... 30 A6
  DEAL CT14 ...... 135 J8
  HYTHE CT21 ...... 206 M3
  RYE TN31 ...... 234 C4
  WGOS CT8 ...... 30 B5
Seasalter Beach *WSTB* CT5 ...... 43 H7
Seasalter CI *IOS* ME12 ...... 24 D7
Seasalter Cross *WSTB* CT5 ...... 43 G8
Seasalter La *WSTB* CT5 ...... 65 G2
Seasalter Rd *FAV* ME13 ...... 63 K4
Seaside Av *IOS* ME12 ...... 15 K6
Sea St *HB* CT6 ...... 46 A3
  RDV CT15 ...... 155 G8
Seathorpe Av *IOS* ME12 ...... 15 K7
Seaton Av *HYTHE* CT21 ...... 205 F3
Seaton Rd *RCANTE* CT3 ...... 89 J4
Sea View Av *BRCH* CT7 ...... 29 H6
Seaview Av *IOS* ME12 ...... 25 C5
Sea View CI *RFOLK* CT18 ...... 191 J5
Sea View Gdns *IOS* ME12 ...... 24 D3
Sea View Rd *BRCH* CT7 ...... 29 H6
  BRDST CT10 ...... 33 H8
  HB CT6 ...... 47 H1
  MSTR CT12 ...... 53 J8
  RDV CT15 ...... 175 F2
Seaview Rd *NROM* TN28 ...... 232 E5
Sea View Sq *HB* CT6 ...... 46 E1
Sea View Ter *MARG* CT9 ...... 2 A3
Seaville Dr *HB* CT6 ...... 47 K1
Sea Wall *LYDD* TN29 ...... 217 F5
  WSTB CT5 ...... 44 H4
Seaway Crs *LYDD* TN29 ...... 227 G2
Seaway Gdns *LYDD* TN29 ...... 227 H2
Seaway Rd *LYDD* TN29 ...... 227 G2
Second Av *BRDST* CT10 ...... 33 H4
  IOS ME12 ...... 14 C5
  IOS ME12 ...... 23 J1
  MARG CT9 ...... 3 F2
  QBOR ME11 ...... 20 A3
  RYE TN31 ...... 234 C4
Segrave Rd *FOLKN* CT19 ...... 13 F3
Selbey CI *HB* CT6 ...... 47 H2
Selborne Rd *MARG* CT9 ...... 3 F5
Selkirk Rd *DVE/WH* CT16 ...... 173 F3
Selling Ct *FAV* ME13 ...... 82 C8
Selling Rd *FAV* ME13 ...... 81 K4
  RCANTW CT4 ...... 103 H3
Selsea Av *HB* CT6 ...... 46 C1
Selway Ct *DEAL* CT14 ...... 135 H3
Selwood CI *IOS* ME12 ...... 15 F8
Selwyn Dr *BRDST* CT10 ...... 55 F5
Semaphore Rd *BRCH* CT7 ...... 29 J6
Semple CI *MSTR* CT12 ...... 52 B7
Sene Pk *HYTHE* CT21 ...... 205 H3
Senlac CI *RAM* CT11 ...... 4 B5
Serene Ct *BRDST* CT10 ...... 55 J2
Setterfield Rd *MARG* CT9 ...... 3 D4
Sevastopol PI *CANT* CT1 ...... 87 H5
Sevenacre Rd *FAV* ME13 ...... 62 B5
Seven Stones Dr *BRDST* CT10 ...... 55 H5
Sevington La *KEN/WIL* TN24 ...... 9 F5
Sewell CI *BRCH* CT7 ...... 29 K8
Sexburga Dr *IOS* ME12 ...... 15 J6
Seymour Av *MARG* CT9 ...... 30 E5
  WSTB CT5 ...... 44 B5
Seymour CI *HB* CT6 ...... 47 C5
Seymour PI *CANT* CT1 ...... 6 B4
Seymour Rd *RDV* CT15 ...... 155 F6
Shadoxhurst Rd *RASHW* TN26 ...... 196 E2
Shaftesbury Av *FOLKN* CT19 ...... 189 K7
Shaftesbury Rd *CANTW/ST* CT2 ...... 86 D5
  RCANTE CT3 ...... 69 K5
  WSTB CT5 ...... 44 A3
Shaftsbury St *RAM* CT11 ...... 5 F4
Shakespeare Rd *BRCH* CT7 ...... 29 K6
  DVW CT17 ...... 173 F8
  MARG CT9 ...... 3 D4
  SIT ME10 ...... 51 K6
Shakespeare Ter *FOLK* CT20 ...... 12 C5
Shalloak Rd *CANTW/ST* CT2 ...... 87 H1
Shallows Rd *BRDST* CT10 ...... 32 D8
Shalmsford Ct *RCANTW* CT4 ...... 104 D5
Shalmsford Rd *RCANTW* CT4 ...... 104 A4
Shalmsford St *RCANTW* CT4 ...... 104 E4
Shamrock Av *WSTB* CT5 ...... 43 J7
Shapland CI *HB* CT6 ...... 47 H3
Share & Coulter Rd *WSTB* CT5 ...... 45 G5
Sharsted HI *RSIT* ME9 ...... 78 E6
Shaw Cross *KEN/WIL* TN24 ...... 161 H1
Shawdon Av *SWCH* CT13 ...... 95 G7
Shearwater Av *WSTB* CT5 ...... 43 K7
Shearwater Av *IOS* ME12 ...... 14 C6
Shear Wy *LYDD* TN29 ...... 216 E1
Shearway Rd *FOLKN* CT19 ...... 190 A6
Sheepfold La *ASH* TN23 ...... 182 B2
Sheerstone *RSIT* ME9 ...... 35 J3
Sheerwater Rd *RCANTE* CT3 ...... 91 G1
Sheerways *FAV* ME13 ...... 61 K8
Sheet Glass Rd *QBOR* ME11 ...... 20 B3
Sheldon CI *RCANTE* CT3 ...... 110 C8
Sheldwich CI *ASH* TN23 ...... 160 D8
Shelley Av *CANT* CT1 ...... 7 F1
Shellness Rd *IOS* ME12 ...... 25 C5
  IOS ME12 ...... 41 K1

Shellons St *FOLK* CT20 ...... 13 D4
Shelvin La *RCANTW* CT4 ...... 149 J2
Shepherd Dr *KEN/WIL* TN24 ...... 162 A6
Shepherd's Close Rd *RCANTW* CT4 ...... 108 E5
Shepherdsgate *CANTW/ST* CT2 ...... 6 C2
Shepherdsgate Dr *HB* CT6 ...... 47 F6
Shepherds Wk *HYTHE* CT21 ...... 204 C6
  WSTB CT5 ...... 45 F6
Shepherds Wy *WSTB* CT5 ...... 45 F6
Shepherdswell Rd *RDV* CT15 ...... 131 H7
Sheppey CI *BRCH* CT7 ...... 29 K7
Sheppey St *IOS* ME12 ...... 14 B4
Sheppey Vw *WSTB* CT5 ...... 43 J8
Sheppey Wy *IOS* ME12 ...... 20 B7
  RSIT ME9 ...... 20 B3
  SIT ME10 ...... 57 F1
Shepway *KEN/WIL* TN24 ...... 161 J1
Shepway CI *FOLKN* CT19 ...... 13 D3
Sheridan Rd *DVE/WH* CT16 ...... 173 F3
Sheron CI *DEAL* CT14 ...... 135 G1
Sherriffs Court La *MSTR* CT12 ...... 51 J8
Sherwood CI *FAV* ME13 ...... 62 A6
  HB CT6 ...... 47 H4
  KEN/WIL TN24 ...... 141 H7
  WSTB CT5 ...... 43 K8
Sherwood Dr *WSTB* CT5 ...... 43 K8
Sherwood Gdns *WSTB* CT5 ...... 43 K8
Sherwood Rd *BRCH* CT7 ...... 51 J1
Ship CI *LYDD* TN29 ...... 216 E6
Shipley Mill CI *ASH* TN23 ...... 182 B2
Shipman Av *CANTW/ST* CT2 ...... 86 A6
Shipmans Wy *DVE/WH* CT16 ...... 172 E5
Ship St *FOLKN* CT19 ...... 13 D3
Shire La *FAV* ME13 ...... 98 E8
Shireway CI *FOLKN* CT19 ...... 12 A2
Shirley Av *RAM* CT11 ...... 5 E1
Sholden Bank *DEAL* CT14 ...... 134 E2
Sholden New Rd *DEAL* CT14 ...... 135 F1
Shooter's HI *DVW* CT17 ...... 10 A2
  RDV CT15 ...... 132 A6
Shore CI *HB* CT6 ...... 46 A3
Shoreham La *TENT* TN30 ...... 194 A3
Shorncliffe Crs *FOLK* CT20 ...... 206 E1
Shorncliffe Rd *FOLK* CT20 ...... 12 A4
  FOLK CT20 ...... 206 E1
Shortlands Rd *SIT* ME10 ...... 58 B2
Short La *LYDD* TN29 ...... 212 B8
  RDV CT15 ...... 171 F5
Short's Prospect *IOS* ME12 ...... 22 E6
Short St *IOS* ME12 ...... 14 C4
  RCANTE CT3 ...... 111 J6
  SWCH CT13 ...... 94 A5
Shottendane Rd *BRCH* CT7 ...... 52 C2
Shottenden Rd *FAV* ME13 ...... 101 G7
Shrimpton CI *RCANTW* CT4 ...... 103 H3
The Shrubbery *DEAL* CT14 ...... 135 J5
Shrubcote *TENT* TN30 ...... 194 A3
Shrub Hill Rd *WSTB* CT5 ...... 45 G7
Shrubsole Av *IOS* ME12 ...... 14 D5
Shuart La *BRCH* CT7 ...... 50 C3
Shurland Av *IOS* ME12 ...... 15 J8
  IOS ME12 ...... 25 C5
  SIT ME10 ...... 58 A5
Shuttle Rd *BRDST* CT10 ...... 55 J2
Shuttlesfield La *RCANTW* CT4 ...... 167 H5
Sibert's CI *RDV* CT15 ...... 151 H1
The Sidings *RFOLK* CT18 ...... 167 G2
Sidney St *FOLKN* CT19 ...... 13 E3
Silver Av *BRCH* CT7 ...... 30 A8
Silver Birch Gv *ASH* TN23 ...... 182 A2
Silverdale Av *IOS* ME12 ...... 15 H8
Silverdale Dr *HB* CT6 ...... 47 J4
Silverdale Gv *SIT* ME10 ...... 57 H5
Silverdale Rd *RAM* CT11 ...... 4 A6
Silver HI *TENT* TN30 ...... 194 B5
Silver Hill Gdns *KEN/WIL* TN24 ...... 162 A5
Silver Hill Rd *KEN/WIL* TN24 ...... 162 A5
Silverlands Rd *RFOLK* CT18 ...... 167 F7
The Silvers *BRDST* CT10 ...... 54 D2
Silver St *DEAL* CT14 ...... 115 K7
Simmonds Rd *CANT* CT1 ...... 6 B4
Simon Av *MARG* CT9 ...... 32 E4
Simone Weil Av *KEN/WIL* TN24 ...... 8 B1
Simon's Av *ASH* TN23 ...... 160 D7
Simpson Rd *SIT* ME10 ...... 57 H1
Singledge La *RDV* CT15 ...... 151 K3
Singleton CI *SIT* ME12 ...... 52 A8
Singleton HI *ASH* TN23 ...... 160 B6
Singleton Rd *ASH* TN23 ...... 160 A5
Sir John Moore Av *HYTHE* CT21 ...... 204 E4
Siskin CI *RFOLK* CT18 ...... 189 K2
Six Fields Pth *TENT* TN30 ...... 194 A7
Sixth Av *IOS* ME12 ...... 23 K1
Skeete Rd *RFOLK* CT18 ...... 166 D7
Skinner Rd *LYDD* TN29 ...... 231 H8
  LYDD TN29 ...... 237 H1
Slade Rd *RMAID* ME17 ...... 97 K6
Slades CI *WSTB* CT5 ...... 45 F6
Sleigh Rd *CANTW/ST* CT2 ...... 68 E8
Slip La *RDV* CT15 ...... 170 D4
Sloe La *BRDST* CT10 ...... 32 C8
Slough Rd *RSIT* ME9 ...... 77 H1
Smallhythe Rd *TENT* TN30 ...... 194 A8
Smarden Rd *HDCN* TN27 ...... 157 G1
Smeed CI *SIT* ME10 ...... 58 C2

Smithy Dr *ASH* TN23 ...... 182 B2
Smuggler's Wy *BRCH* CT7 ...... 29 K6
Snakes HI *RCANTE* CT3 ...... 110 C1
Snargate La *LYDD* TN29 ...... 223 G1
Snargate St *DVW* CT17 ...... 10 B5
Snell Gdns *HB* CT6 ...... 46 A4
Snowbell Rd *ASH* TN23 ...... 182 A2
Snowdrop CI *FOLKN* CT19 ...... 12 C1
Sobraon Wy *CANT* CT1 ...... 87 H5
Soleshill Rd *RCANTW* CT4 ...... 102 E5
Solomons La *FAV* ME13 ...... 62 C7
Somerset CI *SIT* ME10 ...... 57 H2
  WSTB CT5 ...... 44 A4
Somerset Rd *ASH* TN23 ...... 8 B3
  CANT CT1 ...... 7 F3
  DEAL CT14 ...... 135 H3
  FOLKN CT19 ...... 189 K8
Somme Ct *CANT* CT1 ...... 87 H5
Somner CI *CANTW/ST* CT2 ...... 6 A2
Sondes CI *HB* CT6 ...... 47 F4
Sondes Rd *DEAL* CT14 ...... 135 K1
Sotherton *KEN/WIL* TN24 ...... 9 E6
Souberg CI *DEAL* CT14 ...... 115 J6
Southall CI *MSTR* CT12 ...... 52 B7
South Av *RDV* CT15 ...... 130 C3
  SIT ME10 ...... 58 B3
South Barham Rd *RCANTW* CT4 ...... 128 E8
Southbourne *ASH* TN23 ...... 181 H1
Southbourne Rd *FOLKN* CT19 ...... 13 F4
South Brooks Rd *LYDD* TN29 ...... 236 D6
South Canterbury Rd *CANT* CT1 ...... 7 D5
South Cliff Pde *BRDST* CT10 ...... 55 H4
South CI *CANT* CT1 ...... 7 D5
South Court Dr *RCANTE* CT3 ...... 90 C7
Southdown Rd *IOS* ME12 ...... 15 F8
South Eastern Rd *RAM* CT11 ...... 4 C5
Southenay La *RASHE* TN25 ...... 185 H3
  RASHE TN25 ...... 186 C2
Southernwood Ri *FOLK* CT20 ...... 207 F2
Southgate Rd *TENT* TN30 ...... 194 C7
South Lea *ASH* TN23 ...... 181 K3
Southmead CI *FOLKN* CT19 ...... 12 A3
South Military Rd *DVW* CT17 ...... 10 A6
South Motto *ASH* TN23 ...... 182 A1
South Rd *DEAL* CT14 ...... 155 K1
  DVW CT17 ...... 173 F6
  FAV ME13 ...... 62 A7
  HB CT6 ...... 47 F1
  HYTHE CT21 ...... 205 G5
  SWCH CT13 ...... 75 F6
Southsea Av *IOS* ME12 ...... 15 J5
Southsea Dr *HB* CT6 ...... 46 C2
South Stour Av *ASH* TN23 ...... 8 C5
South St *CANT* CT1 ...... 87 G3
  DEAL CT14 ...... 135 K1
  FAV ME13 ...... 82 D5
  LYDD TN29 ...... 231 H8
  QBOR ME11 ...... 20 A1
  WSTB CT5 ...... 44 D6
South View Gdns *IOS* ME12 ...... 14 D6
South View Rd *WSTB* CT5 ...... 44 A8
South Wall *DEAL* CT14 ...... 115 G6
Southwall Rd *DEAL* CT14 ...... 115 H8
Southwold PI *WGOS* CT8 ...... 30 D7
Southwood Gdns *RAM* CT11 ...... 4 B4
Southwood Rd *RAM* CT11 ...... 4 C4
  WSTB CT5 ...... 44 E4
Sowell St *BRDST* CT10 ...... 55 G1
Spanton Crs *HYTHE* CT21 ...... 204 E3
Speke Rd *BRDST* CT10 ...... 33 F8
Spelders HI *RASHE* TN25 ...... 163 G2
Speldhurst Ct *ASH* TN23 ...... 181 H1
Speldhurst Gdns *MARG* CT9 ...... 33 C3
Spence CI *RFOLK* CT18 ...... 190 B2
Spencer Rd *BRCH* CT7 ...... 29 K6
Spencer Sq *RAM* CT11 ...... 5 D5
Spenser Rd *HB* CT6 ...... 46 E2
Spillett CI *FAV* ME13 ...... 62 A7
Spinney La *RCANTE* CT3 ...... 130 A2
The Spinney *ASH* TN23 ...... 160 C3
  DVW CT17 ...... 172 C4
  MARG CT9 ...... 33 F5
Spire Av *WSTB* CT5 ...... 44 C6
Spitalfield La *NROM* TN28 ...... 226 B8
Split La *RCANTW* CT4 ...... 146 D1
Spratling La *MSTR* CT12 ...... 54 A5
Spratling St *MSTR* CT12 ...... 53 K5
Springfarm Rd *LYDD* TN29 ...... 224 B1
Springfield Av *TENT* TN30 ...... 194 B4
Springfield CI *RAM* CT11 ...... 5 E1
Springfield Rd *DVE/WH* CT16 ...... 173 F4
  MARG CT9 ...... 33 F3
  SIT ME10 ...... 58 B3
Springfield Wy *HYTHE* CT21 ...... 206 B3
Springhead Rd *FAV* ME13 ...... 62 B5
Spring Hollow *LYDD* TN29 ...... 227 H2
Spring La *CANT* CT1 ...... 7 F4
  CANTW/ST CT2 ...... 88 A2
  HYTHE CT21 ...... 206 A2
Springvale *RSIT* ME9 ...... 35 J2
Spring Wk *WSTB* CT5 ...... 43 K7
Springwood CI *ASH* TN23 ...... 160 C3
Springwood Dr *ASH* TN23 ...... 160 B3
Sprotlands Av *KEN/WIL* TN24 ...... 9 F4
Sprotshill CI *SIT* ME10 ...... 35 K8

The Square *RCANTW* CT4 .... **167** K2
RMAID ME17 .... **116** D1
Squire Av *CANTW/ST* CT2 .... **86** A6
Squires Ct *IOS* ME12 .... **23** H3
Squires Wy *DVE/WH* CT15 .... **172** E3
Stablemead *FOLKN* CT19 .... **12** A2
Stace Cl *TENT* TN30 .... **194** C6
Stade St *HYTHE* CT21 .... **205** G4
The Stade *FOLKN* CT19 .... **13** E4
Stadium Wy *SIT* ME10 .... **36** D8
Stafford Cl *ASH* TN23 .... **160** D4
Stalisfield Rd *FAV* ME13 .... **80** A8
FAV ME13 .... **99** K3
Stanbury Crs *FOLKN* CT19 .... **13** F1
Stancomb Av *RAM* CT11 .... **4** C6
Standen La *RFOLK* CT18 .... **190** E1
Stanhope Av *SIT* ME10 .... **58** B3
Stanhope Rd *ASH* TN23 .... **160** C7
DEAL CT14 .... **115** K8
DVE/WH CT16 .... **10** A1
Stanley Av *IOS* ME12 .... **16** A7
OBOR ME11 .... **20** B2
Stanley Cl *LYDD* TN29 .... **217** K2
Stanley Gdns *HB* CT6 .... **46** E2
Stanley Rd *BRDST* CT10 .... **33** G8
DEAL CT14 .... **135** K1
FOLKN CT19 .... **189** K8
HB CT6 .... **46** E2
MARG CT9 .... **3** E2
RAM CT11 .... **5** D3
WSTB CT5 .... **44** A7
Stanmore Ct *CANT* CT1 .... **7** E4
Staple Cl *SIT* ME10 .... **35** K8
Staplehurst Av *BRDST* CT10 .... **55** H4
Staplehurst Gdns *MARG* CT9 .... **33** F3
Staplehurst Rd *SIT* ME10 .... **35** H8
SIT ME10 .... **57** H1
Staple Rd *RCANTE* CT3 .... **91** F3
Staplestreet Rd *FAV* ME13 .... **83** F1
Star La *FOLKN* CT19 .... **189** J7
MARG CT9 .... **54** B1
Starle Cl *CANT* CT1 .... **7** E2
Star Rd *KEN/WIL* TN24 .... **9** D3
Starveacre La *RSIT* ME9 .... **57** H4
Station Ap *BRCH* CT7 .... **29** J7
MSTR CT12 .... **74** B1
NROM TN28 .... **226** D8
RCANTE CT3 .... **110** A3
RDV CT15 .... **154** C4
Station Approach Rd *RAM* CT11 .... **4** C3
Station Dr *DEAL* CT14 .... **135** G5
Station Rd *ASH* TN23 .... **8** C3
BRCH CT7 .... **29** J7
DEAL CT14 .... **135** G5
FOLKN CT19 .... **190** A8
HB CT6 .... **46** D3
HDCN TN27 .... **118** E7
HDCN TN27 .... **157** J2
HYTHE CT21 .... **205** H4
LYDD TN29 .... **216** D7
LYDD TN29 .... **231** J7
MARG CT9 .... **2** B3
MSTR CT12 .... **74** B1
NROM TN28 .... **226** C8
RASHE TN25 .... **184** C3
RCANTE CT3 .... **110** A5
RCANTW CT4 .... **107** K5
RCANTW CT4 .... **108** B2
RDV CT15 .... **151** F1
RDV CT15 .... **154** C5
RDV CT15 .... **154** D6
RFOLK CT18 .... **167** G8
RSIT ME9 .... **34** A8
RSIT ME9 .... **59** K4
TENT TN30 .... **194** A4
WSTB CT5 .... **44** B4
Station Rd East *CANT* CT1 .... **6** C4
Station Rd West *CANTW/ST* CT2 .... **6** C2
Station St *SIT* ME10 .... **58** A2
Steeds Cl *ASH* TN23 .... **181** K4
Steeds La *RASHW* TN26 .... **181** K5
Stembrook *DVE/WH* CT16 .... **10** B3
Stempe Cl *RFOLK* CT18 .... **190** C3
Stephen Cl *BRDST* CT10 .... **55** H2
Stephens Cl *FAV* ME13 .... **62** A6
MARG CT9 .... **31** G7
RAM CT11 .... **4** C3
Stephenson Rd *CANTW/ST* CT2 .... **86** D3
Step Style *SIT* ME10 .... **58** C4
Sterling Cl *BRDST* CT10 .... **55** F1
SIT ME10 .... **57** J5
Sterling Rd *QBOR* ME11 .... **20** B1
Stevens Cl *HDCN* TN27 .... **137** F3
Stickfast La *RSIT* ME9 .... **35** F5
Stiles Cl *FOLKN* CT19 .... **12** A2
IOS ME12 .... **15** H8
Stirling Wy *MSTR* CT12 .... **4** A1
Stirling Rd *KEN/WIL* TN24 .... **9** D6
Stisted Wy *HDCN* TN27 .... **137** F3
Stockbury Gdns *MARG* CT9 .... **33** F4
Stockdale Gdns *DEAL* CT14 .... **135** J2
Stockers Brow *RSIT* ME9 .... **58** B7
Stocker's HI *FAV* ME13 .... **82** E2
RSIT ME9 .... **58** B7

Stock La *RASHE* TN25 .... **184** B3
Stocks Rd *TENT* TN30 .... **219** K3
Stoddart Rd *FOLKN* CT19 .... **189** K8
Stodmarsh Rd *RCANTE* CT3 .... **87** K5
Stombers La *RFOLK* CT18 .... **166** K8
Stonar Cl *RAM* CT11 .... **5** E2
SWCH CT13 .... **94** A5
Stonar Gdns *SWCH* CT13 .... **94** A4
Stone Barn Av *BRCH* CT7 .... **29** K8
Stonebridge *RASHE* TN25 .... **163** G1
Stone Br *TENT* TN30 .... **221** J4
Stonebridge Green Rd
HDCN TN27 .... **137** G2
Stonebridge Wy *FAV* ME13 .... **62** A7
Stone Cross Lees *SWCH* CT13 .... **93** K7
Stonedane Ct *FAV* ME13 .... **62** B6
Stone Gdns *BRDST* CT10 .... **55** J1
Stonegate *RASHE* TN25 .... **142** E4
Stonehall Rd *RDV* CT15 .... **151** H6
Stoneheap Rd *RDV* CT15 .... **133** J5
Stone HI *RASHE* TN25 .... **185** H4
Stone Hill Rd *HDCN* TN27 .... **137** F4
Stone Rd *BRDST* CT10 .... **55** J1
Stonestile Farm Rd *HDCN* TN27 .... **118** C3
Stone St *FAV* ME13 .... **62** B7
HYTHE CT21 .... **203** J2
RASHE TN25 .... **166** A8
RCANTW CT4 .... **126** B4
Stoney Rd *FAV* ME13 .... **83** H3
Stour *ASH* TN23 .... **160** C5
RCANTW CT4 .... **105** F4
Stour Ct *SWCH* CT13 .... **93** K5
Stour Crs *CANT* CT1 .... **87** H3
Stourmouth Rd *RCANTE* CT3 .... **71** K7
Stour Rd *RCANTW* CT4 .... **105** F4
Stour St *CANT* CT1 .... **6** C3
Stour Valley Cl *RCANTE* CT3 .... **70** E3
Stour Valley Wk *ASH* TN23 .... **160** A5
CANT CT1 .... **87** J3
HDCN TN27 .... **138** B4
KEN/WIL TN24 .... **9** F5
RCANTE CT3 .... **89** G1
RCANTW CT4 .... **105** F3
RCANTW CT4 .... **123** K5
RMAID ME17 .... **116** D2
RMAID ME17 .... **116** E3
SWCH CT13 .... **75** K5
SWCH CT13 .... **94** B5
Stour Valley Wy *RCANTE* CT3 .... **72** A4
Stowting HI *RASHE* TN25 .... **165** J5
Straight La *LYDD* TN29 .... **223** K4
Strakers HI *RDV* CT15 .... **133** H6
Strand St *SWCH* CT13 .... **93** K4
Stranger's Cl *CANT* CT1 .... **86** A8
Stranger's La *CANT* CT1 .... **86** A8
Strangford PI *HB* CT6 .... **47** G5
Strangford Rd *WSTB* CT5 .... **44** A4
Stream Wk *WSTB* CT5 .... **44** A4
Streete Court Rd *WGOS* CT8 .... **30** E6
Streetfield *HB* CT6 .... **47** G6
The Street *ASH* TN23 .... **160** A6
BRCH CT7 .... **50** C4
BRCH CT7 .... **52** A3
DEAL CT14 .... **114** A2
DEAL CT14 .... **114** B6
DEAL CT14 .... **134** A1
DEAL CT14 .... **135** F1
FAV ME13 .... **62** A4
FAV ME13 .... **79** C8
HDCN TN27 .... **137** F3
HDCN TN27 .... **137** K7
HYTHE CT21 .... **187** J4
HYTHE CT21 .... **203** H4
KEN/WIL TN24 .... **141** J7
RASHE TN25 .... **143** J8
RASHE TN25 .... **164** E6
RASHE TN25 .... **183** K2
RASHW TN26 .... **139** J7
RASHW TN26 .... **178** E1
RASHW TN26 .... **180** D6
RASHW TN26 .... **198** E7
RASHW TN26 .... **211** F6
RCANTE CT3 .... **71** J8
RCANTE CT3 .... **72** B5
RCANTE CT3 .... **89** J4
RCANTE CT3 .... **91** H8
RCANTE CT3 .... **92** B5
RCANTE CT3 .... **109** K6
RCANTE CT3 .... **111** F4
RCANTW CT4 .... **103** H6
RCANTW CT4 .... **108** B3
RCANTW CT4 .... **108** B8
RCANTW CT4 .... **123** H5
RCANTW CT4 .... **125** K3
RCANTW CT4 .... **126** E7
RCANTW CT4 .... **128** C6
RCANTW CT4 .... **129** F6
RCANTW CT4 .... **129** K5
RCANTW CT4 .... **149** H3
RDV CT15 .... **131** F5
RDV CT15 .... **132** A7
RDV CT15 .... **153** J8

RDV CT15 .... **154** A5
RDV CT15 .... **154** B3
RDV CT15 .... **192** C1
RFOLK CT18 .... **189** F7
RFOLK CT18 .... **190** C1
RSIT ME9 .... **34** A3
RSIT ME9 .... **35** K2
RSIT ME9 .... **57** F4
RSIT ME9 .... **59** F3
RSIT ME9 .... **59** H8
RSIT ME9 .... **78** A7
SWCH CT13 .... **93** G7
TENT TN30 .... **219** J4
TENT TN30 .... **221** H1
Stringer Dr *BRCH* CT7 .... **29** K8
Strode Crs *IOS* ME12 .... **14** D4
Strode Park Rd *HB* CT6 .... **47** F4
Strond St *DVW* CT17 .... **10** B5
Strouts Rd *ASH* TN23 .... **160** B7
Stuart Rd *FOLKN* CT19 .... **13** E3
Studfall Cl *HYTHE* CT21 .... **204** B6
Studio Cl *KEN/WIL* TN24 .... **141** H8
Stumble La *ASH* TN23 .... **182** A5
Stuppington Court Farm
CANT CT1 .... **106** C2
Stuppington La *CANT* CT1 .... **106** C2
Sturdy Cl *HYTHE* CT21 .... **205** H4
Sturges Rd *KEN/WIL* TN24 .... **8** B2
Sturmer Cl *CANT* CT1 .... **7** F4
Sturry Court Ms *CANTW/ST* CT2 .... **68** E5
Sturry HI *CANTW/ST* CT2 .... **68** E6
Sturry Rd *CANT* CT1 .... **7** E1
Sudbury PI *WGOS* CT8 .... **30** D7
Suffolk Av *WGOS* CT8 .... **30** C7
Suffolk Dr *ASH* TN23 .... **8** A3
Suffolk Rd *CANT* CT1 .... **87** H6
Suffolk St *WSTB* CT5 .... **44** A4
Summer Cl *HYTHE* CT21 .... **204** D4
TENT TN30 .... **194** C5
Summerfield Av *WSTB* CT5 .... **44** C5
Summerfield Rd *MARG* CT9 .... **33** F4
Summer HI *CANTW/ST* CT2 .... **86** A5
Summer La *CANTW/ST* CT2 .... **67** H8
Summer Leeze *KEN/WIL* TN24 .... **9** E5
Summer Leeze Gdns *KEN/WIL* TN24 .... **9** E5
Summer Rd *BRCH* CT7 .... **50** B5
Summerville Av *IOS* ME12 .... **21** G1
Sumpter Wy *FAV* ME13 .... **61** K7
Sunbeam Av *HB* CT6 .... **45** J2
Sundridge Cl *CANTW/ST* CT2 .... **86** E2
Sun La *BRCH* CT7 .... **50** C4
HYTHE CT21 .... **205** G4
Sunningdale Av *FOLKN* CT19 .... **12** A2
Sunningdale Wk *HB* CT6 .... **46** C5
Sunny Bank *HYTHE* CT21 .... **204** D4
SIT ME10 .... **36** D8
Sunnyfields Dr *IOS* ME12 .... **14** D8
Sunnyhill Rd *HB* CT6 .... **46** A3
Sunnymead *CANTW/ST* CT2 .... **67** G7
Sunnyside Av *IOS* ME12 .... **15** H8
Sunnyside Cl *DEAL* CT14 .... **134** D5
Sunnyside Gdns *SWCH* CT13 .... **93** J6
Sunnyside Rd *FOLK* CT20 .... **206** D3
Sunray Av *WSTB* CT5 .... **43** J7
Sunset Cl *IOS* ME12 .... **17** J8
WSTB CT5 .... **43** K8
Sun St *CANT* CT1 .... **6** C3
Surf Crs *IOS* ME12 .... **17** J8
Surrenden Rd *FOLKN* CT19 .... **190** A8
Surrey Gdns *BRCH* CT7 .... **29** J7
Surrey Rd *CANT* CT1 .... **87** H7
MARG CT9 .... **3** F2
Susan's HI *RASHW* TN26 .... **195** K4
Sussex Av *CANT* CT1 .... **87** H7
KEN/WIL TN24 .... **8** B2
MARG CT9 .... **3** E2
Sussex Border Pth *TENT* TN30 .... **219** K7
Sussex Cl *HB* CT6 .... **46** A2
Sussex Gdns *BRCH* CT7 .... **29** J7
HB CT6 .... **46** A2
WGOS CT8 .... **30** E5
Sussex Rd *FOLKN* CT19 .... **13** D3
NROM TN28 .... **226** D8
Sussex St *RAM* CT11 .... **5** E4
Sutherland Cl *HYTHE* CT21 .... **204** E4
Sutherland Dr *BRCH* CT7 .... **30** A7
Sutherland Rd *DEAL* CT14 .... **115** J8
Sutton Baron Rd *RSIT* ME9 .... **56** E6
Sutton Cl *FOLKN* CT19 .... **12** A2
Sutton La *DEAL* CT14 .... **134** C6
DEAL CT14 .... **155** F1
Sutton Rd *RCANTE* CT3 .... **69** K5
The Suttons *RYE* TN31 .... **234** C5
Swadelands Cl *RMAID* ME17 .... **116** C1
Swain Rd *TENT* TN30 .... **194** B3
Swale Av *IOS* ME12 .... **14** C5
QBOR ME11 .... **20** A3
Swalecliffe Av *HB* CT6 .... **46** A2
Swalecliffe Court Dr *WSTB* CT5 .... **45** G4
Swalecliffe Rd *WSTB* CT5 .... **44** E4
Swale Heritage Trail *FAV* ME13 .... **61** K3
SIT ME10 .... **36** D8
Swallow Av *WSTB* CT5 .... **43** J7
Swallow Cl *MARG* CT9 .... **2** A5
Swallowfield *KEN/WIL* TN24 .... **9** E6

Swamp Rd *LYDD* TN29 ...... **231** F2
Swan Cl *SIT* ME10 ...... **58** C2
Swan Cottages *TENT* TN30 ...... **219** J3
Swanfield Rd *WSTB* CT5 ...... **44** A6
Swan Gn *RASHE* TN25 ...... **185** K5
Swanstree Av *SIT* ME10 ...... **58** C4
Swan St *TENT* TN30 ...... **219** G3
Swanton La *RCANTE* CT3 ...... **88** C5
RDV CT15 ...... **150** E8
Swarling Hill Rd *RCANTW* CT4 ...... **106** A8
Swaynes Wy *SWCH* CT13 ...... **113** F4
Sweechbridge Rd *HB* CT6 ...... **68** A3
Sweechgate *CANTW/ST* CT2 ...... **68** D7
Sweetbriar La *RDV* CT15 ...... **131** K4
Sweetlove Pl *RCANTE* CT3 ...... **90** C6 ⓵
Sweyn Rd *MARG* CT9 ...... **3** E2 ⓵
Swinburne Av *BRDST* CT10 ...... **55** H3
Switch House Av *LYDD* TN29 ...... **239** F8
Sycamore Av *RCANTE* CT3 ...... **130** A1
Sycamore Cl *BRDST* CT10 ...... **54** D2
HB CT6 ...... **47** H1 ⓵
HYTHE CT21 ...... **204** C5 ⓵
LYDD TN29 ...... **231** J7
MARG CT9 ...... **2** B6
Sycamore Gdns *LYDD* TN29 ...... **216** E6
The Sycamores *RCANTE* CT3 ...... **69** K6
Sydcot Dr *DEAL* CT14 ...... **115** J6
Sydenham Rd *DEAL* CT14 ...... **115** K7 ⓵
Sydney Av *SIT* ME10 ...... **57** H2
Sydney Cooper Cl *CANTW/ST* CT2 ...... **85** K4
Sydney Rd *DEAL* CT14 ...... **135** C5
RAM CT11 ...... **5** F3
WSTB CT5 ...... **44** B6
Sydney St *ASH* TN23 ...... **8** C5
Symmonds Dr *SIT* ME10 ...... **58** B1

T

Tabret Cl *KEN/WIL* TN24 ...... **141** H8
Tadworth Rd *KEN/WIL* TN24 ...... **161** H1
Taillour Cl *SIT* ME10 ...... **36** A7
Talavera Rd *CANT* CT1 ...... **7** F2
Talbot Av *HB* CT6 ...... **46** A3
Talbot Rd *MARG* CT9 ...... **3** F5 ⓵
Tally Ho Rd *RASHW* TN26 ...... **180** E5
Tame La *LYDD* TN29 ...... **202** B7
Tamley La *RASHE* TN25 ...... **164** D1
Tams Gdns *IOS* ME12 ...... **16** A8
Tangier Cl *DVE/WH* CT16 ...... **173** J3
Tankerton Ms *WSTB* CT5 ...... **44** B3
Tankerton Rd *WSTB* CT5 ...... **44** B3
Tank Farm St *LYDD* TN29 ...... **239** G8
Tanner's Hl *HYTHE* CT21 ...... **205** G2
Tanner's Hill Gdns *HYTHE* CT21 ...... **205** G2
Tanners St *FAV* ME13 ...... **62** B7
Tannery La *ASH* TN23 ...... **8** C3
SWCH CT13 ...... **93** K5
Tapleys Wy *RCANTW* CT4 ...... **126** E1
Target Firs *DVE/WH* CT16 ...... **172** B1
Tartane La *LYDD* TN29 ...... **216** E6
Taswell Cl *DVE/WH* CT16 ...... **10** C3
Taswell St *DVE/WH* CT16 ...... **10** C3
Tavistock Cl *SIT* ME10 ...... **57** J2
Tavistock Rd *RAM* CT11 ...... **5** E2
Taylor Rd *FOLKN* CT19 ...... **189** K8
LYDD TN29 ...... **235** F3
MSTR CT12 ...... **52** A8
Taylors Cl *LYDD* TN29 ...... **227** G3
Taylors Hl *RCANTW* CT4 ...... **103** H6
Taylors La *LYDD* TN29 ...... **227** G3
Taywood Cl *KEN/WIL* TN24 ...... **9** F4 ⓵
Teddars Leas Rd *RFOLK* CT18 ...... **188** C2
Teddington Cl *CANT* CT1 ...... **7** E1
Teelin Cl *LYDD* TN29 ...... **227** G2
Telegraph Rd *DEAL* CT14 ...... **135** H4
Telford Ct *FOLKN* CT19 ...... **13** E3
Telham Av *RDV* CT15 ...... **4** B3
Temeraire Hts *FOLK* CT20 ...... **206** C3
Templar Cl *DVE/WH* CT16 ...... **172** B1
Templar St *DVW* CT17 ...... **10** C5
Temple Cl *DVE/WH* CT16 ...... **152** D8
Temple Gdns *SIT* ME10 ...... **58** C3 ⓵
Temple Rd *CANTW/ST* CT2 ...... **6** A2
Templer Wy *ASH* TN23 ...... **8** A2
Temple Side *DVE/WH* CT16 ...... **172** B1
Temple Wy *DEAL* CT14 ...... **114** A2
Tennyson Av *CANT* CT1 ...... **87** H3
Tennyson Gdns *RCANTE* CT3 ...... **110** B8 ⓵
Tennyson Pl *FOLKN* CT19 ...... **13** E2 ⓵
Tennyson Rd *ASH* TN23 ...... **160** E8
Ten Perch Rd *CANT* CT1 ...... **6** A5
Tenterden Dr *CANTW/ST* CT2 ...... **86** D2
Tenterden Rd *RASHW* TN26 ...... **210** E6
TENT TN30 ...... **210** B5
Tenterden Wy *MARG* CT9 ...... **32** D5 ⓵
Terminus Dr *HB* CT6 ...... **47** J1
Terrace Rd *RDV* CT15 ...... **131** K5
SIT ME10 ...... **36** C1
The Terrace *CANTW/ST* CT2 ...... **86** D3
RDV CT15 ...... **151** F1
Teynham Cl *MARG* CT9 ...... **33** G4
Teynham Dr *WSTB* CT5 ...... **44** C4

Teynham Rd *WSTB* CT5 ...... **44** B5
Thames Av *IOS* ME12 ...... **14** C5
Thanet Coastal Pth *BRCH* CT7 ...... **29** K6
BRDST CT10 ...... **33** J5
MARG CT9 ...... **3** E2 ⓵
MSTR CT12 ...... **75** H3
Thanet Gdns *FOLKN* CT19 ...... **13** F3 ⓵
Thanet Place Gdns *BRDST* CT10 ...... **33** J8
Thanet Rd *BRDST* CT10 ...... **55** J2
MARG CT9 ...... **3** D3
RAM CT11 ...... **5** F3
WGOS CT8 ...... **30** C5
Thanet Wy *FAV* ME13 ...... **65** F4
FAV ME13 ...... **82** C1
HB CT6 ...... **46** C3
WSTB CT5 ...... **44** C6
WSTB CT5 ...... **65** J1
Thanington Rd *CANT* CT1 ...... **86** A8
Theatre St *HYTHE* CT21 ...... **205** G4 ⓵
Theresa Rd *HYTHE* CT21 ...... **205** F5
Third Av *IOS* ME12 ...... **17** K8
MARG CT9 ...... **3** F2 ⓵
Thirlemere *KEN/WIL* TN24 ...... **141** G8
Thirlemere Av *RAM* CT11 ...... **4** A4
Thirlemere Gdns *RCANTE* CT3 ...... **110** B8 ⓵
Thistle Hill Wy *IOS* ME12 ...... **21** J1
Thomas Rd *FAV* ME13 ...... **62** B7
SIT ME10 ...... **58** C2
Thompson Cl *DEAL* CT14 ...... **135** H6
FOLKN CT19 ...... **12** B2 ⓵
Thomson Rd *KEN/WIL* TN24 ...... **161** F1 ⓵
Thornbridge Rd *DEAL* CT14 ...... **135** G5
Thornden Cl *HB* CT6 ...... **45** K4
Thornden Wood Rd *CANTW/ST* CT2.. **67** H4
Thorndike Rd *LYDD* TN29 ...... **216** E2
Thorne Hl *MSTR* CT12 ...... **52** E7
Thorne Rd *MSTR* CT12 ...... **52** A8
The Thorn Est *HDCN* TN27 ...... **137** H8
Thorneycroft Rd *FAV* ME13 ...... **99** F8
Thorn Gdns *RAM* CT11 ...... **5** E2 ⓵
Thorn Hl *IOS* ME12 ...... **24** C1
Thorn La *RCANTE* CT4 ...... **146** A4
Thornlea *ASH* TN23 ...... **160** C4
Thornton Cl *KEN/WIL* TN24 ...... **162** A5
Thornton La *DEAL* CT14 ...... **112** B8
SWCH CT13 ...... **112** E5
Thread La *FAV* ME13 ...... **85** H1
Three King's Yd *SWCH* CT13 ...... **94** A5 ⓾
Throwley Dr *HB* CT6 ...... **46** B2
Throwley Rd *FAV* ME13 ...... **100** C3
Thrupp Paddock *BRDST* CT10 ...... **33** H5 ⓵
Thruxted La *RCANTW* CT4 ...... **104** C5
Thundersland Rd *HB* CT6 ...... **47** C2
Thurlow Av *HB* CT6 ...... **47** D2
Thurston Pk *WSTB* CT5 ...... **44** B5
Tickham La *RSIT* ME9 ...... **60** A8
RSIT ME9 ...... **78** D3
Tickner's La *LYDD* TN29 ...... **223** K5
Tilden Cl *RASHW* TN26 ...... **177** J7
Tilden Gill Rd *TENT* TN30 ...... **194** C7
Tile Kiln Hl *CANTW/ST* CT2 ...... **85** J1
Tile Kiln La *FOLKN* CT19 ...... **190** A7
Tile Kiln Rd *KEN/WIL* TN24 ...... **141** K3
Tile Lodge Rd *HDCN* TN27 ...... **117** K7
Tillard Cl *RCANTW* CT4 ...... **125** K3
Tillery La *LYDD* TN29 ...... **223** H7
Timperley Cl *DEAL* CT14 ...... **115** H8 ⓵
Tina Gdns *BRDST* CT10 ...... **33** H8
Tithe Barn La *ASH* TN23 ...... **160** B6
Tivoli Brooks *MARG* CT9 ...... **2** C4 ⓵
Tivoli Park Av *MARG* CT9 ...... **2** C4
Tivoli Rd *MARG* CT9 ...... **2** C4
Toby Rd *LYDD* TN29 ...... **233** F9
Todd Crs *SIT* ME10 ...... **36** B6
Tollemache Cl *MSTR* CT12 ...... **52** E4
Toll Ga *DEAL* CT14 ...... **135** G2
Tollgate Cl *WSTB* CT5 ...... **43** K6
Toll La *HDCN* TN27 ...... **119** G7
Tolsford Cl *FOLKN* CT19 ...... **189** J8
RFOLK CT18 ...... **188** B3
Tomlin Dr *MARG* CT9 ...... **32** D7
Tonbridge Wy *RYE* TN31 ...... **234** B3 ⓵
Tonford La *CANT* CT1 ...... **85** K8
CANTW/ST CT2 ...... **85** H7
Tonge Rd *SIT* ME10 ...... **58** C2 ⓵
Tontine St *FOLK* CT20 ...... **13** D4
Tookey Rd *NROM* TN28 ...... **232** C1
Top Rd *TENT* TN30 ...... **221** F3
Tormore Ms *DEAL* CT14 ...... **135** G2 ⓵
Tormore Pk *DEAL* CT14 ...... **135** G2
Toronto Cl *DVE/WH* CT16 ...... **173** F3 ⓺
Torrington Rd *ASH* TN23 ...... **8** C5
Tothill St *MSTR* CT12 ...... **52** J9
Tournay Cl *ASH* TN23 ...... **160** D6
Tourney Cl *HYTHE* CT21 ...... **203** H3
Tourney Rd *LYDD* TN29 ...... **237** G1
Tourtel Rd *CANT* CT1 ...... **7** D2
Tower Est *LYDD* TN29 ...... **217** G4
Tower Gdns *HYTHE* CT21 ...... **205** G5
Tower Hamlets Rd *DVW* CT17 ...... **10** A3
Tower Hamlets St *DVW* CT17 ...... **10** A3
Tower Hl *DVW* CT17 ...... **10** A3
WSTB CT5 ...... **44** B3
Tower Rd *WSTB* CT5 ...... **44** B4
Tower St *DVW* CT17 ...... **10** A3

Towers Vw *KEN/WIL* TN24 ...... **141** G7 ⓵
Tower Wy *CANT* CT1 ...... **6** C3 ⓶⓵
Towne La *RCANTW* CT4 ...... **84** E8
Townley Rd *RAM* CT11 ...... **5** D5 ⓾
Town Rd *RCANTW* CT4 ...... **125** K2
Townsend Farm Rd *RDV* CT15 ...... **155** F8
Townwall St *DVE/WH* CT16 ...... **10** C4
The Tracies *RSIT* ME9 ...... **34** B8
Trafalgar Rd *DEAL* CT14 ...... **135** G2 ⓵
The Tram Rd *FOLK* CT20 ...... **13** E3 ⓷
FOLKN CT19 ...... **13** E4
Transformer Av *LYDD* TN29 ...... **239** F8
Travers Rd *DEAL* CT14 ...... **135** G1
Treasury Vw *RCANTE* CT3 ...... **89** J6
Tribune Cl *IOS* ME12 ...... **14** C6 ⓵
Tribune Dr *SIT* ME10 ...... **36** A8
Trimworth Rd *FOLKN* CT19 ...... **12** A3
FOLKN CT19 ...... **190** A8
Trinity Crs *FOLK* CT20 ...... **12** B6 ⓵
Trinity Gdns *FOLK* CT20 ...... **12** C5
Trinity Hl *MARG* CT9 ...... **3** D2 ⓵
Trinity Pl *DEAL* CT14 ...... **135** G2
RAM CT11 ...... **5** F4
Trinity Rd *FOLK* CT20 ...... **12** B5
IOS ME12 ...... **14** D4
KEN/WIL TN24 ...... **141** G7
KEN/WIL TN24 ...... **161** F1
SIT ME10 ...... **36** A7
Trinity Sq *BRDST* CT10 ...... **33** G7
MARG CT9 ...... **3** D2 ⓵
Tritton Cl *KEN/WIL* TN24 ...... **141** K7
Tritton Flds *KEN/WIL* TN24 ...... **141** J7 ⓶
Tritton Gdns *LYDD* TN29 ...... **217** F5
Tritton La *NROM* TN28 ...... **226** C8 ⓵
Troubridge Cl *KEN/WIL* TN24 ...... **162** A7 ⓷
Troughton Ms *MARG* CT9 ...... **2** B4 ⓵
Troy Town La *RASHE* TN25 ...... **143** H8
Trueman Cl *CANTW/ST* CT2 ...... **66** D7
Truro Rd *RAM* CT11 ...... **5** F4
Tudor Av *LYDD* TN29 ...... **217** F5
Tudor Byway *KEN/WIL* TN24 ...... **141** J7
Tudor Cl *BRCH* CT7 ...... **30** A6 ⓵
Tudor End *KEN/WIL* TN24 ...... **161** H1
Tudor Rd *CANT* CT1 ...... **6** B4
FOLKN CT19 ...... **189** J8
KEN/WIL TN24 ...... **161** H1
Tufton Rd *KEN/WIL* TN24 ...... **9** D3
Tunis Ct *CANT* CT1 ...... **87** H5
Tunis Rw *BRDST* CT10 ...... **55** J1
Tunstall Rd *CANTW/ST* CT2 ...... **86** E2
RSIT ME9 ...... **57** H6
Turketel Rd *FOLK* CT20 ...... **12** C4
Turmine Ct *IOS* ME12 ...... **21** H1 ⓶
Turnagain La *CANT* CT1 ...... **6** C3 ⓷⓹
Turnden Gdns *MARG* CT9 ...... **33** F4
Turner Cl *SIT* ME10 ...... **36** B7
Turners Av *TENT* TN30 ...... **194** B6
Turner St *RAM* CT11 ...... **5** E5
Turnpike Cl *HYTHE* CT21 ...... **204** E3 ⓵
Turnpike Hl *HYTHE* CT21 ...... **204** E3
Twelve Acres *KEN/WIL* TN24 ...... **9** E5
Twiss Av *HYTHE* CT21 ...... **205** H4
Twiss Gv *HYTHE* CT21 ...... **205** H4
Twiss Rd *HYTHE* CT21 ...... **205** H4
Twyne Cl *CANTW/ST* CT2 ...... **69** E2
Tyler Cl *CANTW/ST* CT2 ...... **86** D3
Tyler Hill Rd *CANTW/ST* CT2 ...... **66** D8
Tyler Wy *WSTB* CT5 ...... **45** H3
Tyndale Pk *HB* CT6 ...... **47** G2
Tysoe Ct *IOS* ME12 ...... **21** G1
Tyson Av *MARG* CT9 ...... **31** F5
Tyson Cl *FOLKN* CT19 ...... **13** E2

U

Uden Rd *LYDD* TN29 ...... **217** J2
Uffington Ct *RCANTE* CT3 ...... **110** C4
Ufton La *SIT* ME10 ...... **57** K3
Ulcombe Gdns *CANTW/ST* CT2 ...... **86** C2
Ulley Rd *KEN/WIL* TN24 ...... **141** H7
Ullswater Gdns *RCANTE* CT3 ...... **110** B8 ⓵
Ulster Rd *MARG* CT9 ...... **3** D5 ⓵
Undercliff *FOLK* CT20 ...... **206** E3
Undercliffe Rd *DEAL* CT14 ...... **155** K1
Underdown La *HB* CT6 ...... **46** E4
Underdown Rd *DVW* CT17 ...... **173** F7 ⓹
HB CT6 ...... **46** E2
Underhill Rd *FOLK* CT20 ...... **206** B1
Underwood *RFOLK* CT18 ...... **169** H8
Underwood Cl *CANT* CT1 ...... **7** D6
KEN/WIL TN24 ...... **141** H8 ⓵
Union Crs *MARG* CT9 ...... **3** D3 ⓶⓷
Union Pl *CANT* CT1 ...... **7** D2 ⓶⓷
Union Rd *DEAL* CT14 ...... **115** K4
IOS ME12 ...... **16** A7
RAM CT11 ...... **5** F3 ⓵
RCANTW CT4 ...... **107** K5
Union Rw *MARG* CT9 ...... **2** C3
Union St *CANT* CT1 ...... **7** D2
DVW CT17 ...... **10** B5 ⓵
FAV ME13 ...... **62** B7
IOS ME12 ...... **14** B4 ⓵
RAM CT11 ...... **5** E4 ⓵

Unity Pl *RAM* CT11 .... 5 F4 ⬛
Unity St *IOS* ME12 .... 14 E4
SIT ME10 .... 57 K3
University Rd *CANTW/ST* CT2 .... 86 B3
Upchurch Wk *MARG* CT9 .... 33 F4 ▧
Uphill *RFOLK* CT18 .... 190 C2
Uplands *CANTW/ST* CT2 .... 86 D2
Uplands Wy *IOS* ME12 .... 20 D1
Uplees Rd *FAV* ME13 .... 39 J8
FAV ME13 .... 60 K3
Upper Approach Rd *BRDST* CT10 .... 55 H3 ⬛
Upper Brents *FAV* ME13 .... 62 C5
Upper Bridge St *CANT* CT1 .... 7 D4
RASHE TN25 .... 143 F4
Upper Chantry La *CANT* CT1 .... 7 D4 ⬛
Upper Dane Rd *MARG* CT9 .... 3 E4
Upper Denmark Rd *ASH* TN23 .... 8 C5 ⬛
Upper Dumpton Park Rd *RAM* CT11 .. 5 E4
Upper Field Rd *SIT* ME10 .... 58 C1
Upper Free Down *HB* CT6 .... 47 F4
Upper Gv *MARG* CT9 .... 3 D3
Upper Malthouse HI *HYTHE* CT21 205 F4 ⬛
Upper Rd *DVE/WH* CT16 .... 11 D2
Upper St Ann's Rd *FAV* ME13 .... 62 A8
Upper Strand St *SWCH* CT13 .... 94 A5 ⬛1
Upper St *CT14* 132 E3
DEAL CT14 .... 155 K1
Upper Vicarage Rd *KEN/WIL* TN24.. 141 H7
Upton Cl *FOLKN* CT19 .... 12 A2
Upton Rd *BRDST* CT10 .... 55 G1
Ursuline Dr *WGOS* CT8 .... 30 C7

V

Valebrook Cl *FOLK* CT20 .... 206 C1
Valenciennes Rd *SIT* ME10.. .... 57 K3
Vale Pl *RAM* CT11 .... 5 D5
Vale Rd *BRDST* CT10 .... 55 G2
RAM CT11 .... 4 C5
RDV CT15 .... 134 B7
WSTB CT5 .... 44 A6
Vale Sq *RAM* CT11 .... 5 D5
Valestone Cl *HYTHE* CT21.. .... 206 B2
The Vale *BRDST* CT10 .... 55 G2
Vale View Rd *DVW* CT17 .... 173 F7
RCANTE CT3 .... 130 A1
Valkyrie Av *WSTB* CT5.. .... 43 J6
The Vallance *RSIT* ME9 .... 59 H8
Valley Rd *CANT* CT1 .... 6 B5
DVW CT17 .... 172 C3
FOLK CT20 .... 206 E2
MARG CT9 .... 53 K2
RCANTW CT4 .... 128 E4
Valley Wk *HYTHE* CT21 .... 206 B3
Vanity Rd *IOS* ME12 .... 24 E5
Varne Pl *FOLKN* CT19 .... 13 F3
Varne Rd *FOLKN* CT19 .... 13 F4
Vaughan Dr *SIT* ME10 .... 36 A6
Vauxhall Av *CANT* CT1 .... 87 G3
HB CT6 .... 87 G3 ⬛
Vauxhall Crs *CANT* CT1 .... 87 G3 ⬛
Vauxhall Industrial Rd *CANT* CT1 .. 87 G2
Vauxhall *CANTW/ST* CT2 .... 87 G2
Vectis Dr *SIT* ME10 .... 36 A6
Venture Cl *LYDD* TN29 .... 217 F5
Vere Rd *BRDST* CT10 .... 55 H2
Vereth Rd *RAM* CT11 .... 5 D5 ⬛1
Vernon Pl *CANT* CT1 .... 7 E4
DEAL CT14 .... 115 K6 ⬛
Vesper Ct *HDCN* TN27 .... 156 A5
Vestey Ct *WGOS* CT8 .... 30 D5
Viaduct Cl *MSTR* CT12 .... 4 C3
The Viaduct *DVW* CT17 .... 10 B6 ⬛
Vicarage Gdn *MSTR* CT12 .... 51 F7
Vicarage Gdns *RCANTE* CT3 .... 90 C7 ▧
Vicarage HI *RCANTW* CT4 .... 125 J2
Vicarage La *ASH* TN23 .... 8 C3
DEAL CT14 .... 132 E5
DEAL CT14 .... 135 F1
FAV ME13 .... 80 E1
FAV ME13 .... 82 C8
RCANTW CT4 .... 167 K2
RDV CT15 .... 130 E1
RDV CT15 .... 155 F8
RSIT ME9 .... 34 B3
SWCH CT13 .... 93 K5 ⬛0
Vicarage Pl *MARG* CT9 .... 3 D4 ⬛1
Vicarage Rd *FOLK* CT20 .... 207 F3
IOS ME12 .... 16 A7 ⬛
SIT ME10 .... 55 J7
Vicarage St *BRDST* CT10.. .... 55 G1
FAV ME13 .... 62 C6
Vickers Cl *RFOLK* CT18 .... 190 B2
Victor Av *MARG* CT9 .... 32 E4
Victoria Av *BRDST* CT10 .... 33 F6
HYTHE CT21 .... 205 F4
MARG CT9 .... 3 F4
RDV CT15 .... 155 H8
WGOS CT8 .... 30 E7
Victoria Crs *ASH* TN23.. .... 8 E7
DVE/WH CT16 .... 10 A3 ⬛

Victoria Dr *HB* CT6 .... 46 B1
Victoria Gv *FOLK* CT20 .... 13 D4
HYTHE CT21 .... 206 B4
Victoria Pde *RAM* CT11 .... 5 F4
Victoria Pk *DVE/WH* CT16 .... 10 C3
HB CT6 .... 46 E1
Victoria Pl *FAV* ME13 .... 62 B7
Victoria Rd *ASH* TN23 .... 8 B4
BRDST CT10 .... 33 F8
CANT CT1 .... 6 B4
DEAL CT14 .... 135 K1
DEAL CT14 .... 155 J2
FOLKN CT19 .... 12 C4
HYTHE CT21 .... 205 C5
MARG CT9 .... 3 D4
NROM TN28 .... 233 F1
RAM CT11 .... 5 F4
RFOLK CT18 .... 191 J4
SIT ME10 .... 57 J2
Victoria West *NROM* TN28 .... 232 E1
Victoria Rw *CANT* CT1.. .... 7 D2
Victoria St *DVW* CT17 .... 173 F5
IOS ME12 .... 14 C5
NROM TN28 .... 226 B8 ⬛
Victory St *IOS* ME12 .... 14 C4 ▧
Viking Cl *BRCH* CT7 .... 29 G6
Village Wy *RASHW* TN26.. .... 198 F7
Villiers Av *CANT* CT1 .... 87 H5
Vincent Cl *BRDST* CT10 .... 54 D3
FOLK CT20 .... 206 E2
Vincent Gdns *IOS* ME12 .... 14 D5
Vincent Pl *KEN/WIL* TN24 .... 9 F1
Vincent Rd *MARG* CT9 .... 53 H2
SIT ME10 .... 58 D3
Vine Cl *RAM* CT11 .... 5 E1
Vine Lands *LYDD* TN29 .... 231 G8
Viners Cl *SIT* ME10 .... 57 K5
Viney's Gdns *TENT* TN30 .... 194 C5
Vinson Cl *FAV* ME13.. .... 63 J5
Vinten Cl *HB* CT6 .... 47 G6
Violet Av *MSTR* CT12 .... 4 A4
Virginia Rd *WSTB* CT5 .... 44 D6
Vlissingen Dr *DEAL* CT14 .... 115 J6
Volante Dr *SIT* ME10 .... 35 K7
Vulcan Cl *WSTB* CT5 .... 43 K7

W

Wacher Cl *CANTW/ST* CT2 .... 6 C1
Waddington Dr *RFOLK* CT18 .... 190 B2
Wades Cl *LYDD* TN29 .... 226 C1
Wadham Pl *SIT* ME10 .... 58 C4
Wain Ct *IOS* ME12 .... 21 H1
Wainwright Pl *KEN/WIL* TN24 .... 9 D5 ⬛1
Wakefield Wy *HYTHE* CT21 .... 205 F5
Walcheren Cl *DEAL* CT14 .... 115 J6 ⬛
Waldershare Av *SWCH* CT13 .... 95 G7
Waldershare Rd *RDV* CT15 .... 152 E1
Waldron Rd *BRDST* CT10 .... 55 J4
Walker La *BRCH* CT7 .... 29 G6 ⬛1
Wallace Ms *FOLKN* CT19 .... 13 D2
Wallace Wy *BRDST* CT10 .... 55 F2
Waller Rd *LYDD* TN29 .... 233 F7
Wallers Rd *FAV* ME13 .... 61 K7
Wallis Rd *KEN/WIL* TN24 .... 9 D3
Wall Rd *KEN/WIL* TN24 .... 8 B2
The Wall *SIT* ME10 .... 57 K1
Wallwood Rd *RAM* CT11 .... 5 F3
Walmer Castle Rd *DEAL* CT14 .... 135 J5
Walmer Gdns *DEAL* CT14 .... 135 G4
MSTR CT12 .... 75 H1
SIT ME10 .... 57 J2
Walmer Rd *WSTB* CT5.. .... 44 B6
Walmer Wy *DEAL* CT14 .... 135 J4
Walmsley Rd *BRDST* CT10 .... 55 G1
Walner Gdns *NROM* TN28 .... 226 C7
Walner La *NROM* TN28 .... 226 C7
Walnut Cl *KEN/WIL* TN24 .... 141 H8
Walnut Tree Dr *SIT* ME10 .... 57 J2 ⬛
Walnut Tree La *CANTW/ST* CT2 .... 69 H7
Walpole Rd *MARG* CT9 .... 3 D2 ⬛
Walsby Dr *SIT* ME10 .... 36 B6
Waltham Cl *KEN/WIL* TN24 .... 9 F5
MARG CT9 .... 33 F4 ⬛
Waltham Rd *RCANTW* CT4 .... 125 H5
Walton Gdns *FOLKN* CT19 .... 13 D2
Walton Manor Cl *FOLKN* CT19 .... 13 D1
Walton Rd *FOLKN* CT19 .... 13 D3
The Waltons *FOLKN* CT19 .... 12 C1
Wanden La *HDCN* TN27 .... 136 B5
Wantsum Cl *HB* CT6 .... 48 A1
Wantsume Lees *SWCH* CT13 .... 93 J4
Wantsum Wk *BRCH* CT7 .... 29 F7
BRCH CT7 .... 50 A7
HB CT6 .... 50 B4
Wantsum Wy *BRCH* CT7 .... 50 B4
Warden Bay Rd *IOS* ME12 .... 24 D3
Warden House Ms *DEAL* CT14 .... 135 G2 ⬛
Warden Rd *IOS* ME12 .... 23 H2
Warden View Gdns *IOS* ME12 .... 24 B5
Wardour Cl *BRDST* CT10 .... 55 J2 ⬛
Wards Hill Rd *IOS* ME12 .... 15 J6

Wardwell La *RSIT* ME9 .... 34 B4
Warehorne Rd *RASHW* TN26 .... 198 D7
Warre Av *RAM* CT11 .... 4 C6
Warren Cl *FOLKN* CT19 .... 13 F3
SIT ME10 .... 58 C4 ⬛
Warren Dr *BRDST* CT10 .... 55 F1
The Warren Dr *WGOS* CT8 .... 30 C7
Warren La *KEN/WIL* TN24 .... 8 A1
RDV CT15 .... 151 F7
Warren Rd *FOLKN* CT19 .... 13 F3
NROM TN28 .... 226 E8
Warren St *RMAID* ME17 .... 97 K8
The Warren *RASHE* TN25 .... 185 F1
WSTB CT5 .... 43 K8
Warren Vw *ASH* TN23 .... 160 D2
Warren Wy *FOLKN* CT19 .... 13 F3
Warten Rd *RAM* CT11 .... 5 F2
Warwick Crs *SIT* ME10 .... 57 H1
Warwick Dr *RAM* CT11 .... 4 B6
Warwick Rd *CANT* CT1 .... 7 F3
DEAL CT14 .... 135 K4
KEN/WIL TN24 .... 141 J8
MARG CT9 .... 3 F3
WSTB CT5 .... 44 A4
Washford Farm Rd *ASH* TN23 .... 181 H1
Washington Cl *DVE/WH* CT16 .... 173 F3 ⬛
Washington La *LYDD* TN29 .... 224 A7
Wass Dro *RCANTE* CT3 .... 72 E7
Watchester Av *RAM* CT11 .... 4 C6
Watchester La *MSTR* CT12 .... 74 A1
Waterbrook Av *KEN/WIL* TN24 .... 182 E1
Watercress La *ASH* TN23 .... 160 C6
Waterditch La *RMAID* ME17 .... 97 K8
Waterfall Rd *RASHW* TN26 .... 139 J8
Water Farm *RCANTW* CT4 .... 167 K2
Waterham Rd *FAV* ME13 .... 64 D5
Water La *CANT* CT1 .... 6 C3 ⬛
FAV ME13 .... 62 B7 ▧
FAV ME13 .... 80 E1
Waterloo Crs *DVW* CT17 .... 10 C4 ⬛
Waterloo HI *IOS* ME12 .... 16 A8 ⬛1
Waterloo Pl *RAM* CT11 .... 5 F4 ⬛
Waterloo Rd *FOLK* CT20 .... 206 D1 ▧
SIT ME10 .... 57 J1
WSTB CT5 .... 44 A4
Water Mdw *CANTW/ST* CT2 .... 87 K2 ▧
Watersend *DVE/WH* CT16 .... 172 A1
Waterside *KEN/WIL* TN24 .... 9 F5
Waterside *WGOS* CT8 .... 30 E5 ⬛
Waterside Vw *IOS* ME12 .... 24 D2
Water St *DEAL* CT14 .... 115 K7
Waterworks HI *RDV* CT15 .... 154 B3
Waterworks La *RDV* CT15 .... 154 B3
Watery La *RCANTW* CT4 .... 126 A1
Watkin Rd *FOLKN* CT19 .... 12 C3
Watling Pl *SIT* ME10 .... 58 B3
Watling St *CANT* CT1 .... 6 C3 ⬛⬛
Watsons Cl *RASHE* TN25 .... 141 G6
Watson's HI *SIT* ME10 .... 57 K1
Wauchope Rd *WSTB* CT5 .... 43 G8
Waverley Av *IOS* ME12 .... 15 J7
Waverley Rd *MARG* CT9 .... 31 G6
Wayborough HI *MSTR* CT12 .... 52 C6
Way HI *MSTR* CT12 .... 52 D7
Wayne Cl *BRDST* CT10 .... 55 F1
Wayside *TENT* TN30 .... 194 B4 ⬛1
Wayside Av *TENT* TN30 .... 194 B3
Weald Ct *SIT* ME10 .... 57 J4
Wealden Av *TENT* TN30 .... 194 B4
Wealdhurst Pk *BRDST* CT10 .... 54 E1
The Weald *KEN/WIL* TN24 .... 8 C2
Wear Bay Crs *FOLKN* CT19 .... 13 F4
Wear Bay Rd *FOLKN* CT19 .... 13 F4
Weatherall Cl *FAV* ME13 .... 83 H4
Weatherly Dr *BRDST* CT10 .... 5 F1
DVE/WH CT16 .... **192** E2
Webb Cl *FOLKN* CT19 .... 12 A2
Weddington La *RCANTE* CT3 .... 92 C4
Weeks Ct *OBOR* ME11 .... 20 B1 ▧
Well Cl *CANTW/ST* CT2 .... 69 F8
Wellesley Av *DEAL* CT14 .... 135 J4
Wellesley Cl *BRDST* CT10 .... 55 F3
WGOS CT8 .... 30 D7 ▧
Wellesley Rd *DVE/WH* CT16 .... 10 C4 ⬛
IOS ME12 .... 14 E5
KEN/WIL TN24 .... 8 C3
MARG CT9 .... 3 F4
WGOS CT8 .... 30 D7 ▧
Wellfield Rd *FOLK* CT20 .... 12 A4
Wellington La *WGOS* CT8 .... 30 D5 ▧
Wellington Crs *RAM* CT11 .... 5 F5
Wellington Gdns *MARG* CT9 .... 3 D2 ⬛
Wellington Pde *DEAL* CT14 .... 135 K7
Wellington Pl *FOLK* CT20 .... 206 D3 ▧
Wellington Rd *DEAL* CT14 .... 135 K1
DVE/WH CT16 .... 172 B1
FOLK CT20 .... 206 D1
SIT ME10 .... 57 G1
WGOS CT8 .... 30 D7
Wellington St *WSTB* CT5 .... 66 A1
Wellis Gdns *MARG* CT9 .... 2 A4
Well La *CANTW/ST* CT2 .... 88 A3
FAV ME13 .... 79 K3
RDV CT15 .... 155 F8

Well Rd *QBOR* ME11 .... 20 A3
   QBOR ME11 .... 20 B1
   RFOLK CT18 .... 167 G8
Wells Av *CANT* CT1 .... 7 E4
Wells Cl *NROM* TN28 .... 226 D8
   TENT TN30 .... 194 A6
Wells Rd *FOLKN* CT19 .... 189 K8
Well Winch Rd *SIT* ME10 .... 57 J1
Welsdene Rd *MARG* CT9 .... 31 G6
Welson Rd *FOLK* CT20 .... 207 F1
Wemyss Wy *CANT* CT1 .... 7 F3
Wenham's La *LYDD* TN29 ...... 224 D4
Wentworth Av *MARG* CT9 .... 31 F5
Wentworth Cl *RFOLK* CT18 ... 167 G8
Wentworth Dr *MSTR* CT12 .... 4 A2
   SIT ME10 .... 57 H1
Wentworth Gdns *HB* CT6 .... 46 C4
Wesley Ter *RFOLK* CT18 .... 167 G7
Westbere La *CANTW/ST* CT2 ... 69 G8
Westbourne *ASH* TN23 .... 160 B8
Westbourne Gdns *FOLK* CT20 .. 12 B5
Westbourne St *SIT* ME10 .... 57 K1
Westbrook Av *MARG* CT9 .... 31 F5
Westbrook Cottages *MARG* CT9 .. 2 A4
Westbrook Gdns *MARG* CT9 .... 2 A4
Westbrook La *HB* CT6 .... 46 A3
Westbrook Prom *MARG* CT9 ..... 31 G4
Westbrook Rd *MARG* CT9 .... 2 A3
   MARG CT9 .... 2 A4
Westbury Crs *DVW* CT17 .... 173 F8
Westbury Rd *DVW* CT17 .... 173 F8
   WGOS CT8 .... 30 E6
West Cliff *WSTB* CT5 .... 43 K6
West Cliff Dr *HB* CT6 .... 46 B4
Westcliff Dr *IOS* ME12 .... 16 A7
West Cliff Gdns *FOLK* CT20 ... 13 D5
   HB CT6 .... 46 A3
Westcliff Gdns *MARG* CT9 .... 2 A4
   MARG CT9 .... 31 G5
West Cliff Prom *RAM* CT11 .... 5 D6
West Cliff Rd *BRDST* CT10 .... 55 H3
Westcliff Rd *MARG* CT9 .... 2 A4
West Cliff Rd *RAM* CT11 .... 5 D5
Westcourt La *RCANTW* CT4 .... 130 B7
Westdean Cl *DVW* CT17 .... 172 C4
West Dumpton La *RAM* CT11 ..... 5 E1
Westerham Cl *CANTW/ST* CT2 .. 86 E2
   MARG CT9 .... 33 G4
Westerham Rd *SIT* ME10 .... 57 H3
Westerhout Cl *DEAL* CT14 ...... 115 J6
Western Av *ASH* TN23 .... 8 A3
   HB CT6 .... 46 C2
   IOS ME12 .... 14 E7
   RCANTW CT4 .... 107 K5
Western Cl *DVW* CT17 .... 10 A5
Western Esp *BRDST* CT10 .... 55 J4
   HB CT6 .... 46 B1
Western Gdns *KEN/WIL* TN24 .... 9 E5
Western Link *FAV* ME13 .... 61 K6
Western Rd *DEAL* CT14 .... 115 J8
   MARG CT9 .... 32 D6
Western Undercliff *RAM* CT11 .... 4 C6
Westfield *CANTW/ST* CT2 .... 66 D8
Westfield La *RFOLK* CT18 .... 188 C3
Westfield Rd *BRCH* CT7 .... 29 J7
Westfields *HDCN* TN27 .... 137 K6
Westgate Av *BRCH* CT7 .... 53 F2
Westgate Bay Av *WGOS* CT8 .... 30 C5
Westgate Cl *CANTW/ST* CT2 .... 86 A5
Westgate Court Av *CANTW/ST* CT2 .. 6 A2
Westgate Gv *CANTW/ST* CT2 ..... 6 C2
Westgate Hall Rd *CANT* CT1 ...... 6 C2
Westgate Rd *FAV* ME13 .... 62 D7
Westgate Rbt *CANTW/ST* CT2 .... 6 C2
Westgate Ter *WSTB* CT5 .... 6 C2
West Gn *SIT* ME10 .... 36 A5
West Hill Rd *HB* CT6 .... 46 B1
West Hythe Rd *HYTHE* CT21 ... 203 J6
Westlands Av *SIT* ME10 .... 57 G2
Westlands Rd *HB* CT6 .... 46 A3
Westland Wy *RFOLK* CT18 ...... 190 C3
West La *IOS* ME12 .... 14 B4
   SIT ME10 .... 58 B2
West Lawn Gdns *FOLK* CT20 .. 206 D3
West Lea *DEAL* CT14 .... 115 J7
Westleigh Rd *WGOS* CT8 .... 30 C6
Westmarsh Dr *MARG* CT9 .... 33 F4
Westmeads Rd *WSTB* CT5 .... 44 B4
Westminster Rd *CANT* CT1 .... 87 C2
Westmoors *ASH* TN23 .... 160 B8
Westmoreland Dr *RSIT* ME9 ..... 34 A3
West Norman Rd *DVE/WH* CT16 .. 10 C3
Westonville Av *MARG* CT9 .... 31 G5
Westover Gdns *BRDST* CT10 ..... 33 F7
Westover Rd *BRDST* CT10 .... 33 F7
West Pde *HYTHE* CT21 .... 205 F6
West Park Av *MARG* CT9 .... 32 E5
West Pas *IOS* ME12 .... 14 B4
West Pl *LYDD* TN29 .... 227 C6
West Rdg *SIT* ME10 .... 57 J4
West Rd *FOLK* CT20 .... 206 D4
   MSTR CT12 .... 75 F6
West Side *RDV* CT15 .... 154 A5

West St *ASH* TN23 .... 8 B3
   DEAL CT14 .... 115 J7
   DVW CT17 .... 10 A3
   FAV ME13 .... 62 B6
   IOS ME12 .... 14 B3
   NROM TN28 .... 226 B8
   QBOR ME11 .... 20 A1
   RASHW TN26 .... 139 G7
   RMAID ME17 .... 96 E6
   SIT ME10 .... 57 K2
West Ter *FOLK* CT20 .... 13 D5
West View Cl *HB* CT6 .... 46 B4
Westwell La *KEN/WIL* TN24 .... 140 C8
   RASHE TN25 .... 139 J4
Westwood Pl *FAV* ME13 .... 81 H1
Westwood Rd *BRDST* CT10 ...... 54 D2
Weyburn Dr *MSTR* CT12 .... 4 A2
Weymouth Cl *FOLKN* CT19 .... 189 J8
Weymouth St *FOLKN* CT19 .... 189 J8
Wey St *RASHW* TN26 .... 213 H3
Wharfedale Rd *MARG* CT9 .... 3 E4
Wharton Gdns *KEN/WIL* TN24 .... 9 E5
Whatmer Cl *CANTW/ST* CT2 ..... 69 F8
Wheatcroft Cl *SIT* ME10 .... 58 C2
Wheatley Rd *MSTR* CT12 .... 4 C2
   WSTB CT5 .... 44 B4
Wheatsheaf Cl *FAV* ME13 .... 83 G3
Wheatsheaf La *RDV* CT15 .... 154 B4
Wheatsheaf Gdns *IOS* ME12 .... 14 C5
Wheelwrights Wy *SWCH* CT13 .. 113 F4
Wheler Rd *HDCN* TN27 .... 118 E6
Whimbrel Cl *SIT* ME10 .... 36 A6
Whinfell Av *RAM* CT11 .... 54 A7
Whinless Rd *DVW* CT17 .... 172 E6
Whiston Av *RASHW* TN26 .... 178 D2
Whitby Rd *FOLK* CT20 .... 189 J8
White Acre Dr *DEAL* CT14 ...... 135 H6
Whiteacre La *RCANTW* CT4 .... 145 H2
White Cliffs Country Trail
   DEAL CT14 .... 134 A5
   RDV CT15 .... 133 K8
   RDV CT15 .... 134 A5
   SWCH CT13 .... 94 C5
   SWCH CT13 .... 113 H5
Whitecliff Wy *FOLKN* CT19 ..... 189 H5
Whitefriars Meadow *SWCH* CT13 .. 94 A6
Whitefriars Wy *SWCH* CT13 ..... 93 K5
Whitehall *LYDD* TN29 .... 223 G6
Whitehall Bridge Rd *CANTW/ST* CT2 .. 6 B3
Whitehall Cl *CANTW/ST* CT2 ..... 6 B3
Whitehall Gdns *CANTW/ST* CT2 .. 6 B2
Whitehall Rd *CANTW/ST* CT2 ..... 6 A3
   MSTR CT12 .... 4 B3
   SIT ME10 .... 57 K4
Whitehall Wy *RASHE* TN25 ..... 186 A5
White Hl *RASHE* TN25 .... 139 J4
White Hill Cl *RCANTW* CT4 ..... 106 E6
White Horse Hl *RFOLK* CT18 .. 190 D4
White Horse La *CANT* CT1 .... 6 C5
   RCANTW CT4 .... 166 E3
Whitehouse Dro *RCANTE* CT3 ... 74 C7
Whitelocks Cl *RCANTW* CT4 ... 128 D3
Whitenbrook *HYTHE* CT21 ...... 206 A3
Whiteness Gn *BRDST* CT10 ...... 33 G5
Whiteness Rd *BRDST* CT10 ...... 33 H5
White Post Gdns *RCANTE* CT3 .. 92 B5
Whiteness Hi *DEAL* CT14 .... 132 E4
Whiteway Rd *QBOR* ME11 .... 14 A8
White Wood Rd *SWCH* CT13 ... 113 F5
Whitfeld Rd *ASH* TN23 .... 8 B5
Whitfield Av *BRDST* CT10 .... 33 F7
   DVE/WH CT16 .... 173 F4
Whitfield Ct *DVE/WH* CT16 ..... 152 E4
Whitfield Hl *DVE/WH* CT16 ..... 172 C2
Whiting Crs *FAV* ME13 .... 61 K6
Whitstable Rd *CANTW/ST* CT2 ... 6 A1
   FAV ME13 .... 62 D7
   HB CT6 .... 45 K3
Whybornes Cha *IOS* ME12 .... 15 H1
Whytecliffs *BRDST* CT10 .... 55 H4
Wichling Cl *CANTW/ST* CT2 ..... 86 E3
Wickenden Crs *KEN/WIL* TN24 .. 162 A6
Wicken La *HDCN* TN27 .... 119 G8
   HDCN TN27 .... 139 G1
Wickham Av *RAM* CT11 .... 55 H6
Wickham Cl *RSIT* ME9 .... 34 A8
Wickham Court La *RCANTE* CT3 .. 89 H3
Wickham La *RCANTE* CT3 .... 89 H4
Wickham Rd *RCANTE* CT3 .... 89 H5
Wick La *RCANTW* CT4 .... 129 K7
Widgeon Wk *RFOLK* CT18 ...... 190 C3
Widred Rd *DVW* CT17 .... 10 A3
Wife of Bath Hl *CANTW/ST* CT2 .. 86 A6
Wigmore La *RDV* CT15 .... 132 A6
Wigwam Paddocks *BRCH* CT7 .. 29 K6
Wiltred Rd *RSIT* ME9 .... 58 E4
Wilberforce Rd *FOLK* CT20 ..... 206 E3
Wilbrough Rd *BRCH* CT7 .... 29 K7
Wilcox Cl *RCANTE* CT3 .... 129 K2
Wilderness Hl *MARG* CT9 .... 3 E3
Wildish Rd *FAV* ME13 .... 61 K6
Wiles Av *NROM* TN28 .... 226 C8
Wilfred Rd *RAM* CT11 .... 4 C4
Wilgate Green Rd *FAV* ME13 .... 80 C7
Wilkes Rd *BRDST* CT10 .... 55 F3

Wilkie Rd *BRCH* CT7 .... 29 K6
Willement Rd *FAV* ME13 .... 62 A7
Willesborough Rd *KEN/WIL* TN24 .. 161 K1
Willetts Hl *MSTR* CT12 .... 51 G7
William Av *FOLKN* CT19 .... 12 B2
   MARG CT9 .... 32 D6
William Judge Cl *TENT* TN30 .. 194 D7
William Pitt Av *DEAL* CT14 ..... 115 H8
William Pitt Cl *HYTHE* CT21 ... 205 H4
William Rigby Dr *IOS* ME12 ...... 15 F7
William Rd *ASH* TN23 .... 8 B5
Williamson Rd *LYDD* TN29 ..... 233 F8
William St *FAV* ME13 .... 62 C7
   HB CT6 .... 46 E1
   SIT ME10 .... 57 K3
Willingdon Pl *DEAL* CT14 .... 135 J4
Willis Ct *IOS* ME12 .... 21 G1
Willop Wy *LYDD* TN29 .... 217 H3
Willow Av *BRDST* CT10 .... 54 E2
   FAV ME13 .... 61 K7
Willowbank Cl *LYDD* TN29 ...... 227 H2
Willow Cl *CANTW/ST* CT2 .... 86 E3
   HYTHE CT21 .... 204 C5
   MARG CT9 .... 32 D4
Willow Dr *LYDD* TN29 .... 227 G3
   RASHW TN26 .... 198 E7
Willow Rd *DEAL* CT14 .... 134 C3
   WSTB CT5 .... 65 K1
The Willows *RSIT* ME9 .... 34 A8
   SIT ME10 .... 36 A5
Willow Tree Cl *HB* CT6 .... 47 J1
   KEN/WIL TN24 .... 9 F4
Willow Wy *MARG* CT9 .... 2 A5
Willow Waye *RDV* CT15 .... 132 B7
Willson's Rd *RAM* CT11 .... 4 C5
Wilmott Pl *SWCH* CT13 .... 113 F4
Wilson Av *DEAL* CT14 .... 135 F3
Wilton Cl *DEAL* CT14 .... 135 H1
Wilton Rd *FOLKN* CT19 .... 12 B3
   MSTR CT12 .... 54 A5
Wimborne Pl *MSTR* CT12 .... 4 B3
Winant Wy *DVE/WH* CT16 ...... 173 F3
Wincheap *CANT* CT1 .... 6 B5
Wincheap Rbt *CANT* CT1 .... 6 B4
Winchelsea Rd *DVW* CT17 ...... 173 F7
Winchelsea St *DVW* CT17 .... 173 F7
Winchelsea Ter *DVW* CT17 ...... 173 F7
Winchester Gdns *CANT* CT1 .... 7 D5
Windermere *FAV* ME13 .... 62 D8
Windermere Av *RAM* CT11 .... 44 A4
Windermere Gdns *RCANTE* CT3 .. 110 B8
Windermere Gv *SIT* ME10 .... 57 J5
Wind Hl *HDCN* TN27 .... 118 A7
Winding Hl *FAV* ME13 .... 81 J7
Windmill Av *MSTR* CT12 .... 54 C3
Windmill Cl *CANT* CT1 .... 7 F3
   KEN/WIL TN24 .... 162 A5
   RCANTW CT4 .... 108 A5
Windmill Quay Rd *IOS* ME12 .... 22 A5
Windmill Ri *IOS* ME12 .... 16 B8
Windmill Rd *CANT* CT1 .... 7 F3
   HB CT6 .... 47 F4
   SIT ME10 .... 35 J8
   WSTB CT5 .... 44 A7
Windmill St *HYTHE* CT21 .... 205 F5
Windmill Wk *MSTR* CT12 .... 4 B2
Windsor Av *MARG* CT9 .... 3 F3
Windsor Cl *BRDST* CT10 .... 55 F1
Windsor Dr *SIT* ME10 .... 57 J4
Windsor Gdns *HB* CT6 .... 46 A3
   IOS ME12 .... 24 C5
Windsor Ms *NROM* TN28 .... 226 D6
Windsor Rd *CANT* CT1 .... 106 A1
   MSTR CT12 .... 53 J7
Winehouse La *RFOLK* CT18 ... 191 K3
Wingate Rd *FOLKN* CT19 .... 13 D2
Wingham Rd *RCANTE* CT3 .... 89 J6
Wing Rd *IOS* ME12 .... 25 G5
Wingrove Hl *DVW* CT17 .... 172 C4
Wings Ct *BRDST* CT10 .... 55 J1
Winifred Av *MSTR* CT12 .... 4 C1
Winnipeg Cl *DVE/WH* CT16 .... 173 G3
Winstanley Crs *RAM* CT11 .... 5 D3
Winstanley Rd *IOS* ME12 .... 14 D4
Winston Cl *CANT* CT1 .... 7 F2
Winston Ct *BRCH* CT7 .... 29 K6
Winston Gdns *HB* CT6 .... 47 J2
Winterage La *RFOLK* CT18 .... 168 D7
Winterstoke Crs *RAM* CT11 ...... 55 H6
Winterstoke Wy *RAM* CT11 ...... 55 H6
Winton Wy *LYDD* TN29 .... 227 H1
Wises La *RSIT* ME9 .... 57 F3
The Wish *RASHW* TN26 .... 197 H6
Wittersham Rd *CRBK* TN17 .... 218 C2
   RYE TN31 .... 220 B6
   TENT TN30 .... 219 G1
Wollaston Rd *DEAL* CT14 .... 135 J2
Wolseley Av *HB* CT6 .... 45 K2
Wolseley Pl *KEN/WIL* TN24 .... 8 B2
Wood Av *FOLKN* CT19 .... 13 D2
Woodberry Dr *SIT* ME10 .... 58 C3
Woodbrook *HDCN* TN27 .... 119 F7
Woodbury La *TENT* TN30 .... 194 A7

Index - featured places

Boughton Methodist
   Primary School
   FAV ME13.................................. 83 F2
The Boulevard Designer Outlet
   Village (Under Construction)
   RAM CT11.................................. 5 F5
Brabourne C of E Primary School
   RASHE TN25............................ 164 C6
The Bradley Gallery
   BRDST CT10................................ 55 J2
Bradstow School
   BRDST CT10................................ 33 H8
Bredgar C of E Primary School
   RSIT ME9.................................. 76 A1
Brenzett Air Museum
   LYDD TN29............................. 224 A3
Briary CP School
   HB CT6...................................... 46 B4
Brickmakers Industrial Estate
   SIT ME10.................................. 36 C8
Bridge Country Leisure Club
   WSTB CT5.................................. 43 F8
Bridge & Patrixbourne
   Primary School
   RCANTW CT4............................ 108 A4
Bridge Place Country Club
   RCANTW CT4............................ 108 A6
Bridge Road Business Centre
   ASH TN23................................ 160 D4
The British School
   DEAL CT14.............................. 115 K7
Broadlands Industrial Estate
   CANTW/ST CT2.......................... 66 C7
Broad Oak Industrial Estate
   CANTW/ST CT2.......................... 87 F3
Broadstairs Gallery
   BRDST CT10................................ 55 J2
Broadstairs Health Centre
   BRDST CT10................................ 55 H1
Broadstairs Youth
   & Leisure Centre
   BRDST CT10................................ 55 J1
Brockhill Park School (Lower)
   HYTHE CT21............................ 204 E3
Brockhill Park School (Upper)
   HYTHE CT21............................ 204 E2
Bromstone CP School
   BRDST CT10................................ 54 E3
Brook CP School
   RASHE TN25............................ 163 G2
Brooke House School
   for the Deaf
   MARG CT9.................................. 31 G4
Brookfield Industrial Estate
   ASH TN23................................ 160 D4
Brookland School
   LYDD TN29............................. 223 G6
Buckland Hospital
   DVW CT17................................ 172 E5
Bugsys Ten Pin Bowling
   MARG CT9.................................. 3 E2
B U P A
   HYTHE CT21............................ 205 F4
Bus Depot
   DVE/WH CT16............................ 10 B3
The Butts County Infants School
   SIT ME10.................................. 35 K8
Bybrook County Junior School
   KEN/WIL TN24........................ 161 G1
Bybrook County Primary
   Infants School
   KEN/WIL TN24........................ 161 G1
Bysing Wood CP School
   FAV ME13.................................. 61 K6
CAB
   DVE/WH CT16............................ 10 B3
Canterbury Cathedral
   CANT CT1.................................... 7 D3
Canterbury Christ Church College
   CANT CT1.................................... 7 E3
Canterbury Christ Church College
   CANTW/ST CT2............................ 6 C2
Canterbury Christ Church College
   RCANTE CT3.............................. 87 K5
Canterbury Christ
   Church University College
   MARG CT9.................................... 3 D3
Canterbury City Retail Park
   CANT CT1.................................. 87 H2
Canterbury College
   CANT CT1.................................... 7 E4
Canterbury Golf Club
   CANT CT1.................................. 87 J6
Canterbury Health Centre
   CANT CT1.................................... 7 D4

Canterbury Heritage Museum
   CANT CT1.................................... 6 C3
Canterbury High School
   CANT CT1.................................... 6 A3
Canterbury Indoor Market
   CANT CT1.................................... 6 C2
Canterbury Industrial Park
   RCANTE CT3.............................. 70 B5
Canterbury Pilgrims Hospital
   CANT CT1.................................... 6 C3
Canterbury Road CP School
   SIT ME10.................................. 58 C3
Canterbury Road Health Centre
   MARG CT9.................................... 2 A3
Canterbury & St Augustines
   Magistrates Court
   CANT CT1.................................... 7 D3
Canterbury Tales
   CANT CT1.................................... 6 C3
Capel-le-ferne CP School
   RFOLK CT18............................. 191 K3
Cartwright & Kelsey
   Primary School
   RCANTE CT3.............................. 92 A4
Casino
   MARG CT9.................................... 2 C3
Castle
   CANT CT1.................................... 6 B4
Castleacres Industrial Park
   SIT ME10.................................. 36 C8
Castle Clinic
   DVE/WH CT16............................ 10 C3
Castle High School
   DEAL CT14.............................. 135 J2
Cathedral Gateway
   CANT CT1.................................... 7 D3
Central Surgery
   BRCH CT7.................................. 29 J7
Challock CP School
   RASHE TN25............................ 121 F5
Channel Business Centre
   FOLK CT20................................ 13 D5
Channel High School
   FOLKN CT19.............................. 12 C2
Channel Tunnel
   Exhibition Centre
   RFOLK CT18............................. 189 G6
Charing C of E School
   HDCN TN27.............................. 118 E7
Charing Surgery
   HDCN TN27.............................. 118 D7
The Charles Dickens School
   BRDST CT10................................ 55 F2
Chariton Primary School
   DVE/WH CT16............................ 10 A1
Chariton Shopping Centre
   DVW CT17.................................. 10 A3
Chartham CP School
   RCANTW CT4............................ 104 E5
Chartham Surgery
   RCANTW CT4............................ 104 E3
Chatham House
   Grammar School
   RAM CT11.................................... 5 E4
Chaucer College Canterbury
   CANTW/ST CT2.......................... 86 B3
Chaucer Hospital
   CANT CT1................................ 106 E2
Chaucer Technology School
   CANT CT1.................................... 7 F4
Check-in
   RFOLK CT18............................. 189 G7
Cheriton CP School
   FOLK CT20............................... 189 H8
Chestfield Cricket Club
   WSTB CT5.................................. 44 E6
Chestfield Golf Club
   WSTB CT5.................................. 45 G6
Chestfield Medical Centre
   WSTB CT5.................................. 45 F4
Cheyne Middle School
   IOS ME12.................................. 15 F4
Chilham Gallery
   RCANTW CT4............................ 103 H6
Chilham Surgery
   RCANTW CT4............................ 103 J6
Chilton CP School
   RAM CT11.................................... 4 A5
Chislet C of E Primary School
   RCANTE CT3.............................. 70 D1
Christ Church C of E
   Primary School
   FOLKN CT19.............................. 12 C4
Christ Church High School
   ASH TN23................................ 181 J1

Christ Church School
   RAM CT11.................................... 4 C5
Churchill House School
   RAM CT11.................................... 5 D5
Church of England
   Primary School
   LYDD TN29.............................. 223 K4
Church Road Business Centre
   SIT ME10.................................. 36 D8
Church Road CP School
   KEN/WIL TN24........................ 162 A6
City Business Park
   CANT CT1.................................. 87 G3
Clarendon House
   Grammar School for Girls
   RAM CT11.................................... 5 D5
Cliff St Gallery
   RAM CT11.................................... 5 E5
Cliftonville CP School
   MARG CT9.................................... 3 F3
Cliftonville Surgery
   MARG CT9.................................... 3 E3
Cliftonville Theatre
   MARG CT9.................................... 3 E2
Clock Tower
   CANT CT1.................................... 6 C3
The Coach House Surgery
   HB CT6...................................... 47 F1
Cobbswood Industrial Estate
   ASH TN23.................................... 8 A3
Cobbswood Industrial Estate
   ASH TN23................................ 160 D4
College
   DVE/WH CT16............................ 10 B3
College
   SIT ME10.................................. 57 H3
College Square Shopping Centre
   MARG CT9.................................... 3 D2
The College
   ASH TN23.................................... 8 C3
The Commodore Catamaran
   Yacht Club Ltd
   IOS ME12.................................. 15 G4
Cossington House Surgery
   CANT CT1.................................... 7 D4
Council Offices
   CANT CT1.................................... 7 E2
Council Offices
   DVE/WH CT16............................ 152 E8
County Square Shopping Centre
   ASH TN23.................................... 8 B3
Cricket Club
   BRDST CT10................................ 5 F1
Customs & Excise Offices
   DVW CT17.................................. 10 A3
Dame Janet County
   Infant School
   MSTR CT12.................................. 4 B1
Dame Janet County
   Primary Junior School
   MSTR CT12.................................. 4 B1
Dane Court Grammar School
   BRDST CT10................................ 55 F2
Dane John Mound & Monument
   CANT CT1.................................... 6 C4
Danley Middle School
   IOS ME12.................................. 15 F7
Davington Primary School
   FAV ME13.................................. 62 A6
DC Offices
   RAM CT11.................................... 5 F5
Deal Castle
   DEAL CT14.............................. 135 K1
Deal Mongeham CP School
   DEAL CT14.............................. 135 F2
Deal Parochial Primary School
   DEAL CT14.............................. 115 J8
Deal Rowing Club
   DEAL CT14.............................. 115 K7
Deal Squash Racket Club
   DEAL CT14.............................. 115 K6
Deal Town F S & S Club
   DEAL CT14.............................. 135 H2
Deal Victoria & Barnes
   Cricket Club
   DEAL CT14.............................. 135 H4
Deal & Walmer Community
   Health Clinic
   DEAL CT14.............................. 135 H1
De Bradelei Wharf
   Shopping Centre
   DVW CT17.................................. 10 B5
Delf Stream Gallery
   SWCH CT13................................ 93 K6

Denture Clinic
 SWCH CT13 .... **94** A6
Depot
 RCANTE CT3 .... **71** J6
Diocesan & Payne Smith
 Primary School
 CANT CT1 .... **7** D2
Doddington CP School
 RSIT ME9 .... **78** B7
Dolphin Yard Sailing
 Barge Museum
 SIT ME10 .... **58** B1
Dominican Priory
 CANT CT1 .... **6** C2
Dorset Road Industrial Estate
 IOS ME12 .... **14** B6
The Dover Business Centre
 DVW CT17 .... **173** F7
Dover Castle
 DVE/WH CT16 .... **11** D3
Dover College
 DVW CT17 .... **10** A3
Dover College
 Leamington House
 DVW CT17 .... **10** A3
Dover College
 Preparatory School
 FOLK CT20 .... **12** B4
Dover Grammar School for Boys
 DVW CT17 .... **172** E6
Dover Grammar School for Girls
 DVE/WH CT16 .... **10** A2
Dover Harbour Board Offices
 DVW CT17 .... **10** C4
Dover Health Centre
 DVE/WH CT16 .... **10** B3
Dover Sports Centre
 DVE/WH CT16 .... **10** C3
Dover Town Council
 DVE/WH CT16 .... **10** B4
Dover Town Hall
 DVW CT17 .... **10** A3
Dover Water Sports Centre
 DVW CT17 .... **10** C4
The Downs C of E Primary
 School
 DEAL CT14 .... **135** H4
Downsmead School
 FOLKN CT19 .... **13** D2
Downs View County I
 nfant School
 KEN/WIL TN24 .... **141** J7
Drapers Mill CP School
 MARG CT9 .... **3** E5
Dreamland Amusement Park
 MARG CT9 .... **2** C4
Dreamland Cinema/bingo
 MARG CT9 .... **2** C3
DSS
 RAM CT11 .... **5** D5
D2 Trading Estate
 SIT ME10 .... **36** C8
Duke of Clarence Trading Estate
 IOS ME12 .... **14** B3
Duke of Yorks Royal
 Military School
 RDV CT15 .... **173** K2
Dunkirk CP School
 FAV ME13 .... **83** K3
Dymchurch CP School
 LYDD TN29 .... **216** E6
Eastchurch C of E
 Primary School
 IOS ME12 .... **23** H2
East Court School
 RAM CT11 .... **55** H7
East Kent Community NHS Trust
 CANT CT1 .... **7** D4
East Kent Retail Park
 BRDST CT10 .... **54** C1
East Langdon CP School
 RDV CT15 .... **154** A5
Eastling CP School
 FAV ME13 .... **99** G1
Eastry Medical Surgery
 SWCH CT13 .... **113** F4
Eastry Primary School
 SWCH CT13 .... **113** F4
Eaton Road Surgery
 MARG CT9 .... **2** C3
Eden Business Centre
 ASH TN23 .... **8** B4
Egerton CP School
 HDCN TN27 .... **137** F3

Elham C of E Primary School
 RCANTW CT4 .... **167** K2
Elham Surgery
 RCANTW CT4 .... **167** J2
Ellingham Industrial Centre
 ASH TN23 .... **181** K1
Ellington CP School
 RAM CT11 .... **4** C4
Ellington High School
 RAM CT11 .... **4** C4
Elliott Park School
 IOS ME12 .... **15** J7
Elvington Primary School
 RDV CT15 .... **132** A6
Enterprise Business Centre
 DVE/WH CT16 .... **152** E8
Etchinghill Golf Club
 RFOLK CT18 .... **188** C2
Ethelbert Road Infant School
 FAV ME13 .... **62** A8
Eurolink Industrial Centre
 SIT ME10 .... **58** B1
Eurolink Industrial Estate
 SIT ME10 .... **58** C1
Evegate Business Centre
 RASHE TN25 .... **184** C3
Eversley College
 FOLK CT20 .... **207** F2
Factory
 KEN/WIL TN24 .... **9** F2
Faversham Cottage Hospital
 FAV ME13 .... **62** B7
Faversham Golf Club Ltd
 FAV ME13 .... **80** C8
Faversham Industrial Estate
 FAV ME13 .... **62** E7
Faversham Town Football Club
 FAV ME13 .... **81** H1
Fire Sta
 DVE/WH CT16 .... **10** B3
Fire Station
 CANT CT1 .... **7** D4
Fire Station
 MARG CT9 .... **2** C4
Fire Station
 RAM CT11 .... **5** E5
Fitzroy College
 MARG CT9 .... **32** E5
Fleur-de-lis Gallery
 FOLK CT20 .... **207** F3
Folkestone Cricket Club
 FOLKN CT19 .... **12** A3
Folkestone Gas Sports Club
 FOLKN CT19 .... **13** D3
Folkestone Invicta Football Club
 FOLKN CT19 .... **12** A3
Folkestone Rowing Club
 FOLK CT20 .... **206** E3
The Folkestone School
 for Girls
 FOLK CT20 .... **207** F2
Folkestone Yacht
 & Motor Boat Club
 FOLKN CT19 .... **13** E4
The Foreland School
 BRDST CT10 .... **33** H8
Friars School
 ASH TN23 .... **159** K6
Fulston Manor School
 SIT ME10 .... **58** A4
The Gallery
 DEAL CT14 .... **135** K3
Gap House School
 BRDST CT10 .... **55** H4
Garlinge Infant School
 MARG CT9 .... **2** A5
George Spurgen CP School
 FOLKN CT19 .... **13** E2
Georges Turles House Clinic
 CANTW/ST CT2 .... **6** A2
Gibbs Gallery
 CANT CT1 .... **6** C3
Godington CP School
 ASH TN23 .... **160** B3
Godinton Way Industrial Estate
 ASH TN23 .... **8** A3
Goodnestone C of E
 Primary School
 RCANTE CT3 .... **110** E4
Gore Court Cricket Club
 SIT ME10 .... **57** G1
Grace School
 FOLK CT20 .... **13** D4
Grand Shaft (Lower Entrance)
 DVW CT17 .... **10** A5

Grand Shaft (Upper Entrance)
 DVW CT17 .... **10** A5
The Grange Medical Centre
 RAM CT11 .... **5** D5
Granville Theatre & Cinema
 RAM CT11 .... **5** F4
Graveney CP School
 FAV ME13 .... **63** K5
Great Chart CP School
 ASH TN23 .... **160** B6
Great Chart Cricket Club
 ASH TN23 .... **160** A5
Greatstone Primary School
 NROM TN28 .... **232** E4
Green Park (Cricket Club)
 HYTHE CT21 .... **205** G4
Greystones Special School
 KEN/WIL TN24 .... **9** F4
Grosvenor Casino
 RAM CT11 .... **5** F5
Grove Dairy Farm
 Business Centre
 RSIT ME9 .... **35** F8
Grove Ferry Boat Club
 RCANTE CT3 .... **71** G3
Grovehurst Surgery
 SIT ME10 .... **35** K5
Grove Park CP School
 SIT ME10 .... **35** G8
Guildhall Street Surgery
 FOLK CT20 .... **13** D4
Gulbenkian Theatre
 CANTW/ST CT2 .... **86** B2
Guston C of E Primary School
 DVE/WH CT16 .... **173** J3
Hadlow College
 CANT CT1 .... **7** E3
Haine Hospital
 MSTR CT12 .... **54** B2
Halfway House Primary School
 IOS ME12 .... **14** E8
Hampton CP School
 HB CT6 .... **46** B3
Hampton Pier Yacht Club
 HB CT6 .... **46** A1
Ham Street County
 Primary School
 RASHW TN26 .... **198** D6
Harbour Gallery
 WSTB CT5 .... **44** A4
Harbour Special Day School
 RDV CT15 .... **172** C7
Harcourt CP School
 FOLKN CT19 .... **189** K7
Harden Road Industrial Estate
 LYDD TN29 .... **231** J7
Hartsdown High School
 MARG CT9 .... **2** B5
Hartsdown Leisure Centre
 MARG CT9 .... **2** B4
Harvey Clinic
 FOLK CT20 .... **12** C4
Harvey Grammar School
 FOLKN CT19 .... **12** A3
Hawkes Clinic
 FOLK CT20 .... **13** D5
Hawkinge County
 Primary School
 RFOLK CT18 .... **190** C7
Hawkinge Health Centre
 RFOLK CT18 .... **190** C2
Hawkins Clinic
 DEAL CT14 .... **115** J8
Hawley Health Centre
 MARG CT9 .... **3** D3
Hayesbank Surgery
 KEN/WIL TN24 .... **8** C2
Heath Farm School
 HDCN TN27 .... **117** K7
Hedge End Industrial Estate
 BRCH CT7 .... **50** C3
Henwood Business Centre
 KEN/WIL TN24 .... **9** D3
The Hereson School
 RAM CT11 .... **5** F3
Herne Bay CP Infants School
 HB CT6 .... **46** E2
Herne Bay CP Junior School
 HB CT6 .... **46** E2
Herne Bay Football Club
 HB CT6 .... **46** E3
Herne Bay Golf Club
 HB CT6 .... **46** E4
Herne Bay Museum Centre
 HB CT6 .... **46** E1

Herne Bay West Industrial Estate
HB CT6.................................... **46** B3
Herne C of E (Controlled)
Infants School
HB CT6.................................... **47** G6
Herne Junior School
HB CT6.................................... **47** G6
Hernhill CP School
FAV ME13.............................. **64** B8
Hersden CP School
RCANTE CT3.......................... **69** K5
Highfield Business Centre
CANT CT1............................... **6** A4
Highfield Industrial Estate
FOLKN CT19........................... **13** E3
High Halden C of E
Primary School
RASHW TN26......................... **177** K7
Highsted School for Girls
SIT ME10............................... **58** A4
Highworth Grammar
School for Girls
KEN/WIL TN24....................... **8** A2
Hillborough Business Park
HB CT6................................... **48** B1
The Hill Gallery
BRDST CT10........................... **55** J3
Hillside Industrial Estate
FOLK CT20............................. **206** E2
Hoath CP School
RCANTE CT3.......................... **69** K1
Hollywood Bowl
MARG CT9............................. **3** D3
Holos Clinic
SWCH CT13........................... **94** A5
Holy Trinity C of E
(aided) Primary School
RAM CT11.............................. **55** H5
Holy Trinity & St Johns
C of E Primary School
MARG CT9............................. **3** D3
Homewood School
TENT TN30............................ **194** B5
Honiton House
Preparatory School
MARG CT9............................. **3** E2
Hopewell School
ASH TN23.............................. **160** C7
The Hostel Highworth
School for Girls
KEN/WIL TN24....................... **8** A2
Hothfield CP School
RASHW TN26......................... **139** H7
Hoverspeed Terminal
DVW CT17.............................. **10** C5
Howards Gallery
RAM CT11.............................. **5** E4
Hull Park Sports Club
DEAL CT14............................. **115** F8
The Hunt Gallery
SWCH CT13........................... **94** A5
Hythe Community Clinic
HYTHE CT21.......................... **205** G4
Hythe County Infants School
HYTHE CT21.......................... **205** F5
Hythe & Saltwood Sailing Club
HYTHE CT21.......................... **205** G5
Hythe Town Council
HYTHE CT21.......................... **205** G4
Information Communications &
Technology Centre
Canterbury College
CANT CT1............................... **7** D4
Iwade CP School
RSIT ME9............................... **35** J2
John Goodhew Medical Centre
SIT ME10............................... **35** K5
John Wilson Business Park
WSTB CT5.............................. **44** E5
Joseph Wilson Industrial Estate
WSTB CT5.............................. **44** C7
Joy Lane County Infant School
WSTB CT5.............................. **43** K7
Julias Dance School
CANT CT1............................... **12** C5
The Junior Kings School
CANTW/ST CT2....................... **87** J1
Keep
DVE/WH CT16........................ **11** D3
Kengate Industrial Estate
HYTHE CT21.......................... **204** D5
Kennington C of E
Junior School
KEN/WIL TN24....................... **141** H7

Kennington Cricket Club
KEN/WIL TN24....................... **141** H7
Kent & Canterbury Hospital
CANT CT1............................... **7** D6
Kent College
CANTW/ST CT2....................... **86** A3
Kent College Infant
& Junior School
CANTW/ST CT2....................... **85** J5
Kent County Council
FOLK CT20............................. **12** C4
Kent County Cricket Club
CANT CT1............................... **7** E5
Kent Education
Committee Preston School
RCANTE CT3.......................... **71** K8
Kent Private Clinic
SWCH CT13........................... **94** A5
Keynes College
CANTW/ST CT2....................... **86** B2
The King Ethelbert School
BRCH CT7.............................. **30** B7
Kings Gallery
CANT CT1............................... **7** D2
Kingsmead Leisure Centre
CANTW/ST CT2....................... **7** D1
Kingsnorth C of E
Primary School
ASH TN23.............................. **182** A5
Kingsnorth Industrial Estate
ASH TN23.............................. **161** F8
Kings School Recreation Centre
CANTW/ST CT2....................... **6** C1
The Kings School
CANT CT1............................... **7** D2
Klondyke Industrial Estate
QBOR ME11............................ **20** A2
Lady Joanna Thornhill
Primary School
RASHE TN25.......................... **142** D4
Laleham School
MARG CT9............................. **3** F3
Lansdowne CP School
SIT ME10............................... **58** D3
Lansdowne Gallery
DEAL CT14............................. **115** K7
Latne Barn
LYDD TN29............................ **217** F1
Leadenhall Gallery
CANT CT1............................... **7** D2
Leigh Green Industrial Estate
TENT TN30............................ **194** E8
Leigh House Clinic
CANTW/ST CT2....................... **6** B2
Lifeboat Station
MARG CT9............................. **2** C2
Lighthouse
MARG CT9............................. **2** C2
Linden Grove CP School
ASH TN23.............................. **160** E8
Littlebourne C of E
Primary School
RCANTE CT3.......................... **89** F6
Littlestone Gallery
NROM TN28............................ **226** D8
Little Theatre
FOLK CT20............................. **206** E3
Lodge Harvey Grammar School
FOLKN CT19........................... **12** A3
London Beach Golf Club
TENT TN30............................ **194** A2
London Road Trading Estate
SIT ME10............................... **57** J2
Longport Police Station
RFOLK CT18........................... **189** G7
Lower Halston CP School
RSIT ME9............................... **34** A4
Luddenham CP School
FAV ME13.............................. **61** H5
Lydd County Primary School
LYDD TN29............................ **231** H8
Lydden CP School
RDV CT15.............................. **151** H6
Lydd Town Council
LYDD TN29............................ **231** H8
Lyminge C of E Primary School
RFOLK CT18........................... **167** G7
Lympne C of E Primary School
HYTHE CT21.......................... **203** J3
Lynsted CP School
RSIT ME9............................... **59** H7
Mace Industrial Estate
KEN/WIL TN24....................... **8** C2
Maison Dieu House
DVE/WH CT16........................ **10** B3

Manor Clinic
FOLK CT20............................. **12** C5
Margate Business Centre
MARG CT9............................. **2** C2
Margate Caves
MARG CT9............................. **3** D2
Margate Football Club
MARG CT9............................. **2** B4
Margate Lawn Tennis Club
MARG CT9............................. **2** C5
Marina Office
DVW CT17.............................. **10** B5
Marine Road Clinic
DEAL CT14............................. **135** K1
Maritime Museum
RAM CT11.............................. **5** F5
Market
ASH TN23.............................. **8** B3
The Market Place Surgery
SWCH CT13........................... **93** K5
Market Street Gallery
SWCH CT13........................... **94** A5
Marlborough Road
Industrial Estate
DEAL CT14............................. **135** F4
Marlowe Arcade
Shopping Centre
CANT CT1............................... **6** C3
Marlowe Theatre
CANT CT1............................... **6** C2
Martello Industrial Estate
FOLKN CT19........................... **13** F3
Martello Tower Castle
LYDD TN29............................ **216** E7
Masonic Library & Museum
CANT CT1............................... **6** C3
Maybrook Industrial Estate
CANT CT1............................... **87** G3
Meadow View Industrial Estate
RASHW TN26......................... **199** G7
Melbourne CP School
DVE/WH CT16........................ **173** G2
Mersham CP School
RASHE TN25.......................... **183** K3
Mildmay Surgery
RAM CT11.............................. **5** F4
Mile Town Industrial Park
IOS ME12.............................. **14** B5
Milstead & Frinsted
C of E Primary School
RSIT ME9............................... **76** E5
Minnis Bay Sailing Club
BRCH CT7.............................. **29** F7
Minster Abbey
MSTR CT12............................ **74** B1
Minster College
IOS ME12.............................. **15** G8
Minster In Sheppey CP School
IOS ME12.............................. **15** K8
Minster Primary School
MSTR CT12............................ **74** A1
Minster & Rayment
Rural Life Museum
MSTR CT12............................ **52** B8
Minterne CP School
SIT ME10............................... **57** J4
Model Village
RAM CT11.............................. **5** D6
Montessori School
HB CT6................................... **47** F1
Montgomery Grant
Maintained School
RCANTE CT3.......................... **69** H6
Montgomery House
Doctors Surgery
ASH TN23.............................. **160** D6
Montpelier Business Park
ASH TN23.............................. **160** D5
Morehall CP School
FOLKN CT19........................... **190** A8
Motor Museum
RAM CT11.............................. **5** D6
Mundella CP School
FOLKN CT19........................... **13** D3
Murston County Primary
Infant School
SIT ME10............................... **58** C1
Murston CP Junior School
SIT ME10............................... **58** C1
Museum
DVE/WH CT16........................ **10** B4
Museum
IOS ME12.............................. **16** A7
Nature Reserve
LYDD TN29............................ **238** C5

The Neville Pundole Gallery
CANT CT1 ...... **6** C2

Nevill Gallery
CANT CT1 ...... **6** C3

New Hayesbank Surgery
KEN/WIL TN24 ...... **8** C1

Newington C of E Primary School
RSIT ME9 ...... **34** A7

Newington CP Infant School
MSTR CT12 ...... **4** B3

Newington Gm Junior School
MSTR CT12 ...... **4** A3

Newlands County Primary School
RAM CT11 ...... **5** E2

The New Lyminge Surgery
RFOLK CT18 ...... **167** G8

New Road Industrial Estate
IOS ME12 ...... **14** B5

New Romney C of E Junior & Infant School
NROM TN28 ...... **226** B7

Nonington Primary School
RDV CT15 ...... **130** E1

Northbourne Court
DEAL CT14 ...... **134** A1

Northbourne Park School
DEAL CT14 ...... **113** G8

Northbourne Primary School
DEAL CT14 ...... **133** J1

Northdown CP School
MARG CT9 ...... **32** D5

Northdown Industrial Estate
BRDST CT10 ...... **33** F8

Northdown Surgery
MARG CT9 ...... **32** D5

North Foreland Golf Club
BRDST CT10 ...... **33** H6

Northgate Clinic
CANT CT1 ...... **7** D2

The North School
KEN/WIL TN24 ...... **9** D4

The Norton Knatchbull School
KEN/WIL TN24 ...... **9** E3

Nunnery Fields Hospital
CANT CT1 ...... **6** C5

Oak Hall Surgery
NROM TN28 ...... **226** B8

Oaks County Infant School
SIT ME10 ...... **57** J4

Oak Tree CP School
ASH TN23 ...... **160** D6

Oakwood Trading Estate
BRDST CT10 ...... **32** E7

Old Hospital
RCANTW CT4 ...... **167** K1

Old Priory School
RAM CT11 ...... **5** D5

Old School Surgery
RCANTW CT4 ...... **104** E4

Old Timber Yard Industrial Estate
MSTR CT12 ...... **4** A1

Om Medical Centre
IOS ME12 ...... **14** C4

Orchard School
CANT CT1 ...... **6** C5

Ospringe C of E School
FAV ME13 ...... **61** K8

The Oxford Street Health Clinic
WSTB CT5 ...... **44** A5

Palmarsh CP School
HYTHE CT21 ...... **204** B6

Palm Bay County Primary School
MARG CT9 ...... **32** E3

Park Farm CP School
FOLKN CT19 ...... **12** C2

Park Farm Industrial Estate
FOLKN CT19 ...... **12** B1

Park Farm Recreation Centre
ASH TN23 ...... **181** K2

Park Mall Shopping Centre
ASH TN23 ...... **8** B3

Parkside County Primary School
CANT CT1 ...... **87** H4

The Park Surgery
HB CT6 ...... **46** E2

Passenger Terminal
RFOLK CT18 ...... **189** G6

Pembroke Lodge Museum & Art Gallery
BRCH CT7 ...... **29** J7

Pennypot Industrial Estate
HYTHE CT21 ...... **204** D5

Pent Valley Secondary School
FOLKN CT19 ...... **190** A7

Petham CP School
RCANTW CT4 ...... **126** A3

Pharos
DVE/WH CT16 ...... **11** D3

Picart Gallery
FOLK CT20 ...... **13** D5

Pier
DEAL CT14 ...... **115** K8

Pier Pavilion Sports Centre
HB CT6 ...... **46** D1

Pilgrims Way CP School
CANT CT1 ...... **7** F4

Pinnochios Galleria
BRCH CT7 ...... **29** J6

Pioneer Business Park
RAM CT11 ...... **5** D3

Playhouse Theatre
WSTB CT5 ...... **43** K5

Pluckley C of E Primary School
HDCN TN27 ...... **137** J7

Polo Farm Sports Club
RCANTE CT3 ...... **87** K6

Portal House School
RDV CT15 ...... **155** G8

P & O Stena Line
DVW CT17 ...... **10** A6

Poulton Business Park
DVW CT17 ...... **172** D5

Powell CP School
DVE/WH CT16 ...... **173** F2

Princes Golf Club
SWCH CT13 ...... **95** F3

Priory County Infant School
RAM CT11 ...... **5** D4

Priory Fields School
DVW CT17 ...... **173** F6

Queenborough Business Centre
QBOR ME11 ...... **20** B3

Queenborough CP School
QBOR ME11 ...... **20** C1

Queenborough Yacht Club
QBOR ME11 ...... **19** K1

Queen Elizabeths School
FAV ME13 ...... **62** D6

Queen Elizabeth the Queen Mothers Hospital
MARG CT9 ...... **3** E5

Queens Hall & Winter Gardens
MARG CT9 ...... **3** D2

Queen Victoria Memorial Hospital
HB CT6 ...... **47** G2

R A F Manston History Museum
MSTR CT12 ...... **53** F4

Ramsgate Athletic & Football Club
RAM CT11 ...... **4** B5

Ramsgate Boat Club
RAM CT11 ...... **5** D4

Ramsgate New Port Freight Ferry Terminal
RAM CT11 ...... **5** D6

The Ramsgate School
MSTR CT12 ...... **4** A1

Ramsgate Sports Centre
RAM CT11 ...... **5** D4

Ramsgate Swimming Pool
RAM CT11 ...... **4** C3

Range Road Industrial Estate
HYTHE CT21 ...... **204** E5

Reculver Primary C of E Primary School
HB CT6 ...... **48** B2

Regis Business Park
IOS ME12 ...... **14** B5

Regis Industrial Estate
IOS ME12 ...... **14** B5

Regis Manor County Primary School
SIT ME10 ...... **35** K7

Renaissance Gallery
RAM CT11 ...... **5** D6

Research Development & Business Centre
CANTW/ST CT2 ...... **86** A2

Richborough Business Park
SWCH CT13 ...... **94** A3

Richborough Cas
SWCH CT13 ...... **93** J1

Richmond County Primary School
IOS ME12 ...... **14** E5

The Ripple School
DEAL CT14 ...... **134** C6

Ripple Vale School
DEAL CT14 ...... **134** E6

River Court School
RCANTW CT4 ...... **105** F4

River CP School
DVW CT17 ...... **172** C3

Riverside Business Park
KEN/WIL TN24 ...... **8** C2

Riverside Industrial Estate
CANT CT1 ...... **7** E1

Riverside Industrial Estate
HYTHE CT21 ...... **203** K5

Riverside School
ASH TN23 ...... **160** C5

The River Surgery
DVE/WH CT16 ...... **172** C2

Rodmersham CP School
RSIT ME9 ...... **58** C7

Rodmersham Squash Club
RSIT ME9 ...... **58** B8

Roman Museum
CANT CT1 ...... **6** C3

Roman Painted House
DVW CT17 ...... **10** B4

Romney Warren Golf Club
NROM TN28 ...... **227** F8

Roper House School for the Deaf
CANTW/ST CT2 ...... **6** B2

Rose Street CP School
IOS ME12 ...... **14** C4

Royal Cinque Ports Golf Club
DEAL CT14 ...... **115** J5

The Royal Museum & Art Gallery
CANT CT1 ...... **6** C3

Royal St Georges Golf Club
SWCH CT13 ...... **94** D5

Royal School for Deaf Children
MARG CT9 ...... **3** D3

Royal School for Deaf Children
WGOS CT8 ...... **30** D5

Royal Temple Yacht Club
RAM CT11 ...... **5** E5

Royal Victoria Hospital
FOLKN CT19 ...... **12** C3

RSPB
IOS ME12 ...... **20** E8

Rugby Club
RFOLK CT18 ...... **188** D8

Rutland School of English
MARG CT9 ...... **31** G5

St Alphege C of E Infant School
WSTB CT5 ...... **44** A5

St Annes Surgery
HB CT6 ...... **46** D1

St Anselms RC School
CANT CT1 ...... **7** F6

St Anthonys School
MARG CT9 ...... **32** D5

St Augustine's Abbey
CANT CT1 ...... **7** E3

St Augustines Abbey
RAM CT11 ...... **5** D6

St Augustines Business Park
HB CT6 ...... **45** J3

St Augustines College
WGOS CT8 ...... **30** D6

St Augustines Golf Club
MSTR CT12 ...... **75** G1

St Augustines Roman Catholic Primary School
HYTHE CT21 ...... **205** J4

St Bartholomews School
SIT ME10 ...... **36** A7

St Christophers School
CANT CT1 ...... **7** E5

St Crispins CP School
WGOS CT8 ...... **30** D7

St Edmunds Catholic School
DVE/WH CT16 ...... **10** A1

St Edmunds School
CANTW/ST CT2 ...... **86** A3

St Edwards School
IOS ME12 ...... **14** C4

St Ethelberts RC Primary School
RAM CT11 ...... **5** F3

St Faiths at Ash School
RCANTE CT3 ...... **92** A5

St Georges C of E Middle School
IOS ME12 ...... **16** B8

St Georges Secondary School
BRDST CT10 .... 54 D1
St Gregorys College
WGOS CT8 .... 30 D5
St Gregorys RC Primary School
MARG CT9 .... 2 C6
St James' Church (ruins)
DVE/WH CT16 .... 10 C3
St John Business Centre
MARG CT9 .... 3 D4
St Josephs RC Primary School
RCANTE CT3 .... 130 D1
St Josephs School
BRDST CT10 .... 55 G1
St Lawrence Industrial Estate
RAM CT11 .... 4 B4
St Leonards C of E Junior School
HYTHE CT21 .... 205 F4
St Margarets-at-cliffe CP School
RDV CT15 .... 155 G8
St Margarets Hotel
& Country Club
RDV CT15 .... 174 E1
St Martins CP School
DVW CT17 .... 172 E7
St Martins Hospital
CANT CT1 .... 87 H6
St Martins Primary School
FOLK CT20 .... 206 B1
St Mary of Charity C of E
Junior & Infant School
FAV ME13 .... 62 C7
St Marys C of E (aided)
Primary School
FOLKN CT19 .... 13 F3
St Marys C of E
Controlled Primary School
RCANTW CT4 .... 103 H6
St Marys C of E Primary School
ASH TN23 .... 8 A2
St Marys C of E Primary School
DVE/WH CT16 .... 10 C3
St Marys Primary School
WSTB CT5 .... 44 C4
St Marys RC Primary School
DEAL CT14 .... 135 F3
St Michaels C of E
Primary School
TENT TN30 .... 194 B3
St Mildreds CP Infant School
BRDST CT10 .... 55 H2
St Nicholas at Wade
C of E Primary School
BRCH CT7 .... 50 B4
St Nicholas C of E
Primary School
DEAL CT14 .... 155 J1
St Nicholas Court
BRCH CT7 .... 50 A4
St Nicholas Special School
CANT CT1 .... 6 C5
St Peter In Thanet C of E
Junior School
BRDST CT10 .... 33 G7
St Peters Methodist
Primary School
CANT CT1 .... 6 C5
St Peters RC Primary School
SIT ME10 .... 57 J3
St Peters School of English
CANT CT1 .... 7 D3
St Philip Howard RC
Primary School
HB CT6 .... 46 D1
St Radegund's Abbey
RDV CT15 .... 171 K6
St Radigunds CP School
DVW CT17 .... 172 E5
St Richards RC Primary School
DVE/WH CT16 .... 10 B2
St Saviours School
WGOS CT8 .... 30 D6
St Simon of England
RC Primary School
ASH TN23 .... 8 A5
St Stephens CP Junior School
CANTW/ST CT2 .... 86 D3
St Teresas School
KEN/WIL TN24 .... 8 A1
St Thomas' Hall
CANT CT1 .... 7 D3
St Thomas School
SIT ME10 .... 58 D4
Salmestone CP School
MARG CT9 .... 2 C5

Salmestone Grange
MARG CT9 .... 2 C5
Saltwood C of E Primary School
HYTHE CT21 .... 205 F2
Salvation Army
DVW CT17 .... 10 A3
Sandgate CP School
FOLK CT20 .... 207 F2
Sandgate Road Surgery
FOLK CT20 .... 12 A5
Sandown Clinic
DEAL CT14 .... 115 K6
Sandown CP School
DEAL CT14 .... 115 J7
Sandwich County Infant School
SWCH CT13 .... 93 K5
Sandwich County Junior School
SWCH CT13 .... 93 K7
Sandwich Lawn Tennis Club
SWCH CT13 .... 94 B5
Sandwich Sailing
& Motor Boat Club
SWCH CT13 .... 93 J6
Sandwich Sports
& Leisure Centre
SWCH CT13 .... 94 A7
Sandwich Technology School
SWCH CT13 .... 93 K8
Seabrook Primary School
HYTHE CT21 .... 206 B4
Seasalter Sailing Club
WSTB CT5 .... 42 C7
Sea Street Industrial Estate
HB CT6 .... 46 B3
Sellindge CP School
RASHE TN25 .... 185 K5
Sellindge Sports Club
RASHE TN25 .... 186 A5
Selling C of E Primary School
FAV ME13 .... 82 B8
Selsted C of E Primary School
RDV CT15 .... 149 J8
Sene Valley Golf Club
HYTHE CT21 .... 205 J2
Shatterlocks CP School
DVE/WH CT16 .... 173 F4
Sheerness Clinic
IOS ME12 .... 14 D5
Sheerness Golf Club
IOS ME12 .... 15 G7
Sheldwich CP School
FAV ME13 .... 81 G8
Sheppey College
IOS ME12 .... 14 C3
Sheppey Community Hospital
IOS ME12 .... 15 K7
Sheppey Little Theatre
IOS ME12 .... 14 E4
Sheppey Rugby F C
IOS ME12 .... 15 H7
Sheppey Yacht Club
IOS ME12 .... 15 F3
Shepway District Council
FOLK CT20 .... 12 C5
Shiva Medical Centre
IOS ME12 .... 15 J8
Sholden C of E Primary School
DEAL CT14 .... 134 E1
The Shopping Centre
MARG CT9 .... 2 C3
Shorncliffe Industrial Estate
FOLK CT20 .... 206 D2
Sibertswold Primary School
RDV CT15 .... 151 G2
Sibton Park (School)
RFOLK CT18 .... 167 F6
Simon Langton Girls School
CANT CT1 .... 7 F6
Simon Langton Grammar
School for Boys
CANT CT1 .... 106 E2
Simon Langton Grammar
School for Girls
CANT CT1 .... 7 E6
Singleton Medical Centre
ASH TN23 .... 160 B6
Sir Roger Manwoods School
SWCH CT13 .... 94 B4
The Sir William Nottidge
Technology School
WSTB CT5 .... 44 C6
Sittingbourne Industrial Park
SIT ME10 .... 57 H1
Sittingbourne Industrial Park
SIT ME10 .... 58 A1

Sittingbourne Memorial Hospital
SIT ME10 .... 58 A3
Sittingbourne & Milton Regis
Golf Club
RSIT ME9 .... 56 A3
Sittingbourne Sports Centre
SIT ME10 .... 58 B3
Ski Slope
FOLKN CT19 .... 12 A3
Smarden CP School
HDCN TN27 .... 156 A5
Smeeth CP School
RASHE TN25 .... 184 E1
Solomons Temple
RSIT ME9 .... 97 K1
South Avenue County
Infant School
SIT ME10 .... 58 B3
South Kent College
ASH TN23 .... 8 C4
South Kent College
ASH TN23 .... 8 A5
South Kent College
ASH TN23 .... 160 D8
South Kent College
FOLK CT20 .... 12 B4
South Kent College
of Technology
FOLK CT20 .... 12 B4
South Kent Hospital
FOLK CT20 .... 206 E1
Spring Grove School
RASHE TN25 .... 142 C4
Stalham Business Centre
OBOR ME11 .... 20 B3
Stanhope CP School
ASH TN23 .... 181 K1
Stanhope Surgery
KEN/WIL TN24 .... 9 F4
Stella Maris RC Primary School
FOLKN CT19 .... 12 C3
Stelling Minnis C of E School
RCANTW CT4 .... 126 D8
Stone Bay Special School
BRDST CT10 .... 33 J8
Stour Leisure Centre
ASH TN23 .... 8 C4
Stour Retail Park
CANT CT1 .... 87 H3
Stour Valley Industrial Estate
RCANTW CT4 .... 105 G2
Stowting C of E Primary School
RASHE TN25 .... 165 K6
Sturry C of E Primary School
CANTW/ST CT2 .... 69 F7
Summerhill Surgery
MSTR CT12 .... 4 C2
Summerlands Special School
HDCN TN27 .... 139 F2
Sun Lane Surgery
HYTHE CT21 .... 205 G4
Superstore
CANTW/ST CT2 .... 7 D2
Swalecliffe County Infant School
WSTB CT5 .... 44 E4
Swalecliffe Junior School
WSTB CT5 .... 44 E4
Swimming Pool
HYTHE CT21 .... 205 H5
Swinford Old Manor
Residential School
ASH TN23 .... 159 K2
Synagogue
MARG CT9 .... 3 E2
Tara Gallery
BRDST CT10 .... 55 J2
Technical Procurement
Sports Club
RASHE TN25 .... 141 F6
Temple Ewell C of E
Primary School
DVE/WH CT16 .... 172 B1
Tenterden C of E Junior School
TENT TN30 .... 194 A7
Tenterden County
Primary School
TENT TN30 .... 194 B7
Tenterden Golf Club
TENT TN30 .... 194 D5
Tenterden Leisure Centre
TENT TN30 .... 194 B7
Terence Macklin Gallery
WSTB CT5 .... 44 C3
Teynham Medical Centre
RSIT ME9 .... 59 K4

Page 3

D2
1 Booth Pl
2 Clifton Gdns
3 Clifton Pl
4 Ethelbert Gdns
5 Fort Paragon
6 Trinity Hl
7 Trinity Sq
8 Walpole Rd
9 Wellington Gdns

D4
1 Addiscombe Gdns
2 Alma Rd
3 Arnold Rd
4 Charlotte Sq
5 Churchfields
6 Church Rd
7 Church St
8 Cowper Rd
9 Homestead Cl
10 Osborne Ter
11 Oxford St
12 Setterfield Rd
13 Shakespeare Rd
14 Vicarage Pl

Page 5

D6
1 Clifton Lawn
2 The Cloisters
3 Paragon St
4 St Benedict's Lawn

F3
1 Beechcroft Gdns
2 Frances Gdns
3 Lillian Rd
4 Montefiore Cottages
5 Mulberry Cl
6 Union Rd

Page 6

C3
1 Adelaide Pl
2 All Saints La
3 Beer Cart La
4 Best La
5 Black Griffin La
6 Butchery La
7 Church La
8 Gravel Wk
9 Guildhall St
10 Hawk's La
11 High St
12 Hospital La
13 Jewry La
14 Mercery La
15 Mulberry Ct
16 Orange St
17 Parade
18 Rosemary La
19 St Edmunds Rd
20 St John's La
21 St Margaret's St
22 St Mary's St
23 St Peter's St
24 St Peter's Gv
25 Sun St
26 Tower Wy
27 Turnagain La
28 Water La
29 Watling St
30 White Horse La

C4
1 Castle Rw
2 Gas St
3 Gordon Rd
4 Marlowe Av
5 Riding Gate Rbt

Page 7

D2
1 Albion Pl
2 Alma Pl
3 Artillery Gdns
4 Church La
5 Clyde St
6 Cobden Pl
7 Duck La
8 High St
9 Northgate Borough
10 Old Ruttington La
11 St Gregory's
12 St Radigund's Pl
13 Union Pl

D4
1 Cossington Rd
2 Ersham Rd
3 The Hoystings Cl
4 Martindale Cl
5 Oaten Hill Pl
6 Upper Chantry La

D5
1 George Roche Rd
2 Milton Rd
3 Randolph Cl

Page 10

A3
1 De Burgh St
2 East St
3 Peter St
4 Priory Gv
5 Victoria Crs
6 West St

B4
1 Adrian St
2 Albany Rd
3 Bench St
4 Cambridge Rd
5 Cowgate Hl
6 Durham Cl
7 Durham Hl
8 Lancaster Rd
9 Military Rd
10 Princes St

C4
1 Camden Crs
2 Dolphin La
3 Fishmonger's La
4 Flying Horse La
5 Mill La
6 St James La
7 St James St
8 Waterloo Crs
9 Wellesley Rd

Page 12

A2
1 Berkeley Cl
2 Cherry Garden Av
3 Gainsborough Cl
4 Norrington Mead
5 Papworth Cl
6 Stablemead
7 Sunningdale Av

Page 13

D4
1 Bellevue St
2 Bradstone New Rd
3 Bradstone Rd
4 Cambridge Gdns
5 Connaught Rd
6 Copthall Gdns
7 Darby Pl
8 Darlington St
9 Devon Rd
10 Dover Rd
11 Foord Rd South
12 Gloucester Pl
13 Grace Hl
14 Ingles La
15 Mount Pleasant Rd
16 New St
17 Payers Pk
18 Rendezvous St
19 St Eanswythe Wy

E5
1 Lower Sandgate Rd

Page 29

K6
1 Constable Rd
2 Leslie Rd
3 Nasmyth Rd
4 Wigwam Paddocks
5 Wilkie Rd
6 Winston Ct

Page 32

A4
1 Addington Rd
2 Addington Sq
3 Brockley Rd
4 Carroway's Pl
5 Dane Hill Gv
6 Dane Hill Rw
7 Dane Park Rd
8 Danesmead Ter
9 Hawley Sq
10 Lausanne Rd
11 Park La
12 Prince's St
13 Union Crs

A5
1 Addiscombe Gdns
2 Alma Rd
3 Arnold Rd
4 Charlotte Sq
5 Churchfields
6 Church Rd
7 Church St
8 Cowper Rd
9 Homestead Cl
10 Osborne Ter
11 Oxford St
12 Setterfield Rd
13 Shakespeare Rd
14 Vicarage Pl

A7
1 Chapel Hill Cl

B3
1 Cliftonville Ms
2 Dalby Sq
3 Gordon Rd
4 Percy Rd
5 Queens Ct
6 Queens Pde
7 Stanley Rd
8 Sweyn Rd
9 Thanet Coastal Pth

C4
1 Arundel Rd
2 Crawford Gdns
3 Laureate Cl
4 Lower Northdown Av
5 Lyndhurst Av
6 Talbot Rd

D3
1 Avenue Gdns
2 Hodge's Gap
3 Palm Bay Gdns
4 Sackett's Gap

Page 33

F4
1 Egerton Dr
2 Hadlow Dr
3 Hanover Cl
4 Ivychurch Gdns
5 Roseacre Ct
6 Stockbury Gdns
7 Upchurch Wk
8 Waltham Cl
9 Westmarsh Dr

Page 54

D7
1 Claremont Gdns
2 Ellington Pl
3 Hallcroft Ct
4 Nursery Cl

E6
1 Bolton St
2 Gordon Rd

E7
1 Belgrave Cl
2 Belmont Rd
3 Bristol Pl
4 Eagle Hl
5 Elmstone Rd
6 Fortuna Ct

E8
1 Albert St
2 Beresford Rd
3 Clarendon Gdns
4 Cumberland Rd
5 Ethelbert Rd
6 Florence Rd
7 Ivy La
8 James St
9 Spencer Sq
10 Townley St
11 Vereth Rd

Page 55

F2
1 Fairfield Pk

F5
1 Hawthorn Cl
2 Heathwood Dr
3 Stonar Cl
4 Thorn Gdns

F7
1 Alfred Cottages
2 Alma Pl
3 Belmont St
4 Brunswick St
5 Chatham Pl
6 Cleaver La
7 Meeting St
8 Newcastle Hl
9 Packer's La
10 Portland Ct
11 Union St

F8
1 Adelaide Gdns
2 Albion Ms
3 Albion Pl
4 Camden Rd
5 Cliff St
6 Coleman's Yd
7 Guildford Lawn
8 Leopold St
9 Liverpool Lawn
10 York St

G1
1 Beaconsfield Gdns
2 Bradstow Wy
3 St Christophers Gn

G6
1 Beechcroft Gdns
2 Frances Gdns
3 Lillian Rd
4 Montefiore Cottages
5 Mulberry Cl
6 Union Rd

G7
1 Arklow Sq
2 Augusta Pl
3 Balmoral Pl
4 Dreste Rd
5 Irchester St
6 Shaftsbury St
7 Truro Rd
8 Unity Pl
9 Waterloo Pl

H6
1 Winterstoke Wy

J2
1 Alexandra Rd
2 Buckingham Rd
3 Croft's Pl
4 John St
5 Nash Gdns
6 Prospect Pl
7 St Mary's Rd
8 Serene Ct
9 Wardour Cl

Page 62

B7
1 Beckett St
2 Caslocke St
3 Fielding St
4 Mendfield St
5 Millstream Cl
6 Runnymede Ms
7 Water La

Page 86

A8
1 Manciple Cl

C7
1 Grove Ter
2 Ivy Pl
3 St Andrews Cl
4 St Mildreds Pl
5 Seymour Pl

D4
1 Coppergate
2 Roper Rd
3 St Stephen's Cl

D5
1 Abbots Pl
2 Becket Ms
3 Carriage Ms
4 The Causeway
5 The Friars
6 King St
7 Knott's La
8 Linden Gv
9 Mill La
10 North La
11 Orient Pl
12 Palace St
13 St Alphege La
14 St Peter's La
15 St Stephen's Flds
16 Shepherdsgate
17 Westgate Gv
18 Westgate Hall Rd
19 Westgate Rbt

D6
1 Adelaide Pl
2 All Saints La
3 Beer Cart La
4 Best La
5 Black Griffin La
6 Butchery La
7 Church La
8 Gravel Wk
9 Guildhall St
10 Hawk's La
11 High St
12 Hospital La
13 Jewry La
14 Mercery La
15 Mulberry Ct
16 Orange St
17 Parade
18 Rosemary La
19 St Edmunds Rd
20 St John's La
21 St Margaret's St
22 St Mary's St
23 St Peter's St
24 St Peter's Gv
25 Sun St
26 Tower Wy
27 Turnagain La
28 Water La
29 Watling St
30 White Horse La

E5
1 Albion Pl
2 Alma Pl
3 Artillery Gdns
4 Church La
5 Clyde St
6 Cobden Pl
7 Duck La
8 High St
9 Northgate Borough
10 Old Ruttington La
11 St Gregory's
12 St Radigund's Pl
13 Union Pl

E6
1 Burgate
2 Burgate La
3 Canterbury La
4 Church Street (St Pauls)
5 Iron Bar La
6 Ivy La
7 Lady Wootton's Gn
8 Link La
9 Long Market
10 Longport
11 Love La
12 Monastery St
13 St Georges La
14 St Georges St
15 St Pauls Ter
16 South Cl

E7
1 Cossington Rd
2 Ersham Rd
3 The Hoystings Cl
4 Martindale Cl
5 Oaten Hill Pl
6 Upper Chantry La

Page 87

F7
1 Lincoln Av
2 Magdalen Ct

H5
1 Albuhera Sq
2 Blenheim Av
3 Burma Crs
4 Sangro Pl
5 Sevastopol Pl
6 Somme Ct

Page 93

K5
1 Bowling St
2 Cattle Market
3 Cottage Rw
4 Guildcount La
5 Loop Court Ms
6 Mulberry Fld
7 Paradise Rw
8 St Mary's
9 Stour Ct
10 Vicarage La
11 Whitefriars Wy

Page 94

A5
1 Austins La
2 Bell La
3 The Butchery
4 Church St
5 Potter St
6 Quay La
7 St Clements
8 St Peter's St
9 Short St
10 Three King's Yd
11 Upper Strand St

Page 115

K7
1 Bridge Rd
2 Bulwark Rd
3 Capstan Rw
4 Clarence Pl
5 Dibdin Rd
6 Dolphin St
7 Enfield Rd
8 Farrier St
9 George St
10 Golden St
11 Hengest Rd
12 New St
13 Silver St
14 Sydenham Rd

Page 135

G1
1 Diana Gdns

J2
1 Chater Cl
2 Maxwell Pl
3 Woodstock Rd

Page 142

E4
1 The Close
2 The Forstal
3 The Green
4 Old Vicarage Gdns
5 St Ambrose Gn

Page 160

C8
1 Broadmead
2 Charminster
3 Collingbourne
4 Holdenhurst

Page 161

F2
1 Blackdown Dr
2 Brecon Rl
3 Cotswold Cl
4 Exmoor Rl
5 Pennine Wy

F4
1 Drum La
2 Edinburgh Rd
3 Hempsted St
4 Marlowe Rd
5 Middle St
6 Queen St
7 Regents Pl

G3
1 The Chimes
2 Haventhorpe
3 Northbrooke

H4
1 Pemberton Rd

K1
1 Atkinson Wk
2 James Haney Dr
3 John Newington Cl

K5
1 Hewitts Pl
2 Holmlea Cl
3 Taywood Cl
4 Willow Tree Cl

Page 173

F4
1 Brookfield Pl
2 Maresfield Cl
3 St Andrews Gdns
4 Springfield Rd

G5
1 Bartholomew St
2 Barton View Ter
3 Branch St
4 Churchill St
5 Leighton Rd
6 Limes Rd
7 Matthew's Pl
8 Paul's Pl
9 St Alphege Rd
10 Shooter's Hl

H6
1 Biggin St
2 Edwards Rd
3 Effingham Crs
4 Goodfellow Wy
5 Maison Dieu Pl
6 Norman St
7 Priory St
8 Queen's Gdns
9 Stembrook
10 Worthington St

J3
1 Corunna St

J7
1 Camden Crs
2 Dolphin La
3 Fishmonger's La
4 Flying Horse La
5 Mill La
6 St James La
7 St James St
8 Waterloo Crs
9 Wellesley Rd

K6
1 Athol Ter
2 East Roman Ditch

Page 205

G4
1 Bank St
2 Douglas Rd
3 Great Conduit St
4 Marine Walk St
5 Market Hl
6 Mount St
7 Prospect Rd
8 Theatre St

Page 207

K1
1 Bellevue St
2 Bradstone New Rd
3 Bradstone Rd
4 Cambridge Gdns
5 Connaught Rd
6 Copthall Gdns
7 Darby Pl
8 Darlington St
9 Devon Rd
10 Dover Rd
11 Foord Rd South
12 Gloucester Pl
13 Grace Hl
14 Ingles La
15 Mount Pleasant Rd
16 New St
17 Payers Pk
18 Rendezvous St
19 St Eanswythe Wy

Notes

Notes

Notes

Notes

Notes